INDUSTRIAL FLUCTUATIONS

Also Published In

REPRINTS OF ECONOMIC CLASSICS

By A. C. PIGOU

ESSAYS IN APPLIED ECONOMICS [1923]

Edited by A. C. PIGOU

MEMORIALS OF ALFRED MARSHALL [1923]

INDUSTRIAL
FLUCTUATIONS

BY

A. C. PIGOU, M.A.

PROFESSOR OF POLITICAL ECONOMY IN THE UNIVERSITY OF CAMBRIDGE
AUTHOR OF
"THE ECONOMICS OF WELFARE," ETC.

SECOND EDITION

REPRINTS OF ECONOMIC CLASSICS

AUGUSTUS M. KELLEY · PUBLISHERS
NEW YORK · 1967

First Edition 1927

(London: Macmillan & Co., *St. Martin's Street*, 1927)

Reprinted 1967 by
AUGUSTUS M. KELLEY PUBLISHERS
From Second Edition of 1929
For Frank Cass & Co., London, by permission

Library of Congress Catalogue Card Number

67-21689

PRINTED IN THE UNITED STATES OF AMERICA
by SENTRY PRESS, NEW YORK, N. Y. 10019

PREFACE

In the first edition of my *Economics of Welfare* (1920), Part VI., containing 112 pages, was entitled "The Variability of the National Dividend ". In the second edition (1924)— and, of course, also in the new third edition—this Part was omitted, because I was anxious to undertake a more comprehensive study of industrial fluctuations. The present volume is the result of that study. It is written throughout with a constructive purpose, and the (not very numerous) criticisms of the work of others contained in it are strictly subordinate to that purpose. The conditions prevailing in the great post-war boom and subsequent depression have been so abnormal that I have not examined them here.

The charts embodied in the text are worked to a slightly rougher approximation than the tables in the Appendix, on which they are based, and there are, therefore, occasional small discrepancies. Owing, however, to the kind assistance of Miss Elkin, I trust that all serious inaccuracies have been eliminated from both charts and tables.

For exhibiting the relation between the movements of various time-series over the period studied I have relied in the main upon the method of graphic representation. In a criticism of my first edition in the *Quarterly Journal of Economics* for August, 1928, Professor Persons, whose authority on these matters is high, urges that this method is misleading. He points out, for example, that, as between the series of unemployment percentages and bank clearings, shown opposite p. 132, out of the 43 pairs of annual differences nearly a third are of like algebraic sign, so that in reality there is a much less definite inverse correlation between the two series than mere inspection suggests. When, however,

v

we are concerned, as I am, with the relation between wave-movements extending over a number of years, counts of annual differences are liable to conceal the essential fact. Thus, if the annual differences of like sign are small and those of unlike sign large, the like signs may be equally or even more numerous than the others, and yet the broad movements of the two series may be similar — a state of things which the graphic method at once reveals. No doubt, if I were fortunate enough to possess Professor Persons' mastery of modern statistical technique, I should have called that weapon to my aid. Nevertheless, for the purposes of this study I doubt whether the information and suggestions which the graphic method yields would have received any important supplement.

In this second edition I have, I hope, succeeded in improving the analysis in several respects and carrying it a little further. The principal modifications and new material will be found in Part I., Chapters II., X., XI. and XVIII., and Part II., Chapters III., IV., V., VIII. and IX. As in the first edition, so also here I owe much to the criticism and suggestions of Mr. D. H. Robertson, of Trinity College, Cambridge.

A. C. P.

KING'S COLLEGE, CAMBRIDGE,
  February 1929.

CONTENTS

CONTENTS

CHAPTER XXIII

PART II

REMEDIES

CHAPTER I

CONTENTS

CHAPTER XV

CHAPTER XVI

CHAPTER XVII

CHAPTER XVIII

APPENDIX

STATISTICAL TABLES

CHARTS

xxi

* These charts are to be found in back cover pocket.

* These charts are to be found in back cover pocket.

INTRODUCTORY CHAPTER

§ 1. At every moment of the working day workers by hand and brain, in association with the capital equipment available for them, are engaged in rendering economic service. Some of them are constructing and some maintaining capital goods, such as railways and ships, machinery, tools and buildings: others are extracting raw material from the earth or looking after crops and animals on its surface: others advancing material on its way from the raw state nearer to the final form designed for it, as the makers of pig-iron or of cotton yarn: others finishing consumable goods of various sorts, as the makers of clothes, bicycles and boots: others transporting goods: others dealing with them in warehouses and shops: others operating such services as the provision of gas, water and electricity: yet others rendering personal services to individuals and groups of individuals, for example, doctors, lawyers, teachers and domestic servants. At the same time that all this is happening, a stream of goods, the final fruit of a substantial portion of this process, is always flowing into warehouses and shops—institutions which we may regard, if we will, as a lake into which these things pass and in which they stay for a while. At the opposite, or purchasers', end of this lake there is also always proceeding an outflow of goods to the various persons who have claims on them. This outflow goes, in great part, to the controllers of business, who retain some of it for their own consumption or their own use as machines, hand over some to the persons to whom they are under contract to pay interest on past loans, and hand over another part to workpeople in the form of wages to induce them to carry on further work. Out of the portion going to each of these groups some is transferred, before being used, to government authorities in the form of taxes and loans, to be paid by them to various persons, not against work—this part is counted already—but to finance debt service, pension schemes, insurance schemes, poor law relief and so forth. Of course, this account is only rough and approximate ; for, though most of what are usually called consumable goods flow through warehouses and shops, the important part of them constituted by direct services does not do so : while, of instrumental or capital goods, those that are made to order go from producer to purchaser without any intermediary. Broadly, however, what has been said represents the facts.

§ 2. If the life of industry was steady and continuous, the rates of movement and the volumes of these several streams would always be the same ; or, more exactly, since the numbers of the population are not constant, they would change gradually in proportion as population changed. Thus, allowing for growth of population, there would be a steady flow of production from the farms and factories into warehouses and shops ; a steady flow from warehouses and shops into factories of things to make good the wear and tear of machinery and, so far as new capital is being created to match the growth of population, of new machinery, new buildings and so on ; a steady flow from these same warehouses and shops into the homes of business men (and those to whom they are indebted) of things for their own consumption, and a steady flow into their control of the things that constitute the real wages they are offering every week in payment for the services of workpeople. In actual life, however, there is not this kind of steadiness. On the contrary, the modern world is characterised by large and frequent industrial fluctuations.   Thus Professors Mitchell and King have roughly estimated, after making allowance for the factor of growth, that in the United States production " in the worst years runs something like 15 to 20 per cent behind the best, and something like 8 to 12 per cent behind the moderately good years ".[1]

§ 3. In my book *The Economics of Welfare* abstraction

[1] *Business Cycles and Unemployment*, p. 39.

is made of this very important fact. That work deals with the relation of economic welfare to the size of the national dividend, or real income, of the country, and to the way in which this is distributed among people of different degrees of wealth. The point of view taken is a static one, in the sense that, though, of course, causes tending to alter the size and distribution of the dividend are discussed, the relation between economic welfare and the actual process of change is not brought under review. As a consequence of certain causes the dividend, on the average of some assigned period, is conceived to be of such and such a size and to be distributed in such and such a way ; and this is all. A study so limited plainly requires a supplement.

§ 4. To be complete, that supplement would need to cover all types of change, the broad movements that extend over long periods, the oscillations of shorter wave-length extending over several years and the short-time movements that accompany the shifting seasons of the normal year. Long-period movements are outside my present scope : their study would demand so great an equipment of historical knowledge that nobody would expect a review of them in a work of this character. With seasonal fluctuations the case is different. The regularity of their recurrence makes them a fit subject for study by the methods available to economists. As compared, however, with the wave movements extending over several years, though very important for certain special industries, they are not very important for industry as a whole. Thus, over the period 1887–1913 in the United Kingdom, if we take averages of the unemployment percentages for Trade Unionists making returns for all the Januarys, all the Februarys and so on, we obtain a range with a minimum of 4·1 per cent for June and a maximum of 5·1 per cent for January, grouped round an annual average of 4·5 per cent. If, however, we take annual averages, the range extends from a minimum of 2 per cent in 1899 to a maximum of 7·7 per cent in 1909, the annual average for the whole period being, of course, as before, 4·5 per cent. Thus the monthly range has a downward sweep equal to 8·9 per cent and an upward sweep equal to 13·3 per cent of the mean rate ; whereas the annual range has a downward sweep equal to 55 per cent and an upward sweep equal to 71 per cent of the mean rate.   Moreover, the very regularity of the seasonal variations, by making it easy for people to protect themselves by moving between one seasonal occupation and another complementary one, *e.g.* between building in summer and gas-stoking in winter, much reduces the social evil involved in these variations.   Partly for this reason I shall leave them, as well as long-period movements, unexamined.   The present volume will be confined to a study of those industrial fluctuations extending over short spans of years which are sometimes called " cyclical ".   An attempt will be made to elucidate the causes of these fluctuations, the consequences that follow from them and the means available for obviating or mitigating whatever in these consequences is inimical to social well-being.   The inquiry will not deal with the detailed history of particular fluctuations, but will aim, so far as may be, at generality.

PART I

CAUSATION

CHAPTER I

THE GENERAL CHARACTERISTICS OF INDUSTRIAL FLUCTUATIONS

§ 1. THE productive or income-getting power of any community at any time consists of its land, its people, its capital equipment and its organisation. This income-getting power changes in amount with changes in the numbers of the population, developments of scientific knowledge and industrial skill, and the construction of new capital appliances. Alongside of changes in the amount of income-getting power there also occur from time to time changes in the proportion of the income-getting power that is engaged in work. These changes, intra-annual seasonal movements being disregarded, constitute the class of industrial fluctuations with which this volume is concerned. For complete accuracy, indeed, account should be taken, and allowance made, for the fact that the proportion of income-getting power engaged in work is subject to some long-period changes of a non-cyclical character. Thus during the last hundred years the normal length of the working day for manual labour in the United Kingdom has been largely reduced. For short periods, however, the changes that occur in the length of the normal working day, for the average of the whole community, are, in general, very small in comparison with those changes in the application of income-getting power that are associated with overtime, short time and unemployment. For the present purpose, therefore, they may be disregarded without serious error. We may rest satisfied with the statement that industrial

7

fluctuations are fluctuations in the proportion of the community's income - getting power that is actually engaged in work.

§ 2. Since income-getting power consists in a number of different factors, and since the proportions of these several factors at work from time to time need not all vary in the same way, no measure of industrial fluctuations, thus interpreted, can be provided that is at once simple and exact. Plainly, however, it is desirable, if we can, to secure some rough-and-ready statistical index of the movements which we wish to study. Such an index must be looked for either in records of production or in records of employment. It is clear, however, that records of production cannot serve in their crude form ; for they reflect changes in the amount of income-getting power in existence as well as changes in the proportion of it at work, so that, in a community where income-getting power is increasing in amount, production may continue to expand even when the proportion of income-getting power at work is being seriously contracted. In actual fact, " the curve of aggregate production rises strongly during periods of prosperity, and describes during periods of depression slight undulations, in such wise that it hardly departs from a nearly straight, or slightly inclined, line. To the increase in periods of prosperity there is opposed stagnation in periods of depression." [1] Hence, if records of production are to be used as a measure of industrial fluctuations, they must first be " corrected " in such a way as to eliminate long - period trends. Various devices are available by which this can be done in a fairly satisfactory manner. The result is an index of production with the trend removed. Either this or an index of the percentage of workpeople employed will serve as a rough measure of industrial fluctuations.

§ 3. It may be thought at first sight that a " corrected " production index and an employment index, if properly constructed and covering the same industries, must, on account of their close causal connection, necessarily move together. That they will move together, in the sense that

---

[1] Aftalion : *Les Crises périodiques de surproduction*, vol. ii. p. 29.

their upward and downward turning points will roughly synchronise, is true. Evidence of this is afforded by the annexed chart showing together the unemployment percentage and the pig-iron consumption of the United Kingdom since 1850. But they will not move together in the sense that their swings are similar in amplitude. On the one hand, the fluctuations of output about the trend depend upon the extent to which income-getting power as a whole, including mechanical equipment and the brains of technical experts, is set to work. In periods of depression the amount of *intelligence* put into production is, in general, larger, partly because relatively inefficient business men are compelled to sell out to others, but mainly because those persons who remain in business " are put on their mettle, and exert themselves to their utmost to invent improved methods, and to avail themselves of the improvements made by others ".[1] In like manner, workpeople, since they are earning less, are likely, if on piece-wages, to work harder and more intelligently. Thus, in coal-mining, the late Lord Rhondda has shown : " The better-off men were, the more easily they could obtain the means of subsistence, the less energy they put forward ; there was a very considerable diminution in the output per man per annum. On the other hand, when prices fell and wages followed, the fact that the men worked harder accentuated the depression which followed from the number of mines opened during the period of boom." [2] These considerations suggest that, when the trend is eliminated, production will be found to fluctuate less extensively than employment. On the other hand, employment figures ignore the *under-employment* that

---

[1] Marshall, *Evidence before the Gold and Silver Commission* [Cd. 5512], Q. 9816 ; cf. Aftalion, *Les Crises périodiques de surproduction*, vol. i. p. 230.

[2] *Statistical Journal*, Jan. 1914, p. 174. Cf. Mitchell, *Business Cycles*, p. 478. It should be remembered that output per man is not, in these circumstances, at all an adequate test of energy, since in good times inferior men will be added to the normal staff, and, after a point, many firms will be working beyond the output yielding maximum efficiency, and so under conditions of increasing supply price, the workmen having to work with too little machine-power per man. M. Aftalion quotes statistics to show that in coal-mines, iron-mines and blast furnaces, output per head is less in times of prosperity than in times of depression (vol. i. p. 195).

is common in depressions and the overtime that is common
in booms. According to Mr. Berridge's investigations in
the United States for 1919–22, the net result of these con-
flicting influences was that production varied from one
and a half times to twice as much as employment. As he
himself suggests, however, this rather surprising result may
be due to the fact that the production data used by him
related, in large measure, to industries concerned with basic
materials, which are probably more responsive than others
to the course of the business cycle.[1] For the United Kingdom
Mr. Rowe has constructed a production index, referred, like
Mr. Berridge's, in the main to basic industries, from 1907
to 1913 and from 1920 onwards.[2] In the following table this
index is set beside the employment (*not* unemployment)
percentage yielded by the Trade Union returns :

	Production Index.	Trade Union Employment.
1907	100·3	96·3
1908	93·3	92·2
1909	96·8	92·3
1910	97·1	95·3
1911	101·3	97·0
1912	103·6	96·2
1913	107·5	97·8
1920	100·2	97·6
1921	67·5	84·6
1922	80·9	84·6
1923	88·7	88·5
1924	90·9	92·1
1925	87·2	90·3

For the present purpose the year 1921 must be ignored on
account of the prolonged coal strike, which practically
stopped coal production during the second quarter. For the
unemployment statistics, from which the second column in
this table is derived, do not take account of workpeople who
are unemployed because they are engaged in an industrial
dispute, and, consequently, in years of abnormal industrial

[1] Cf. Mitchell, Berridge and others, *Business Cycles and Unemployment*,
p. 61, and Berridge, *Cycles of Unemployment*, chap. v.
[2] *London and Cambridge Economic Service*, Jan. 1924, p. 8, and Jan.
1926, p. 14. For the period of 1920 Mr. Rowe's figures are given by
quarters ; to obtain yearly figures I have taken simple arithmetic averages
of these.

conflict the two indices are not properly comparable. Apart from that year the table shows a relation very similar to that found by Mr. Berridge for the United States—to be explained perhaps in the same way. This, however, is a side-issue. The precise quantitative relation between the movements of production indices and of employment indices does not greatly concern us. The point of practical importance is that, even when the trend is eliminated, production indices and employment indices have swings of *different* amplitude. Consequently, if, as is obviously convenient, we desire to provide ourselves with a single principal measure of industrial fluctuations, choice must be made between the two sorts of index.' This choice is fortunately not difficult, at all events for a student in this country. For, as it happens, while statistics of employment, useless indeed as absolute measures but of high value as measures of change, are available over a long period and a wide range of occupations, statistics of production are exceedingly deficient—so deficient that little or nothing can be done with them. In this book, therefore, variations in the volume of employment in particular industries and in the general body of industry will be taken as the main statistical criteria of those industrial fluctuations which it is our business to investigate.

§ 4. Having thus obtained a rough definition and a rough measuring-rod for our subject-matter, we are ready to set out the principal characteristics which that subject-matter presents. We notice, first, that in recent times industrial fluctuations have not occurred independently in different countries, but have as a rule affected at the same time and in the same sense the whole, or nearly the whole, of the industrially developed part of the world. In the earlier years of the nineteenth century the fortunes of different nations were less closely interdependent, but recent industrial fluctuations, those whose peaks were reached in 1872, 1882, 1890, 1900 and 1907, have all been world-wide in scope. Of this fact indirect evidence is afforded by the close parallelism of the price movements, shown in the accompanying chart, in the United Kingdom,

Germany, France and (in a lesser degree) the United States ; for, as will be shown presently, price cycles and industrial cycles are closely connected.   There is also available direct evidence from import and export statistics and, though unfortunately here foreign material is exceedingly deficient, from statistics of unemployment.

§ 5. Secondly, concentrating attention upon this country and making use of the returns of unemployment furnished by Trade Unions—the statistics obtained under the National Insurance Act do not extend sufficiently far back for our purpose—we are able to set out certain facts as to the range of industrial fluctuations throughout the general body of industry. The chart printed as frontispiece to this volume gives from 1850 to 1914 the annual percentage of unemployment over the average of all the industries for which returns are available. That chart displays a clearly marked rhythmic or wave-like succession of fluctuations. The waves are not of equal length nor yet of equal amplitude. As regards length the figures yield the following results.   From 1860 till 1914 the intervals between successive years of minimum unemployment are 7, 10, 7, 10, 7, 7 and 5 years respectively ; the intervals between successive maxima 6, 11, 7, 7, 11 and 4 or 5 years respectively ; the average length of periods of lessening employment being $\frac{2.6}{6}$ years and that of periods of improving employment $\frac{2.1}{6}$ years. As regards the amplitude of the fluctuations the differences between the maximum positions and the succeeding minimum positions were : 4·2, 5·8, 9·1, 8·1, 5·5, 2·4 and 5·7 per cent respectively. The general movement is thus rhythmic, both in respect of wave-length and of amplitude. The successive cycles are broadly similar to one another. A " typical " cycle constructed by making, as it were, a composite photograph of all the recorded cycles would not differ in form very widely from any of them. Its duration from minimum to minimum would be $7\frac{4}{7}$ years and its range from minimum to maximum employment 5·8 per cent. But this typical cycle is not an exact replica of any individual cycle. The rhythm is rough and imperfect. All the recorded cycles are members of the same family, but among them there are no twins.[1]

§ 6. So far attention has been directed to industrial activity in the mass. The mere fact, however, that industry as a whole moves up and down in waves tells us nothing about the way in which the waves are constituted. If, for instance, we find a 5 per cent upward swing, that might come about because some one industry expands 100 per cent while many others contract 1 per cent ; or because all industries expand exactly 5 per cent ; or because most industries expand, but some expand more and some less than 5 per cent. The last of these three possibilities is the one that is in fact realised. The third characteristic to be noted, therefore, is a general concordance in timing and direction between the wave movements in different occupations. In periods of prosperity nearly all industries show better employment than usual ; in periods of depression nearly all show worse employment than usual. The swings of the different industries are not independent and inchoate. They are concordant in direction. We may fairly speak of common swings of expansion and contraction in the main body of industries taken separately, and not merely in the aggregate or average of industries.

§ 7. But, fourthly, the amplitudes of the swings in different occupations are very far from concordant ; some are much larger than others. The industries (among those for which records are available) with the largest amplitude are shipbuilding and engineering—constructional industries ; other industries show much smaller amplitudes. Over the period 1860–1913 the average differences between the maximum unemployment figure and the succeeding minimum figure were, for engineering and shipbuilding 9·1 per cent, for building 4·1 per cent, for woodworking and furniture 3·7 per cent, and for printing and bookbinding 1·5 per cent.

---

[1] The Harvard University Research Bureau, on a more extended statistical basis, concludes that hitherto the lengths of the cycles have not " in any country been sufficiently uniform to warrant the prediction of major turns in business activity on the basis of a constant time interval between crises " (*Economic Barometers*, International Labour Office, 1924, p. 12).

The facts are clearly brought out in the accompanying chart. In view of these facts it is not surprising to find that industrial booms have nearly always been characterised by large and conspicuous investment in construction of some kind. A main feature of the boom culminating in 1825 was investment in Mexican mines and other enterprises in the South American countries recently freed from Spain. In 1833–6 there was large investment in railway building in England and in the United States. The crisis of 1847 was associated with a tremendous boom in English railway building ; the amount of money turned into railways rising from under seven millions in 1844 to over forty millions in 1847. Prior to the 1857 crisis we had made large investments in, and had exported much material for, American railways.[1] In the early 'sixties there was another British railway boom and in the early 'seventies another American one. The Baring crisis followed large investments in railways in Argentina. The beginning of the twentieth century witnessed a great expansion of electrical enterprise, especially in Germany, and the 1907 crisis, initiated in the United States, followed upon a similar development there. Thus industrial expansions have always been, in the main, expansions in the building of means of production. What means of production are selected depends upon circumstances. "At the beginning of the nineteenth century it was the means for sewing and spinning ; in a word, all kinds of textile machinery ; a little later it was the formidable apparatus of railways and railway material and of steel steamships to take the place of wooden sailing vessels ; in our own day it is electrical energy and its manifold industrial applications, tramways, electric railways, electric furnaces, electric light, and so on."[2] But always *some* form of construction dominates the stage. Thus Jevons wrote : "A characteristic of boom periods is that the proportion which

---

[1] As Mr. C. K. Hobson's study of twentieth-century figures shows, "in the case of railways at any rate British foreign investments, over a wide portion of the globe, are very largely represented by orders to British manufacturers of railway materials and railway stock" (*The Export of Capital*, p. 15).

[2] Cf. Lescure, *Les Crises générales et périodiques*, p. 413.

the capital devoted to permanent and remote investment
bears to that which is but temporally invested soon to
reproduce itself " [1] is increased.   Thus, again, Mr. Robertson
finds : " The most characteristic feature of an industrial
boom is the utilisation of an abnormally large proportion
both of past accumulations and of the current production
of consumable goods to elicit the production, not of other
consumable goods, but of constructional goods." [2]   Thus,
finally, Mr. Hull writes : " The difference between periods
of prosperity and periods of depression is . . . chiefly a
decrease in the rate of production of permanent wealth,
such as buildings, railways, ships, goods, materials, etc." [3]
Distinguishing between necessary construction, *i.e.* repairs
and such new construction as is associated with the growth
of population, and optional construction, he puts the latter
at about one-third of the whole in periods of maximum
activity, and finds the dominant note of industrial fluctuations in the large changes that it undergoes.

§ 8. If we look in detail at such statistics of output as
are available, there is suggested an even sharper contrast
between production and consumption industries than was
indicated in the preceding section.   For, while a diagram
showing the output of the instrumental industries would
be a curve with large rises and large falls, one showing
the output of consumers' industries would consist of rises
interspersed with horizontal movements, like the outline
of a flight of stairs.   Evidence for this statement is afforded
by railway statistics, which indicate great expansion in
boom periods, but hardly any contraction in periods of
depression.[4]   The statistics of coal consumption [5]—in this
differing from the statistics of iron consumption—and the
statistics of the quantities of foreign trade are of like
character.   There may, indeed, be a momentary contraction
due to shock in some crises, such as that of 1870, but this
does not generally last long.[6]   M. Aftalion, summarising a

[1] Jevons, *Investigations in Currency and Finance*, p. 28.
[2] *A Study of Industrial Fluctuations*, p. 157.
[3] *Industrial Depressions*, p. 27.
[4] Cf. Aftalion, *Les Crises périodiques de surproduction*, ii. p. 23.
[5] *Ibid.* ii. p. 157.   [6] *Ibid.* ii. p. 26.

considerable inquiry, writes : " Perhaps reductions in the manufacture of objects of consumption have taken place on the morrow of crises. Perhaps also the production of goods of this kind declines in those industries which are only slightly capitalistic and make use of hand-work and home-work. But during a good part of the depression, for a number of industries making consumable goods, manufacture progresses rather than diminishes." [1] This continuing progress in the output of industries making consumption goods when instrumental industries are markedly depressed might suggest that, in times of depression, *employment* also in consumption industries must, contrary to what was said above, continue to increase ; workpeople, perhaps, being transferred into them from instrumental industries so as to make this possible. The facts, however, make no such inference necessary. The continuing progress or, at least, comparatively small regress in the output of consumption goods during periods of depression does not imply continuing progress in the amount of work done in them. It is due rather to the continuing influx of new machinery, on which work was started in the preceding booms and the delivery of which has been delayed owing to the long period involved in its manufacture. We need not, therefore, distrust the direct evidence of our statistics. Whatever may be the case with output, employment in consumption trades varies in the same sense as, though in a much less degree than, employment in instrumental trades.

§ 9. In the sixth section of this chapter it was stated that there is a marked concordance in the timing as well as in the direction of the movements of the several industries that go to make up the aggregate movement. In a broad sense the curves that face p. 14 show that, for England at all events, that is true. These curves do not, however, prove that the turning-points of the several movements exactly coincide. Obviously, since they are based on annual averages, it is impossible that they should do this, and the need for a closer study is suggested. Such a study reveals evidence—not, indeed, conclusive, but sufficient to

---

[1] Cf. Aftalion, *Les Crises périodiques de surproduction*, vol. ii. pp. 174-5.

establish a probability—that the turning-points in instrumental trades tend to precede by a short interval the
turning-points in consumption trades. Thus Sir William
Beveridge notes that in Great Britain the turning-points
of employment in engineering, shipbuilding and metals
preceded those of employment in other groups in the bad
years about 1868 and 1893-4 and in the good years about
1872 and 1890.[1] Again, M. Aftalion notes that in 1858,
1874, 1901 and 1908 the prices of all metals fell on nearly
every occasion in the first year of the depression, but that
the prices of several textile materials and those of a considerable proportion of other things did not do so.[2] Yet
again, Professor Mitchell, after studying *monthly* figures
for the United States, writes : " Producers' goods reached
their highest point and began to fall earlier in 1907 than
consumers' goods, and were on the down grade several
months before the panic broke out. Their decline in 1908
was also greater in degree, their recovery began sooner
and proceeded at a faster pace." [3] There are, of course,
pitfalls in comparisons of monthly figures in view of the
divergent *seasonal* influences to which different occupations
are subject. Still, on the whole, it seems fair to conclude
that movements in the instrumental industries are not
only larger than the corresponding movements in the consumption industries, but also often precede them by a
short interval.

[1] Cf. *Unemployment*, p. 40.
[2] Cf. Aftalion, *Les Crises périodiques de surproduction*, i. p. 24.
[3] *Business Cycles*, p. 99.

CHAPTER II

§ 1. PART I. of my book deals with causation. That the problem to be attacked under this head is difficult is shown by the number and variety of the explanatory theories that have, from time to time, won adherents among economists. It is well, therefore, to attempt some lightening of our task by framing for ourselves at the outset a definite and limited objective. The fundamental fact to be emphasised is the curious wave-like movement, which industrial activity in modern industrial communities everywhere undergoes, and which is excellently depicted for this country in the annual percentages of unemployment summarised in my frontispiece chart. These fluctuations of unemployment are intimately associated with fluctuations in the aggregate amounts of real wages that are annually paid out by the controllers of industry to workpeople. There is, we may conceive, a supply schedule representing the numbers of days' work that will be supplied by workpeople in response to different rates of real wages ; and a demand schedule representing the number of days' work in return for which employers will offer different rates of real wages. The interaction of these two schedules at any moment determines at once the size of the real wages bill and the curve of employment. If both schedules swing up or down parallel to one another, the amount of the real wages bill will alter, but the amount of employment will remain unchanged. If, however, one of the schedules moves relatively to the other, the amount of employment will certainly alter, while the size of the real wages bill, though, as will appear presently, it *may* remain stationary, will *in general* alter also.

Our fundamental index of industrial fluctuations being fluctuations in employment, parallel movements of the two schedules do not, therefore, interest us. Industrial fluctuations, as here defined, are brought about if, and only if, one of the schedules moves relatively to the other.

§ 2. Let us first ignore the fact that workpeople are split up into a large number of groups, each specialised to a particular sort of production, and imagine that they are all engaged in making a single kind of commodity or various commodities each in equal proportions. In these conditions the supply schedule of work, in terms of the commodity or complex of commodities, is the joint result of the workpeople's attitudes of aversion from work and of desire towards the fruit of work : and the demand schedule is determined by the fact that it will pay employers to offer for any rth unit of work a rate of pay equal to the anticipated net product (discounted to allow for the interval, if any, between wage payment and final production) of the rth unit.[1] If workpeople come to dislike work less or to like the fruit of work more, the supply schedule of work will fall. If, through changes of method or otherwise, work becomes more efficient, in such wise that any rth unit of work yields a larger output than before, the demand schedule for work will rise. Now it is reasonable to suppose that, from

---

[1] Let $F(w)$ be the workpeople's aggregate aversion from performing w units of work. Let $\psi(w)$ be the discounted quantity of produce yielded by w units of work. Let $\phi\{\psi(w)\}$ be the workpeople's aggregate desire for the fruit of w units of work.

Then it is easy to see that the supply price of w units of work in terms of product

$$= \frac{dF(w)}{dw} \div \frac{d\phi\{\psi(w)\}}{d\psi(w)},$$

and the demand price
$$= \frac{d\psi(w)}{d(w)}.$$

Equilibrium is attained when these two quantities are equal ; and a disturbance of equilibrium will in general occur if any of F, ψ or ϕ is altered.

It will be noticed that the term " work " is here used as equivalent to effort, so that, when a man becomes stronger or more skilful and functions for the same length of time, we say, not that more work is being done, but that the productivity of a given quantity of work has become larger. With this use of language increased strength or skill on the part of workpeople signifies a rise in the demand schedule, not a fall in the supply schedule of " work ".

the short-period standpoint relevant to so-called cyclical movements, workpeople's attitude of aversion from work and desire for the fruits of work will remain fairly stable ; and, therefore, that, abstraction made of population changes, the supply schedule of labour will not undergo significant autonomous variations.[1] It follows that the proximate causes behind cyclical industrial fluctuations can only be such variations in the real demand schedule for labour as do not themselves indirectly bring about parallel movements in the supply schedule. It is further reasonable to suppose that, from the standpoint of periods relevant to industrial fluctuations, the supply schedule of labour, conceived as distributed over the production of things in general, is of such a character that increases in real price are associated with increases in quantity supplied. It follows that upward movements in demand increase, and downward movements diminish, at once the volume of employment and the aggregate real wages bill.

§ 3. This simple analysis is not directly applicable when workpeople are separated into specialised groups making different things. For, whereas in our imaginary world the demand schedule and the supply schedule both express relations between quantities of work and quantities of one commodity or of a collection of commodities combined in defined proportions, in the actual world the supply schedule for each group of workpeople expresses a relation between quantities of work and quantities of those " goods in general " that are paid in wages, while the demand schedule expresses, primarily at all events, a relation between quantities of work and quantities of the particular commodity which each group severally produces. Plainly, demand schedules for work in different industries, so conceived, cannot be added together to yield a demand schedule for work as a whole. A conception of an aggregate demand schedule is, however, essential for any satisfactory treatment of industrial fluctuations. In order to make this possible, we must frame for ourselves the notion of a unit of wage goods in general. This must be con-

---

[1] Variations that are not autonomous but are brought about by monetary disturbances are studied in Chapter VIII.

ceived as a collection of so many physical units of the various
sorts of goods that are actually handed to wage earners
in the proportion in which they are so handed.   It is, of
course, impossible to make this conception watertight—for
the reason, among others, that different groups of workpeople
consume various sorts of goods in different proportions.   But
the precise constitution of our unit does not, for the present
purpose, greatly matter.   We need not, indeed, even build
it exclusively of wage goods.   If we will, it can be the total
collection of things bought by all the £s expended on some
specified day, divided, as to each element comprised in it,
by the number of £s then expended.   The essential thing
is to construct mentally *some* definitely conceived generalised
unit, so to speak, of objective value.   When we have done
this, it is easy to express both the supply schedule and the
demand schedule for days' work of each group of workpeople
in terms of this generalised unit ;   whereupon it becomes
possible to sum the separate schedules into aggregated supply
and demand schedules for work as a whole.   When this is
done, it remains true, as in the simplified case considered in
the preceding section, that, from the standpoint of industrial
fluctuations, the aggregated supply schedule of work is not
likely to undergo any autonomous movements ;   that it is
elastic from the standpoint of periods relevant to our
problem ;   that the proximate causes of industrial fluctuations, as here defined, can only be such variations in the
demand schedule for labour as do not themselves indirectly
bring about parallel movements in the supply schedule ;   and
that these proximate causes will make the volume of employment and the real wages bill vary in the same sense.   The more
complex analysis of this section does not lead to any different
result in this matter from that attained in the simpler one.

§ 4.   Now, if in any community the demand schedule for
labour is moving upwards or downwards at a constant rate—
which means, of course, that the real aggregate wages offered
per day for any r units of work is altering at a constant rate,
—it is reasonable to suppose that this movement will indirectly bring about a definitely related movement of the
supply schedule.   If the numbers of the people are stationary,

their standard of comfort will alter with the altering environment, and, hence, also the rate of real wages which is required to call out the supply of a given quantity of work. The aggregate amount of employment will, therefore, not change : there will be no industrial fluctuations in my sense. If the numbers of the people are not stationary, the reaction of the supply schedule will be somewhat more complicated in character. The aggregate amount of employment will not remain stationary : but the reaction, it is fair to suppose, will be of such a kind that the percentage of employment so remains. Again, therefore, there are no industrial fluctuations. In general, then, the proximate causes of the fluctuations that actually occur may be defined more precisely, not as movements of the demand schedule for labour, but *as deviations in the movement of the demand schedule away from its general line of trend.*

§ 5. It must, indeed, be conceded that, in employing the concept of a line of trend in this way, we are artificially simplifying the facts. The purely technical difficulty that a demand schedule is a list of quantities, and not a single quantity, is, indeed, easily overcome. For, on the assumption that the shape of the demand schedule does not change, its condition at any moment can be *represented* by a single quantity, namely, the quantity of work demanded, *i.e.* the demand for work, at a defined real price P. There is, however, also a difficulty of substance. The line of trend in the movement of demand is not given in advance, in such wise that the supply schedule can adapt itself to it in a mechanical and rigid manner. What the line of trend has become can only be discovered when we look backwards over history ; no reliance can be placed on forward extrapolations. Moreover, even from the standpoint of a student looking backwards, there will seldom be a single unambiguous line of trend, about which all experts would agree. It is only when a series mounts in rough arithmetical progression that the trend can be represented by a straight line. For more complex progressions curved lines are needed, and to determine the precise form of curve that is most appropriate will not always be easy. Moreover, it may well happen that, from time to time, the general direction of the trend alters abruptly, so that, in effect, a new line of trend has supplanted the old one. All this must be conceded. But, nevertheless, the conception is adequate for our present purpose. It is true that the supply schedule of labour does not adjust itself with any exactness to the trend of demand, and it is also true that the state of demand, which would conform to the trend at any particular moment, cannot often be unambiguously determined. But the supply schedule does adjust itself to the trend of demand in a rough general way, and states of demand substantially out of conformity with the trend can be detected. This is all that we really need.

§ 6. Industrial history does not display merely alternations of excesses in the demand for labour above the line of trend, associated with good employment, and deficiencies in the demand below the line of trend associated with bad employment. Rather the alternations are of *periods* of gradually improving and of gradually worsening employment. Thus, according to our analysis, there must be present upward deviations in the demand for work from the line of trend, which are at first small, and then, over a period of one, two or possibly three years, become larger and larger till a maximum is reached. Thereafter the demand gradually falls again to the line of trend, passes below it, and reaches a minimum some years later than the maximum ; and so on in successive cycles. When, therefore, we endeavour to pass beyond proximate to more ultimate causes, our problem will not be merely to discover the causes of alternations between excesses above and deficiencies below the line of trend on the part of the demand for labour, but the causes of alternations possessing this peculiar progressive and cumulative character.[1] Furthermore, these causes must also be such as will explain the much more marked fluctuations which we have seen to take place in the demand for work in productive industries than in that for work in consumption industries.

---

[1] Thus, let the demand schedule per month be represented by the quantity of stuff offered for labour at a wage rate r. Call this the demand. Let t be the number of months that have elapsed since zero month. Let $\phi(t)$ be the actual demand and $f(t)$ the demand conforming to the line of trend in month t. Then, starting from the point of minimum demand, we

Movements about the line of trend of the demand for labour, possessing these characteristics, are the proximate causes of industrial fluctuations. To what are they themselves due ?

§ 7. If and when we have discovered the answer to this question, we shall not by any means have exhausted our problem. The influences behind variations in the real demand schedule for labour are, we may say, the initiating causes of industrial fluctuations. But every initiating cause, when it comes into play, operates upon a certain complex of industrial and monetary conditions. Given the initiating cause, these will determine the nature of the effect that it produces, and are, in this sense, themselves causes of industrial fluctuations. The initiating cause is the dropping of a match : the consequences are determined by the nature of the material with which it comes in contact. It is reasonable to expect *a priori*, and the rough similarity of form among successive industrial wave movements confirms the expectation, that in the modern world the conditions which are present when successive matches fall, or at all events when they fall in such a way as to ignite the surrounding material, are more or less alike. In regard to these conditions, therefore, it may be possible to conduct an analysis that will be applicable, not merely to particular industrial fluctuations, but to industrial fluctuations in general. A considerable part of my work will consist in an inquiry along these lines.

§ 8. There remains yet a third problem. As was shown in the last chapter, industrial fluctuations succeed one another in a rough rhythmical sequence. This fact has led a number of writers to search after the cause of this rhythm or regularity. They admit, of course, that the rhythm may be " accidental ", that is to say, the result of

---

have four phases in a normal cycle, each lasting one year, two years or possibly more :

In phase (1) $\phi(t) < f(t)$ and $\phi'(t) - f'(t)$ is positive.
In phase (2) $\phi(t) > f(t)$ and $\phi'(t) - f'(t)$ is positive.
In phase (3) $\phi(t) > f(t)$ and $\phi'(t) - f'(t)$ is negative.
In phase (4) $\phi(t) < f(t)$ and $\phi'(t) - f'(t)$ is negative.

These distinctions enable us to give an exact definition to Professor Mitchell's terms revival, prosperity, recession and depression, as employed in *Business Cycles, The Problem and its Setting*, p. 381.

the concatenation of a number of small independent causes, which have " happened " to bring it about. But, they hold, the rhythm is so marked that it is more likely to be due to some special dominant cause or small group of causes, " accident " accounting only for its failure to attain to complete regularity. This is not, indeed, admitted by all writers. Thus Mr. Hull declares : " There is literally nothing in periodicity, as applied to the industries, except the simple fact that, when the industries increase from their lowest point to their highest point and in turn fall from their highest point to their lowest point, a period of time necessarily elapses." [1] Most students of industrial fluctuations, however, do not dismiss the seeming regularity of succession among industrial cycles so lightly as this, but hold that it requires some special explanation. This matter is discussed in the final chapter of Part I.

[1] *Industrial Depressions,* p. 57.

CHAPTER III

CHANGES IN EXPECTATIONS AS PROXIMATE CAUSES OF
CHANGES IN THE DEMAND FOR LABOUR

§ 1. THE demand schedule at any time for labour in general
in terms of stuff in general is determined by the anticipated
yield of various quantities of labour, discounted for the period
that must elapse between the payment made for the labour
and the emergence of its fruit. More precisely, the real
demand price for any rth unit of labour is equal to the
difference which it is anticipated that this unit will make
to the total product, discounted in the above manner. Thus
there are two ways in which changes in the demand for
labour may come about : (1) through changes, whether
warranted or not, in expectations about yield ; and (2)
through changes in the rate of discounting. A doubling in
the anticipated rate of return on investment and a halving
in the rate of discounting have the same effect. This latter
type of change in turn can come about in either of two ways :
(1) through changes in people's general attitude towards the
future ; or (2) through changes in the size of the income
stream that is flowing in to them. From the short-period
standpoint relevant to industrial fluctuations, the former type
of change may legitimately be left out of account. Hence
variations in the real demand for labour must find their
proximate cause [1] either in changes in the expectations entertained by industrialists as to the real yield to be got from
employing given quantities of new capital or in changes in
the size of the real income accruing to the community as a

---

[1] Apart from autonomous changes on the side of money.

whole.[1] There is, of course, nothing to prevent these two
types of cause from being present at the same time. Indeed,
it is probable that they will often be combined and will
support one another. Thus an expectation of an enlarged
yield from labour, leading to an increased demand for and
employment of labour, will, if it has been soundly based,
lead presently to an enlarged flow of production, which will
enable the demand for labour to be expanded further. Again,
an enlargement in the stream of product, due to some " act
of God "; is likely to have psychological reactions and so
to stimulate optimistic expectations as to the yield from
labour. Though, however, the two types of cause are intimately connected, it is to be presumed that one of them
plays a larger part than the other in generating the industrial fluctuations of real life. It is important for my
purpose to discover, if possible, which of them is thus predominant, so that we may know where further investigation
can most usefully be concentrated.

§ 2. Some light is thrown on this issue by the relation
between variations in industrial activity and variations in
the stocks of consumable goods—we are not here concerned
with production goods—in warehouses and shops. In order
that this may be brought out clearly, I shall indicate briefly
what the relation between the inflowing stream and the
stock of these goods might be expected to be if no fluctuations occurred. When the stream flows from the industrial
machine, it is not turned instantly to its final uses. Rather,
as was observed in the Introductory Chapter, it passes at first
into the reservoir constituted by warehouses and shops, and
every drop comprised in it stays there for some finite period
of time. If the volume of flow per day were constant and the
period of time for which a representative drop stayed in
the reservoir were constant, the stock standing in the reservoir would also be constant. It would be equal, of course,
to the volume of water that flows in during the period of

[1] Strictly speaking, account should also be taken of changes in the
distribution of a given income, by which more or less comes into the hands
of persons (*e.g.* the very rich) more likely than others to turn it to capital
uses. For our present purpose, however, it is not necessary to go into
this.

time for which a representative drop occupies the reservoir : for, if the drops flowing in each day stay there (on the average) for six months, there must obviously always be there six months' inflow of drops. The fraction of a year constituted by a representative drop's " period of residence " and the fraction of the annual flow constituted by the permanent stock are, in stationary conditions, equal : they are, in fact, two ways of expressing the same thing. What this fraction shall be is determined by a balancing on the part of warehousemen and shopkeepers of the advantage, which the marginal unit of stock affords in enabling the requests of their customers to inspect goods to be satisfied and their orders to be filled promptly, against the loss of interest involved in holding it. As I have said, we may expect it to remain constant in stationary conditions. When, however, conditions are not stationary, but causes initiating industrial fluctuations are at work, there is no reason to expect this. It is *prima facie* more probable that the size of the stock held in warehouses and shops will undergo variations of one kind or another. If the dominant influence behind expansions in the real demand for labour were increases, and that behind contractions in this real demand decreases, in the stream of produce flowing into the hands of the controllers of industry, we should expect to find expansions preceded by an increase in the stocks of consumable goods stored in warehouses and shops : for it does not seem likely that the reaction in the demand for labour, due to the enlargement of the stream of goods accruing to controllers, would be instantaneous.

§ 3. M. Tugan Baranowsky maintains that these preliminary agglomerations of consumable goods in fact take place, and, furthermore, that they " explain " industrial fluctuations. According to his view, during depressions there is an accumulation of capital, in the sense of wage goods and materials, seeking investment, which, after a time, is turned into industry and brings about expansion. Unused savings of these things are gradually piled up, and, as soon as they are massed in sufficient quantities, are thrown forward into industry, being there used to hire extra labour for the manufacture of capital instruments. Munitions are, as it were, built up during several years of trench warfare and then discharged in a great attack, and this attack, in turn, is followed by another period of quiescence and accumulation. Thus M. Tugan Baranowsky draws a parallel for industry from a steam engine. Capital, in the form of unused stocks of consumable goods, accumulates, he says, like steam behind a piston ; when the pressure attains a certain intensity, it drives the piston forward, and exhausts itself in doing so ; then a new accumulation takes place, until the piston is again driven forward; and so on continually.[1] This conception may be set out thus. Imagine Robinson Crusoe on his island and, alongside of him, a number of men, who normally produce—perhaps with a little help from Robinson's charity—enough to maintain themselves alive, but who ordinarily possess a good deal of unemployed labour power. Robinson saves, in the sense of accumulating a mass of consumable goods. When he has been doing this for some years, it occurs to him to entice his neighbours' unused labour power into activity by the offer of some of his accumulated goods in return for the manufacture of certain productive instruments. If he does this, his savings are converted into productive capital. There need not be any shifting of industrial effort from making consumables to making instrumental goods ; but, under the influence of Robinson's offer, new industrial effort, destined to the production of instrumental goods, is called into play. Thus a previous expansion in the store of consumable goods is followed by, and, in a sense, causes, a boom in the amount of labour that is hired to make productive instruments. So soon as the accumulated savings of consumable goods have been " used up " by conversion into fixed capital—railways and so on—the boom must break. There is no free capital —unhypotheticated savings—left with which to carry it on, and it thereupon comes to an end.

§ 4. In attempting to bring this theory to the test of facts we have, of course, to recognise that, in the short period which immediately follows the breaking of a boom, whole-

[1] Cf. *Les Crises industrielles en Angleterre*, p. 273.

salers' and retailers' stocks are bound to pile up ; for, *ex hypothesi*, the outflowing stream of wage goods going to workpeople is reduced—and the reduction cannot be more than partly offset by an increase in unemployment benefits and so on—while, since the first cut in labour will be made in the earliest stages of production and not in respect of partially finished goods on order that are nearly completed, the inflowing stream is not at once affected.[1] In like manner, in the short period which immediately follows the ending of a depression and the beginning of a revival the wholesalers' and retailers' stocks are bound to dwindle ; for an enlarged stream is flowing out in payment of workpeople—the growth being larger than the reduction in the stream that was flowing out before to unemployed persons and so on [2]—and, since the workpeople's efforts do not bear fruit instantaneously, no enlarged stream is for the moment flowing in. These, however, are only the first and the last stages, and they quickly pass. A knowledge of what happens at these stages does not enable us to say whether, during a period of depression, unused real savings—stocks of consumption goods—go on

---

[1] Thus, though it is true that, on these occasions, " the shops with unsold goods on their shelves and diminished takings in their tills, cannot give their usual orders to the merchants and manufacturers who supply them " (*Report of the Royal Commission on the Poor Laws*, p. 331), these unsold stocks are a symptom, and not a cause of the fundamental industrial malady. Moreover, it should be noted, in view of the fact that the fruits of past orders are pouring in, the temporary growth of stocks in dealers' hands does not prove that the turn of the tide has been started by something in the nature of a " consumers' strike ". It *may* be so started, as apparently happened in the United States in 1920. (Cf. Withers, *Bankers and Credit*, p. 166.) But it may also be started by the spontaneous birth among dealers of an expectation that consumers' demands will shortly fall off. It may be noted that, when the initiative is taken by retailers, retail prices do not necessarily fall before wholesale prices. The retailers may hold their prices while the reduction in their orders forces wholesale prices down. The fall in wholesale prices may cause the public to expect a fall in retail prices, and so may itself become a part cause of that contraction in the public demand which the retailers have anticipated. In the post-war boom in the United Kingdom retail prices went on rising for some seven months after wholesale prices had turned (July to January 1920). This fact suggests that retailers stopped off their orders in expectation of a slackening of consumers' purchases rather than as a result of it. It is not, however, conclusive ; for retailers *might*, of course, have held prices up in spite of a falling off of consumers' demand, supporting themselves by borrowing.

[2] Cf. *post*, Chapter XI.

accumulating till their volume is so great that they burst their way, as it were, into productive industry. In order to answer that question, we need to know whether, over the main body of a representative period of depression, the exit from our lake continues to be blocked up more thoroughly than the entrance to it. Evidence on this matter is very scarce. On the whole, however, it appears that, speaking generally, this does not happen. As a depression proceeds, " the accumulated stocks of goods carried over from the preceding period of prosperity are gradually disposed of. Even when consumption is small, manufacturers and merchants can reduce their stocks of raw material and finished wares by filling orders chiefly from what is on hand, and confining purchases to the small quantities needed to keep full assortments." [1] Thus, in spite of the fact that the consumption of wage-earners is lower than it was before, stocks of consumable commodities go on falling until after revival has begun. More generally, booms are characterised by the " production of goods in excess of the current rate of consumption, with consequent accumulation of stocks ", and depressions by " curtailment of production below current consumption, with consequent depletion of stocks ".[2] If this view is correct, the later part of the period of depression is responsible, not only for no accumulation of stocks of consumable goods, but for an actual reduction in the stocks left over from the preceding period of boom. Consequently, the theory that, as depressions progress, unused real savings go on accumulating till their growing pressure bursts the dam that holds them back from industry is inconsistent with the facts.

§ 5. The preceding paragraph does, indeed, ignore one aspect of a community's life, namely, its trade relations with other communities. If account is taken of this, our conclusion is somewhat modified. When there is a depression in one country, not merely absolutely, but also relatively to the rest of the world, the low prices that rule in that

---

[1] Cf. Mitchell, *Business Cycles,* pp. 565-6 ; cf. also *Business Cycles and Unemployment,* p. 8.

[2] Persons, Hardy and others, *The Problem of Business Forecasting,* p. 305.

country cause imports of goods to diminish and exports of goods to increase. They, therefore, cause either an import of gold—if the country is on a gold standard—or an increase in the country's credit holdings abroad, or both these things together. The extra gold and foreign credits constitute real accumulated savings. In effect manufacturers and others have sold goods to foreigners and taken gold and credits, instead of goods, in exchange for them. The gold and credits are not, of course, themselves either consumable goods or instrumental goods ; but they constitute a power to purchase from foreigners either sort of goods, if their owners choose to make use of it. Thus, when account is taken of foreign trade, the " unused savings " that accumulate during depressions — when the depressions are peculiar to particular communities—are not wholly imaginary, but are represented by a growing power in the community as a whole to make effective claims upon foreign communities. This qualification to our general conclusion is, however, clearly of no significance from the standpoint of industrial fluctuations that are spread over the world, as, in fact, in greater or less degree, most large movements are. Even from the standpoint of movements private to a particular country it is probably of secondary importance. The things that chiefly matter are goods stored in warehouses and shops. Of these, as has already been observed, not only does no continuing accumulation take place during periods of depression, but the stocks that are left over at the end of the preceding booms, if the scanty evidence which is available may be trusted, are dissipated rather than increased.

§ 6. As was observed at the end of § 2, if the initiation of industrial expansions were due to enhancements in the stream of produce accruing to the controllers of industry, these expansions would probably be preceded by expansions in the stocks of consumable goods. They would not, however, *necessarily* be so preceded. The reaction of the controllers of industry to an enlarged income might be so rapid that there was no time for any preliminary accumulation. Hence, though what

has been said makes, *pro tanto*, against the view that variations in the stream of produce flowing to the controllers of
industry are the predominant initiating causes of industrial
fluctuations, it falls short of proof. The rival claims of
changes in income and changes in expectations must, therefore, be submitted to further tests. Two such tests are
available, provided respectively by movements of the price
level and movements of interest rates. First, if expansions
in the real demand for labour were predominantly due to
expansions in the stream of production, periods of expansion should, other things being equal, be associated with
low prices and periods of contraction with high prices : for
in the former there would be a surplus, in the latter a
dearth of consumable goods in relation to money. In fact,
however, expansions in the real demand for labour are, in
general, characterised by rising prices and industrial depressions by falling prices. Again, if expansions in the stream
of production were the dominant influence making for
expansions in the real demand for labour, the rate of
interest should be low in good times and high in bad
times ; whereas in fact, as the accompanying chart clearly
shows, expansions are, in general, associated with high rates
for money and depressions with low rates.[1] These considerations prove that the dominant causal factor is not
on the side of the inflowing stream of production, but on
the side of expectations of yield. When these are good,
they lead business men to increase their borrowings, in
part from the banks, thus directly pushing up the rate
of interest and indirectly, by bringing more purchasing
power into circulation, pushing up prices : when they are
bad, they have converse effects. Thus, while recognising
that the varying expectations of business men may themselves be in part a psychological reflex of such things

[1] It should be noticed, however, that, as a careful study of the preceding
chart shows, the turning points in interest rates tend to lag a year or so
behind the turning points in the employment percentage. This is in
agreement with Mr. Snyder's findings for the U.S.A. There the upward
turns in business activity, as inferred from bank clearings, usually anticipate the upward turns of interest by from ten to fifteen months, while
the interval for the downward turns is still longer. (Cf. *Business Cycles
and Business Measurements*, p. 223.)

as good and bad harvests—while not, indeed, for the
present inquiring *how* these varying expectations themselves
come about—we conclude definitely that they, and not
anything else, constitute the immediate and direct causes
or antecedents of industrial fluctuations. We shall turn
then in the following chapters to a study of the causes
behind changes in the expectations of business men.

CHAPTER IV

REAL CAUSES BEHIND VARYING EXPECTATIONS OF PROFIT
FROM INDUSTRIAL SPENDING AMONG BUSINESS MEN

§ 1. In the title of this chapter I have used the term industrial spending instead of the more usual investment, because the latter is sometimes taken to mean the employment of mobile resources in securing the construction of more or less durable instruments of production. That is not what is intended here. For the present purpose the decision of a cotton-spinner to spin more yarn, or of a boot-maker to make more boots, stands on the same footing as the decision of an engineering firm to make more machines or of a shipbuilder to build more ships. The use of the term industrial spending will, it is hoped, prevent any misunderstanding on this point.

§ 2. The causes of varying expectations of return from industrial spending may conveniently be separated into three groups, labelled for brevity real causes, psychological causes and autonomous monetary causes. For the moment I shall ignore this last group, reserving the discussion of it to Chapter VIII. Real causes consist in changes that have occurred, or are about to occur, in actual industrial conditions ; and expectations based on these are true, or valid expectations. Psychological causes, on the other hand, are changes that occur in men's attitude of mind, so that, on a constant basis of fact, they do not form a constant judgment. In a stationary state, or, more accurately, a state of steady self-repeating movement, real causes of varying expectations could not, by definition, exist. Nor, as a matter of fact, though not of logic, could psychological causes exist, because, with everything repeating itself regularly, rational beings would be bound to realise that this was happening, and so could not fall into error. In a non-stationary state peopled exclusively by perfectly intelligent persons psychological causes, as defined above, could not exist, since they imply error ; but there would be nothing to prevent real causes from existing. In the actual world both sorts of cause are present. Moreover, they react on one another. On the one hand, real causes *may* set going psychological causes : actual prosperity, for example, leading people to take an unduly optimistic view of the future. On the other hand, psychological causes *must* set going real causes, for an error of expectation made by one group of business men, leading to increased or diminished output on their part, alters the *facts* with which other groups are confronted. Nor is this all. The reactions set up may, when once started, be reciprocating and continuous : a real cause calling a psychological cause into being : this in turn adding something further to the real cause : this in turn adding something further to the psychological cause : and so on. Of the method of these reactions something will be said at a later stage. In the present chapter our task is to disentangle the principal real causes that play a significant direct part, without reference to the question whether they also play an indirect part mediated through psychology, in causing the expectations of business men to vary, and so bringing about actual industrial fluctuations.

§ 3. For this task help may be obtained along three lines of inquiry. First, we ask ourselves what *sort* of changes are likely to affect the expectations of yield from industrial spending entertained by business men, and, through them, the volume of industrial activity ; what sort of changes, in fact, are *prima facie* relevant. Secondly, we ask whether the changes that actually take place under the several heads thus distinguished are sufficiently *large* to warrant a belief that their causal influence is significant. Thirdly, we ask whether there exist and are recorded any

statistical correlations between the several sorts of change
and the industrial fluctuations of history — correlations
which, if our analysis so far has been correct, would, of
course, imply corresponding correlations between the several
sorts of change and the underlying movements of industrial expectations. These three lines of inquiry must
be followed, so far as may be, together. It is sometimes
supposed that, when the third line is fully open, it is
sufficient by itself without resort to the other two : that
these other two are only useful as a *pis aller* when the
third is closed. This is a serious error. The absence of
statistical correlation between a given series of changes
and industrial fluctuations does not by itself disprove,
and the presence of such correlation does not by itself
prove, that these changes are causes of the fluctuations.
This statement has now to be elucidated.

§ 4. The negative part of it is, for our present purpose,
comparatively unimportant. Plainly, however, it is possible,
in certain circumstances, for causal action to be present
and yet completely masked. This will happen if a factor
making for industrial depression is always introduced at a
time when, for other reasons, industry is expanding. As
will be mentioned presently, there is some reason to believe
that industrial disputes occur most frequently in times of
prosperity ; a circumstance which would tend to prevent
the occurrence of a positive correlation between disputes
and depressions, even though disputes have in fact exercised
a depressing influence. A more striking illustration from
another field is afforded by the fact that in India there is
not merely no positive correlation, but actually a strong
negative correlation between inoculation for plague and
freedom from attacks by it : the explanation, of course,
being that inoculation is undertaken principally in places
where, and at times when, plague is severe.

The other part of our statement, that the presence of
correlation between a given series of changes and industrial
fluctuations does not by itself prove that these changes
are causes of the fluctuations requires a further defence.
First, it is possible that the series of changes may be effects

of industrial fluctuations, and not causes of them. This possibility is not excluded even though the changes in question *precede* the fluctuations ; for, if these are antici-pated, foreknowledge of their occurrence may bring about effects before they themselves occur. Thus, suppose that we found a positive correlation between variations in the aggre-gate volume of crops and industrial fluctuations, and had no statistics of yield per acre. The causal process—if this was the only information we had [1]—*might* be that farmers, foreseeing industrial booms and depressions brought about by causes independent of their action, increased and decreased the area of crops sown to match the anticipated variations in the demand for their products. A more striking illustration is furnished by the annexed chart. In Curves I and II on this chart there are brought to-gether British unemployment percentages and the quotients obtained by dividing for each year the index of mineral prices into the index of the prices of vegetable foods as set out by Sauerbeck. Except for the decade 1885–95, the correspondence between the two curves is extremely close. It is natural to infer that, when vegetable food-stuffs are abundant on account of good harvests, the consequent pros-perity of farmers leads to an increased real demand for the products of industry, so to improved expectations on the part of business men, so to an expansion of industry, and so to a high price for minerals. This inference is, however, over-hasty ; for expansions of industrial activity are sure to in-volve increases in the demand for minerals much more than proportionate to the increases in the demand for food ; and, therefore, the observed correspondence between the curves might be expected even though no causal action took place from the side of varying harvests. The sugges-tion that cheapenings of foreign food in terms of British manufactures *must* be causes of expansions in British in-dustry, because, as shown in the Curve III of the chart,

---

[1] In fact, of course, we have other information also, namely, that (in the United States) a substantially similar correlation exists between yield of crops *per acre* and industrial fluctuations (cf. *post*, p. 43). This rebuts the particular suggestion of the text, but does not affect the theoretical point it is meant to illustrate.

such relative cheapenings in fact accompany expansions, is defeated by the same criticism.

Secondly, it is possible that the given series of changes may be correlated with industrial fluctuations, because both they and industrial fluctuations are the joint effects of a common cause. Thus, when we find, as in fact we do, a considerable correlation between the yield of crops *per acre* and industrial activity in the United States, the explanation *may* be that variations in climatic conditions affect in the same sense both the productivity of the soil and the keenness of business men.[1] The statistics by themselves cannot possibly rebut this suggestion. It can only be rebutted by resort to general common-sense judgements of relevance and probability. It is on the strength of these, and not of the statistics, that I reject this explanation and conclude that much stronger evidence than any that has so far been forthcoming would be required to warrant us in entertaining it.

Thirdly, even though the two sorts of explanation suggested above are both excluded, we are still not entitled to conclude, from statistical correlations alone, that our given series of changes are causes of industrial fluctuations. We have ruled out the possibility that the industrial fluctuations themselves cause the series of changes, and the possibility that both the industrial fluctuations and the series of changes are effects of a common cause. But we have not excluded the possibility that there is no causal connection at all between the two series, the correlation between them being due to a number of small independent factors, after the manner of what is usually called "accident" or "chance". In view of this possibility we have to recognise that a statistical correlation by itself, however perfect it is, can never prove a causal connection. The utmost it can accomplish is to suggest that such a connection is prob-

---

[1] Cf. Hexter, *Social Consequences of Business Cycles*, p. 169. Dr. Hexter supports this explanation by observing that in the city of Boston cyclical fluctuations in conceptions (which, of course, precede births by nine months) among women *precede* fluctuations in wholesale prices by about eight months. Dr. Hexter's suggestion is not supported by the statistics of the United Kingdom, which show a lag of two or three years in birthrates behind the business cycle (cf. Thomas, *Social Aspects of the Business Cycle*, p. 98).

able.   If, *apart from this evidence,* the existence of such a
connection, or its existence in any significant measure,
seems to us to be highly improbable, either because the
alleged causal factor seems irrelevant or because it seems
quantitatively too trivial, even a very high degree of correlation may fail to make it probable on the whole.   A perfect
correlation, for instance, between the daily number of deaths
in South Africa and the daily number of words uttered by
the Archbishop of Canterbury would still leave us sceptical
as to the presence of anything other than " coincidence ".
These considerations make it apparent that the temptation
to rely on mathematical rules of thumb must be avoided,
and that judgement must be based on *all* the evidence that
is available, including our intuitive feelings as to relevance
and adequacy.

§ 5. Acting on this conception of the right method of
approach, I propose to consider in turn several sorts of
incident, which, on a *prima facie* view, it is plausible to suspect of being causal agents in making the expectations of
business men, and so the volume of industrial activity,
undergo fluctuations.   We are not here concerned with anything that involves merely relative changes in the expectations entertained by different groups of industrialists, but only
with absolute or aggregate changes of expectation, when there
is a net balance of gain or loss on the whole.   *Prima facie* the
principal real causes to this type of change are : (1) variations
in the yield of harvests, enabling industrialists to obtain
better or worse terms for their products from the agricultural
community ; (2) technical inventions or improvements, enabling a given amount of effort employed in some industry to
yield a new product, or more of an existing product, and also
enabling people engaged in other industries to sell their
goods on better terms against this product ; (3) the discovery
and exploitation of mineral deposits and so on, with consequences similar to the above; (4) industrial disputes; (5)
net changes—not mere transfers—in taste, involving increased
keenness of desire, on the part of none-wage-earners,[1] for

---

[1] If we are to maintain the thesis of Chapter II. § 2 that, for periods
relevant to the study of industrial fluctuations, the net supply schedule of

some commodity or class of commodities, not balanced by
a corresponding falling-off of desire for other commodities,
or *vice versa*.   From the point of view of a particular community, one or more of these several causes may operate
through foreign demand and may be modified on occasions
by tariff changes.   In the present chapter some discussion
will be offered of all the above causes, the consideration
of psychological causes being reserved for Chapters VI. and
VII., and that of autonomous monetary changes, as already
stated, for Chapter VIII.

1. CROP VARIATIONS

§ 6. I begin with variations in the yield of crops per acre,
—since the trend of change is here slow and slight, we need
not trouble to say variations about the trend—for which,
as is well known, some writers have claimed, not merely
some causal efficacy in determining industrial fluctuations,
but *sole* causal efficacy.   The occurrence of an exceptionally
good harvest means, of course, that agriculturalists find
themselves with an exceptionally large amount of their
produce on hand.   They thus have an opportunity to consume more of it themselves, to increase the volume of the
stocks that they carry, and to offer more in purchase of the
products of industry.   It is certain that they will devote
some of the extra produce—we do not as yet ask how large
a proportion of it—to this last use.   In other words, it is
certain that they will offer a larger demand in terms of
agricultural produce—will raise their real demand schedule
—for the products of industry.   At first sight it might be
supposed that this *must* affect the expectations of profit
to industrialists in such wise as to call out an increased
volume of industrial activity.   But this is not necessarily so.
Reflection shows that, if the general demand for agricultural
produce is highly inelastic, *i.e.* has an elasticity less than
unity, the enlarged amount of agricultural produce obtainable
from the output of any rth workman employed in industry

---

labour does not undergo autonomous changes, we must rule out alterations
of taste in the above sense on the part of wage-earners.

would represent, not an enlarged, but a diminished amount of things in general, and that the expectation of profit to be got by hiring any rth workman would, therefore, be not improved, but worsened. In like manner, if this demand has an elasticity equal to unity, the amount of things in general so obtainable, and, hence, the expectation of profit would be unaltered.[1] Something further will be said upon this matter in the next chapter. For the moment, however, it is sufficient to note that an elasticity of demand exactly equal to unity is a limiting case exceedingly unlikely to occur in practice. Therefore there is good ground for expecting, as it were *a priori*, that harvest variations will be a direct cause of alterations—either for better or for worse—in the expectations of profit obtainable from setting men to work in industry. That is to say, harvest variations are *prima facie relevant* to industrial fluctuations. Moreover, we know that these variations are substantial in amount. The tests of relevance and adequacy are then both satisfied. What of the evidence from statistics ?

§ 7. In the United States of America there is a fairly

---

[1] The problem discussed in the text presents a curious example of the way in which diagrams, if carelessly handled, may mislead. If, in an ordinary price-amount diagram, we represent the offer of the group whose output has expanded by a supply curve, and the offer of the other group by a demand curve, the conclusion of the text is immediately established. But, if we represent the offer of the group whose output has expanded by a demand curve and the offer of the other group by a supply curve, it appears at first sight that a raising of the demand curve must, in all circumstances, cause an increase in the output of the other group, and, therefore, that the conclusion of the text is invalid. This appearance is false. The explanation of it is that we are accustomed to employ the price-amount diagram to represent the quantity of a single commodity demanded and supplied at various money prices. Since variations in the supply of individual commodities cannot in ordinary circumstances react appreciably upon the marginal desiredness of money, it is impossible for the supply curve in this type of diagram to bend backwards towards the left in such a way as to cut a vertical line more than once. In the face of a supply curve bound by this condition it is true that a raising of the demand curve must, in all circumstances, cause an increase in output. But, when this type of supply curve is used to represent the offer of things in general for some one thing, there is no presumption that the marginal desiredness of this thing will be approximately unaffected by variations in the amount of it that is purchased. Consequently, there is no presumption that the supply curve will not bend backwards towards the left, and no ground for the thesis that a raising of the demand curve must, in all circumstances, cause an increase of output.

well-marked correlation between changes in the yield per
acre of the principal agricultural crops (combined together)
and immediately subsequent changes in business activity.
Professor Jevons writes concerning this matter : " The
production of pig-iron is the best evidence of the state of
the iron and steel trades, and these themselves vary with
the general state of industry in the country (*i.e.* the United
States), though perhaps in a somewhat exaggerated manner
—I mean that fluctuations of the iron and steel business
synchronise closely with those of other trades, but tend on
the whole to be more violent.　On calculating the production of pig-iron per head of population in the United States
year by year, and plotting it as a curve beneath that of the
total agricultural production, the connection between the two
sets of figures is obvious.　The abundant crops of 1870 and
1871 were followed by a great production of iron in 1872
and 1873 ; the big harvests of 1879 and 1880 were followed
by an increased production of iron, which, again, culminated
two years later, in 1882 ; and the bountiful harvest of 1884
produced a spurt in the iron trade two years later.　In the
years 1888 to 1895 the curve of pig-iron production follows
closely that of agricultural production, one year later ; and,
from 1893 onwards, the correspondence of the two curves is
most remarkable, making due allowance for the rapid growth
of the iron and steel industry." [1]　The same point is made,
as Professor Jevons notes, by Professor Piatt Andrew.　Summarising a careful study of the influence of crops on business
in America, that writer observes : " One cannot review the
past forty years without observing that the beginnings
of every movement towards business prosperity, and the
turning-points towards every business decline (movements
which frequently, it will be remarked, have antedated the
actual outbreak of crises by several years), were closely
connected with the out-turn of crops." [2]　Lastly, Professor
H. L. Moore has worked out, for the period 1870–1907, the
correlation coefficient between changes in the yield per
acre of certain American crops and changes (in the subse-

---

[1] *Contemporary Review*, August 1909, pp. 177-8.
[2] *Quarterly Journal of Economics*, 1906, p. 351.

quent year) in the quantity of pig-iron produced, and has found this coefficient to be very high.[1]

§ 8. A subordinate but interesting point must be mentioned here. If the products of agriculture were instantly perishable, it would be impossible for any reaction to occur, except in so far as the variations in their yield could be foreseen ; for, apart from this, no group of non-agriculturalists would have time to alter their own output with a view to the altered opportunities offered for the purchase of agricultural products. Since, however, agricultural products are not in fact instantly perishable but are capable of being stored, variations in their amount are able to react upon the expectations of business men and so upon industrial activity, even though they are not foreseen in any degree. Thus the feasibility of forecast does not affect the nature of the reactions that are produced. But it does affect the interval of time after which they occur. Clearly this must depend on the *extent* to which crop prospects are capable of being foreseen. If no fore-knowledge were possible, no reaction could occur until the harvest has actually been reaped. In modern conditions, however, some considerable measure of foreknowledge is possible. In the United States reports on the prospects of the crops are issued monthly on the basis of widespread official inspection.[2] Mr Brace finds a close relation between prices on the produce exchanges and visible supply. He adds : " Furthermore, it is seen that prices have a tendency to move sooner than the visible supply, thus indicating that the market leaders, from the reports of crops and acreage, together with other indications of prospective change in demand and supply, were able to predict what the visible supply would be, and, hence, to initiate a price movement before the demand and supply of the actual commodity were reflected in the visible supply." [3] Nor is this all. Means of forecast additional to those furnished by inspection of the standing crops have recently become available. Thus, Dr. Shaw has shown that in England the wheat crop in any

---

[1] Cf. *Economic Cycles*, p. 110.
[2] Cf. Babson, *Business Barometers*, p. 317.
[3] *The Value of Organised Speculation*, p. 133.

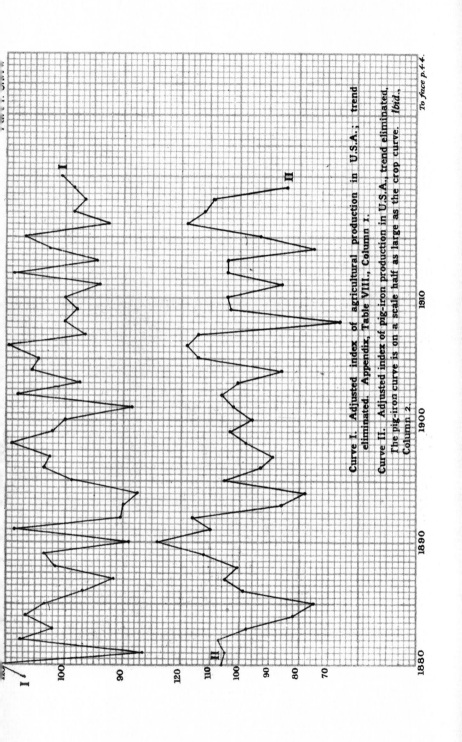

Curve I. Adjusted index of agricultural production in U.S.A.; trend eliminated. Appendix, Table VIII., Column I.

Curve II. Adjusted index of pig-iron production in U.S.A., trend eliminated. The pig-iron curve is on a scale half as large as the crop curve. *Ibid.*, Column 2.

To face p. 4.

year depends upon, and can, within close limits of error, be deduced from, the rainfall of the preceding autumn ; [1] and Professor Moore has found a similar correlation between the harvest and the rainfall of the preceding " critical period " in the principal grain-growing areas of the United States.[2] As a result of this increased power of forecast, the interval between harvest causes and industrial effects appears in recent years to have diminished. Thus Professor Jevons writes : " In the 'seventies it took two years for abundant harvests to work their full effect upon the iron industry. By the early 'nineties the activity of industry lagged but one year behind the harvests, while, in recent years, its movement has become simultaneous. At the present day the growing crops are discounted — literally turned into money as they stand—either by the farmers themselves or by the merchants to whom the farmers have sold their crops in advance. Relying upon Government crop estimates, too, manufacturers and wholesale merchants anticipate the demand which will arise from an abundant harvest, and railways the call for rolling stock ; and they place orders accordingly." [3]

§ 9. The general statements of the two preceding paragraphs are borne out by the evidence which is summarised in visual form on the charts that face p. 44 and p. 46. The statistics there exhibited refer exclusively to the United States, which is at once a great industrial and a great agricultural country. Obviously it is useless to seek for a similar connection between industrial fluctuations in the United Kingdom and variations in the harvests here ; for, in view of our large importations of agricultural produce, any effects that local crop changes might tend to bring about are liable to be swamped in larger world changes.

§ 10. The evidence adduced above does not, of course,

----

[1] " An Apparent Periodicity of the Yield of Wheat in Eastern England ", *Journal of the Royal Statistical Society*, vol. lxxviii. pp. 69-76.

[2] Cf. *Economic Cycles*, chap. iii.

[3] *Contemporary Review*, August 1909, pp. 177-8. Professor Moore finds, for the period he has examined, an average lag of between one and two years (*Economic Cycles*, p. 110). This, of course, is not incompatible with Professor Jevons's view that the lag has now disappeared.

show that good harvests are always associated with industrial activity or bad harvests with industrial depressions. M'. Tugan Baranowsky draws emphatic attention to cases in which there is no such connection. "In England the period of prosperity from 1820 to 1823 embraced exactly the years of bad harvests, and the industrial stagnation coincided with good harvests. The industrial boom of the years 1845-7 took place during a great dearth, and the depression of 1848 accompanied a good harvest. The world crisis of 1857 took place at the same time as an excellent harvest. The high prices of bread in 1870-73 did not prevent an industrial boom : nor was the stagnation which followed prevented by good harvests. The industrial stagnation which came about 1885 coincided with cheap bread." [1] Our evidence does, however, show that, on the whole, the yield of crops is correlated positively in a substantial measure with the activity of industry. This fact, coupled with the general considerations set out in earlier paragraphs, entitles us to conclude that harvest variations occupy a significant place among the real causes of variations in the expectations of business men, and so of industrial fluctuations, good harvests tending to promote expansions and bad harvests contractions of industrial activity.[2]

2. Inventions and Improvements in Method : and the Discovery of Mineral Deposits

§ 11. The second type of real cause to be considered is associated with industrial inventions. Here the abstract argument is of a similar character to that set out as regards harvest variations. If it becomes possible for a given group to produce more of its output with the same amount

[1] *Les Crises industrielles en Angleterre*, p. 237.

[2] This is not to deny that a good harvest *confined to wheat alone* may have a depressing effect on industry. Mr. Jackson (*Canadian Historical Review*, vol. iii. No. 3) argues with some force that a part cause of the depressions in Canadian industry in 1913-14 and 1920-21 was that good world harvests of wheat had reduced the aggregate real value of the wheat which the Canadian farmer had to offer to Canadian manufacturers, and that this was not made up for by an increase in the real value of what the farmers of other countries had to offer to them.

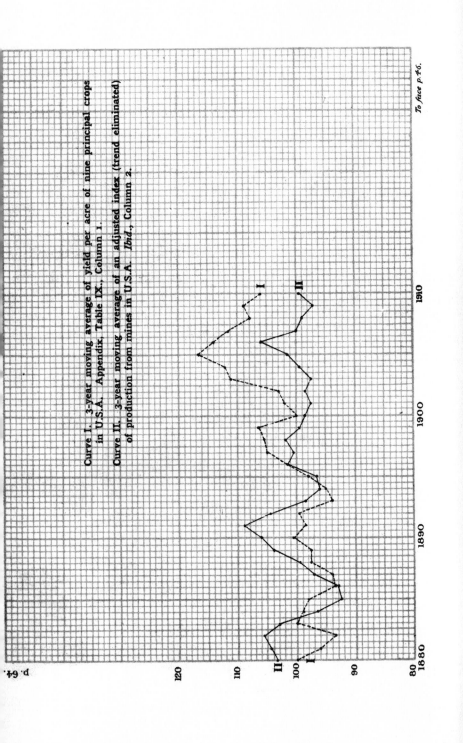

Curve I. 3-year moving average of yield per acre of nine principal crops in U.S.A. Appendix, Table IX., Column 1.

Curve II. 3-year moving average of an adjusted index (trend eliminated) of production from mines in U.S.A. *Ibid.*, Column 2.

p. 64.

To face p. 46.

of work as before, then, provided that the demand of other groups for this output has an elasticity greater than unity, other groups will enjoy an improved expectation of profit from setting labour to work : and also—and here there is something additional to what happens with a good harvest —in the group primarily affected there will be an improved expectation of profit. If the demand of other groups for the product of a group in which improved methods have been introduced has an elasticity less than unity, there will be a worsened expectation of profit, and less work will be done both in the other groups and in this group. Apart, therefore, from the limiting case of a demand with an elasticity exactly equal to unity, there is an *a priori* probability that industrial inventions and improvements in particular occupations will act as initiating causes of general industrial disturbance.

§ 12. It is important to recollect, however, that, for our present purpose, there is, broadly speaking, no significance in a *steady stream* of invention ; for, though this is highly relevant to the trend of progress, it cannot, of itself, set up any wave-movements. Moreover, an abnormal development of invention in one particular occupation is of no significance for us, if this is offset by a corresponding diminution of invention in another : just as an abnormally good harvest in one agricultural crop is of no significance if it is balanced by an abnormally bad harvest in another crop of similar importance.[1] If the spirit of discovery merely wanders

---

[1] This statement, along with the corresponding statement concerning changes of taste in § 19, is subject to a qualification, which, though of some theoretic, is of little practical interest, and is, therefore, relegated to a footnote. Nobody, of course, disputes that relative variability of demand between different occupations, even when accompanied by constancy of aggregate demand, inflicts social damage. For, granted, as is in fact the case, that wage rates are fairly rigid in the face of changing demand (cf. *post*, Chap. XX.) and that the mobility of labour is imperfect (cf. *post*, Chap. XXI.), it must lead to the formation at various points of pools of labour, among which (taken collectively) there is always a considerable mass of unemployment. Thus, to take an extreme instance, if in occupation A 1000 men are wanted in summer and only 500 in winter, while in occupation B these numbers are reversed, and if labour cannot move from the one to the other, 2000 men must be attached to the two occupations to fulfil their requirements, whereas, if there were no relative variations, 1500 would suffice. In this case the relative variations of demand are responsible for 500 men—the individual men are, of course, different at different times—being always unemployed. This effect of relative vari-

from one occupation to another, maintaining always a constant activity, or a constant rate of progress, on the whole, the shifting of its incidence from time to time will cause,

---

ability, important as it is from the broad standpoint of economic welfare, is not, however, an effect on industrial fluctuations : and it is widely believed that, so long as aggregate demand remains constant, no effect of that kind *can* be associated with it, contractions of activity in one occupation being always offset by expansions of equivalent size in others. Closer analysis shows, however, that this opinion is not entirely accurate. The issue can be set in a clear light by the help of symbols. Let A, B, C, D, etc., be the average number of workers demanded at a given (say the average ruling) wage in each several occupation. Suppose that there is no variation in aggregate demand, so that the sum of the numbers demanded at the given wage in all occupations is always $(A + B + C + D \ . \ . \ .)$. At any given moment, the number at A need not be A, nor the number at B be B. Let the numbers in fact be $(A + a)$, $(B - b)$, $(C + c)$, $(D - d)$ and so on. Then $(a - b + c - d \ . \ . \ .)$ is necessarily equal to zero : while $(a + b + c + d \ . \ . \ .)$ added together without regard to sign may conveniently be taken to measure the extent to which, at the given moment, there has been a relative movement of demand away from the average. With these symbols in mind it is easy to see that, if labour were perfectly mobile between different occupations, no fluctuation in the aggregate number of workpeople employed could occur in consequence either of the existence of relative changes in demand or of changes in the rate at which relative changes are occurring. If, however, labour is not perfectly mobile between different occupations, this is no longer necessarily so. To simplify the argument, suppose that labour is absolutely immobile between occupations. If the supply of labour in each occupation were perfectly inelastic—that is to say, if the workpeople there would be prepared to let the wage-rate fall to zero, or even below it, rather than suffer any unemployment, no unemployment could occur in any event, and, therefore, relative changes of demand—and absolute changes also for that matter—could never cause the volume of employment to fluctuate. In actual life, however, wage-rates are, as was indicated above, somewhat rigid. Moreover, as a rule, rigidity is much greater, and the supply of labour is much more elastic, against substantial decreases of demand than against increases. Thus, to take an extreme case, if there are 1000 people attached to an occupation, and in normal times 950 are employed, while small increases and small decreases in demand may affect the numbers employed to about the same extent, the largest possible increase cannot raise the number by more than 50, while a quite moderate decrease may easily reduce it by more than 50. From this consideration it can be deduced that, when, as, of course, in practice must always happen, relative changes in demand are going on, they may bring about fluctuations in the aggregate amount of employment, even though the rate of relative change, as calculated by our measure $(a + b + c + d \ . \ . \ .)$ remains constant. They are likely to do this if a few large relative movements accompanied by a few very small ones take the place of many moderate ones—if, for example, instead of a, b, c and d being each equal to 10, a and b are each equal to 19 and c and d each equal to 1, or *vice versa*. An easy extension of this reasoning shows that, if the rate at which relative changes in demand are going on (as measured by $a + b + c + d \ . \ . \ .$) increases, the volume of unemployment is likely to increase, and in the reverse case to decrease.

indeed, *relative* expansions and contractions in different parts
of the country's industry, but will leave the level, or, more
strictly, the trend of industrial activity as a whole unchanged.
There is, moreover, a strong probability that invention
as a whole will fluctuate very much less than invention
in any given representative occupation. In view of this
fact, and in view of the imperfections of our records, it is
quite impossible to distinguish periods, if there are any such,
in which ordinary minor inventions and improvements in the
aggregate are being made at a more rapid rate than usual ;
and therefore, in regard to these, no statistical support for
the *a priori* proposition set out in the preceding section can
be forthcoming. Common sense suggests that this class of
invention is, from the point of view of general industrial
fluctuations, a minor factor that may safely be left out of
account.

§ 13. There are, however, from time to time large and
dominating inventions, such as those associated with railway
development, electrical development, and so on, which cannot
be ruled out of court in this way. Our records show that
inventions of this order are sometimes associated with very
large industrial disturbances—witness the British railway
boom in the 'forties following the invention of steam transport, and the German iron and steel boom from 1895 to 1900
following the invention of electric transport—booms which,
of course, affected not merely the people directly concerned
in the exploitation of these inventions, but also the providers
of the materials that enter into them. There is here, however, a serious difficulty. It is not the making of an invention
or a discovery that sets up either the reactions of which we
have just been speaking in the industry primarily concerned
or the reactions in other industries : it is the *adoption and
actual working* of the invention or discovery that does this.
But there is no close connection in time between the *discovery*
of these things and their exploitation. In the United Kingdom, for example, the Stockton and Darlington railway was
opened in 1825, Huskisson was killed by " The Rocket " in
1830, and the most important railway mania developed in
1845–7. Thus, while it is, of course, true that, if Stevenson's

invention had not been made, a railway mania could not have occurred in 1845–7, we are not entitled to infer that there would have been no general industrial boom in 1845–7. Railway development may have been merely a channel, into which expanded industrial activity, caused in some quite different way and due to come into play whether or not this invention had been made, found it convenient to flow. If it were possible to demonstrate a close statistical correlation between the making of industrial inventions and *neighbouring* disturbances in general industrial activity, this line of criticism would not be open. But it is not in fact possible to do anything of the sort. On the contrary, there is evidence that in slack periods technical devices and improvements accumulate in the sphere of knowledge, but are not exploited till times improve. In these circumstances it seems proper to conclude that, though, no doubt, on occasions, large and dominating inventions are direct causes of booms, the part which inventions play as primary impulses in the causation of industrial fluctuations is, on the whole, small.[1] A very similar analysis and conclusion holds good of the discovery of new mineral deposits.

3. INDUSTRIAL DISPUTES

§ 14. In studying the evidence concerning the relation of industrial disputes to industrial fluctuations it must be remembered that, as was noticed in Chapter I., in the United Kingdom persons unemployed because they are directly involved in a strike or lock-out are not counted in the published figures of unemployment. These figures refer to unemployment other than that suffered by persons involved in industrial disputes (or idle on account of sickness).

§ 15. It seems plain that, whenever the number of men involved in industrial disputes is larger than usual, this must make *pro tanto* for a decline in the prospects of profit elsewhere, and so in aggregate industrial activity, and that, whenever the number so involved is smaller than usual, there is *pro tanto* an impulse towards industrial expansion. For a

---

[1] But cf. *post*, p. 92 and footnote.

shortage of the goods produced by one industry, if it lasts long enough to trench seriously upon, not to say to exhaust, accumulated stocks, is bound to lessen the yield, in terms of things in general, of work done in other industries. In view of these considerations there can be little doubt that industrial disputes—or rather excesses and deficiencies in industrial disputes as against the average—are a genuine cause of industrial fluctuations.

§ 16. In attempting to gauge how important this cause is we naturally look in the first instance to the statistics of days lost by persons involved in stoppages over a series of years. Between 1894 and 1913 once, in 1912, 40 million working days were lost by persons involved in disputes; twice, 1898 and 1904, between 14 and 16 millions were lost; five times, 1894, 1897, 1908, 1910 and 1913, between 9 and 12 millions were lost; in all the other years except 1894 (5·7 millions) and 1904 (1·5 million) the number of days lost lay between a little over 2 and a little over 4 millions. If, for a rough average of the period, we reckon the industrial population at 10 millions, 10 million working days in a year represents about one-third per cent of the working power of the community. Plainly, therefore, the variations in the amount of working time annually lost by persons involved in industrial disputes are, in general, very small, relatively both to the average of unemployment annually suffered by other persons and to the variations in this annual average.

§ 17. Moreover, it is a vital fact that industrial disputes do not usually involve stoppages that last individually a very long time. There is thus often scope, in the same year in which a stoppage occurs, for a compensatory effect. Since a stoppage in any industry involves a shortage of stocks and a delay in the fulfilment of orders, it is to be expected that a stoppage occurring now will cause a high degree of activity soon afterwards. If, therefore, there is a stoppage for, say, two months in January and February of any year, the total of work during the year in the industry will not be cut down by the full amount of these two months' idleness. Hence the total damage inflicted on

the expectations of profit in other groups that have dealings
with this one will be less than that inflicted during the actual
period of the stoppage. If the stoppage occurs in the earlier
months of any year, the figures for the full year may take
account of these compensatory effects, but, if it occurs at
the end, they cannot do so. This is statistically confusing.
The main point, however, is that stoppages of work due to
industrial disputes involve, for the reasons explained, smaller
contractions of industrial activity elsewhere than they might
be thought to do at first sight.

§ 18. To elucidate this matter further, I have brought
together in the accompanying chart the percentages of
unemployment (exclusive of persons directly involved in
stoppages) and the number of persons so involved over
the years 1894–1913. It will be seen that there is no
positive correlation between the scale of industrial disputes
and the recorded percentages of unemployment. Indeed,
in the two periods covered by the chart, 1897–8 and 1910–13,
in which disputes were largest, the unemployment percentage was exceptionally low. It would be wrong to lay
much stress upon this fact. For there is reason to suspect
that prosperity in a sense causes disputes, because it stimulates workpeople to try to force a rise of wages more strongly
than depression stimulates employers to try to force a fall.
If this factor were at work alone we should expect to find
a negative correlation between industrial disputes and unemployment. Hence the absence of a correlation of the
opposite sort is not decisive. Moreover, it must be remembered that any compensatory expansion, that takes place
after the close of a dispute in the industry where it has
occurred, enters into our unemployment figures, though the
contraction during the dispute itself in this industry does
not. On the whole body of evidence, however, it seems
reasonable to conclude that, in recent times at all events,
industrial disputes have not played any significant part in
causing industrial fluctuations. It is not, of course, incompatible with this conclusion to recognise that a stoppage
of work in a fundamental industry, such as coal-mining or
railway transport, would inevitably, if it were sufficiently

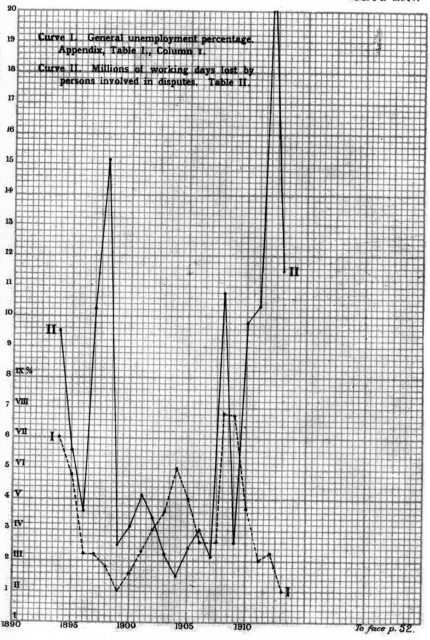

Curve I. General unemployment percentage.
Appendix, Table I., Column I.

Curve II. Millions of working days lost by
persons involved in disputes. Table II.

prolonged, inflict great damage on business prospects, and bring about a great contraction in employment all round.

4. CHANGES OF TASTE

§ 19. Changes of taste or fashion are in a position very similar to that occupied by inventions and improvements of method. *A priori* it is easy to see that an increase in the desire of non-wage-earners for the product of any group must lead to an increase in the activity of these persons in order to provide the wherewithal to express their increased desire. If, as is likely, the general demand for the services that these persons offer has an elasticity greater than unity, it must lead also to an increase in the expectations of profit, and so in the industrial activity of this group. Thus, if other things remain the same, an enhancement in the public taste for anything is likely to cause an increase in aggregate industrial activity. In actual life, however, an enhancement in the public taste for one thing is often offset by a corresponding decline of taste for another thing. When this happens we have to do with a mere transference of taste, not with a net change. Plainly, however, from the standpoint of general industrial fluctuations, it is only *net* changes that count.[1] This consideration rules out of account the great bulk of fashion changes. Moreover, even in respect of changes that are not mere transfers, there is a presumption that a good deal of cancelling will take place : that peoples' taste for some things will happen to be declining at the same time that that for others is expanding. Yet again, it must be borne in mind that luxury goods, the principal subjects of fashion changes, constitute a very small part of the total production of any ordinary country. Even in France, the great producer of luxuries, it has been estimated that " only about $\frac{1}{210}$th of the total volume of normal production is subject to the influences of fashion ".[2] From the point of view of our present inquiry, therefore, very little importance would seem to attach to this matter.

[1] But cf. *ante*, p. 47, footnote.
[2] Robertson, *A Study of Industrial Fluctuations*, p. 72.

§ 20. There is, however, one kind of change in desire that stands on a different footing. It is logically proper to think of wars as operating on the activity of industry through the alteration of taste among commodities that accompanies them. Here, however, we have to do with something very different from those changes of fashion — mostly mere transfers—that were discussed in the preceding section. When war breaks out, the general body of the people, functioning in this instance through the Government, do not merely want soldiers' work and shells and guns instead of other things : they do not merely want to get these things by transferring effort to making them away from making other things : they also want to enhance the supply of them by increasing the aggregate sum of effort, and by increasing this in an enormous degree. To this end they set in motion complex financial processes that create greatly improved expectations of profit to those who can serve their need, while at the same time much extra work is done without regard for profit at all. In these circumstances there must be an enormous expansion of industrial activity. This expansion is, of course, much larger than appears in unemployment statistics, because a very large number of persons hitherto not engaged in industry are drawn into it. The activity of soldiering should, of course, be counted for this purpose as an industry.

5. Changes in Foreign Demand

§ 21. This completes our analysis so far as concerns changes *internal* to a community. A community set in the midst of other communities is, however, also liable to be affected by changes initiated outside itself. It is easy to see that the analysis appropriate to the main part of these changes is implicit in what has been said. If there is a good (or bad) harvest abroad in a country trading with England, or if there is an invention abroad that cheapens production in some occupation, the effect in England will be the same as it would have been had the initiating change occurred here, except that that part of the effect which concerns the industry of primary impact is eliminated. Similarly, if the taste of foreigners for a particular English commodity is enhanced, expectations of profit and the amount of work done in respect of that commodity are increased in the same way as they would have been if the change of taste had occurred among other Englishmen; but the effect on the work of those groups whose taste has changed is, so far as England is concerned, eliminated. We need not, therefore, go over again, in connection with changes initiated from outside a community, ground which has already, in effect, been covered. It is proper to observe, however, that, in the special case of England, since this is a country abnormally dependent on foreign countries for food and raw materials, external causes of disturbance are exceptionally important. We need not, therefore, be surprised to learn that, over the only period so far examined in detail, namely 1903–13, the employment cycle in England followed from six months to a year behind the corresponding cycle in the United States.[1] It should be added that the expectations of profit, and so the activity of industry, in one country is also liable to be affected by changes in the customs or export duties imposed by other countries. Since, however, such a country as England trades in a great number of commodities with a great many other countries, and since not many of these are likely to change their tariffs in the same sense at the same time, the chance of our experiencing suddenly from this cause a significant percentage change in the aggregate foreign demand for our goods is not very great.

6. SUMMARY

§ 22. It is obvious that the various groups of initiating causes that have been distinguished above cannot be put into a list arranged in order of importance : for in each group some individual members will be much more important than others. It would be ridiculous, for instance, to lay it down in an abstract general way that harvest variations are more important causes of industrial fluctuations than inventions,

[1] Cf. Berridge, "Employment and the Business Cycle", in the *Review of Economic Statistics*, January 1922, p. 4.

or wars than industrial disputes : for, while a large harvest variation will certainly be more important than a trifling invention, and a large war than a strike in an occupation employing fifty men, a minute harvest variation will be less important than an epoch-making invention and an insignificant war settled by a few naval shells than a coal strike lasting a year.　On this matter, therefore, it is only possible to speak in rough general terms on the basis of the foregoing analysis and of recent experience.　In this sense then we may conclude that fashion changes, ordinary industrial disputes, and the general run of inventions, improvements and mineral discoveries may, for practical purposes, be disregarded.　Large inventions, on the other hand, may be important, and harvest variations are certainly so : while the great war of 1914–18 brought about an upheaval in industry enormously greater than anything ever experienced before.

CHAPTER V

§ 1. In the preceding chapter we attempted to gauge, by a combined use of common sense and statistical data, the significance, as initiating causes of general industrial fluctuations, of certain sorts of change. In that discussion a distinction was noted between the effect that an initiating cause may produce directly upon a given basis of business judgement and the effect that it may produce indirectly by causing business judgement to swing unduly towards optimism or towards pessimism. In the present chapter it is proposed to leave the second of these two classes of effect wholly on one side and to inquire whether it is possible to obtain any sort of quantitative knowledge about the direct effects taken by themselves.

§ 2. An initiating cause of industrial disturbance may be focussed on a particular group of producers from either of two sides. On the one hand, the productive activity of the group itself may be altered from within, whether on account of a change in its technical efficiency or on account of a change in the desire of its members for the output of other groups. On the other hand, the productive activity of the group may be altered from without in consequence of a change in the demand for its product, brought about by altered technical efficiency or altered desire in other groups. We have seen in the last chapter that, apart from the special case of wars, changes of desire for particular commodities need not be reckoned as important impulses towards general (as distinct from relative) industrial fluctuations. Attention may, therefore, be confined to changes in technical efficiency, including, of course, the technical efficiency of Nature as represented in harvest yields.

§ 3. Let us then consider a particular group A within our community confronted with the remainder of the community, which we may call B. Two cases have to be distinguished. First, the *output* of A changes in such wise that no consequential changes occur in the *activity* of A. This condition is roughly satisfied for changes in harvest yield ; they arc, as it were, *ex post facto*, and do not affect the quantity of labour employed on the land. Secondly, the method of work or the mechanical technique available at A changes in such wise that a given amount of labour becomes capable of yielding a larger (or smaller) amount of output than before. In the first of these cases we have to reckon with changes in industrial activity in B only ; in the second with changes in both B and A. Neglecting differences in the quality of workpeople, the supporting capital equipment per man, and so on, as between A and B, suppose that normally 10,000 workers are engaged at A and exchange their product against the product of 10,000 among the workers included in B. Then, *if B is a homogeneous group*, it is possible to determine, in terms of what has happened at A, the maximum change that can be brought about in the activity of A and B together. Suppose that A's output is increased by 20 per cent—the equivalent of what would normally be yielded by 2000 workers. Then in case 1 employment at A will, of course, remain unchanged, and the maximum possible addition to employment at B—occurring if, and only if, B's demand for A's product is perfectly elastic —will be 2000 workers. For, were the consequent increase in B larger than this, B would be offering better terms per unit for a larger than for a smaller quantity of A's goods. In case 2, the maximum possible addition to employment at B is again 2000 workers ; but in this case, if the elasticity of A's demand for B's goods also approximates to perfect elasticity, the extra output at A will imply an addition there also (consequent upon the improved technique) of just under 2000 workers. Thus in case 1 the maximum aggregate increase of activity in our community which is theoretically possible is measured by 2000 workers ; in case 2 it is measured by 4000 workers. Of course, in practice it is quite certain that we shall not find demands of anything approaching perfect elasticity. Consequently, what may for convenience be called the practical maximum is in both cases very much smaller than the theoretical maximum. Our main result may be expressed in a rougher but perhaps more easily appreciated form in the language of money, it being assumed that the purchasing power of the monetary unit in terms of things in general is somehow kept stable. Suppose that the expenditure of the community upon the products of group A is increased by £1,000,000 on account of the extra output in A, and that this £1,000,000 represents, as perhaps in England it does, $\frac{1}{4000}$th part of the aggregate annual income of the community. It is then impossible that the associated increase in the aggregate activity of the community can exceed $\frac{1}{4000}$th part, or $\frac{1}{40}$th per cent, in case 1 ; and $\frac{1}{2000}$th part, or $\frac{1}{20}$th per cent, of this aggregate activity in case 2.[1]

§ 4. It will be seen that the method of analysis just developed should, if it is valid, enable us to assign limits to the *direct* action of certain important initiating causes in bringing about industrial fluctuations. The argument may be illustrated thus. Professor Day has constructed an adjusted index, that is to say, an index from which the secular trend of increase is eliminated, of physical production for agriculture in the United States from 1879 to 1920; and we know from other sources that this index, which embraces twelve important crops, moves in substantial accord with a corresponding index (trend also eliminated) of yield per acre. The maximum value attained by this index is 110·8 in 1880 and the minimum value 86·8 in 1881. These are extreme values rarely ap-

---

[1] We have spoken in the text only of limits to the *expansion* of activity in B associated with increases in A's product. If B's demand for A's product has an elasticity less than unity, an increase in A's product will, *caeteris paribus*, be associated with a contraction of activity in B. If the elasticity of B's demand for agricultural produce were zero, the price in B's products of agricultural produce might theoretically, as the result of a good harvest, fall to zero, and B's activity contract correspondingly. Our conclusion, however, to be set out on p. 62, that the elasticity of demand for agriculture produce is greater than unity, makes it unnecessary for us to examine this type of limit.

proached.[1] We may therefore, I think, fairly conclude that, over the average of agricultural crops in the United States, the yield, after allowance has been made for secular trend, is not liable to vary from the mean by more than 10 per cent in either direction, *i.e.* 20 per cent in the aggregate. Now, it has been calculated by Professor King (for 1910) that, of the national value product of the United States, about 22 per cent belongs to agriculture.[2] Even then, if the portion of agricultural produce that is consumed by agriculturalists be ignored, and if it be assumed that the demand for agricultural produce is infinitely elastic, the maximum possible range of industrial fluctuations due to crop variations is $\frac{22}{78}$ths of 20 per cent, *i.e.* $6\frac{1}{2}$ per cent, or $3\frac{1}{4}$ per cent on either side of the mean. Since it is certain that, with commodities that are not perishable, the supplies coming to sale will vary considerably less than those produced—more being held for stock in good than in bad years—we may safely cut this figure down at the very least to 6 per cent, or 3 per cent on each side of the mean.

§ 5. We should like, of course, to step on from this to a more decisive result by determining how elastic the demand for agricultural produce as a matter of fact is. There is a preliminary difficulty in the fact that the *conception* of this elasticity is ambiguous ; for agricultural produce embraces a number of different sorts of things, for which there is no reason to suppose that the elasticity of demand is the same. A further complication arises out of the fact that the elasticity of the demand of any group for the whole of any kind of produce is different from the elasticity of its demand for that part of the produce that is grown in a particular country. Since the supply from other countries can be substituted for the supply from any one country, the elasticity of the demand for the part that comes from one country is always greater than the elasticity of the demand for the whole. But the relation between the two elasticities is not fixed. That relevant to the produce of one country falls more nearly to that relevant to the whole, as the proportion which that country's crop bears to the world crop increases. Thus,

---

[1] Cf. *Review of Economic Statistics*, vol. ii., 1920, p. 259.
[2] Wilfrid King, *Wealth and Income of the United States*, p. 138.

though the demand for wheat in the aggregate is probably less elastic than the demand for cotton in the aggregate, yet, since America provides a much larger share of the world's cotton than of the world's wheat, the demand for American cotton is less elastic than the demand for American wheat. The most useful form in which the question of elasticity can be posited from our present point of view is probably the most general form. With a given percentage expansion in harvest yields throughout the world as a whole, by what sort of a percentage would industries in general, and English industries in particular, increase their expenditure (in terms of real things) on the purchase of agricultural products ? Obviously, no exact answer can be given to this question, because aggregate harvest yields may expand in a great number of different ways, sometimes through a crop of inelastic demand and sometimes through one of elastic demand. Perhaps, however, the difficulty is not really so important as it seems. For some degree of positive correlation appears to exist between the variations that occur in the yields of different crops in the same country. On the strength of this fact we may attempt a step forward. It is established that, when correction has been made for secular trend, there is a strong negative correlation between agricultural output and agricultural prices. In thirty out of the thirty-four years from 1879 to 1913 the output and the price of twelve important crops of the United States combined together moved in opposite directions, the inverse correlation between the year-to-year changes being expressed by the coefficient − ·88, where a coefficient of − 1 would indicate perfect disagreement.[1] There is, however, no clear connection between changes in output and changes in aggregate value. " In eighteen cases the two series moved in the same direction from year to year ; in seventeen years they moved in opposite directions. The degree of correlation is numerically expressed by the coefficient − ·04, when 0 denotes lack of either direct or inverse correspondence." [2] These statistics are somewhat surprising. It must, however, be remem-

---

[1] Cf. Persons, *Review of Economic Statistics*, 1921, p. 34.
[2] *Ibid.* p. 36.

bered that our aggregate values are values at the farm,[1] that values *after transportation* to the consumer would be more satisfactory for our present purpose, and that, since railway rates are likely to increase, or, at all events, not to diminish, with growing traffic, these values, if obtainable, would be more directly correlated with output than farm values are. That there is in fact a positive correlation, signifying an elasticity of demand greater than unity, is also strongly suggested, though, since psychological reactions might account for the facts, it is not definitely proved, by the association between industrial expansions and good harvests set out in the preceding chapter. On pre-war evidence as a whole I conclude that the elasticity of demand for agricultural produce in general is greater than unity, but that it only exceeds unity by a little. It will follow, then, from the argument of the last section, that the direct effect of good harvests in inducing industrial expansions and of bad harvests in inducing industrial contractions must be very small. We have seen that with infinite elasticity—*i.e.* when a fall of real price of 0 per cent follows from an increase of output of 1 per cent—the range of industrial fluctuation due to harvest variations could not exceed 3 per cent on either side of the mean. We may now add, as the result of an easy arithmetical calculation, that, with an elasticity of 2, the maximum range works out at one-half of this amount ; with an elasticity of 1·5, at one-third ; with an elasticity of 1·2, at one-sixth. It seems improbable that, if the elasticity of demand were larger than this last figure, which implies a change of roughly one-sixth per cent aggregate value as a direct consequence of a change of 1 per cent in output, there would be no sign of correlation between output and aggregate values—duly corrected on Professor Persons's method—in our statistics. The inference is that harvest changes in the United States are not *directly* responsible for industrial fluctuations of more than one-half per cent on either side of the mean.[2]

[1] Cf. Persons, *Review of Economic Statistics*, 1921, p. 34, footnote.

[2] It may be worth noticing that, if (for small changes) $\frac{\text{proportional change of output}}{\text{proportional change of price}}$, which is, on the usual notation, elasticity of

§ 6. If the method of analysis which has been illustrated above were valid, it might be possible to pursue it into various ramifications, and it seems probable that we should be warranted by it in inferring that the direct effects of the several initiating causes of fluctuations described in the preceding chapter are, in general, too small to account for more than a very small part of the fluctuations which actually occur. Unfortunately, however, there are two assumptions underlying the use of this method, which do not conform to the facts, and in the absence of which the above clear-cut conclusion is not warranted. The first assumption is that B, the part of our community other than the group A in which an impulse is initiated, is a homogeneous body and deals with A as a single unit. This excludes the possibility that glass-makers, for example, may obtain the wheat they need, not directly by exchanging wheat against glass (or, alternatively, if they find that it is boots that wheat-makers want, by transferring a part of their efforts to making boots), but indirectly by exchanging glass against boots and then re-exchanging boots against wheat. The second assumption is that what A sells to B is a finished product, and not something which some among the members of B must have as a raw material in order to make the exercise of their own activity possible. When these assumptions are removed the way is opened for certain *repercussions*—we are still, of course, excluding psychological factors and reactions due to them—which may greatly enlarge the scale of effects due to the various impulses under review.

§ 7. As a preliminary it is well to clear out of the way a type of so-called repercussion which is illusory and unreal. Thus Bagehot, after arguing, in a passage which I shall cite immediately, that in the actual world a change initiated in one occupation propagates itself through a long line of other occupations, adds that the impulse set in motion " in a certain sense rebounds " upon the occupation in which it originated. This contention is independent of the number

---

demand, be represented by η, a negative quantity, then $\dfrac{\text{proportional change in aggregate value}}{\text{proportional change in output}}$ is approximately equal to $\left(1 + \dfrac{1}{\eta}\right)$.

of occupations that are set in line, and so can be fully explored in a community consisting of A and B only without any further members. The thesis is in substance that an enhanced real demand on the part of A for B goods makes B better off, and that, therefore, B is able to display an enhanced real demand for A goods, thus in turn making A better off. Thus a sort of reciprocating spiral of mutual expansion (or contraction) is set up, which need never cease, nor apparently, if we press things to extremes, need ever even lessen in intensity. It may well be that Bagehot had in view those psychological reactions which we have just excluded and which would warrant his conclusions. Apart from them, expressed in money, the suggestion is that A offers B £2000 more for further supplies of B goods; this enables B to offer, if not £2000 more, at all events some considerable sum more for further A goods ; this again enables A to offer more for further B goods ; and so on for ever. Whether expressed in real terms or in money terms, this is a fallacy. If A makes his offer in the form of £2000, he makes it in substance in the £2000 worth of A goods that B buys with the £2000. When B has handed over his extra product, received £2000 for it, and spent the £2000 in buying A goods, the money counters return to their old seats, and the real transaction has been completed. There is a *response* on B's part to A's increased demand, but there is no secondary effect on A. In short, the extra output which takes place in A is wholly cause and not at all effect. There is, that is to say, no " rebound ". The half of Bagehot's thesis which asserts that there is, if it is interpreted without reference to psychological reactions, is invalid. This sort of repercussion is illusory.

§ 8. The case is different, however, with the sort of repercussion which comes into view when the assumption of homogeneity, as defined above, is removed. What has to be said on this matter is best introduced by reference to another and more important part of the passage cited from Bagehot. This runs : " There is a partnership in industries. No single large industry can be depressed without injury to other industries ; still less can any great group of industries.

Each industry, when prosperous, buys and consumes the produce probably of most (certainly of very many) other industries, and, if industry A fail and is in difficulty, industries B and C and D, which used to sell to it, will not be able to sell that which they had produced in reliance on A's demand; and in future they will stand idle until industry A recovers, because, in default of A, there will be no one to buy the commodities which they create. Then, as industry B buys of C, D, etc., the adversity of B tells on C, D, etc., and, as these buy of E, F, etc., the effect is propagated through the whole alphabet." [1]   Here we are called upon to envisage a number of different groups, B, C and D, engaged in different kinds of production. What has been said already will have served to display the direct effect of a change in A's output or prosperity upon the activity of B, C, D, and so on. A will obtain from each of these groups so much more of their product in return for so much more of its own product handed over to each of them to *hold and use*. But—and this is the point—in so far as B is dealing with C, A's prosperity, making B more prosperous, would enable B to demand more of C's product, so that, alongside of its direct effect on B's activity, A's prosperity would also have a mediated effect on C's. In like manner, in so far as C is dealing with B and D, A's prosperity directly expands C's activity and indirectly B's and D's. Thus the aggregate effect of an enhancement of A's output or prosperity upon the activity of B, C and D is larger than the immediate effect, and may much exceed what it would have been if B, C and D could be treated as a collective unit in the way contemplated in § 3. This is the thesis we have now to examine.

§ 9. To clarify the issue, it is convenient to conceive industrial groups in the following abstract form. Industry A manufactures finished goods, and has, subordinated to it and producing the materials and the machinery that it needs, sub-industries a_1 and a_2; the sub-industries in turn having other sub-sub-industries a'_1 and a'_2, which provide their materials and machinery. Alongside of A there is another finishing industry B, with a similar series of sub-

---

[1] *Lombard Street*, pp. 125-6.

industries, and yet others, C, D, and so on. Of course this
rigid division and specialisation of sub-industries does not
exist in real life, but the conception is none the less of
service for analysis.

§ 10. When the demand for B's products in terms of
A's stuff (for which we assume B has an elastic demand)
expands, B, in order to increase his output so as to take
advantage of the increased demand for his products, will need
more materials and machines. It is plain, therefore, that a
stimulus to expansion will be given to sub-industries b_1 and
b_2 and to the sub-sub-industries below them.   " To construct
a factory or a railway it is necessary to procure materials of
construction (wood, tiles, iron, etc.), machines and tools, and
to engage workpeople. The materials of construction, like
the machines, do not fall from the sky ; they are furnished
by other branches of production. Thus, the more numerous
new enterprises are, the greater is the demand for means of
production."[1]   So far, therefore, as the sub-industries b_1,
b_2, and so on are concerned, it is true that A's prosperity
propagates itself through B among further industries. But
this propagation is, so to speak, analytic and not synthetic.
That is to say, in its dealings with A, B is partly a principal
and partly an intermediary for b_1, b_2, and so on, distributing
what A pays between itself and its subordinates according
to their respective contributions towards the final B product.
Thus, if A hands over 100,000 additional bushels of wheat
in payment for B products, he is not offering 100,000 bushels
for an equivalent extra supply of B work, but for an equivalent extra supply of B work plus b_1 work plus b_2 work, and so
on. If B hands on 50,000 bushels to b_1 and keeps 50,000
for himself, the effect on B's activity and on b_1's activity is
the same as if A had dealt with each of B and b_1 separately,
or as if B and b_1 had constituted a single homogeneous
group. There is nothing, therefore, in this sort of propagation
to suggest that the aggregate effect on other people's activity
can in real life exceed the limit that is set to it in § 3. So
far as it means only this, Bagehot's thesis is explicative of
our earlier discussion, but nothing more.

[1] Tugan Baranowsky, *Les Crises industrielles en Angleterre*, p. 258.

§ 11. Bagehot suggests, however, that A's prosperity propagates itself through B, not merely inside B's own family, so to speak, among the b_1's, b_2's, and so on, but also outside the B family among C, D, and so on.   This is a very different and much more important matter ; for the propagation here conceived of *is* synthetic.   To elucidate it let us make A stand for the complete A family, including the a_1's and the a_2's, and similarly, let us make B and C stand for the complete B and C families.   Let us then suppose that A is so constituted that, having an enlarged output, he concentrates the whole of its extra purchasing power on B goods, not desiring any increase at all of C goods or D goods.   It is conceivable that B is so constituted as to desire no further goods except A goods.   In this case the whole of what happens is that A produces his (say) 100 extra units of A goods and exchanges them against (say) 100 more units of B goods ; C and D are not affected in any way.   It is, however, also conceivable that B desires only C goods, C only D goods, and so on till we reach Z, who desires only A goods. In this case the extra 100 A goods, that A has handed to B in exchange for 100 B goods, are retransferred to C in exchange for (say) 100 C goods, and so on all down the line until we come to Z, who is content to retain the A goods. In this case, instead of A's prosperity leading only to a new effort on B's part, represented by 100 B goods, it leads to an equal effort all down the line, which manifests itself in an addition of 100 B goods *plus* 100 C goods *plus* 100 D goods *plus* . . . 100 Z goods.   The contrast between this case and that contemplated in the analysis of § 3 can be illustrated by a simple analogy.   A, who is about to move forward 100 yards, may be considered as attached by a chain to Z directly, or as attached by a chain to B, who is attached to C, and so on till we get to Z.   In the first case the reaction to A's movement is an equal movement by Z alone ; in the second case it is an equal movement by every member of the series. The analysis is easily extended to the case in which A desires, not merely 100 units of B goods, but also 100 units of each of the other sorts of goods.   Then, on the assumptions taken, his demand for C goods adds 100 units to the output, not only of C, but of each group down to Z. It thus appears that the aggregate effect of A's demand for an extra 100 units from each of the twenty-five groups is to provoke an additional output as under :

$$
\begin{array}{rll}
100 \text{ units from} & B, \\
200 & ,, & ,, & C, \\
300 & ,, & ,, & D, \\
. & . & . & . \\
2500 & ,, & ,, & Z ;
\end{array}
$$

namely, 32,500 units in all, instead of 2500 units in all. Hence the reaction on aggregate employment, due to the change initiated in A, depends for its extent, not merely on the mutual demand relations of A and B, A and C, A and D and so on, but also on the mutual demand relations of B and C, B and D, C and D, and so on.

§ 12. The preceding argument shows that, when A is confronted, not with a single homogeneous B, but with a number of separate specialised groups B, C, D, E, and so on, the reaction induced by variations in A's offer is not limited in the way described in § 3. It is important to determine, if we can, how far in the conditions of real life specialisation and isolation of groups are likely to enlarge the scale of this reaction beyond the limit there set out. Let us begin by supposing that A somehow becomes possessed of more wheat or gold or anything else whatever, whether through a good harvest, an improved process, or in any other way. If, after he has made his purchases from B, C, D . . ., the comparative marginal utilities of A goods and of other goods to each of B, C, D . . . are unaltered—provided that B, C and D were exactly alike, and that A were to distribute his extra money evenly among them, this condition would be satisfied—no secondary movement will occur, and the result will be the same as though B, C, D . . . were a single homogeneous group. If there is any one of the groups B, C, D . . . from which A makes no purchases, there is bound to be some secondary movement ; and, if he makes some purchases from all, but the adjustment is not exactly right, there is also bound to be some secondary movement. For example, suppose that cotton people, having somehow become more prosperous than hitherto, spend a larger proportion of their new income than the community as a whole spends of its total income on beer. The people engaged in making beer will obtain more extra money per head than the people engaged in making furniture do. Consequently, they will seek to buy more furniture, and so indirectly the services of more furniture makers ; and these persons, to whom, *ex hypothesi*, relatively little of the new money has yet flowed, and to whom, therefore, the marginal utility of money is as yet but slightly altered, will provide more furniture and more furniture makers' work in response to this demand. The point may be put otherwise and more generally thus. The groups, to which the cotton people pay over the money they have received in extra earnings, start at first as holders of extra money confronted with things whose prices have not yet changed ; they are thus being offered higher real payment, and so stimulated to greater activity. When they in turn spend their new money, some of the people selling to them may be buyers of something that has not yet been touched by the upward swing of prices ; and, therefore, the extra money offered may, for them too, imply an extra real offer. Thus, though in the long run all the successive layers of people who are touched by the stream of money come back to their initial relative positions, a real impetus to greater effort has been given in the process to a large number of them, though not, of course, to the last in the row. If, from the sum of money added to the earnings of cotton people, those people pay out to the makers of each several sort of goods—all the groups being supposed to be of the same size—£1, £1000, £10,000 and £80,000 respectively, re-transfers of money against further work will take place from the more favourably to the less favourably affected of these groups. It is, of course, possible that the cotton people's new expenditure may be distributed in such a way as to affect the relation between the marginal utility of money and of things in exactly the same way for all other groups ; but this is *a priori* improbable. If it does not happen—if there is need for re-transfers—repercussions or secondary movements will take place. The magnitude of these secondary movements will be measured roughly by the amount of the re-transfer of A's stuff that takes place between B, C, D . . . after A has paid for his purchases ; it being understood that, when B re-transfers to C and C again to D, there are here two re-transfers and not one. It is evident that, if there are n groups other than A, there cannot be more than n re-transfers of each of A's original purchase payments ; and also that an aggregate of re-transfers enormously smaller than this is much more probable than one approximating closely towards this.

§ 13. I turn to the sort of repercussions which come into view when account is taken of the fact that productive groups do not always hand over to others completely finished goods, but sometimes raw materials to be worked up by them. This sort does not need any lengthy elucidation. The coal industry sells, let us suppose, x tons of coal to the iron industry, which, we assume for simplicity, employs one ton of coal in making each ton of iron. The iron industry pays for the coal with hx tons of iron (made by means of hx tons of coal), and uses the remaining $(x - hx)$ tons of coal to help it make other iron goods, which it exchanges against boots and textiles. If its supply of coal is cut off, there is done away, not merely the activity of the coal industry and that part of the activity of the iron industry which used to buy the coal, but also activity in the iron industry represented by the value that this industry used to add to the coal it employed in manufacturing iron to exchange for things other than coal ; because, if it cannot get coal, its capacity for making iron has no scope, and, being specialised, must be thrown into idleness. In so far as iron is itself the raw material of some other industries, a further check to industrial activity of the same sort occurs in these other industries. It is obvious that the percentage effect on industrial activity throughout the country may be many times more than twice the fraction yielded by dividing the percentage reduction of expenditure on coal by the normal national income.

§ 14. The foregoing analysis of " repercussions ", both

parts of which, it will be noticed, are made necessary by the fact that capital and labour are specialised into different occupations, separated by barriers impassable except at heavy cost, destroys the hope, which the earlier sections of this chapter suggested, that we might be able to estimate quantitatively, or at least to establish an outside limit for, the direct effects (as distinguished from indirect effects operated through the psychology of business men) of the various causes previously distinguished in promoting industrial fluctuations. Had we been able to accomplish this, a long step forward would have been taken. In view, however, of the existence of these repercussions, the force of which it seems impossible to gauge by any generalised method, or, indeed, to estimate at all otherwise than by guess-work in particular cases, further advance along this route, unless other students are more fortunate than the present writer, cannot as yet be made.

CHAPTER VI

§ 1. Up to this point we have spoken as though an increase
(or decrease) in A's productivity or in A's desire for the
products of other groups could only react on B when it was
actually consummated in changes in real demand for B
products. If all work realised itself instantaneously this
would be so. But in fact most sorts of work precede by
a considerable interval the product to whose creation they
contribute. Therefore there is room for work to be done in
anticipation of the demand of those who ultimately use the
fruits of it. Producers in group A may enhance their output
on their own initiative because they think that there is going
to be an increased offer from B, C and D. It is not, indeed,
necessary that articles which take time to manufacture
should be made in anticipation of the demand of those
who are going to use them. Thus producers' goods are
often made to the order of the manufacturers needing
them. In like manner, some consumers' goods, such as ball-
dresses, bridges, large houses and buildings which have
to be adjusted to individual requirements, are almost
always made to the order of the ultimate purchasers.
Many producers' goods, however, and the bulk of consumers' goods are manufactured in advance of the ultimate
demand. With the supersession of hand-work by machine-
work some goods, which were formerly in the other
class, are passing into this one. Boots and shoes are an
instance of this tendency. Moreover, even when completed articles are still built to the specifications of indi-

vidual customers among the public, standard parts, that enter into a number of different finished articles, are often manufactured in advance. These goods are not, indeed, often made in large quantities by manufacturers entirely on their own initiative. On the contrary, they are made to order. Thus, a recent Report on unemployment in Philadelphia observes : " Twenty years ago a manufacturer made carpet or hosiery or cloth and then went out and sold *that* carpet or hosiery or cloth. To-day the order comes in for a particular design, with a certain kind of yarn or silk and a certain number of threads to the inch, and the manufacturer makes that particular order. Formerly a manufacturer produced standard makes of his particular line, and simply piled up stock in his warehouse in the off-season. . . . To-day manufacturers make, as a rule, very little to stock and run chiefly on orders." [1] The orders, however, come, not from ultimate purchasers but from middlemen, in the form of wholesale and retail dealers, who undertake the office of forecast, and order from A what they think B, C and D will ask for presently. When, after this, or, indeed, after any manner, expected facts are substituted for accomplished facts as the impulse to action, the way is opened for a second group of causes of industrial fluctuations, namely, psychological causes, which, at the beginning of Chapter IV., I distinguished from the " real " causes there discussed. These causes consist in variations in the tone of mind of persons whose action controls industry, emerging in errors of undue optimism or undue pessimism in their business forecasts.

§ 2. There are a number of ways in which these variations of tone and the associated errors may come about. They may arise " spontaneously ", which means as a result of the interplay of a number of small independent causes. They may arise as a psychological reflex from the actual experience of good and bad fortune, good fortune breeding errors of optimism, bad fortune errors of pessimism. Thus they may be a consequence of good and bad harvests, inventions, the

<hr />

[1] " Steadying Employment ", *Annals of the American Academy of Political Science*, May 1916, pp. 6-7.

discovery of mineral deposits, industrial disputes or the settlement of such disputes, political events, and so on. Again, in accordance with the suggestion of Mr. Hexter, referred to in Chapter IV., they may come about as a direct result of climatic changes upon human psychology, thus being associated with harvest changes, not as effects of them, but as joint-effects with them of a deeper underlying cause.[1] Yet again, they may be induced by monetary movements set going by monetary causes (*e.g.* the discovery of a gold mine, resort by a needy government to the printing press or the enactment of a new law about bank reserves); by monetary movements set going by harvest variations, industrial disputes or industrial inventions; or, in part, as a reflex effect of monetary movements set going by themselves. There is in all this food for reflection and a source of difficult problems. For the present, however, leaving the question of origin on one side, I proceed to investigate the various factors by which the *scope* of these errors is controlled.

§ 3. First, in a class by itself may be set the fact that industrial conditions are neither stationary not yet progressive in a continuous line, but that productivity and desire move in jerks. In a sense this fact may be regarded as *the* cause of errors; because, if everything were absolutely stable, recurring every year with exact similarity or in a perfectly regular progression, people could not fail to be aware of the relevant facts and to form correct judgements.[2] If the price of wheat is always the same, no speculator will be stupid enough to make a mistaken forecast. Thus errors in forecast *result* from inconstancy in facts. With increased stability in the facts the range of error would be lessened, just as in times of large social change, such as followed upon the Great War, when rule-of-thumb experience is rendered worthless, that range is abnormally large.

§ 4. Some instability in the facts being assumed, among the factors governing the scope of error must be put—and that in a high place—the capacity and mental calibre of the persons by whom forecasts operative in action are made. These persons include the proprietors of private business

---

[1] Cf. *ante*, p. 39.   [2] Cf. *ante*, p. 36.

concerns, the managers and directors of joint-stock companies, and the promoters and financial agents who from time to time, with the help of the investing public, float new enterprises.   Plainly, in a country such as America, where it is the custom for the best brains to go into business (in a wide sense) rather than into politics, the Church or the profession of arms, the mental quality of business leaders is likely to be higher than it is in a country in which business holds a lower place in people's interest.

§ 5. When the actual distribution of intellectual capacity among the different agencies concerned directly and indirectly with production is given, much depends on the extent to which they severally take a hand in framing the forecasts that will be operative. This consideration is very important in connection with the floating of joint-stock companies. Most members of the general public, from whom the funds for these ultimately come, are, if left to their own devices, quite incapable of giving any reasoned opinion upon the various propositions that are, on different occasions, put before them.   Hence " one of the chief sources of disturbance is the action of the general public in providing funds for joint-stock companies ".[1] The damaging effect of this unregulated action is the greater because the short-period prospects, in which promoters are interested, may easily be much rosier than the ultimate prospects ; and it may, therefore, be to the advantage of these experts deliberately to mislead their clientèle.   Attempts have sometimes been made to mend this situation by regulations designed to prevent uninstructed members of the general public from dealing in the shares of new companies. The pre-war German rule forbidding the issue of shares of a low face value was directed to this end. A more fundamental remedy is to keep the work of promotion in the hands of bankers—whose reputation depends upon the *permanent* success of the business undertakings that they father, and whose intervention, therefore, constitutes an effective buffer between the irresponsible promoter and the irresponsible subscriber of capital. It is not customary for banks in the United

[1] Marshall, *Money, Credit and Commerce*, p. 261.

Kingdom to take charge in this way of business enterprises, and it is obvious that such action on their part might lead to a dangerous lock-up of their resources. On the whole, the practical difficulties in the way of extruding uninstructed persons from company financing and concentrating the work upon experts are probably too great to be overcome. It may be hoped, however, that, long before the general public have become competent to form for themselves sound judgements about investments, they will have at least discovered that they are not competent to do this, and will avail themselves, before placing their money, of the consultation and advice, and not merely of the mechanical mediation, of brokers or other experts.

§ 6. A further factor, by which the range of errors in industrial forecasts is influenced, is the measure in which relevant information is accessible to the makers of forecasts. Business secrecy plainly handicaps forecasts, while publicity helps them. In Marshall's words, " those causes of discontinuity which lie within our scope, and are remediable, are chiefly connected in some way or other with the want of knowledge. . . . Better and more widely diffused knowledge is a remedy for that excessive confidence which causes a violent expansion of credit and rise of prices, as it is also a remedy for that excessive distrust which follows." [1] In this matter legal rules enforcing upon company promoters the full disclosure of all relevant facts to those from whom they solicit subscriptions of capital, public control over the prospectuses of new companies, and effective administrative action against fraudulent promotion are obvious means of betterment. The position would be further improved if it were possible to secure the publication, at short intervals, of full statistics about the stocks of various sorts of commodities on hand in warehouses and shops ; and if Mr. Hull's suggestion were carried out, that the State should publish monthly " all pertinent information in relation to the existing volume of constructions under contract for future delivery ".[2] It may be added that the steadying influence

---

[1] *Money, Credit and Commerce*, pp. 260-61.
[2] *Industrial Depressions*, p. 218.

of publicity would be strengthened if the practice of cancelling orders when a depression has set in could be checked either by custom or by law : for this practice makes the depression worse than it need be both directly and also indirectly by encouraging reckless orders during booms.

§ 7. Whatever steps are taken on the above lines, it is, of course, certain that there will be a great deal of important information which is *not* published. In view of this, the division of industrial groups into a number of separate units acting independently of one another and, therefore, not pooling their knowledge, is a factor tending to promote errors of forecast. If production and sale were an instantaneous process, this division of control could not promote errors, because, the moment an error occurred, it would be unmasked. But in actual life it is responsible for large errors. The individual producer of anything, or the dealer who orders from the individual producer, or the manufacturer of finished goods ordering, say, machines, is usually without information as to the supply of these things that will be forthcoming from other producers or dealers to confront the prospective demand for which he is himself preparing. Since the processes of manufacture generally take some little time, the actual appearance on the market of the rival's product or the fruit of the rival's order is delayed. Consequently, when a particular producer or dealer expects the public demand for the product in his hand to expand or to contract, he usually pays too little attention to the fact that his rivals are likely to have formed the same opinion and to be acting on it. He *may* even be blind to the fact that he himself, by his own preparations for increased output, is setting supply in chase of demand. " If," writes M. Aftalion, " to remedy the deficiency of heat in a room, one revives the fire on the hearth, it will be necessary to *wait for some time* before the desired temperature is obtained. As the cold continues and the thermometer continues to register it, one would be led, if one were not instructed by experience, to throw more fuel on to the fire. One would do this even though the quantity already accumulated there were such that, when it is all ignited, it would give out an unbearable amount of heat. In letting oneself be guided by the sensation of present cold—by the present indications of the thermometer —one would fatally overheat the room." [1] This sort of blindness, however, is not likely to prevail widely : nor, when the individual producer or dealer is a small part of the market, would it matter much if it did. The really important point is that other people, besides himself, are piling coal on the fire, and that he has no adequate means of knowing to what extent they are doing this. This ignorance leads to an under-estimate of their activity in boom times—an under-estimate that inevitably calls new competitors into industries in which there is not really room for them—and an over-estimate of their activity in times of depression. Errors generated in this way would, of course, be mitigated by the official publication of information about contracts in the manner contemplated in the preceding section.

§ 8. The division of the control over any form of production among a number of hands opens the way for errors on the supply side as well as on the demand side. The great bulk of producers are not integrated businesses completing the whole process of manufacture from raw material to finished article. For the most part the entrepreneur in control of an industrial concern has to buy raw materials and half-manufactured goods, to engage labour and to borrow capital ; and the persons from whom these things have to be obtained are not exclusively bound to him. When undertakings, such as works of construction, occupy a long time in execution, contracts are usually made in connection with them months, or even years, before much of the labour and material employed upon them will be required. Thus there arises the practice of " forward buying ", firms engaged in the more advanced processes of production contracting to make, at a future date, certain purchases at certain rates from those engaged in the less advanced processes. It is not, however, in general, practicable for advanced contracts to be entered into for labour or for certain raw

---

[1] Aftalion, *Les Crises périodiques de surproduction*, vol. ii. p. 361.

materials. Consequently, in reflecting on the terms at which they are prepared to sell for future delivery, most of the firms affected must be content with guess-work concerning a considerable part of their costs. Each firm, however, in making its guess, is, as has been observed above, usually without information as to the future contracts undertaken by other firms. It is, therefore, apt to ignore the effect which the execution of these contracts, when they fall due, will have upon the real price of labour and materials. Hence a general movement towards optimistic expectations is likely to be carried further than it would be if the making and the execution of contracts synchronised. These tendencies, it will be observed, are not dependent upon the modern practice of manufacture in anticipation of final demand, but occur in respect of commodities that are made to consumers' orders. An excellent illustration is afforded by the history of the English munition contracts in the earlier part of the Great War. Firms contracted to deliver large quantities of shells on the assumption that they would be able to sub-contract a part of their orders to other works, and then discovered that these works were also being sought after for a like purpose by rival firms ; with the result, incidentally, that the aggregate of shells actually delivered fell enormously below the aggregate for which contracts had been made.

§ 9. What has been said of raw materials and labour applies also to capital. Particular concerns are apt to neglect the fact that the response made by other concerns to a rising demand will force up the rate of interest against them in the later stages of their own work. This is well set out by Professor Cassel. " What is over-estimated ", he writes, " is the capacity of the capitalists to provide savings in sufficient quantity. We must bear in mind that this capacity has to be estimated several years in advance, since, on the average, there are several years between the time when the work is planned and the time when it makes its full demand upon the community's savings. The individual employer has no other means of judging the condition of the capital market except the rate of interest.

During the depression and the first part of the high conjunc-
ture, however, the rate is low, or at least moderate. The
demands for capital-disposal which result from the increased
activity of employers in the sphere of the production of
fixed capital do not yet make themselves fully felt. It is,
therefore, quite possible that enterprises, such as the
construction of houses, railways, etc., will be planned, and
even begun, in such quantities that, when their need of
capital afterwards makes itself felt, it cannot be satisfied.
. . . This wrong estimate of the future condition of the
capital market would not lead to such a catastrophe if
the individual employer secured in advance the whole of
the capital he needs to carry out his plans. Under present
conditions this can rarely be done. Share-capital, which
is subscribed for the purpose of realising a large undertaking,
represents, as a rule, only a part, sometimes only a very
small part, of the whole of the capital needed. People
generally persuade themselves that in the future it will
be possible to get the requisite capital by the issue of debentures, by bank-credits, and so on." [1]

§ 10. There is yet one other way in which division of
control promotes error. When operative forecasts are made
by dealers, and the thing in question is something that it
takes a long time to make, these dealers, in a period of expansion, finding that manufacturers at first are only able to
supply a proportion of their orders, may deliberately give
much larger orders than they want to have filled, in order to
improve their chance of getting what they do want. Moreover, failing to get an immediate supply from one manufacturer, they may make application to several. These proceedings on their part involve a false inflation in the demand
that actually comes to manufacturers' order books, of a sort
that would not occur at all if ultimate consumers manufactured for themselves, and would not occur in so high
a degree if manufacturers dealt with consumers direct
without any intermediary.[2] This adds to the expansion of

---

[1] *The Theory of Social Economy*, vol. ii. pp. 626-7.

[2] Ultimate consumers might, of course, over-order to some extent,
just as members of the public, subscribing to some new loan, may apply
for more shares than they hope to get.

industry in boom times, and afterwards adds to the depression by leading either to a cancellation of dealers' orders or to an overstocking of the warehouses and shops, in consequence of which demand is reduced later on.[1]

§ 11. The discussion of the two preceding sections necessarily leads on to a further point. If what is needed for the reduction of error is that each forecaster in a particular industry should have information about what is being done by all, it is evident that by far the most effective means to that end is that all the firms engaged in any given form of production should be combined under a single head in a Trust or in a Kartel possessing a central office entrusted with the regulation of output. This circumstance must not, however, be taken to prove that the " trustification " of industries makes for stability of output on the whole. In Chapter XIX. one reason for scepticism on this matter will be set out. Apart from this, however, it must be remembered that attempts at trustification often lead to multiple monopoly rather than to simple monopoly. If this happens, fluctuations may be made extremely great by causes other than those specified so far. Even if there is no cut-throat competition, we may get fluctuations over a wide range of indeterminateness ; [2] and, if cut-throat competition supervenes, the range of possible fluctuations is still further enlarged. Finally, even if a single monopoly is formed for a time, it may presently break up again, and so cause a large fluctuation.

§ 12. Hitherto we have been concerned with influences of a general sort and have not considered at all differences between different industries. We have now to observe that the range of error in operative forecasts, whether these are made by retailers, wholesalers, manufacturers, company promoters or subscribers of capital, will be larger for things that it takes a long time than for things that it takes a short time to make ; for the reason that it is always easier to see a little distance ahead than a long

---

[1] Cf. Mitchell, " Competitive Illusion as a Cause of Business Cycles ", *Quarterly Journal of Economics*, August 1924, p. 631 *et seq.*

[2] Cf. *The Economics of Welfare*, Part II. chap. xv.

distance. For example, a man who tries to forecast on the present data how many ships or houses will be wanted at the time when ships or houses started now would be ready is much more likely to make a mistake than one who similarly tries to forecast how many pairs of gloves will be wanted at the time when gloves started now would be ready. It is true, no doubt, that many of the things that take a long time to make, such as ships, or houses, or locomotives or elaborate machines, are made, neither speculatively by manufacturers nor to the order of intermediate dealers, but to the order of the ultimate purchasers ; and, therefore, it might seem, error in forecast on the side of production is precluded. Apart, however, from dwelling-houses, it so happens that nearly all the things that it takes a long time to make are instruments of production, and the ultimate purchasers people who want to use them, not for consumption, but for further production. When a thing of this sort, say, a textile plant, which takes two years to construct, is ordered, though the producer of the plant makes no forecast, nevertheless a forecast *is* made and acted on—a forecast, namely, by the giver of the order, of the demand for cotton goods that will rule two years hence. Thus, despite the fact that the things are made to the order of the ultimate purchasers, the length of time which they take to make is a factor determining the range of error to which operative forecasts are subject.

§ 13. Besides the length of time that things take to make, another very important factor affecting the range of error about future demand to which an industry is liable is the area of the market from which this demand comes. In a primitive community, where each family, or small group, is more or less self-sufficing and directs the main part of its activity to the production of things to be consumed by itself, the forecast it would have to make on the demand side (*i.e.* apart from prospective costs of production) would refer exclusively to its own future tastes. In modern conditions, however, with industry conducted on the basis of division of labour and exchange of products, each producer's forecast must refer both to the tastes of other people and also to their real income and purchasing power. Naturally, this sort of forecast is exposed to much larger error than the primitive forecast ; and the difficulty of right judgement is enhanced as the relevant market comes to include more and more remote groups of purchasers, about whose circumstances the ordinary producer has great difficulty in informing himself. In so far as the demands of different parts of this market are subject to independent influences, he is, indeed, entitled to assume that, the more markets he secures, the greater is the chance that variations in their several demands will partly cancel one another. But this consolation is not available in respect of those general fluctuations of demand associated with trade cycles. Nor is it available in industries in which, because of their novelty, there is no secure basis of past experience to serve as a guide. " Large errors are especially liable to occur in enterprises in new fields, whose limitations have not been accurately measured by investors, or even by capitalists of proved judgement and experience. . . . New discoveries and the opening up of new continents have contributed greatly to these mistakes during the modern commercial age." [1]

§ 14. We have now to consider the way in which errors in different industries are related to one another. If they arise independently, there is a presumption that they will tend more or less to neutralise one another, an error of optimism in one place being balanced against an error of pessimism in another, so that large *net* errors are only likely to occur at rare intervals. No doubt, neutralisation will be far from complete. Even if it is true that an equal distribution of individual errors between undue optimism and undue pessimism is more probable than any other *specified* distribution—a proposition that is open to doubt—it is not true that an equal distribution is more probable than *some* (unspecified) other distribution. On the contrary, it is much less probable. It is practically certain that, at any moment chosen at random, the distribution of individual errors on the two sides of truth will be unequal, and that, at some moments, it will be very unequal. Still, the inequality of distribution is likely to be much less if the different persons

---

[1] Conant, *The History of Modern Banks of Issue*, p. 461.

concerned act independently than if they draw one another
on in the same direction. A tendency towards *common*
action among them enormously increases the mean range of
error. If the passengers on a ship always walk about independently, there is little danger of their causing much disturbance to its equilibrium, but, if they rush in combined
panic from side to side, there is very great danger. It is,
therefore, important for us to inquire how far, in the matter
of expectations concerning the future, those persons whose
action controls business do, in fact, tend to act in droves.

§ 15. Before this problem is attacked, however, it will be
well to clear away a confusing suggestion which would make
it appear that *generalised* errors of forecast are, in the nature
of things, impossible. The suggestion is that, if everybody
at the same time formed the ungrounded opinion that everybody else was about to be prosperous (or the reverse),
the very universality of this error would transmute it into
truth. For A, thinking that B is about to be prosperous
and so to exercise an increased real demand for his products,
increases his output, and B, dominated by the corresponding
thought about A, does likewise. These increased outputs,
created in error though they are, nevertheless constitute
increased reciprocal demands for one another. Therefore,
the argument runs, the fact of A's error causes A so to act
that B's error becomes the truth ; and the fact of B's error
causes B so to act that A's error becomes the truth. The
fact that *all* expectations have been false causes *each* expectation to be true ! This reasoning, paradoxical as it is in form,
is not obviously fallacious in substance. It is, however, in
fact, fallacious. The nature of the fallacy involved can be
set out as follows. It is perfectly true that an increase in
the output of A, however caused, makes worth while some
increase in the output of B. Professor Mitchell seizes this
point when he writes : " As it spreads, the epidemic of
optimism helps to breed conditions which both justify and
intensify it. The mere fact that a growing number of business men are gaining confidence in the outlook becomes a valid
reason why each member of the group, and outsiders also,
should feel confident. For the hopeful mood means greater

readiness to make new purchases, enter into new contracts, etc.—in fine, means that the incipient revival of activity will be supported and extended." [1] All this is true. But it is not true that a given false expectation on the part of A justifies an *equal* false expectation on the part of B, and *vice versa*. The two false expectations jointly create for one another *some* justification, but not a *sufficient* justification. This can easily be proved. The general laws of demand inform us that A will be prepared to offer a lower real price per unit for B's goods the larger the quantity offered becomes ; and that B will stand in a like relation to A's goods. Hence, if A thinks that B is going to offer twice his normal supply of goods, A will reply by producing, not twice his normal supply, but, say, one and a half times his normal supply ; and B, under the influence of a similar opinion about A, will act in the same way. Hence both A and B, as a result of their false opinions, produce one and a half times their normal output. But, *ex hypothesi*, A is willing to give one and a half times his normal output in exchange, not for one and a half times, but for twice B's normal output ; and B is in like case. Hence the error of the one, though it makes the error of the other less glaring than it would otherwise be, does not convert it into a truth. A and B are both disappointed and both find that their expansion of output was a mistake. The situation is exactly similar if each of A and B falsely expects the other to contract his output, and contracts his own in consequence. In these circumstances, as Marshall observes, " the chief cause of the evil is want of confidence. The greater part of it could be removed almost in an instant if confidence could return, touch all industries with her magic wand, and make them continue their production and their demand for the wares of others." [2] In lack of such revivification of confidence, both A and B will find, when their product

---

[1] *Business Cycles*, p. 455.

[2] *Principles of Economics*, p. 711. Cf. Kinder (*The Effects of Recent Changes in Monetary Standards upon the Distribution of Wealth*, p. 499) : " In a community where the individual members are working only half their time, any inducement, though illusory in itself, which sets them at work their full time, may benefit all without necessarily injuring any." Mr. Kinder is thinking of the possible effects of a rise of prices due to monetary causes.

comes to be sold, that their real receipts per unit are larger than they expected, and will realise that contraction of output was a mistake. Thus the doubt whether all-round over-estimates and under-estimates of future real demand are possible may be dismissed. The same result may be reached from the side of money prices. For, even though everybody is certain that the general level of prices is going to remain constant, everybody may also be convinced, without any internal inconsistency, that the price of his own particular product is going to rise or to fall.

§ 16. The generalisation of errors being thus recognised as possible, we have next to inquire whether there are any influences at work liable to promote it. I suggest that there are three such influences.

First, among business men, even when engaged in different occupations, there often exists a certain measure of psychological interdependence. A change of tone in one part of the business world diffuses itself, in a quite unreasoning manner, over other and wholly disconnected parts. An expansion of business confidence " propagates itself by that sympathetic and epidemic excitement which so largely sways communities of men ".[1] There comes into play a quasi-hypnotic system of mutual suggestion :

> One with another, soul with soul
> They kindle fire from fire.

" Perhaps the buoyancy of a grocer gives a lumber dealer no adequate reason for altering his conservative attitude towards the business projects upon which he must pass. Yet, in despite of logic, he will be the readier to buy if his acquaintances in any line of trade have become aggressively confident of the future. The fundamental conditions affecting his own business may remain the same ; but his conduct is altered because he sees the old facts in a new emotional perspective." [2] This tendency is the more marked in so far as business men are congregated in close physical proximity to one another in the business sections of large cities.[3]

---

[1] Kemmerer, *Money and Prices*, p. 83.
[2] Mitchell, *Business Cycles*, p. 455.
[3] Cf. Jones, *Economic Crises*, p. 204.

Secondly, as was explained in the preceding section, an error of optimism on the part of one group of business men itself creates a justification for some improved expectation on the part of other groups. For the group primarily affected has more product to sell, which means, in effect, that it offers a higher real demand for the goods of other groups. The real increment of prosperity thus given to these others stimulates in them a spirit of optimism, and makes it more probable than it would otherwise be that they too will lean unduly to the sunnier side of doubt. The fact that A's erroneous optimism is a ground of some small justified optimism on the part of B, C and D adds a material link to the link of sympathy which we have already seen to bind business men in different occupations together. Exactly analogous considerations hold good of errors of pessimism.

Thirdly, yet another connection is set up between business men in different occupations by the debtor-creditor relation which prevails extensively in the modern world. The great bulk of industrial concerns are both borrowers and lenders. They borrow from one set of people by buying materials from them on credit, and they lend to another set by selling the fruits of their workmanship on credit. Of course, in actual life these credits are expressed in terms of a money of variable value, and in a later chapter it will be shown that this fact has important consequences. For the present, however, we may ignore it, assuming rather that the credits are in terms of things in general, or that the value of money as against things in general is stable. We have thus, as it were, a series in the form A, B, C, D, each member of which is debtor to the one preceding, and creditor to the one succeeding, himself. Manufacturers of raw materials are borrowers from the banks and lenders to manufacturers of finished goods ; manufacturers of finished goods are borrowers from manufacturers of raw materials and lenders to wholesale dealers ; wholesale dealers are borrowers from manufacturers of finished goods and lenders to retailers ; and retailers are borrowers from wholesale dealers and lenders to customers who buy on credit. This fact implies that, if any good or evil chance happens to one, its effects are likely to be passed on to the others. Furthermore, the measure of this financial interdependence among business men is increased by every development of business practice towards longer or larger credits between manufacturers of raw materials and manufacturers of finished products, between manufacturers of finished products and wholesalers, and between wholesalers and retail tradesmen.[1] Hence it is significant that, at all events in some industries, as the tide of profits advances, credits do in fact tend to become both larger and longer. Some sorts (though not all sorts) of collateral, being of higher price, will command a larger advance, and, when no collateral is employed, A, looking more optimistically on B's prospects, will regard with less critical eyes his request for credit. Thus Sir Sydney Chapman observes: "The longer the period of good trade, the further is forward buying drawn out and the more involved do traders become. If normally the rule is to buy in October for January deliveries, towards the end of a period of good trade dealers will be buying for January deliveries, say, in July, under the pressure of demands crowding in in the face of only slightly elastic production."[2] Moreover, there is reason to believe that, in nearly all industries in times of boom, there is an enormous increase in forward buying against informal promises to pay—a development which links the fortunes of different business men still more closely together. But the forecasts made by business men are almost certainly coloured by their present fortune. It follows that interdependence

---

[1] It may be noted that, as between brokers and their clients, credits are kept low by the system of "short settlements". This system "aims at reducing the risk of loss due to the assumption by weak dealers of risks greater than the funds at their disposal enable them to cover, and, thus, at rendering business more secure, and, being more secure, capable of being carried on with narrower profits. The parties to the contract may (or in some cases must) deposit a sum of money sufficient to cover any probable loss due to variation of price for a short time, and, if prices vary beyond what the deposit can make good, must increase the deposit." (*British Association Report*, 1900, p. 4.) This system, in effect, prevails both among those who speculate on margins on the Stock Exchange and among those who deal in futures on the Produce Exchanges.

[2] *Unemployment in Lancashire*, p. 95.

of fortunes carries with it some degree of interdependence of forecasts.

The three links between business men, which we have thus distinguished, act as conducting rods along which an error of optimism or pessimism, once generated, propagates itself about the business world. By their joint action they exert a powerful influence, in favour of action in droves. This means that large net errors of forecast are liable to occur much more frequently than they would do if these links were lacking : and large net errors may be expected to carry with them large fluctuations in the aggregate volume of industrial activity.

CHAPTER VII

THE MUTUAL GENERATION OF ERRORS OF OPTIMISM
AND ERRORS OF PESSIMISM

§ 1. HITHERTO we have considered errors of optimism and pessimism as simple, self-contained and independent. They are not, however, in fact of this character. On the contrary, errors of either sort, in whatever way they may have come about, have the characteristic of generating, after a while, errors of the opposite sort. The process is not difficult to understand. The activity which is developed in industry under the influence of an error of optimism finally materialises in the form of commodities seeking a market. So long as these are in process of being created —as we may say, throughout their period of gestation— exceptional activity continues. Some of them, of course, are completed sooner than others. Even for the same sort of thing the period of gestation is not the same when factories are fully occupied as when they are slack : and for different sorts of things it varies greatly. A boom involves, as it were, the sowing of a great number of different kinds of seed, the crops from which are scattered over a considerable range of time. Some of the seed will spring up and flower immediately ; some in one year, some in two, some in three, some perhaps in ten. The period of gestation for ordinary consumable goods, such as cotton cloth, is very short. Construction goods in general take a good deal longer to make. Mr. Hull states that it takes a year to build an iron furnace. M. Aftalion suggests that the gap between ordering and completion is, for the rolling stock of railways some one and a half years, for locomotives some three years, and for shipping some two years. Houses, according to their size, may take from one to three years to build. Steam-engines for industrial works in France may take one, two or three years. The period of gestation of a coffee plantation is some five years. That of a coal mine is probably, in present conditions, even longer. The above are not designed to be more than illustrations. The essential fact is that the period of gestation varies greatly for different things, and is especially likely to be long for elaborate constructional instruments. We cannot, therefore, say generally that the period will always be of such and such a definite length. But we can say that, for all things, there is some period of gestation, the conclusion of which brings forecast to the test of fact. When this test has been applied to a fair number of things and found wanting for a fair number, confidence is shaken. The fact that errors of optimism have been made and prospective profits exaggerated is discovered and recognised widely. By the fact of discovery on a large scale the tendency to errors of optimism is necessarily destroyed. As a consequence the flow of business activity is checked. The check does not, indeed, operate instantaneously, because business men who find themselves in difficulties are tempted to extend their borrowings and make a desperate throw to restore their fortunes. After a little while, however, those people who have made and acted upon errors of optimism have to confess them—at least to themselves,—to sell a mass of products at a lower real price than they had anticipated, and to pocket the consequent loss. This leaves them in no mood for any further errors of optimism. Nor is this all. Partly in consequence of the financial interdependence of different businesses discussed in Chapter VI., they are apt to fall into a strong reaction. The ill-fate that has occurred to the direct victims of optimistic error strikes indirectly at a great number of other people. Traders who have done bad business, being impoverished, endeavour to draw in their debts from other houses directly associated with them. This action on their part causes the other houses in turn to adopt a like policy. Hence a fairly general liquidation of

bad business sets in. " Once begun, the process of liquidation extends rapidly, partly because most enterprises, which
are called upon to settle their maturing obligations, in
turn put similar pressure upon their own debtors, and
partly because, despite all efforts to keep secret what is
going forward, news presently leaks out and other creditors
take alarm." [1] This movement inevitably reacts upon
business confidence. Under its influence the dying error of
optimism gives birth to an error of pessimism. This new
error is born, not an infant, but a giant. For an industrial
boom has necessarily been a period of strong emotional
excitement, and an excited man passes from one form of
excitement to another more readily than he passes to
quiescence. The error of pessimism thus established implies
an unduly depressed view in all industries of the prospective
demand of other industries for their products. Therefore
in all of them but little activity is expended, and dullness
supervenes. After an interval, equal, as before, to the
period of gestation of the principal instrumental goods *plus*
the time necessary for their products to get to market,
the error of undue pessimism, like the previous error of
undue optimism, is discovered. Those who have ventured
to order these things, or to make them in anticipation of
orders, find themselves in receipt of good profits. Moreover,
after a time the continued using up of dealers' stocks reduces
them to a point below which no further reduction can be
made, so that, henceforth, new orders must be given to
cover the whole, and not merely a part, of the current
purchases of consumers. In these circumstances certain of
the bolder spirits in industry begin to make preparations
for an enlarged output, or to venture upon some hitherto
untried type of enterprise, for which scientific advance has
opened up the way.[2] The pioneers, who thus undertake

[1] Cf. Mitchell, *Business Cycles*, p. 576.
[2] Professor Schumpeter finds the origin of all the most important
booms of the last 100 years in this latter type of action. "Those booms
consist in the carrying out of innovations in the industrial and commercial
organism. By innovations I understand such changes of the combinations
of the factors of production as cannot be effected by infinitesimal steps or
variations on the margin. They consist primarily in changes in the
methods of production of a new article, or in the opening up of new markets

and expand enterprises, at once fill a social need and lay up treasure for themselves. Gradually, as no disaster happens to them, other less bold spirits follow their example ; then others and yet others. Professor Schumpeter well writes : " Whenever in a given situation new things have been successfully done by some, others can, on the one hand, copy their behaviour in the same line—whence prominence of one industry at the time—and, on the other hand, get the courage to do similar things in other lines, the spell being broken, and many details of the behaviour of the first leaders being applicable outside their own field of action. And, therefore, the first success draws other people in its wake." [1] All these people are further encouraged by the fact, noted by Professor Mitchell, that, during the preceding period of depression, there has probably been an accumulation of " technical improvements, of which new plants can take advantage, and, therefore, the greater becomes the inducement to invest in new equipment ".[2] Advance thus takes place all along the line. " There is, of course, no formal agreement between the different trades to begin again to work full time, and so make a market for each other's wares. But the revival of industry comes about through the gradual and often simultaneous growth of confidence among various trades." [3] The first-comers make an addition to industrial energy that is really needed to correct the error that has hitherto prevailed. Perhaps those who come in and expand their business directly after the beginnings of revival are also in this class. The first year or two, say, is taken up with a wholly justified expansion. But, after the first year or two, further expansion represents, not a correction of the past error, but the creation of a new one, and, thereafter, any further expansion represents a growth of unjustified optimism. The turn of the tide from ebb to flow is a slow and gradual process. Cautiously and

---

or of new sources of material. *The recurring periods of prosperity of the cyclical movement are the form progress takes in capitalistic society.*" (*Economica*, Dec. 1927, p. 295.)

[1] *Economica*, Dec. 1927, p. 298.   [2] Mitchell, *Business Cycles*, p. 567.
[3] Marshall, *Principles of Economics*, p. 711.

hesitatingly the first steps on the return journey towards the correct route are taken ; some time elapses before that route is reached ; when it is reached it is passed, and a new false track on the opposite side is entered upon, down which industry runs at an accelerating pace, until once more the presence of an error of optimism is revealed and, on revelation, destroyed. An error of pessimism is then again generated in the way we have described, and presently, when it in turn has died, a new wave of optimism begins to gather on the same pattern as before.

§ 2. The extent of the revulsion towards pessimistic error, which follows when optimistic error is disclosed, depends, in part, upon the magnitude of the preceding optimistic error. The larger this has been the larger also the reaction is likely to be. But the extent of the revulsion does not depend only upon this. It is also affected by what we may call the detonation, which accompanies the discovery of a given mass of optimistic error. The detonation is greater or less according to the number and scale of the legal bankruptcies into which the detected error explodes. These legal bankruptcies, or business failures, are not, in themselves, of great industrial importance. It seldom happens that, as a result of them, any business enterprise is abandoned ; the normal course is for it to pass, through sale or through a receivership in the interest of bond-holders, into the control of other—very probably more energetic and more able—men, with the net result that a relatively competent entrepreneur is substituted for one who was relatively incompetent. It is, thus, a true saying which Mr. Burton quotes from John Mills : " As a rule, panics do not destroy capital ; they merely reveal the extent to which it has been previously destroyed by its betrayal into hopelessly unproductive works." [1] But business failures necessarily and always breed fear among industrialists that their own debtors may fail. The more extensive they are—that is to say, the louder the detonation—the more they shatter business confidence. The influences by which the detona-

[1] Burton, *Financial Crises*, p. 20.

tion that accompanies any given discovery of error is determined are, therefore, real causes affecting the amplitude of industrial fluctuations.

§ 3. Among these influences are the methods by which industry is normally financed. When people (not otherwise in debt) make unsuccessful investments with resources belonging to themselves, the failure of their ventures cannot involve legal bankruptcy. But, when they employ borrowed resources, failure may involve this. From this point of view, therefore, the highly developed credit arrangements of the modern world constitute a danger. The danger is especially great when loans have been taken up in a form that requires periodic renewal, so that the venturer may find himself, in his hour of need, forced to pay back the principal of his loan. In the United States a large share of the capital required in manufacturing establishments and in other enterprises " is furnished by discounts obtained from banks instead of by permanent capital or by long-time loans or bonds ".[1] This is a risky arrangement. If businesses find it necessary to raise floating loans, prudence requires that they should fund them as soon as possible.[2] There is danger, again, when creditors are ill-advised enough, or when their fortunes are so far bound up with those of potentially insolvent debtors that they are practically forced, to add loan to loan for firms which, whether by making new plunges of rash investment or by holding up goods against liquidation, are heading for the rocks. When this happens the eventual collapse will be all the more severe, just because it has been delayed. For not only is there a presumption that a business house, which has committed errors large enough to render it potentially insolvent, is incompetently managed and is likely to commit further errors in the future, even if its business practice is not worsened ; but also this practice is, in fact, likely to be worsened, because, since the house is already insolvent, further losses will fall, not upon it, but upon its creditors. This danger can be partly

[1] Burton, *Financial Crises*, p. 263.

[2] The increase in the issue of securities that often occurs after a crisis is due in the main to this process of funding. (Cf. Mitchell, *Business Cycles*, p. 405.)

mitigated by embodying in the bankruptcy laws stringent provisions against various forms of fraud and sharp practice. In Germany an attempt is made to do more than this. As soon as the balance sheet of a company—the balance sheet must take account of depreciation of capital—shows an excess of liabilities over assets, compulsory winding-up is required and enforced by penalties. English law allows a company to continue in business till it actually becomes bankrupt.

§ 4. The above influences go far to determine over how wide a range, at any given turning-point of confidence, business failures will be threatened. They do not, however, by themselves determine what proportion of the threatened failures shall actually occur. This is settled principally by the capacity and willingness of the country's banking system to save houses which are really sound—in the sense that their assets are more than sufficient to cover their liabilities—but which cannot at the moment secure sufficient money to meet obligations immediately payable in that form. For, of course, on these occasions it is money, and money only, that is wanted. Commodities and securities are both useless for the purpose. Money alone will save, and the repositories of money are the banks. Hence, other things being equal, the actual occurrence of business failures will be more or less widespread, according as bankers' loans, in the face of crisis demands, are less or more readily obtainable.

§ 5. Now at the time when errors of optimism are discovered bankers are often beginning to realise, not merely that their liabilities relatively to their cash reserves have become exceptionally large, but also that an exceptionally large proportion of their loans are being used in financing constructional enterprises, as distinguished from commerce proper, and have, therefore, become, as it were, solidified, instead of liquid, assets. Therefore it is natural that they should hesitate to swell their liabilities still further, whether by lending to sound houses or in any other way. They are themselves under contract to meet all liabilities with legal tender upon demand, and anything that widens the gap between liabilities and reserves lessens their assurance of

being able to do this. It may, therefore, be argued, and
was argued by earlier bankers, that, though the public
interest requires them to lend freely, their own private
interest commands, rather, a calling-in of their loans.   Under
a many-reserve system, when the separate banks are isolated
from one another, this reasoning *may*, on occasions, be
sound.   Though it would pay *all* banks to lend freely, it
need not pay any particular bank to do so.   For, if it lends
freely, the whole of its reserve may be drawn out and paid
over into the coffers of its rivals ; whereas, if it holds its
hand, it may possibly stand a rare survivor amid the general
ruin.   Even under a many-reserve system, however, and
still more under a one-reserve system, a selfish policy is
dangerous to the banks that practise it, as well as highly
injurious to the community as a whole.   If loans are withheld and sound houses fall, their fall will drag down others.
Panic will grow wilder and wilder and will eventually lead
to distrust of the banks themselves.   When this happens
and depositors begin to insist on their legal right to actual
currency, the safety of the banks generally—of the selfish
equally with the public-spirited—is threatened far more
seriously than it would have been had loans been made
with sufficient freedom to nip the panic in the bud.   It
follows that the self-interest of the banks, looked at broadly
and generally, requires them to lend freely in the face of
crisis demands.   In other words, bank loans in these circumstances, so far as bankers recognise their own interest, will
be readily granted.   They will be refused only if bankers
fail rightly to analyse the situation and are timid by mistake.
They must lend freely.   Where there is a central banking
institution, that institution especially must lend freely,
either directly to the other banks through rediscounting,
as in the United States, or, as in England, to bill brokers,
by whose repayments of called-in loans out of the proceeds
the balances of the other banks at the Bank of England
are enhanced.[1]   To lend freely does not, of course, mean
to lend cheaply.   On the contrary, since panic generally
comes at the apex of an exaggerated boom, when high

[1] Cf. Withers, *Banks and Credit*, pp. 36-7.

prices have led to expanded imports and are inducing a heavy foreign drain, the rates charged must be high. But at high rates loans must be forthcoming. This is Bagehot's celebrated advice to the Bank of England : " The end is to stay the panic ; and the advances should, if possible, stay the panic. And for this purpose there are two rules. First, that these loans should only be made at a very high rate of interest. . . . Secondly, that at this rate these advances should be made on all good banking securities, and as largely as the public ask for them." [1] The policy thus recommended has become a recognised part of Bank of England practice. It necessarily exercises a powerful effect in lessening the detonation of financial crises. It may, therefore, be credited with considerable influence in restricting the amplitude of errors, and, therewith, of industrial fluctuations.

[1] *Lombard Street*, p. 199.

CHAPTER VIII

AUTONOMOUS MONETARY CAUSES OF INDUSTRIAL FLUCTUATIONS

§ 1. In Chapters XII.-XVII. I shall examine monetary and credit arrangements as *conditions* upon which initiating causes, real and psychological, act, and which, by the response they make, largely determine the scale of the effect that is produced upon the activity of industry. The response, as will be shown, is made through changes in the volume of credit and the level of general prices. Such changes, however, it is plain, may come about otherwise than as a response to the above impulses. When this happens events affecting money are themselves initiating causes of industrial disturbance, on a par with the real causes and psychological causes discussed above. The manner in which they operate is, of course, very similar to the manner in which monetary movements set going as a secondary effect of some other initiating cause operate. A full study of that difficult subject will be found in later chapters, and to anticipate it here would involve needless repetition. In this chapter, therefore, I shall confine myself in the main to a discussion of the principal ways in which autonomous monetary causes come into play. To obtain a complete view of them, this chapter must be read in conjunction with Chapters XII.-XVII.

§ 2. These causes, which may, of course, act synchronously with other causes affecting industrial activity in the same sense, or synchronously with other causes affecting it in the opposite sense—as would happen if a gold mine were discovered at a time when industry was depressed in consequence of a bad harvest—or entirely alone, are less easy to set in a clear light than they might seem to be at first sight. If we had to do with a community in which there was never any general trend upwards or downwards in the supply schedule of money or bank credit, they would consist simply of all causes that bring about changes in the supply schedules of these things. In fact, however, in all communities the supply schedules of money and banking facilities are subject to trends as well as to fluctuations about the current line of trend. When changes in the supply schedule of monetary instruments are adjusted to their general trend, we may not say that there is any independent cause on the side of money making for industrial fluctuations. Such causes are present when the supply schedule of any year diverges, not from the supply schedule of the year before, but from what the supply schedule of that year would have been had it conformed exactly to the general trend. Thus, the trend of the demand schedule for money being supposed steady, if the trend of the supply schedule is such as to bring about an annual increase of 3 per cent in the supply of money, and if the conditions governing the supply schedule between any two years change in such a way as to cause the supply to grow by more or less than 3 per cent—changes due to variations in the conditions of demand are not here relevant—there is, to the extent of the divergence from 3 per cent, a monetary cause making for industrial fluctuations.[1]

§ 3. In a country with a free paper money, that is one not tied, after the pattern of the gold exchange standard, to the monies of other countries, autonomous monetary causes of industrial disturbance can only arise inside the country itself. The Government, in order to save itself from the unpopular task of levying new taxation to balance an inflated budget, may print and use extra currency ; or, in response to popular demands for cheap money, it may print

---

[1] The somewhat cumbrous language of the text is made necessary by the fact that the quantity of money units supplied (the supply) may be altered either by a change in demand (*i e.* the position of the demand schedule), the conditions of supply (supply schedule) remaining constant, or by a change in the conditions of supply (a movement of the supply schedule). We are not here concerned with changes in the supply consequent upon changes in demand, but only with changes in the supply schedule.

extra currency and lend it to bankers, so as to make it possible for them to increase their loans to customers without the risk of finding themselves unable to meet cheques drawn upon them.   Practices of this sort are only resorted to in times of financial catastrophe, and have little bearing upon normal industrial fluctuations.   In normal times it may be presumed that countries with paper currencies will either tie them to some gold standard money, in which case the autonomous impulses impinging upon industry from the side of money will be the same as under a gold standard : or that they will regulate them with a view to keeping the general price level in some sense stable, in which case there will be no impulses from the side of money which can properly be called autonomous.   It is not, of course, suggested that, in a country whose money consists of paper not linked to gold, no effects at all are produced on industrial activity by movements in the value of gold outside.   Just as abundant harvests or large industrial inventions abroad, by enhancing the real demand for our exports on the part of foreigners, would bring about industrial expansion here whatever our monetary system was, or even if all trade was conducted by means of barter, so also will large alterations in the circumstances of the world gold market.   For, even though gold plays no part here as money, we shall still be concerned to purchase it for the arts.[1]   When, however, gold is used as a standard of value, changes in the supply of it, besides giving an impulse to industrial fluctuation after the same manner as changes in the supply of any other commodity, give also an additional impulse by modifying the standard in which contracts are made.   It is *this* sort of impulse from the side of gold that is eliminated under an independent paper standard.   So much being understood, we may concentrate attention upon gold standard monies.

[1] Careful students will observe that, besides eliminating *monetary* impulses associated with changes in the gold market, the substitution of a free paper standard for a gold standard would also *reduce* the size of the *non-monetary* impulses associated with it.   For a country making no use of gold as money will hold less of it and will vary its import of it by a less (absolute) amount in response to given variations in its value outside ; with the result that, *other things being equal*, the activity of the export industries with which it buys gold will vary less.

§ 4. It will simplify our exposition, without obscuring any essential factor, if we discuss this matter from the point of view of Great Britain, where, of course, there are no gold mines, and if we assume, further, that the general principles of banking policy here are permanently fixed. In these circumstances no impulses from the side of money can originate inside the country,[1] but all must come from outside. I proceed to distinguish the most important among these.

§ 5. Mention may be made first of the discovery and the closing down of gold mines and of the invention of new methods of extracting and refining gold. These things affect the annual output of new gold and, through this, the rate at which the world's stock of gold increases. Other things being equal, if this rate exceeds the trend rate, the value of gold will diminish (which is the same thing as saying that gold prices will rise) more rapidly than usual or increase (which is the same thing as saying that gold prices will fall) less rapidly than usual throughout the world. In converse conditions the opposite results will follow. Thus throughout the world, first in countries near the gold mines and subsequently in others, an impulse, in the one case towards an expansion, in the other towards a contraction of industry will come into being, and this impulse will in due course impinge upon Great Britain. Seeing, however, that

---

[1] For complete accuracy a small exception should be made from this statement in connection with the peculiar relations that subsist between the Government and the Bank of England on the one hand, and the Bank of England and the Joint-Stock Banks on the other. At those periods of the year when it becomes necessary for the Treasury to pay out large sums in interest on the national debt resort is had to Ways and Means Advances from the Bank of England. Cheques drawn on the Bank of England are then paid by the holders of the National Debt into their banks, with the result that the balances of these banks with the Bank of England are increased in a much bigger proportion than their liabilities to customers, and these banks, therefore, become free, if they wish, without exceeding their normal proportion, to make large further loans to these customers. As things are at present, however, the Ways and Means Advances to the Government are paid off out of revenue very rapidly. They are not—indeed apart from a co-ordinated growth in the number of currency notes they could not be—progressive from year to year, as they were during the war ; and, therefore, though relevant to intra-annual seasonal fluctuations, do not sensibly affect those industrial movements of wider scope with which alone this volume is concerned.

the average annual output of new gold is only about 3 per
cent of the existing stock, *variations* in the annual output
will rarely amount to any significant proportion of that
stock.   The impulses to industrial fluctuations that come
to our country—I do not say to the gold-producing countries
—are bound, therefore, on all ordinary occasions to be
slight.

§ 6. Secondly, the money of a gold standard country
may be subject to shocks from outside through changes in
the monetary or banking policy of foreign countries, involving
changes in the amount of their gold holdings.   Thus between
1871 and 1873 Germany absorbed a large quantity of gold in
order to establish a gold standard, and in the years following 1878 the United States did likewise in connection with a
law making the inconvertible Government bank notes, which
had been issued during the Civil War, convertible into
gold at the Treasury.   Converse effects are likely to be produced when a country changes from a many-reserve banking system to something more akin to a one-reserve system,
as the United States did immediately before the war ; for,
other things being equal, much less gold is needed to support
a given volume of credit when it is concentrated than when
it is scattered.   A similar economy of gold is effected when
a country, while retaining the gold standard, substitutes
paper for gold for internal circulation.   Plainly, changes of
this type in other countries may involve a substantial dis-
placement of gold, and so may affect in a significant degree
the value of gold in this country.   It should be noted, moreover, that, in this matter, pre-war experience does not fully
cover the field of possibility.   Before 1914 there was a very
large free world market for gold, and the currency traditions
of most important countries were firmly established.   In the
period immediately following the war the position was quite
different.   The large reservoirs of gold in the currencies and
banking systems of the world, which formerly had been open
and available to keep gold values fairly steady in the face
even of considerable changes in demand, were, many of
them, sealed up by Government action.   In 1921 Professor
Cassel wrote : " The European countries have locked up

their gold funds and prohibit, more or less stringently, all export of gold. Even when they are unable to meet their foreign obligations, countries refuse to part with their gold : and, curiously enough, the claimants do not insist upon having it, for any considerable reduction of their gold holdings is believed to be impossible without causing a serious economic crisis in the debtor country, and so, of course, impairing its ultimate capacity to pay. In these circumstances, European gold funds are, for all practical purposes, locked away from the world's market." [1] Moreover, certain of these countries with locked-up gold had large international debts. It was always possible that some of the countries so situated might change their policy and fling gold on the markets of the world. *Per contra*, countries whose paper money had broken down might at any time try to get gold to start a gold currency. Yet again, countries in receipt of large gold imports in payment of debts might change their policy as to the relation between gold reserves and liabilities. Thus the United States banks have recently made large arbitrary changes in the proportionate stock of gold which they keep as a foundation for given liabilities. In 1920–21, when low prices drew gold to the United States, the lowness of prices was not counteracted, because the Federal Reserve Banks simply piled up the gold without, in consequence, increasing their loans or lowering their rates. This policy might be reversed suddenly and the ratio of reserve to liabilities lowered, with the result of a general fall in the value of gold. In the last few years, of course, the world monetary situation has become much less uncertain. The restoration of a free gold market in the United Kingdom was followed by similar action elsewhere. As a recent League of Nations' memorandum puts it, " by the middle of 1925 there were, in all, some thirty countries whose currencies were legally or *de facto* based on gold ".[2] Since that date Italy and France have stabilised their currencies in terms of gold. Hence the era of post-war monetary disturbance may fairly be treated as closed. Plainly, however, the chances that this, or any other country, may be

---

[1] Cassel, *The World's Monetary Problems*, p. 123.
[2] *Memorandum on Currency and Central Banks*, 1913–24, vol. i. p. 6.

subjected to shocks by changes in the monetary or banking policy of foreigners is, at best, no smaller than it was before the war.

§ 7. A third sort of monetary disturbance, to which a gold standard country may be subjected from outside, consists in short-period drains and influxes of gold in connection with foreign financial operations. The United Kingdom before the war was very markedly exposed to disturbances of this kind. The tradition of a market for gold in London, in practice if not in theory much more free than elsewhere, made us liable to exceptionally large drains. A direct consequence of the existence of that free market was that, when a foreigner had a claim on London and wished to realise it, he was not prevented from realising it in gold. An indirect consequence was that many foreign traders, who expected to want gold to finance their international transactions, regularly purchased credits on London, while some Continental institutions, which expected to want gold for their reserves, " always kept a portfolio stocked with bills on London, constantly replaced as they matured, so that, in time of need, they might take gold from London to replenish the basis of their note issues ".[1]   A further indirect consequence was that trade between England and the rest of the world was, in general, financed by bills drawn on London, and not on the places to which English traders sell.   In short, London was the regular centre, to which, along routes carefully prepared beforehand, foreigners, who needed gold, were accustomed to present their claims. English acceptors and discounters were, of course, paid for the services which they rendered—some estimates put these services before the war at eighteen millions annually—but, as a penalty for rendering them, we were liable in a higher degree than other nations to foreign drains of gold.

§ 8. There remain to be considered expansions and contractions of bank credit in foreign countries, which, from our present point of view, are, in effect, creations and destructions there of acceptable substitutes for gold.   There can be little doubt that, for the sort of period which cyclical

[1] Withers, *The Meaning of Money*, pp. 171-2.

movements of industry normally cover, these things, in
general, have a far more potent influence upon the external
value of gold than any of the factors hitherto examined.
As was indicated in § 5, variations in the output of gold
mines during a single year or a few years can never amount
to more than a very small proportion of the accumulated
stock of gold. Fundamental changes in monetary policy
or banking organisation on the part of important countries
occur but seldom. Short-period drains and influxes of gold
of the type considered in § 7 are, as a rule, compensated
very quickly. Creations and destructions of bank credit
are, on the other hand, large, recurrent and liable to last
for a substantial length of time. A credit expansion involving a fall in the value of gold abroad necessarily tends
to drive gold here, until the influx, whether on its own
account or on account of credits built upon it, has forced
the value of gold here to a correspondingly low level, and a
credit contraction abroad, involving a rise in the value of
gold there, has a converse effect. In these ways the general
level of prices is altered by external events, and an impulse
is given from the side of money to industrial expansion or
contraction here. Of course, in practice this impulse is
tangled up with impulses acting in a similar sense, associated,
in the case of credit expansions, with abnormally large
foreign production, which implies abnormally large real
purchasing power in the hands of foreigners, and, in the
case of credit contractions, with abnormally small foreign
production and real purchasing power in foreign hands.
Thus the *monetary* impulse to disturbance will be smaller
and have smaller effects than the sum total of impulses
with which it is associated. Plainly, however, there is
nothing in this to prevent it from being itself large.

CHAPTER IX

INSTRUMENTAL AND CONSUMPTION TRADES

§ 1. Up to this point we have been studying the nature of the various initiating causes of disturbance that lie behind industrial fluctuations. Before we pass on to an analysis of the conditions under which these causes function it seems desirable to interpose a chapter upon an issue of narrower range. In Chapter I. it was pointed out that industrial fluctuations are manifested predominantly in the instrumental and constructive industries. This shows that the swing of expectations in respect of these industries is much larger than in respect of others. It was also pointed out that the turns from expansion to contraction and *vice versa* often come a little earlier in instrumental than in consumption industries. On the strength of this fact some writers have maintained that the instrumental industries are the true seat of varying expectations ; and that industrial activity in consumption industries only alters as a secondary reflex of the primary movement, the makers of consumption goods finding the demand for these goods improved or worsened simply because more or fewer workpeople are employed, and more or less money is being paid out in wages, in the instrumental trades.[1] The purpose of the following pages is to examine this thesis.

§ 2. It is easy to see that the thesis does not follow from the fact that fluctuations are larger in instrumental than in consumption trades. For the facts fit equally

---

[1] Cf. Tugan Baranowsky, " Ce n'est pas parce que la consommation s'accroît que la production se développe dans la phase de prospérité ; au contraire, l'accroissement de la consommation provient de l'extension de production " (*Les Crises industrielles en Angleterre*, p. 277).

well with the contrary thesis ; *i.e.* that the origin of industrial fluctuations lies in changes in the actual and expected demand of purchasers (whether for use or stock) of consumption goods. Broadly speaking, instrumental goods are goods the purpose and use of which is in producing, possibly at one or more removes, consumable goods. If, like raw materials, they were used up in the process of making the related consumable goods, changes in the demand for new consumables would carry with them proportionate changes in the demand for new instruments. But in actual life instruments are not used up in a single act.[1] They continue to function for a number of years, and, consequently, there is always a stock of instruments that have already been made, alongside of the annual flow of new instruments. If, then, it is decided to increase the production of, say, cotton goods by 20 per cent in conditions such that, in order to do this, the supply of cotton machinery has to be increased by 10 per cent, the 10 per cent increase in the *supply* of cotton machinery will involve a very much larger increase, perhaps an increase of 80 per cent or 100 per cent, in the *new production*, including, of course, that part of the new production (perhaps two-thirds of the whole in busy years) which is needed for replacements and repairs, of that machinery. Thus there is, *prima facie*, reason to expect that a given boom in the production of consumable goods will involve a larger (percentage) boom in the production of instrumental goods.[2]

§ 3. Nor is this all. When for any reason the aggregate demand is increased for commodities that are durable and

---

[1] The distinction between commodities which are, and commodities which are not, destroyed in use is not equivalent to that between commodities which are, and commodities which are not, inherently durable in their own nature. Thus radium emanation is essentially of short life, but it is not destroyed by being used, whereas wheat or coal, which, if left to themselves, may last for thousands of years, are so destroyed.

[2] Of course, if a maker of cotton goods only looks forward to a short boom, he will hesitate to buy new machinery, and will try, so far as may be, to secure extra output by working his existing machinery harder. This, *pro tanto*, weakens the argument of the text. When, however, a boom is actually in progress, it requires great self-control on the part of business men to act on the presumption that the boom will soon give place to a depression.

are not destroyed in the act of use, the resultant extra production of these commodities in the years of high demand involves the existence of a correspondingly enlarged stock of them in later years. Consequently, if and when the aggregate demand returns to what it used to be, it is confronted with this enhanced stock, and so gives rise to a smaller demand for new production of these commodities than it used to give rise to before. Thus the upward fluctuation of industrial activity above the normal carries with it a subsequent downward fluctuation below the normal when the stimulus is removed, and not merely a subsequent return to the normal. For, in effect, in depressions a rival supply is called out that has been piled up in booms ; the magnitude of this varying directly with the average intensity, multiplied by the length, of the preceding boom period.[1] Obviously this state of things prevails, not only as regards production goods, but also as regards those consumption goods (*e.g.* pianos), which are both durable and not destroyed in a single act of use. Less obviously, the same thing holds good of those consumption goods which *are* destroyed in a single act of use, provided that they are durable in their own nature and are of such a sort that they can be held in store without great cost or risk ; for dealers pile up stocks of them in booms, and in depressions are forced to offer them out of their stocks in competition with the current output of industry. But the characteristics of not being destroyed in a single act of use and of being durable in their own nature belong much more largely to production goods than to consumption goods — to the category embracing ships, machines, factory buildings, railways and works of construction generally than to the category embracing bread, meat, boots, clothes and personal services. Here, then, we have a second reason for expecting that instrumental industries will fluctuate more than others, even though it is in the others that the cause of fluctuation lies.

§ 4. The argument for the thesis we are discussing, which is derived from the fact that the turning-points *from expansion*

[1] Cf. Babson, *Business Barometers*, p. 96.

to contraction in instrumental trades often precede by a little those in consumption trades, seems at first sight strong. In reality, however, it also fails. This can be shown as follows. If the demand for consumption goods is constant, the demand for new instruments in place of those that become worn out will be constant. If the demand for consumption goods grows at a constant rate, the demand for new instruments to provide for new production will be constant, and the demand for new instruments to make good wear and tear will gradually increase, so that the demand for new instruments as a whole will gradually increase. If, however, the rate at which the demand for consumption goods is increasing decreases, the demand for new instruments for new production *must* decrease, and the demand for new instruments in the aggregate will very probably decrease. But the rate of increase in the demand for consumption goods will often decrease while the amount of the demand is still growing. Hence the *amount* of demand for instrumental goods, being associated with the *rate of increase in* the demand for consumption goods, will often fall off *before* the amount of demand for consumption goods falls off. Even, therefore, when the cause of a turn in the tide from boom to depression acts from the side of consumption goods, the actual downward move may begin first in instrumental goods. Thus, in the 1902–8 cycle, both in the United States and in Germany, " the prices of consumers' goods began to decline about seven months after the decline in the prices of producers' goods ". Of course, a movement initiated from the side of consumers' goods does not necessarily mean one initiated by the final purchasers of these goods. Dealers, whether wholesale or retail, anticipating such movements, may themselves take the initiative.[1] This, however, is irrelevant to the issue as between the two classes of producers' goods and consumers' goods.

§ 5. The fact that the turning-points *from contraction to expansion* come earlier in the instrumental than in the consumption trades cannot be explained on the lines of the preceding section ; for clearly, in order to an increase in the demand for instruments, there must be an increase in

[1] Cf. *ante*, footnote to Chap. III. § 5.

the quantity of consumable goods demanded in a year : a mere decrease in the rate at which this quantity was decreasing from year to year would not suffice. For example, if the demand has been for 1000, 900 and 800 units of a consumable commodity in three successive years, the occurrence of a demand for 750 units in the fourth year would not involve any increase in the demand for instruments. It is, however, still possible that a slackening in the rate of decrease in the demand for consumption goods is the initiating cause. It may react on the instrumental industries, not directly, but by creating in those persons who control them a belief that the tide has turned and that the demand will presently increase.

§ 6. These critical considerations do not stand alone. Against the claim that the initiation of industrial fluctuations lies with the capital-making or instrumental industries the following argument may be advanced. There is no difficulty in seeing how a movement of expansion or contraction initiated in an industry making consumption goods will be reflected back into the industries which make the producers' goods relevant to that industry. The consumption goods being in greater demand, so also will be the services of the workpeople who make the machines employed in their manufacture. But how precisely is an expansion or contraction in an instrumental trade to be reflected in an increased demand for the services of workers in consumption trades, so that expansions in the two sorts of trades may, as history shows that they in fact do, accompany one another ? How, for example, is a boom that is started in railway building to propagate itself among consumption trades ? At first sight the answer seems plain. The railway employees, being increased in numbers and receiving an enlarged aggregate wage, will buy more food and clothes and other wage-goods from the shops ; these will, therefore, give increased orders to the manufacturers of these things, who will in turn engage more workpeople. This reasoning would be well enough if the railway builders were producing anything that workpeople in other industries would accept as part of their wages. While the work of building is still incomplete, they can, however, offer nothing but railway securities, and for these, broadly speaking, wage-earners have no use. Consequently, in consumption trades, so long as the real wage-rate in terms of wage-goods stands at W and the productivity of labour in the industry is unchanged, there will be no inducement to employers to hire more labour than before. The point may be put in detail thus. Let a hundred thousand men be working at the manufacture of a particular kind of wage-good— say, wheat—their marginal net product per unit of time being one bushel of wheat. They are paid a wage of half a bushel of wheat, three-quarters of a pound of meat and two pounds of cotton. If meat becomes more abundant, their employer can obtain more meat than before for a given quantity of wheat, and, therefore, would make an extra profit, were he to continue to produce the same quantity of wheat and to pay the same rate of real wage. He is, therefore, stimulated to increased output. But, if railway securities— which, *ex hypothesi*, his workpeople do not want—become more abundant, they will fall in value in equal measure relatively to the real wage that he is paying and to what he is getting in return for it. The relation between this real wage and its fruit remains exactly what it was before, and there is no inducement to him to employ more labour in wheat making. Indeed, strictly speaking, since the profitableness of railway making has increased, there will be a tendency for him to divert his investment from wheat making to railway making, thus actually diminishing the activity of consumption industries. It follows that the extra wage-goods which railway workers obtain come exclusively from diminished consumption on the part of non-wage-earners, and not at all from an increased output of wage-goods. Hence it is impossible that the initiating cause of an industrial expansion, that involves consumption trades as well as instrumental trades, should have its seat in the instrumental trades ! This argument would, I think, be valid in a world of barter. In the actual world, however, as we shall see presently, an industrial expansion, wherever initiated, is usually associated with the creation of additional monetary purchasing power, which causes prices to rise and rates of real wages for a time to fall. If such a fall occurs, it will pay employers in consumption trades to set more workpeople to work. Moreover, psychological reactions are liable to be set up, which expand the expectations of business men, and so enhance their demand for labour. Hence it is *not* impossible for an expansion initiated in instrumental trades to set up secondary expansions in consumption trades.

§ 7. There remains, however, a further reason—slender, perhaps, but less dubious than the preceding argument—for believing that the origin of industrial fluctuations is not always, or even usually, to be found in the instrumental industries. For, if these movements did originate there, in periods of boom the stocks of consumption goods in warehouses and shops would be drained upon to provide wages for workers in the constructive industries, expanding activity in the consumption industries resulting from this drain and mitigating, but not cancelling, it. In depressions in like manner the stocks of consumption goods would pile themselves up. In actual fact, however, as was argued in Chapter III., stocks tend to accumulate, not in depressions, but in booms. Of course we have no ground for asserting that this happens always. On some occasions, when, for example, means of making some new important capital instrument, *e.g.* railways, have been discovered, it may well happen that the initiative comes from the side of the instrumental trades. But on other occasions, perhaps on most, it seems that the first stage towards a boom is an expansion in dealers' forecasts of the public demand for consumption goods and, therefore, in their own orders for them, and that the associated expansion of demand for instrumental goods is an effect of this.

CHAPTER X

§ 1. WHENEVER an industrialist pays wages to a workman, he is, we may imagine a popular writer saying, turning income into capital : the provision of a given amount of wages is only possible if somebody is prepared to turn that amount of income into capital : the wages bill cannot be increased in any year above what it was in the year before unless somebody is prepared in the second year to turn into capital an extra amount of income equivalent to the amount of the increase. These sentences embody a mass of confusion which it is vital to sweep away if the task of this volume is to be successfully carried through. In the present chapter an attempt will be made to do this.

§ 2. We may conceive the general situation thus. There is a vast area surrounded by a wall, which belongs, so to speak, to industry. Inside this area there is an immense collection of varied mechanical apparatus—fixed capital—of materials and goods in process—working capital or circulating capital—and also of human beings—workpeople. Into this area there is continually pouring a stream of wage-goods, which enters into the mouths and homes of the workpeople as food, clothes and so on, and gives rise in them to activities, which, in conjunction with the fixed capital and working capital, yield further goods. These further goods during the process of their up-building stand for a time inside the walled area. As they come to completion they flow out at the far end of the area in a new enormous stream, one part of which is retained by the controllers of industry for the use in consumption of themselves and of persons to whom they are indebted, while the other part flows round again into the walled area in such wise that the process there enacted is endlessly maintained. This rough description has now to be filled in more fully.

§ 3. the vital point for our present purpose is that each item of wage-goods that flows into the walled area of industry ultimately, in some form or other, flows out again, and that there is for each item a definite interval before the outflow—which need not, of course, be instantaneous, but may be spread over a period of time—takes place ; the length of the interval depending on the use to which the item is put. This is true equally whether it goes to pay workpeople who make or repair machines or to pay those who forward the working capital of goods in process towards their final form for consumption. What ultimately flows out is not, of course, physically identical with what flows in, but may be conceived in a somewhat vague way as the " virtue " embodied in this. Unless, when it flows out, an inflow exactly equivalent to the inflow to which it was due takes place, the quantity of capital stock held inside the walled area will be altered. Of course, even when capital is maintained intact, the *value* of what flows out as consumable goods is not equal to the *value* of what flows in as wages (including the wages of those who bring in raw materials). On the contrary, it exceeds this value by the earnings due to the services of workers other than wage-earners and of the stock of fixed and working capital. The extent of the excess depends on the quantity of those other factors that are present and on the rate of pay they require. My " virtue " is thus by no means equivalent to " value ". We may consider it, if we will, as a sort of disembodied essence of the entering wage-goods, to which, while it is in the industrial area, other elements due to capital and so on are joined, and which flows out materially bound up with, though analytically distinct from, these elements. Without attempting to make this conception more precise, I shall endeavour to draw out its implications as regards the relation that subsists in various circumstances between capital stock and the daily real wages bill—to be called henceforward, for brevity, the daily wages bill.

§ 4. Let $F(t)$ be the aggregate real wages bill expended since zero hour, and t the interval of time that has elapsed since then. This implies that $\Delta t F'(t)$ is the wages bill per small interval of time, that is, paid at time t. Let k be the average period that elapses between the inflow of wages and the outflow of the virtue that they yield. It follows that the stock of capital, as measured by the real wages that have gone to build it up,

$$= F(t) - F(t - k)$$

$$= kF'(t) - \tfrac{1}{2}k^2F''(t) + \frac{1}{2\cdot3}k^3F'''(t). \quad . \quad . \quad .$$

From this equation the following conclusions can be drawn. (1) In a " stationary state " $F'(t)$ is constant, and all further differentials are zero. Hence both the wages bill *per* small interval of time and the stock of capital are constant : and, if k be a number of days, the stock of capital is equal to k times the daily wages bill, or to $\dfrac{k}{365}$ times the annual wages bill. (2) In a state of things where expansion is taking place at a constant rate, $F''(t)$ is constant, and all later differentials zero. Hence neither the wages bill *per* small interval of time nor the stock of capital are constant. The stock of capital existing on any given day is less than k times the wages bill of that day. But the rate of increase in the stock of capital, measured by $kF''(t)$, is equal to k times the rate of increase in the wages bill : both rates of increase being, of course, constant. For example, if $k = 18$ months, the annual rate of increase in the stock of capital (as represented in the wages that went to building it) is equal to one and a half times the annual rate of increase in the real wages bill. If $k = 0$, that is to say, if the fruit of work realises itself instantly in consumable products, there will, of course, be no capital stock, and consequently, whatever happens to the wages bill, there is no associated process on the side of capital stock.

§ 5. There is a relation between k, the average interval that elapses between the inflow of wages into the industrial area and the outflow of their virtue, and the period of production of the commodities which embody this virtue. The nature of this relation is clearest when the work done for the wages is devoted to building up goods in process towards consumption. For let k_1 be the interval and p_1 be the period of production in days. Then, if technical conditions are such that the labour for which the wages are paid is all used on the first day, and Nature is thereafter left alone to mature the product, $k_1 = p_1$. If, on the other hand, very little labour is used on the first day, then none until the last day, and on that day practically all that is employed at all, $p_1 =$ (approximately) 0. In general, if work is so distributed that the rth day from the end is, so to speak, the centre of gravity of the whole of it, $k_1 = r$. It is reasonable to suppose that, on the average of consumable goods in general, the distribution of work over the period of production is uniform. Then $r = \frac{1}{2}p_1$ and $r = k_1$, so that $k_1 = \frac{1}{2}p_1$. When the work done for wages is devoted to making instruments, which, when made, are used to help the production of consumable goods, let the interval and the period be k_2 and p_2 respectively. If we write l for the length of life of the instruments, and assume that throughout their life they contribute equally to the production of consumable goods ; and if we write p'_2 for the period of production of the instruments themselves ; then $p_2 = p'_2 + \dfrac{l}{2}$, and, on the same assumptions as before, $k_2 = \frac{1}{2}(p'_2 + \dfrac{l}{2})$. If we write w_1 for the wages paid for making consumables, and w_2 for those paid for making instruments, then, k being the average interval for all sorts of consumable goods, the time needed to make the instruments to make these being counted in,

$$k = \frac{w_1 k_1 + w_2 k_2}{w_1 + w_2} = \frac{\frac{1}{2}\{w_1 p_1 + w_2(p'_2 + \dfrac{l}{2})\}}{w_1 + w_2}.$$

§ 6. What has been said so far, though essential to the clarification of our ideas, has no direct bearing on the problem of industrial fluctuations : for, if the argument of Chapter II. be accepted, these fluctuations do not come into play, either with the wages bill constant, or with the wages bill undergoing a constant rate of increase or decrease. From the standpoint of industrial fluctuations, we are interested exclusively in the kinks and bends, so to speak, in the movements of the demand for labour as represented by the wages bill. In order to get into direct contact with our problem, we have to study the relation of these kinks and bends to the process of capital building. The appropriate analysis is substantially the same whether the norm, from which the kinks and bends are deviations, is a stationary state or a state of expansion at a constant rate.

§ 7. Let us consider first the case in which the line of trend of the wages bill is horizontal, so that the fluctuations which take place are fluctuations about a constant mean, and the stock of capital, as measured by the real wages engaged in making it, is, from a long-period standpoint, constant. This implies that, if in one period there are daily excesses aggregating in the whole period to, say, a hundred thousand pounds' worth of wages above what is "proper" to that period, there must be another associated near-by period, not necessarily equal in length, in which there are daily deficits aggregating also to a hundred thousand pounds' worth. Suppose that we start on a day following a long period of stability. The stock of capital is then C and the daily wages bill W. For m days, let us suppose, the stock of capital continues to expand till it becomes $C + c$: for n days thereafter it remains stationary; and thereafter, during q days, it declines; till at the end of $(m + n + q)$ days from the beginning of the movement it again stands at C. Let h be the interval that, in existing technical conditions with the particular sort of capital in question, must elapse after the decision to turn extra real wages into the industrial area, before any of them flow out of that area in resultant completed goods. Then, during the first h days (h must be $< m$), the excesses of the daily wages bill above the norm must be equal to the additions that are being made to capital, as measured by the real wages engaged in making it. During the following $(m - h)$ days the wages bill and the daily addition to capital will both be growing, but the excess of the daily wages bill above the norm will be greater than the daily addition to capital. In the next n days the daily wages bill will throughout exceed the norm by a constant amount, and the stock of capital will remain constant. During the final q days, the daily wages bill will exceed the norm throughout, but the extent of the excess will be continually diminishing : and the stock of capital will be diminishing, till on the $(m + n + q)$th day both the daily wages bill and the stock of capital stand again at the original norm. Thus during the first m days of the period some amount of capital will have been created, and during the last q days an equal amount will have been destroyed : but the amount that was created will, in general, be much less than the hundred thousand pounds' worth of aggregated excess wages bill. In like manner, over the corresponding period when the wages bill stands below the norm, during the first r days a certain amount of capital will have been destroyed, to be replaced in the later days : but the amount of capital thus destroyed (and subsequently replaced) will, in general, be much less than the aggregated one hundred thousand pounds' deficiency in the wages bill that is manifest in that period. The reason for these inequalities, put broadly, is that the wages bill at any moment is made up of two parts : (a) wages devoted to producing or maintaining capital, and (b) wages devoted to operating (i.e. extracting income out of) existing capital. Consequently, when capital is expanding, the aggregate daily wages bill grows more rapidly, and when capital is contracting, declines more rapidly than the part of it that is comprised under the heading labelled (b).

§ 8. A word should be added as to the shape which the kinks and bends embodying industrial fluctuations will assume in different circumstances. We suppose that, after a period of stability, it is decided by a single person at a single instant to turn into the industrial area an extra £100,000 worth of real wages. These are to be there transformed into some form of capital, whether fixed capital, as machinery or a ship, or circulating capital, as materials or goods in process. As we have seen, over our interval h the addition made to capital and the excess above the norm of the wages bill must be exactly equal : it is impossible for them to differ in any way, either in the aggregate or in respect of any individual day. The way in which the additions and excesses are distributed over the several days will, however, vary according to the nature of the capital object that is being constructed. Whatever this object is, a ship, or a building, or a piece of machinery, or a collection of elements in various stages of becoming cotton cloth or loaves of bread, technical considerations will determine the relative quantities of work to be done on it on the various days of the process of construction. On a ship, for example, not much work can be done till the keel is laid : then a great deal ; and in the last days, when the finishing touches are being added, probably not much. Again, with agricultural products, after the work of sowing, little more is needed till the harvesting. Whatever the technical conditions may be, there will be associated with them some definite distribution of work through time. A different formula will apply to each several set of conditions. The simplest of these formulae may be set out by way of illustration. This is applicable when we are concerned with a type of entity or collection of entities, which takes h days to make, and *in the making of which equal amounts of work are employed on each of the days*; for example, a range of goods in various stages of process, fitted together so that a constant inflow of appropriately adjusted work will cause a constant equivalent outflow of consumable goods to be emitted. In these circumstances, since it is impossible to apply a second day's work to any item of material before a first day's work has been applied to it, and it is wasteful to apply the first day's work until the second is ready to follow, we may expect the extra work and wages bill to be distributed in the following proportions : on day 1, one first day's work ; on day 2, one first day's work and one second day's work ; on day 3, one first day's work, one second day's work and one third day's work ; and so on. Thus, for an aggregate addition to the wages bill, and to the stock of capital (as measured by the wages devoted to it), of $\frac{1}{2}qh(h+1)$, the contribution of the successive days will be q, $2q$, $3q$ . . . hq. If the aggregate is £100,000, q is equal, of course, to $\dfrac{£200,000}{h(h+1)}$.

When the h days are over, let us suppose that it is decided to make no further additions to capital, but to maintain intact for a while the extra capital that has been made. So long as this is done, it is certain, in accordance with the reasoning of the preceding section, that the daily wages bill will be larger than it was before the h days began. But it is not certain whether it will be larger or smaller than it was on the last of the h days. Thus, if what has been made is an instrument, such as a machine or a ship, the daily wages bill will no longer include what was expended on the last of the h days in manufacturing this, but will include instead the wages paid to the persons who now operate it, as well as whatever is necessary to keep it in repair. According to circumstances the new daily total may be larger or smaller than the old. In the special case set out at the end of the preceding paragraph, the daily wages bill throughout the period of maintenance will evidently be equal to what it was on the last of the days of construction, namely, to the aggregate extra capital which has been created divided by $\frac{1}{2}(h+1)$.

When the time comes to let the extra capital disappear, what happens will again vary with the nature of this capital. If it is an instrument such as a ship or a machine with a fairly long life, its disappearance will be slow. Wages will at once cease to be paid for repairs and renewals, and, as it becomes less useful, the wages bill due for operating it will gradually fall off. In the special case cited above, the period of decline, if there is to be no waste, will be equal to the period of construction, namely, h days. Moreover, just as in the period of construction, the wages bill is on successive days q, $2q$ . . . hq; so in the period of disappearance it is on successive days hq, $(h-1)q$ . . . q. The capital stock will decline to the same extent as the wages bill declines.

Of course, in practice we do not have to do with single decisions instantly taken by single persons. On the contrary, it is probable that, if on the first day one man decides to turn an extra £100,000 into the industrial area, other men will take similar decisions on the second and later days, so that on the hth day, not only will the capital begun on the first day come to completion, but also the capital begun on later days will be still under construction. The case is similar with decisions to let capital run down. The result is that the whole kink movement is somewhat smoothed out, and extends over a longer period than the preceding analysis suggests ; but its essential characteristics are not thereby affected.

§ 9. When kink movements are imposed, not on a horizontal trend, but on one that is rising at a constant rate, the substance of the analysis given in §§ 7-8 still holds good. There is no reason why the form of the movements or their general nature should be other than they are in the simpler case.

CHAPTER XI

THE SUPPLY OF NEW CAPITAL

§ 1. WE are now in a position to review the *conditions* under which the various initiating causes of industrial disturbance distinguished in earlier chapters exercise their influence. The analysis of those chapters has shown that expansions relatively to the line of trend in the aggregate real wages bill always imply, during the period when the expansion is taking place, expansions, relatively to the trend, in the stock of capital (circulating or fixed) as measured by the sum of wages devoted to making it, that is held by industrialists. The excess of real wages bill, as against the trend quantity, expended during a year does not, indeed, necessarily carry with it an addition to the capital stock equal to the excess. In certain sorts of industrial spending it does so, but in others it carries a much smaller— it can in no circumstances carry a larger—addition than this. When the expansion (relatively to the trend) in the real wages bill ceases, the expansion (relatively to the trend) in the stock of capital will also cease, but both wages bill and capital stock will continue to stand above the trend levels. When the expansion (relatively to the trend) in the wages bill is in process of being cancelled, the expansion relatively to the trend in the stock of capital will also undergo cancellation. The studies of quantity made in the preceding chapter are, for our present purpose, of secondary interest. The vital fact is that expansions in the wages bill beyond the line of trend cannot occur without expansions in the stock of capital held in industry beyond the line of trend also occurring ; that an excess of wages bill cannot be

123

maintained without an excess of capital stock being maintained ; that contractions below the line of trend in the
wages bill imply contractions below the line of trend in the
capital stock held in industry; and that the maintenance
of an abnormally low wages bill implies the maintenance of
an abnormally low capital stock.　Moreover, since the dis-
tributors of merchandise to the public will presumably try
to increase or diminish their stores of goods as their turn-
over waxes or wanes, what has been said of the stock of
capital in industry probably holds good also of the stock
of capital in industry and the distributing trades together.

§ 2. It follows from this that given variations in the
scheme of business men's expectations of yield from industrial spending carry with them different variations in
their demand for labour—as represented by the real wages
bill they are prepared to fill at given wage-rates—according
to the conditions of supply of resources available to be transformed into new capital—more briefly of new capital.　The
demand price for any rth unit of labour is equal, it will be
remembered, to the anticipated *discounted* value of its
marginal net product; so that, when the anticipated actual
value changes in given measure, the measure in which
the demand price changes approaches more or less closely
to this according as the rate of discounting is altered little
or much in consequence of the associated change in the
demand for new capital.　If it is thought that, in consequence of some technical improvement, the discounted
marginal net product of 1500 workers at the present rate
of discounting will, henceforward, be as large as the discounted marginal net product of 1000 workers used to be,
the question how many extra workers are in fact engaged
—whether 500 or none at all or some intermediate number—
will depend entirely on how far the rate of discounting has
to be raised in order to attract given additional quantities
of new capital.　That is to say, the extent to which the
demand for labour, and so industrial activity, fluctuates in
consequence of given fluctuations in the expectations of
business men depends upon the elasticity of the (annual or
monthly) supply of new capital to industry.　If this supply

was perfectly inelastic, no variation, however large, in expectations would modify at all the demand for labour. This is one extreme possibility. If the supply of new capital were perfectly elastic, there would be a swing in the demand for labour exactly corresponding to the swing of expectations. This is the opposite extreme possibility. In real life the annual or monthly supply of new capital available to employers is neither perfectly elastic nor perfectly inelastic, but something between the two. Hence a given upward (or downward) swing of expectations will carry with it some, but not a proportionate, swing in the real demand for labour. Given the original swing, this induced swing will be larger, the more elastic is the supply of new capital available for industry. Anything that enables the supply to be increased (or decreased) by a given amount for a smaller inducement enhances the scale of the swings in the demand for labour, and so in industrial fluctuations, consequent upon a given change in expectations (whether justified or not) as to the fruits of industrial spending. It is, therefore, very important to elucidate the influences upon which the elasticity of the supply of new capital depends.

§ 3. To provide variations in the flow of new capital— or, more strictly, in wage-goods earmarked for conversion into new capital—in response to variations in the demand for it, there are available, to be drawn upon during any week or month, four principal sources. First, the extra work that is being done may bring about an increase in the production of consumable goods adequate to provide for the extra wage payments. Secondly, the flow of goods to the workpeople secured for their own consumption otherwise than through wages, may be cut down below its normal level. Thirdly, the flow for their own consumption that entrepreneurs and rentiers absorb may be cut down.[1] Lastly,

---

[1] To facilitate our exposition we ignore the fact that what entrepreneurs and rentiers take out for their own consumption is not the whole of what they take out otherwise than for industry, but that they also take something to pay over against personal services by chauffeurs, gardeners and so on ; and that, so far as this is cut down in order to provide new capital for employers, the aggregate real demand for labour is increased somewhat less than it appears to be. We also ignore the fact that, when entrepreneurs and rentiers cut down their consumption, the items they

the stock of consumable goods in warehouses and shops may be depleted and reduced below its normal level. In an isolated community there are no other ways in which the supply of new capital can be altered, *i.e.* through which it can have any elasticity at all. In a country situated among, and in contact with, others there are also available drafts from abroad. Let us examine these several ways in detail.

§ 4. Consider first new production consequent upon extra work. When a boom comes, a large part of the impact is always, as was shown in Chapter IX., likely to be upon industries engaged in instrumental trades: and, plainly, extra work there will not lead to an addition to the flow of consumable goods available for conversion into new capital for a considerable time. The same thing is true, in a less degree, of the extra work which is devoted to growing, extracting or transporting raw materials, and of that devoted to pushing goods towards, but not actually into, their finished state. Thus the main part of the additional resources that are turned into industry in periods of expansion does not immediately pass through industry, shooting out an equivalent to itself at the farther end, but becomes, as it were, bunched up inside the industrial machine, being transmuted partly into new fixed equipment and partly into an additional volume of all sorts of goods in process of manufacture. Only a small part of the extra work that is being done is likely to be employed in finishing goods and making them ready for consumption. It appears, therefore, that in the first instance, when an extra stream of new capital is turned into the industrial machine, no significant additions to the outflow will appear at the other end. The analysis of the preceding chapter has shown, however, that this state of things will not continue indefinitely. In the later parts of a period of

cease to buy are not the same as the items that wage-earners begin to buy. If we look at things in the aggregate, this does not matter. It means that shopkeepers will find their stores of luxury goods depleted less than usual, and their stores of staple goods more than usual : and that, therefore, orders for staple goods will expand relatively to orders for luxury goods. But the sum of the two together will be affected in the same way as if everybody consumed the same classes of goods in similar proportions.

unusual activity the outflow will reflect the extra exertions of the earlier parts, so that there is more•stuff than before available to be turned per month or week into new capital. How much more there is after any given interval from the beginning of the expansion depends, of course, upon the kind of operations into which the extra industrial spending has been turned and the interval of time which divides work done from fruit achieved. There is also relevant here another circumstance, of which hitherto nothing has been said. So long as the supply of labour is perfectly elastic, a given percentage expansion in the real wages bill implies an equal percentage expansion in the quantity of work done in return for wages. After a certain degree of expansion has been attained, however, practically all the labour power available in the country will be at full work, and the supply in respect of further amounts will have practically no elasticity ; so that additions to the wages bill call out no more work at the moment and, therefore, no more produce in the future.

§ 5. Turn next to the resources that, in bad times, go to wage-earners in a form other than that of wages. Many elaborate arrangements exist which enable workpeople, who are out of work, nevertheless to obtain real income. They obtain it partly through credits at shops, partly through receipts from the unemployment insurance fund in excess of current payments out of wages into that fund, partly through Poor Law Authorities—all methods which, by one road or another, set up a drain on the stream of goods available for conversion into new capital. This implies a peculiar linkage between the demand for wage-goods on the part of employers to provide wages [1] and the demand on the part of the State and other institutions that deal with unemployed workpeople. This linkage is of such a sort that, when employers' demand expands, the supplanting demand falls off. Hence, to put the point roughly, the supply to employers of resources for turning into new capital is made more elastic by the exist-

[1] The implication here made, for simplicity of exposition, that wages are paid in kind makes no difference to the present argument, but, of course, the fact that money is used has important effects in other connections (cf. *post*, Chap. XII. *et seq.*).

ence of this source, up to the point at which all labour is
absorbed into employment.   After that point has been
passed, this factor making for elasticity will cease to function, for the bulk of non-wage consumption by wage-earners
will have disappeared.   Here too, then, we have an element
of elasticity which is operative only up to a certain stage
of industrial expansion.   To determine its importance we
should need to know how much wage-goods are obtained by
wage-earners when out of work relatively to what they would
have purchased if in work.   Some of the means of obtaining
them, for example credit and pawning, are exhaustible—in
the nature of a stock of private purchasing power rather than
a flow—and so become less significant the longer a depression
lasts.   But this is not true of Poor Law Relief, nor—always—
of Unemployment Insurance.

§ 6. Before leaving this matter, we have to notice a
somewhat subtle difficulty.   It is certainly true that there
is in bad times a flow of resources going to labour in
the way described.   But how is this flow to be tapped
by new would-be employers ?   It may be argued that, if an
additional business borrower comes into the market, he
will, indeed, get new capital from rentiers, but merely
at the expense of what would have appeared as new
capital through some other agency ; that he cannot, in fact,
directly tap the afore-mentioned flow.   This is, in substance,
Mr. Hawtrey's reply to the suggestion that a municipality,
undertaking public works in bad times, will be able to draw
on real resources that are being used in the form of unemployment benefit to the unemployed.[1]   I do not think the
difficulty is a real one.   The optimistic business man, or the
Government, or whatever the agent is, pays over more money
to shops, and hands over the stuff so obtained to the new workpeople it employs.   This causes a reduction in the money
demand upon shops that is financed out of unemployment
benefit.   There is thus, in effect, a flow into the shops of
what would have been an outflow to drawers of unemployment benefit.   It is true that, if there were no shops as a
buffer, there would be a difficulty : for *ex hypothesi*, since

[1] Cf. *Economica*, March 1925.

we are not now considering the possibility of cuts in the personal consumption of rentiers, the optimistic business man, or the Government department, could not raise more real stuff from rentiers except by causing a corresponding cut in what other business men raise from them.   In that case the only line of connection would be for the Government to divert its benefit money, or some of it, for direct use as wages.   Mr. Hawtrey would hardly deny that this must produce a real addition to aggregate real wages; though, of course, it might leave some unemployed persons without benefit.

§ 7. Thirdly, consider cuts in consumption on the part of entrepreneurs and rentiers. It may be assumed that these classes would need a considerable inducement in order to make them reduce their consumption voluntarily in a significant proportion ; for the standards of most of them are likely to be well set and not readily modified except under compulsion.   Even when there is compulsion, through creations of bank credit which raise prices and so secretly tax persons with fixed incomes, a good deal of the enforced variation in expenditure on the part of these people is likely to be a variation, not in expenditure upon consumption goods, but upon capital equipment (*i.e.* investments). So far as this is so, any addition made to the real wage fund—to be wielded by the State or by business men financed through banks—at the expense of these people comes from what would have been new capital in any event, and is, therefore, no addition to the fund as a whole. We have, however, to observe that for some people there are no normal annual investments to cut into.   Moreover, there is a continuing *trend* towards increased output of consumption goods, due to the growth of capital relatively to population.   There is, thus, in each year a *new* flow, which rentiers, ordinary shareholders, and so on, have available either for increased consumption or for investment.   So far as this flow goes, their choice is not hampered by a rigid standard of life.   In booms, when the rate of interest is high, it may well be that a larger part of it will be turned over to business men as new capital, and a smaller part devoted to consumption by its owners, than in depressions. How elastic is the supply of new capital available from this source obviously depends in part on how large are the normal incomes of rentiers relatively to the normal wages bill. The larger this proportion is, the smaller will be percentage cut in their consumption required to provide a given percentage addition to the real wages fund.[1]

§ 8. Fourthly, consider the store of consumption goods normally held in warehouses and shops. *A priori* we should expect an increase in the demand on the part of business men for new capital to be met in part by a depletion of this store, *i.e.* in capital held *outside* industry : in other words we should expect the existence of this store to make the supply of new capital available for them *inside* industry more elastic than it would otherwise have been. If, as an illustrative guess, we assume that stocks of wage-goods held by dealers on the average amount to one month's consumption, an addition of 5 per cent to consumption over a period of a week would involve a reduction of stocks by one-eightieth part, and the additional consumption could be maintained for forty weeks before they were reduced to one-half of their normal amount. This consideration suggests that the existence of stocks makes a substantial contribution towards rendering elastic the supply of new capital available to business men engaged in industry. The statistical evidence cited in Chapter III. indicates, however, that stocks increase when business expectations are good, and, except for a short

---

[1] If resources were all of a single sort, there being no distinction between the things paid out in wages to workpeople and other things, nothing further would need to be said upon this matter. In actual life, however, wage-goods (the goods in which workpeople take out their wages) are, of course, a special and limited class of goods. Consequently, a given proportionate change in the wage fund in terms of things in general, *i.e.* from the point of view of employers, does not necessarily represent an equal proportionate change in this fund in terms of wage-goods, *i.e.* from the point of view of wage-earners. In so far as the supply of wage-goods, as against things in general, is inelastic from the standpoint of the period of the trade cycle, fluctuations in the wage fund, and so in the demand for labour, in the only sense that is significant to labour, will be smaller than they appear to be when expressed in terms of general value. This matter might repay further study. It does not appear, however, on the face of things, to be practically very important.

interval after the turn of the tide, contract when they are bad. If these statistics are to be relied upon, the elasticity-promoting faculty of stock accumulation may, indeed, still exist, but it is completely masked by other factors.

§ 9. There remains finally the resource of drawing new capital from abroad. It is plain that business men, in a country which is not isolated and in which an *independent* demand is springing up, are able, by an offer of improved interest, to borrow money abroad, which, if they will, they can convert into wage-goods there and import in that form. This international mobility of new capital makes the supply of it in any one country much more elastic than it would otherwise have been, provided that fluctuations in expectations are confined to that country alone. If, however, similar fluctuations are occurring synchronously in all countries, this resource is not available to any of them. One further point may be added, though it involves some anticipation of later analysis. Under a gold standard régime an improvement in the expectations of business men sets going processes which lead to a rise in prices— that is to say a lowering of the value of gold in terms of things—and this, provided again that the movement is confined to a particular country, involves the importation of a certain extra quantity of things (including, we may presume, some things of a kind that can be converted through wage-payments into new capital) in exchange for exports of gold.

CHAPTER XII

§ 1. UP to this point, apart from Chapter VIII., our discussion has been carried on without reference to the
mechanism of money. Obviously a discussion so limited
must be very incomplete. In modern conditions the whole
movement of industry and business is conducted in terms of,
and, in large measure, through the agency of, money or some
representative of money. The entrepreneurs, financiers, and
so forth, by whom the stream of goods that comes to completion every year is legally owned, sell these goods for money
to wholesale houses and shopkeepers. The proceeds of this
sale they employ, partly as personal income for their own use,
partly in payment of interest to those persons from whom
they hold loans, and partly in the hiring of labour to be
employed in their enterprises. The money thus distributed
is then used by all parties as a means of purchasing
commodities from shopkeepers ; and in this way the final
distribution of the inflowing dividend is annually effected.
In short, in the modern world industry is closely enfolded
in a garment of money.

§ 2. This fact is brought out very clearly in the accompanying chart, which sets side by side unemployment
percentages and the sum of bank clearings recorded by the
London clearing-house. It will be observed that between
1870 and the middle of 1900 good employment and large
clearings and bad employment and small clearings are associated together very closely. After the middle 'nineties the
rapid upward trend in clearings renders the correlation less

obvious, but leaves it still visible to any one who looks carefully.

§ 3. The intimate part played by money is brought out still more clearly when the employment percentages are set beside an index of price movements. When price index numbers in an undoctored form are used, the connection between industrial activity and price change over the period of normal trade cycles is obscured by the long-period fall of prices between 1871 and 1896. To obviate this masking I have, in the chart that follows, eliminated the trend from the price figures by a rough device. Sauerbeck's original figures have first been reduced so that the number for 1900 stands at 100. I have then subtracted 1 from the number for 1895, 2 from that for 1894, and so on down to 1872, prior to which date 24 is subtracted from the figure for each year ; and I have further subtracted 1 from the figure for 1897, 2 from that for 1898, and so on till 1914. In the curve representing price indices thus doctored the short-period connections between unemployment and prices are brought out more clearly than they would have been in an undoctored chart. It will be seen at a glance that there is consilience between low unemployment and high prices and high unemployment and low prices. Except for the drop in employment between 1860 and 1863, which was, no doubt, due to the cotton famine consequent upon the American Civil War, there is no main movement in one curve unaccompanied by a movement in the opposite sense in the other.

§ 4. In a perfectly steady state, or, more accurately, in a state of perfectly steady self-repeating movement, there is no reason to suppose that the mediation of money would modify in any respect the results ultimately achieved. The quantity of money passing from shopkeepers to entrepreneurs, as likewise the quantity of goods passing in exchange from entrepreneurs to shopkeepers, is the same every year ; the distribution of the money by entrepreneurs is the same ; and so also is the quantity of purchases effected by it when distributed. The quantity of commodities annually consumed by each several class and the quantity held in store are not only identical with themselves in every year, but are also, at all times, identical with what they would have been had the process involved been direct. When, however, there is motion, the fact that industry is wrapped in a money garment seems likely *a priori* to render its reactions to the various impulses applied to it different from what they would have been had its limbs been bare. The money garment will, we may suspect, constitute a condition modifying the effects of these impulses ; for the fact that its own movements are themselves caused by these impulses is, of course, no reason why they should not also exercise a causal influence. How far and in what precise ways this suspicion is justified the six following chapters will endeavour to determine in detail. Since the issues raised are complex, I shall, in this preliminary chapter, prepare the ground by sketching out the general character of the reactions to be studied.

§ 5. If we are to gauge satisfactorily the way in which modern monetary and banking arrangements modify the course of industrial fluctuations—make this course different, that is to say, from what it would otherwise have been— it is plainly essential to envisage clearly what " otherwise " means. As things are, people are accustomed to hold a certain average of real value in the form of money and bank balances, with a view partly to convenience in business and partly to security against bad debts and sudden calls. We are free, if we will, to contrast this arrangement with one under which there is no money and banking and people hold no fund analogous to this. It is, however, I think, more proper to suppose that, in the absence of a monetary and banking system, they would still need a store of readily available resources ; and I shall postulate that they would hold, either in their own hands or with business men as agents, a store equivalent to what they hold now, but in the form of actual consumable goods and materials, *i.e.* real stocks of stuff. In making this assumption I am, of course, abstracting from the very important indirect influence which the monetary and banking system has had in smoothing the wheels of industry and enlarging the whole scale of production. From the present point of view, however, that does not matter.

§ 6. When we conceive things in this way, it becomes apparent that an important portion of the reactions which take place through the monetary and banking system during industrial fluctuations, and which are associated with changes in the stock of real capital held by business men, are merely mediating links, not causal factors. That is to say, on the assumptions set out in the preceding section, if the monetary and banking systems were eliminated, equal changes in the stock would be brought about in other ways. Thus, when the expectations of business men improve, they come to desire more keenly things and services to *use* in industry—because, as we have seen, the extra new capital which they turn into the industrial machine does not at once reproduce itself in their hands, but becomes, as it were, bunched up there [1]—and at the same time, since they now have less fear of bad debts or other ill-fortune, they come to desire less keenly a store of value with which to protect themselves against these eventualities. If there is a money and banking system, they will in these circumstances expend a part of their store of money in buying things and services to use in industry from other people, and, by so doing, will add to the stock of real capital under their control. But this addition is *not* an addition to the stock of capital in industry, as against what it would have been had there been no monetary and banking system, because in that event business men would have drawn directly to an equivalent extent upon an equal store of value, in that case consisting, not of money and bank balances, but of real things. A corresponding statement holds good of the happenings that take place when the expectations of business men worsen. This type of reaction—we are supposing here that it takes place as a consequence of changes in business men's expectations, and not as a secondary reflex effect of price movements [2] —is not relevant to the elasticity of supply of new capital available to business men for the conduct of industry.

§ 7. When, however, the expectations of business men

---

[1] Cf. *ante*, Chap. XI. § 4.   [2] Cf. *post*, Chap. XV. § 10.

alter for any reason, they do not confine themselves, in their endeavour to alter correspondingly the volume of capital in industry, to the method just described. When their expectations improve they resort also to two other means, new borrowings of unusual amounts directly from the public and new borrowings of unusual amounts from the banks. Their borrowings from the public are not affected by the fact that they are accomplished in terms of money ; the money acts, subject to a qualification which I shall introduce in a moment, as a mere ticket conveying a right to things. But their borrowings from the banks are different. Business men are able to achieve extra borrowings of this type, because the banks (conceived in the widest sense as embracing the banking system as a whole) are ready, in response to offers of higher interest, to allow the ratio of their reserves to their liabilities to decrease.[1] The ability to make these extra borrowings enables business men to enlarge the amount of new capital that becomes available for them in good times more than they would have been able to do otherwise. That is to say, modern practice in the matter of money and bank- ing renders the supply of new capital available to business men more elastic in response to given variations (whether warranted or not) in their outlook than it would be in the absence of such practice. This reaction is independent of associated changes in the general level of prices.

§ 8. The extra borrowings from banks, resorted to by business men when their expectations are roseate, set forces in motion which cause the general level of prices to rise. A further rise is induced by the action of these men in drawing upon their store of value for use in industry ; because, since under modern conditions this store is held in the form of money—mainly, of course, bank-money—

---

[1] Thus in England the "proportion", which the joint-stock banks maintain between liabilities and reserve of cash and balances at the Bank of England, seems to be kept fairly constant, but the joint-stock banks are still free to increase the aggregate amount of their liabilities, even though the gold in the Bank of England is unchanged, because they can always exchange securities against further balances there. (Cf. *post*, Part II. Chap. VII. § 8.)

the process of drawing on it can only be accomplished by offering money against commodities in the market. When business men's expectations become gloomy the same two-fold influence comes into play to push prices down. These price movements will not, as a rule, have been fully fore-seen when contracts for loans and, in a less degree, wage-agreements were entered into. Hence business men, who are, in the main, borrowers and wage-payers, find them-selves in times of prosperity in receipt of a windfall gain, consequent upon what is, in effect, a doctoring in their favour of past contracts. They are thus in a position to add to the volume of new capital to be turned into industry. In bad times the position is reversed. In con-sequence of these doctorings of the terms of past contracts, which movements in the general price level involve, the elasticity of the supply of new capital available for industry is enhanced a second time.

§ 9. A third reaction, for which monetary and banking organisation is responsible, acts, like that just discussed, through the price level, but is of an entirely different char-acter. In good times the fact that prices have risen creates an expectation that they will continue to rise, and this implies, in a manner to be explained presently, the expectation of a sort of bounty to business men, partly in respect of any new loans that they may raise and partly in other ways. Moreover, the mere fact of " prosperity ", due in part to the doctoring of past contracts in their favour, makes business men more inclined than usual to look upon the sunny side of doubt. Hence, partly with and partly with-out warrant, their expectations of profit from industrial spending grow brighter. They, therefore, borrow still more from the banks and draw still more heavily upon their store of value, with the result that prices again rise ; the rise reacting in turn upon their expectations. In this way a cumulative tendency towards expansion is set up, which continues under its own impulse until it encounters some external obstacle. A corresponding process takes place in periods of depression. This important subject will be studied in Chapter XVII.

CHAPTER XIII

CREATIONS OF BANK CREDIT

§ 1. In this chapter I propose to examine the direct effects
on the quantity of real new capital available to business
men in good and bad times, when their expectations of profit
are given, which are brought about through the power of
banking systems, in the common phrase, to create credit.
That phrase is, indeed, somewhat ambiguous. A man is
said to possess good credit if people trust him and are ready
to lend him money. In this sense credit is a quality attaching
to people and institutions on account of their reputation.
Nobody claims that banks can create credit in this sense.
For the present purpose credit means something objective,
namely a quantity of purchasing power " credited " to a
borrower and held at his disposal. It is the power to create
credit understood in this way that we have now to investigate.
Before that task is entered upon it is necessary to consider
certain utterances upon this subject by Professors Cassel and
Cannan. I hope and believe that my difference with these
eminent writers is concerned with words and not with substance ; but in a matter so intricate words are important.

§ 2. Professor Cassel draws a distinction between an
increase in the real savings of the people and the creation
of artificial purchasing power, thus suggesting that, when
command over new capital is put into the hands of business
men by the latter method, this new capital is something
other than the embodiment of real savings. It cannot be
that Professor Cassel's *thought* is confused when he uses
this language, but the language, I think, is confused. For
what he must mean by " real savings ", if his distinction

is to be accurate, is not " real savings " at all as ordinarily understood, but savings of money. He must be distinguishing between a banking system, which receives £100 in currency from depositors and hands it over to a Government or business man, and a banking system which hands over £100, or a claim to £100, without having first received any corresponding currency deposits, thus in a sense " creating " the money it hands over. Of course there is a distinction between these two things, and the distinction is important from the point of view of prices : in the former case prices are left intact, in the latter they are raised. But, so far as " real savings ", in the natural sense of savings of real stuff, are concerned, there is no distinction. In either event what the Government or business man gets is an addition to the real stuff, the wage-goods and materials, at his command. If the £100 is provided by customers bringing currency to the banks, they relinquish voluntarily for the bankers' use command over this value of stuff ; if it is provided by credit creation, they relinquish command over an (approximately) equivalent amount under the suasion of a concealed tax.[1] The Government or business man gets, and gets only, an addition to its resources equivalent to what other people go without. When Professor Cassel contrasts the real savings of the people and the creation of artificial purchasing power as rival sources of finance, he appears to deny this fact. In truth, the creation of artificial purchasing power, so far from being an alternative to real savings, is simply a particular piece of mechanism through which, in some communities, real savings are taken hold of and transferred.

§ 3. I pass to Professor Cannan's round assertion that the whole conception of bankers " creating credit " is confused and fallacious. " If ", he writes, " cloak-room attendants managed to lend out exactly three-quarters of the bags entrusted to them, we should not be surprised to find that the number of bags on deposit was exactly four times the number in the cloak-room ; we certainly should not accuse the cloak-room attendants of having ' created ' the

---

[1] For a more exact account of this matter, cf. *post*, §§ 8-10.

number of bags indicated by the excess of bags on deposit over bags in the cloak-rooms." [1]　There seems to be some confusion here. The quantity of purchasing power existing at any time may be measured in either of two ways.　On the one hand, it may mean the number of units of money over which people have control—the quantity, in £s sterling, of legal tender money *plus* bank-notes *plus* bank balances in their possession.　On the other hand, it may mean the quantity of stuff over which this quantity of £s sterling gives command.　As was observed in § 5 of the preceding chapter, in any given set of general conditions, the public of any country find it convenient to keep, on the average, a certain definite proportion of their real wealth in an immediately available form as legal tender money, bank-notes or bank balances ; for, by so doing, they are enabled to conduct their daily transactions without trouble or friction, and are also safe-guarded, in a measure, against embarrassment by sudden calls.　The proportion of their wealth that they choose to hold in these forms will, indeed, vary from time to time, but, in general, the causes of these variations are outside the control of bankers.　So far as this is so, the quantity of purchasing power, measured by its value in terms of real things, that is in existence at any time is unaffected by anything that bankers can do.　If they were to double the quantity of purchasing power measured in £s sterling, each £ sterling would become worth half what it was before, and the aggregate stuff-value of the sum total of £s sterling in existence would be unaltered.　Subject to qualifications which are not relevant to the present purpose, it is generally agreed that bankers cannot create purchasing power in the sense of augmenting the aggregate stuff-value of extant purchasing power.　They can, however, create purchasing power in the other sense.　Their action in doing this does not create any new real capital, but it does enable them to hand over to customers titles or claims to capital.　Pro-fessor Cannan's own analogy helps us to see this.　What actually happens is that the banking system receives, let us say, one million bags from people who want to put them on

[1] *Economica*, 1921, p. 31.

current account or on deposit, gives them in exchange one million tickets, and then " creates ", say, three million other tickets and hands over these tickets to customers. We then have four million deposit tickets in the hands of the public. Of these tickets those who have borrowed them present, say, four hundred thousand, and withdraw four hundred thousand bags ; the final position being that there are outstanding three million six hundred thousand deposit tickets and six hundred thousand bags in depôt. It is clear that the banks have not " created " bags, but equally clear that they have created three million deposit tickets against non-existent bags ; and these tickets have a purchasing power in the market. The whole point is that the receipts or tickets handed out by bankers to customers, whether against deposited money or by way of loan, constitute, as the receipts of, say, Savings Banks do not, units of purchasing power that have currency in the business world. Of course, it is open to Professor Cannan to reply that the people who accept unbacked tickets and do not present them are really lending to the banks what the banks have lent to the people to whom they give the tickets. This is true. Obviously the banks can only create credit for customers on condition that these customers or others lend to them in *this* sense—the sense of being ready to accept and use their promises to pay. The extent to which a banker can induce them to do this limits the extent of his lending. If his promises were not accepted, or if, being accepted, they were instantaneously presented for encashment, no new purchasing power could come into being. But this is a formal point. It gives no ground for quarrelling with the convenient phrase credit creation. What in substance has happened is that the bankers have transferred to business men purchasing power, and, through purchasing power, real stuff in the form of wage-goods and so on, formerly belonging to other people. They have done this by giving new money titles to business men while leaving the money titles in other people's hands untouched, in exactly the same way as they would have done had they taken money titles from other people and handed them to business men. There is, therefore, no reason why the phrase credit creation should not be employed, and I propose in what follows to employ it.

§ 4. It is well at the outset to get clear upon certain arithmetical points. First, when a particular bank credits a customer with £1000 in its books, whether against specific securities or by way of overdraft, this creation of credit does not necessarily imply any net creation of credit by the banking system as a whole; for the customer may use it to pay off a debt to another banker, or, more probably, may pay it to some creditor who, in turn, uses it to pay off a bank debt. Since some part of the credits created by particular banks in any period is almost certain to be used in this way, we may expect that the total of bank credit created in any period will be somewhat less than the sum of the credits created in that period by individual banks. Secondly, there is a somewhat intricate relation between the net amount of credit created by the banks for the public (including the Government) in any period, e.g. a month, and the addition made during that period to bank deposits. It is clear at the outset that, in so far as recorded bank deposits include deposits of one bank with another bank, they are not relevant to credit creations in the above sense. In England banks other than the Bank of England do not, in general, hold deposits either for one another or for the Bank of England, but the Bank of England does hold deposits to the credit of other banks. Hence changes made in any period in that part of the Bank of England's deposits which consists of bankers' balances ought to be eliminated before we attempt to infer the amount of credit creations made during that period from the additions made to aggregate bank deposits. Unfortunately no records of the amount of bankers' balances at the Bank of England have been published between 1878, in which year these balances stood at £9,500,000, and 1928, when, in connection with the transfer of Treasury notes to the Bank of England, the form of its return was changed. Yet again, the deposits of the banking system will be increased if gold is "deposited" with them, whether the gold is imported from abroad or drawn in from circulation outside the banks; *per contra* they will be diminished if gold is taken away from the banks either for export or for circulation outside the banks.[1] Changes in deposits induced in these ways do not, of course, imply any creation (or destruction) of bank credits to the public. For simplicity, bank loans made to the public directly in currency without any mediation of deposits may be regarded as deposit credits immediately drawn upon for currency. Subject to these qualifications the sum of net credit creations made in any period for the public (including the Government) may be measured by the addition made in that period to aggregate bank deposits, a net credit destruction being represented, of course, by a corresponding diminution in aggregate bank deposits. Thirdly, the net credit creations made by the banks in any period are not necessarily equal to the credit creations made in favour of, and handed over to, industrialists. When a nation's budget is not balanced, such creations may be made on occasion even for the purpose of enabling the Government to pay interest on its internal debt; and, apart from this, some credit creations are likely to be made for non-industrial purposes. Normally, however, the non-industrial credits outstanding are not likely to vary very much, and it is reasonable to regard the sum of new credit creations made in a year and the sum handed over to industrialists as not very far from equal—it being understood, of course, that some of the new credits may be handed over indirectly in the form of advances to members of the public who wish to take up new industrial shares. In the light of this discussion, and subject to the several cautions contained in it, we may treat the addition made to bank deposits in any year as a rough index of the quantity of bank credit created for industrialists during that year.[2]

[1] If gold is drawn by the other banks from the Bank of England and kept in their tills, the deposits of the Bank of England, and so of the banking system as a whole, will, of course, be diminished ; but this we have already allowed for in what was said about bankers' balances ; aggregate deposits *minus* bankers' balances are not affected.

[2] Mr. Joseph Sykes, to whom I owe valuable criticisms on this chapter as it appeared in my first edition, suggests, no doubt rightly, that a better index could be constructed from statistics of advances and bills. He is, I understand, at present working at these statistics.

§ 5. From 1877 onwards there are available records of the deposits held by the joint-stock banks of the United Kingdom in the October of each year ; and, since 1892, there are records of the deposits of private banks. The deposits of the Bank of England are, of course, recorded, and so also are the amounts of gold held by it. We are without information, however, as to the deposits of private banks before 1892 and as to the gold holdings of banks other than the Bank of England. In these circumstances it is not possible to make a completely satisfactory table to display the credit creations made for industry in successive years. The best that can be done is, I think, this. For 1892 and later years the additions made to the deposits of the Bank of England, the joint-stock banks, and the private banks are summed, and the addition made to the gold holdings of the Bank of England are subtracted. For the years before 1892 it is assumed that the deposits of the private banks bore the same ratio to the deposits of the joint-stock banks and the Bank of England that they bore in 1892, and the same procedure is adopted. The gold holdings of banks other than the Bank of England are ignored throughout. Our inability to take account of changes in these gold holdings and of any transfer of deposits (by absorption or otherwise) from private banks to joint-stock banks before 1892 are the chief sources of weakness in Table XIII., as printed in the Appendix. It may, perhaps, be thought that the last column of that table should have been drawn up after the total of deposits *minus* gold for each year had been corrected to allow for price changes. This, however, is not so. The credit creations in previous years were made in previous years, and, if total credit creations stood last year at 500 and this year at 510 millions, there has been a new creation of 10 millions of credit this year, even though the real value of 510 millions now is less than that of 500 millions then. The table, therefore, is properly drawn.

§ 6. In the last column of that table it will be observed that a minus sign appears only three times. This means that good times differ from bad, not in that the former witness creations, and the latter destructions, of credit, but that the former witness larger, and the latter smaller, creations. That is to say, the banks do not in bad times reduce the stream of new real capital flowing to business men below what it would have been had there been no banks, but merely increase it to a smaller extent than they do in good times. At first glance a hasty reader may perhaps feel some embarrassment about this asymmetry. A moment's reflection, however, shows that there is no cause for this. What concerns us is the effect of variable credit creations in augmenting the variations in the volume of new capital flowing to industry as between good times and bad. This effect is obviously no different whether it results from a credit creation of 25 millions this year followed by a credit destruction of 25 millions next year, or from a credit creation of 120 millions this year followed by a credit creation of 70 millions next year. Credit creations will be without effect upon the amplitude of industrial fluctuations if, and only if, allowance being made for price changes, they are equal in amount in successive years, or, in other words, if, this allowance made, the figures in the final column of our table increase *at a constant rate*—whether positive, negative or zero.[1]

§ 7. The accompanying two charts set out my index of credit creations alongside of the unemployment index inverted —turned, that is to say, so that the peaks of the curve represent minima of unemployment. The curves in the first chart are drawn from annual figures; those in the second from moving three-year averages, with a view to smoothing out sudden year-to-year variations. It will be seen that in both charts the swings of the two curves are very closely associated; the showing of the moving average chart being better than that of the other, because in it the sudden declensions of the credit index in 1890 and 1906 are smoothed out. Indeed, on the moving average chart the only significant lapse from parallelism is the continuation of good employment for longer than might have been expected from 1896–1900. The appearance of the credit creation index suggests

---

[1] In view of this consideration it is evident that no purpose would be served by comparing indices of industrial activity with aggregate amounts of deposits, as distinguished from rates of increase in deposits.

that the employment curve should have turned down some two years earlier than it did. This lapse from parallelism may, however, well be accounted for by the South African war. In the charts there is thus a clear proof that in times of industrial activity the contribution to the stream of new capital provided through the creation of new bank credits is larger than it is in times of depression.

§ 8. When the comparative amounts, in terms of money, of the new credits created by the banks for industrialists in successive years is known, the comparative amounts of resources available for transformation into new capital that are handed over through these credits can be calculated in a rough way by dividing the money figure for each year by the price index for that year ; and it might seem at first sight that, when we have done this, we have ascertained, in absolute terms, the extent to which credit creations have made the quantities of new capital available for business men in each of a series of years different from what they would have been had no credit creations taken place. This, however, is not so. The difference in this sense made by credit creations is only discernible when we have subtracted, for each year, from the new capital handed over to business men through credit creations the new capital which would have been contributed in other ways if the banks had not been there, and which, as things are, is not contributed on account of the banks' action. Under this head two separate deductions have to be made, one obvious, the other somewhat obscure. Of these the latter has precedence in logical order, and will be considered first.

§ 9. The need for this deduction was demonstrated in effect—though his analysis was not directed to this particular end—by Mr. D. H. Robertson in his little book *Banking Policy and the Price Level.* Consider a rentier who holds no currency in his house, does not owe money to any bank, and is not prepared for the moment to buy securities. When the rate of interest goes up, the only way in which such a man can respond is by leaving balances unspent in the bank—putting, say, £100 on deposit account there to earn the improved interest offered—instead of spending it and so transferring it to the balances of other people. From the rentier's point of view, this action comes to exactly the same thing as refraining from spending £100 and paying it into a bank in discharge of a bank loan. In either event the rentier is intending to do without a £100 worth of consumption, and to make £100 worth of investment instead. Here, therefore, the banks are mere intermediaries. But it is impossible for them, in the conditions supposed, to perform their mediating function except by the process of creating £100 worth of new credits. For *this* action by the rentier does not, as the repayment of a bank loan would do, diminish his (or anybody else's) bank balances, and does not, therefore, allow an addition to be made to the balances of business men except on condition that an equal addition is made to the sum total of balances. If the banks do not create an extra £100 of credits for business men, the intention of the rentier is, so to speak, defeated. His conduct reacts to lower prices slightly all round, but does not lead, as he had intended, to any real saving. Hence—and this is the point—such part of credit creations by the banks as offsets this sort of action by rentiers does not involve any net addition to the new capital available for business men over what would have been provided had there been no banking machine. This part of credit creations merely constitutes a route along which, in actual conditions, rentiers provide something which they intended to provide, and would have provided directly, had they been accustomed to keep their store of value in real form instead of in bank balances. The size of this part of credit creations can be determined as follows. If rentiers or others, for no matter what reason, refrain from spending £100, which otherwise they would have spent, correct mediatorial action on the part of the banks requires that they shall create £100 of new credits for business men.[1] If they do this, they convey to them exactly what the rentiers intended to convey to them—no more and no less. More-

---

[1] As Mr. Robertson points out, this is equally true whether the intention to provide more real savings in money form arises from a desire to hold in this form a larger proportion of an unchanged real income or an unchanged proportion of a real income which has become larger. (Cf. *Economica*, June 1928, p. 138.)

over, if they do this, their action will exercise an upward
pressure on the price level exactly equal to the downward
pressure which the rentiers' action exerts. Hence the part
of credit creations which is purely mediatorial is such part
as is required in the circumstances in order to keep the
price level constant. In other words, it is such part as is
required to cancel changes brought about by action on the
part of the banks' customers, other than business men,[1]
in what we shall learn to know presently as the average
income velocity of monetary circulation. The quantity of
new capital carried by this part of the created credit must
be deducted from the total when we attempt to estimate
the extent to which the supply of new capital to business
men in good times is enhanced above what it would have
been in the absence of modern banking machinery.

§ 10. The second deduction to be made can be described more easily. When, in consequence of improved
expectations among business men, improved rates of interest
are offered, extra command over stuff, available for use as
capital, is handed to them by the general public through
several channels. The two most important of these lie
outside the banks' purview altogether. One of them consists in the additions which companies make to their own
reserves before profits are distributed, thus, in effect, compelling their shareholders to make new savings in their
behalf. The other consists in the transfer of bank balances to
them from the public against issues by them of new securities.[2]
The transfer need not, of course, be direct : a rentier may buy
in the market an existing security from a financier and the

---

[1] This distinction needs explanation. When rentiers expend their
balances less freely, they are trying to add to the store of stuff held for
them, as we may suppose, by business men and thus available for industry.
But, when business men expend their balances less freely, they are trying
to release resources from the task of making capital goods for industry to
the task of standing in store. This latter purpose can be accomplished
without any help from the banks, whereas, apart from such help, the
rentiers' purpose will be defeated.

[2] It should be noted that sometimes companies raise new funds in the
first instance by borrowing from banks, and subsequently shift their debt
to the public by issuing securities, with the proceeds of which they repay
the bankers. A substantial part of the " new capital issues " in bad times
is probably of this character.

financier may buy the new security with the proceeds of his sale. These proceedings stand entirely apart from the action of banks in creating new credits for business men. Plainly, however, we are not entitled to assume that they will be carried on in exactly the same way if banks create credits as they would have been if they did not do this. On the contrary, it may well be asked : When new capital is raised for business men by the agency of credit creation, will not the real funds so obtained simply take the place of real funds that would otherwise have come to business men by these other means ? Have we not merely substituted one channel of supply for another without making aggregate supply different from what it would have been had there been no such thing as credit creation ? Apart from credit creation business men would have raised in a year 1000 units of stuff for capital uses from rentiers, out of the, say, 1500 units in their hands, by the offer of 5 per cent interest : now they absorb 200 units from them by a forced levy operated through credit creation : will it not follow that the 5 per cent offer will now raise only 800, instead of 1000, units of voluntary supply ? Rentiers suffer just as much by dispensing with the 1000th unit of food and so on, whether all the previous 999 units are provided voluntarily or some are taken by force ; why should they now dispense with it for less than 5 per cent, and, if they do not dispense with it for less than this, how is the aggregate of new capital available to business men made any different from what it would have been in any event ? This argument is plausible, but it is invalid. It ignores the fact that the desire of rentiers to invest at interest is keener in respect of the 800th unit of investment than in respect of the 1000th. This point is easily illustrated by a parallel case. Suppose .that rentiers hitherto, out of an income of 1500 apples, have been accustomed to consume 500 themselves and to exchange 1000 against 1000 oranges. By some agency 200 apples are forcibly taken away from them. They will not now consume 500 themselves and exchange 800 against 800 oranges ; for the 800th orange means more to them than the 1000th orange. They will consume themselves less than 500 apples, and will offer more than 800 apples against oranges at a rate somewhat higher than one apple against one orange. It is exactly the same with the supply of new capital. Rentiers, having been deprived by force of 200 units of resources, will be prepared to offer *more* than 800 additional units for a 5 per cent interest rate. Credit creation by banks is thus not merely a channel into which new capital that would come to business men in any event is diverted ; it is a means by which a bigger aggregate of new capital is made available to them in response to a given offer of interest. In other words, the second deduction, which, in order to estimate the total effect of credit creations, we have to make from the direct contribution of new capital handed to industrialists in any period through credit creations, is less than the whole of that direct contribution—as diminished, of course, by the first deduction described in the preceding section. It is easy to see that it will be larger in absolute amount the more elastic is the business world's demand for, and the more elastic is the general supply of, new real capital.

§ 11. We conclude then that in any year the *difference* made to the stream of resources available to become new capital in industry by credit creations is smaller than the direct yield of the credit creations. What proportion of the gross contribution due to credit creations constitutes a net contribution we are unfortunately without means to determine : and we cannot even say that this proportion will be the same in different years. It is, therefore, not certain that the *variations*, as between good times and bad, in the net contributions made to the volume of available new capital by bank action will be smaller than the variations in the gross contributions so made. It is, however, in my judgement, *probable* that they will be smaller.

CHAPTER XIV

CREDIT CREATIONS AND THE ASSOCIATED REAL LEVIES

§ 1. THE present chapter is an interlude in the main argument and may be omitted by readers who are not interested in theoretical niceties. When we know how much credit has been created over a given period and what the price level was at the times when the various component parts of this credit were expended by the persons to whom they were handed over, we can, as was indicated in the preceding chapter, ascertain by simple arithmetic how large an amount of real goods and services the created credit commands. But, if we take our stand, not after the event but before it, and ask how much real goods and services a given sum of created credit will yield gross (*i.e.* apart from the deductions discussed in the preceding chapter), *if no other new factor except the creation of the credit and the reactions to which it leads is introduced,* we find ourselves confronted by a curious and interesting analytical problem. In the pages that follow I shall investigate this problem. To simplify the exposition —no difference is made in principle—I shall assume that money consists exclusively of bank-money, *i.e.* balances in the books of bankers, on which cheques are drawn. In the first part of my inquiry I shall also assume, but this assumption will be withdrawn at a later stage, that the act of credit creation does not affect at all the productivity of industry or the amount of real value which the public, as a whole, desire to hold in the form of money.

§ 2. At first sight there appears to be no difficulty. If the money income of the country be represented by £3600 millions, and if, during a year, the banks create and spend

£300 millions of new money—money, of course, includes deposits subject to cheque as well as currency—it seems clear that, by this process, they will make a levy on the public in terms of real income (of goods and services) equal to $\frac{300}{3600 + 300}$, *i.e.* $\frac{1}{13}$th of the total real income of the year: this levy being handed on by them to those persons to whom the £300 millions of new money has been handed on. There is, however, a pitfall here. In the above statement it is tacitly assumed that the price level is altered in proportion to the addition made to the *stream* of money appearing as money income during the year; whereas, according to generally accepted monetary theory, this level ought to be altered in proportion to the addition made to the *stock* of money; and, as a matter of fact, the stream of money appearing as money income during a year is not equal to the stock of money. It seems, therefore, that some other and less simple line of inquiry must be found. The procedure which naturally suggests itself is that we should take as a fundamental unit of time —to be called the *circulating period*—a period of such length that, during the course of it, the stream of money appearing as money income is equal to the stock of money. This period will obviously constitute a fraction of the year equal to the fraction of their real (annual) income that people choose to hold in money form. It will be understood that the stream of money appearing as money income is not the same thing as the sum of money expenditures made against commodities. When A buys a commodity for £10, sells it for £10 to B, who in turn sells it for the same sum to C, and so on, only £10, and not £30, appears as income. More generally, the circulating period, as here defined, is independent of the number of times that representative units of money change hands during the year against representative units of commodity—a number which must, of course, be equal to the number of times that representative units of commodity change hands against representative units of money. With the aggregate (annual) money income of the country standing at £3600 millions and the stock of money standing at £1800 millions, the circulating period will, on this understanding, be six months. If, then, so many units of new money are created by the banks during a circulating period, and if this new money circulates with the same rapidity as the money already existing, the proportionate additions made to the stream of money and to the stock of money respectively will be equal. Thus in the first six months of our year £150 millions will be added to £1800 millions, raising both stream and stock to £1950 millions. The price level will rise to $\frac{13}{12}$ of what it was before, and the new money created and spent by the banks will bring in to them $\frac{1}{13}$th part of the real income of goods and services accruing to the community in six months. In the second six months £150 millions will be added to a stream and stock which now stand at £1950 millions. The price level will become $\frac{14}{13}$th of what it was, and the banks will secure a real levy consisting of $\frac{1}{14}$th part of six months' real income. Thus over the year the real levy made on the public will be $\frac{1}{2} \left\{ \frac{1}{13} + \frac{1}{14} \right\}$ times the aggregate real income of the year.

§ 3. If, for simplicity, we suppose that the period during which the banks go on (at a constant rate) creating new money is n times as long as the period of circulation of money, *and that n is a whole number*, these results can be generalised as follows :

Let M be the stock of money initially.

Let R be the real income of the country per circulating period.

Let Y be the total amount of new money created.

Let n be the number of circulating periods during which it is being created (at an even rate throughout) : n being a whole number.

Let P be the price level initially.

Let $P_1, P_2 \ldots P_n$ be the price levels in each of the n successive circulating periods.

Let $L_1, L_2 \ldots L_n$ be the real levies raised in each of these periods through the expenditure of the new money.

Then we have (from the general theory of money) $P = \dfrac{M}{R}$.

$$P_1 = \frac{M + \dfrac{Y}{n}}{M} P = \frac{M + \dfrac{Y}{n}}{R}.$$

$$P_2 = \frac{M + 2\dfrac{Y}{n}}{M} P = \frac{M + 2\dfrac{Y}{n}}{R}.$$

$$L_1 = \frac{Y}{n} \div P_1 = R \frac{\dfrac{Y}{n}}{M + \dfrac{Y}{n}} = R \frac{Y}{nM + Y}.$$

$$L_2 = \frac{Y}{n} \div P_2 = R \frac{\dfrac{Y}{n}}{M + 2\dfrac{Y}{n}} = R \frac{Y}{nM + 2Y}.$$

Hence the aggregate real levy made by the banks

$$= \Sigma^n L = R \left\{ \frac{Y}{nM + Y} + \frac{Y}{nM + 2Y} + \ldots \text{ to } n \text{ terms} \right\}.$$

$$= R \left\{ \frac{1}{n\dfrac{M}{Y} + 1} + \frac{1}{n\dfrac{M}{Y} + 2} + \ldots \text{ to } n \text{ terms} \right\}.$$

This sum, it will be noticed, varies, when M and Y are given, with the value of n : that is to say, with the number of monetary circulating periods, or, more roughly, the length of time, over which a given act of credit creation is spread. It can be proved [1] that the sum continually increases as n increases, from which it may be inferred that, the longer the period covered by a given credit creation, the larger will be the resultant command over real goods and services. It is easy to see, however, that, whatever the value of n, the above

sum is greater than $R \left\{ \dfrac{1}{\dfrac{M}{Y} + 1} \right\}$ and is less than $R \left\{ \dfrac{1}{\dfrac{M}{Y}} \right\}$.

---

[1] The proof involves mathematical difficulties. Mr. Ramsey of King's College, Cambridge, kindly constructed one for me : but it is too complicated for reproduction here.

Hence, so long as the amount of credit creation is small relatively to the previously existing stock of bank (and other) money, even a very great extension of the time over which the credit creation is spread can only make a very small difference to the amount of real resources secured. For example, if Y is $\frac{1}{10}$th of M, an increase in n from 1 to ∞ would only cause Σ^n L to increase from $\frac{1}{11}$ R to something less than $\frac{1}{10}$ R. The length of the period covered by a given act of credit creation, provided that the sum of credit creation is small, does not, therefore, matter much.

§ 4. If n is not a whole number, provision has to be made for the loose end by which it hangs beyond a whole number, or, should it be less than 1, beyond 0. Since in our formulae we have implied that, when the creation of new money is spread over a complete circulating period, the price level relevant to the *whole* of that period is the same, namely a level adjusted to the addition that will have been made to the stock of money at the end of the period, we are bound also to take that view as regards new creations of money which cover only a part of a circulating period. To do anything else would involve the paradoxical thesis that the price level in one month is affected by an event not necessarily foreseen, namely, the cessation of new money creations, which takes place in a *subsequent* month. Thus in a part-period the price level must be taken as equal to what it would have been during the whole period had the creation of new money continued at the same rate throughout the period ; and the levy made through it will be equal to what, at that price level, the new money actually created is able to purchase. This conclusion stands on all fours with, and depends on, the same hypotheses —to be discussed immediately—as are required to sustain our main formula. In the following paragraphs, however, I shall, for simplicity of exposition, ignore these loose ends.

§ 5. Apart from this matter, the general method of attack that has been outlined seems satisfactory so long as we are considering each period of circulation as a whole without analysing it into parts. So soon, however, as we do that, a serious difficulty emerges : because over any part of a circulating period, the money stream is necessarily smaller than the money stock. Thus let us suppose, as before, that the period of circulation is six months and that £300 millions of new money are being created at a constant rate over a year. As before let the money income of the year be £3600 millions and the money stock £1800 millions. Then in the first month of the first circulating period, £$\frac{300}{12}$ millions of new money are created. This increases the money stream of that month in the proportion

$$[\left\{ \frac{300}{12} + 300 \right\} \div 300] = \frac{13}{12}.$$

But it increases the money stock in a different proportion, namely,

$$[\left\{ \frac{300}{12} + 1800 \right\} \div 1800] = \frac{73}{72}.$$

It follows that, if, as in the preceding solution we supposed, the price level is to be raised throughout the first circulating period in the proportion $\frac{13}{12}$, during the first month of that period it must be raised much more than in proportion to the addition, which, in that month, has been made to the money stock ; and the same thing is true of all the other months except the last. Attention was called to this difficulty for the first time by Mr. D. H. Robertson in his *Banking Policy and the Price Level.*

§ 6. The way in which he attempts to meet it is as follows. He conceives each circulating period to be divided into a number of small atomic intervals, finite but indivisible, which he calls days. Let there be k such intervals within a circulating period. Mr. Robertson assumes that the whole of the money newly created in each interval appears as income once during that interval, and that, as has been happening hitherto, $\frac{M}{k}$ parts of the previously existing stock of money appear as income once. Let us write $\frac{Y}{n}$ in our notation (namely the amount of new money created in a circulating period) $= X$: so that the new money created during an interval $= \dfrac{X}{k}$. The money stream in the first interval becomes then $\dfrac{M+X}{k}$ instead of $\dfrac{M}{k}$, and the price-level rises in the proportion $\dfrac{M+X}{M}$. This implies that the new money created by the banks is circulating, in the sense of appearing as money income, more rapidly than the existing stock of money ; in other words that the circulating period of a representative unit of money is shortened. The previous length of circulating period was, however, calculated so as to enable the public to hold in the form of money stocks a given real value R, namely, the real income accruing during the number of days that a representative circulating period has hitherto occupied : and nothing has happened to make the public wish to hold a different aggregate real value in the form of money stocks. Therefore they will immediately take steps to cancel the shortening which has taken place in the circulating period of the representative unit of money, by cutting down the proportion of the original stock of money that is allowed to appear in the stream. Mr. Robertson assumes that, to this end, they succeed, during the second interval, in holding back from circulation an amount of the original stock of money equal to the amount that has been added to the stock in the first interval, so that the stream in the second interval, as augmented by the new money created then, is equal to the stream in the first interval : and so on throughout the course of any one circulating period. If these assumptions are made, we are able to hold without paradox that throughout each circulating period the price level is uniform, in spite of the fact that the stock of money is continuously increasing ; and the formulae set out in § 3 can be successfully defended.[1]

§ 7. When this ingenious analysis is studied carefully, it will be noticed that Mr. Robertson's reasoning depends upon two propositions : (1) the general proposition that,

[1] Cf. *Banking Policy and the Price Level*, Appendix H, Chapter V.

when, through the action of the banks, the real value of the aggregate money stock is diminished, the public endeavour to restore this real value to what it was before ; and (2) the more special proposition that they achieve their end *at a particular rate of speed.* With the first of these two propositions everybody will agree. The second, however, is more difficult. The matter may be put in another way thus. If a given sum of new money is created in, say, a week, the " proper " response—the response that, given the habits of the people, must ultimately be made—is an increase of the price level by a fraction equal to this sum divided by the former stock of money. But, since adjustment to the new conditions can hardly be instantaneous, the *immediate* response is likely to be an increase by a fraction somewhere between this and the fraction yielded when the sum of new money is divided by the *stream* of money which formerly flowed into income per week. In order to make the " somewhere between " definite for all relevant conditions, Mr. Robertson has to assume a particular law as to the speed with which the public reacts to protect the real value of its money stock against depletion. Unfortunately it is not possible to establish *any* particular law on this matter by evidence. Mr. Robertson's law is admittedly an assumption, adopted because *some* assumption *must* be made, because it is *prima facie* not unplausible, and because it enables a simple and manageable formula—that set out in § 3—for determining the real effect of new money creations to be deduced. There is, of course, nothing illegitimate about this procedure. In the circumstances no other procedure is available. But, if the results attained by it are to have significance, it is essential to secure some estimate of the amount of error to which they are subject on account of the unavoidable insecurity of their foundations.

§ 8. Mr. Robertson postulates that the reaction of the public takes place at a certain speed. It is open to us to suppose that it takes place more rapidly than this, thus causing the price level in the earlier parts of a monetary circulating period, during which new money is being created, to be more nearly adapted than his formula indicates to the altered stock of money. In his language, the public, instead of withdrawing from expenditure in the second atomic interval an amount of money equal to the amount that the banks created in the preceding interval, may withdraw rather more than this. The limit of what is possible in this direction is reached if we suppose the public to react instantaneously, so that the price level in each atomic interval is adjusted to the stock of money in that interval, the newly created money being made *instantly* to circulate at the same pace as previously existing money. Let P_1', P_1'' . . . be the price levels in each of the k successive intervals of the first circulating period, and let L_1', L_1'' . . . be the corresponding real levies. Then, with our previous notation,

$$P_1' = \frac{M + \dfrac{X}{k}}{M} \cdot P = \frac{M + \dfrac{X}{k}}{R},$$

$$P_1'' = \frac{M + 2\dfrac{X}{k}}{M} \cdot P = \frac{M + 2\dfrac{X}{k}}{R}.$$

$$L_1' = R\frac{X}{kM + X}.$$

$$L_1'' = R\frac{X}{kM + 2X}.$$

Hence the aggregate real levy made by the banks in the first circulating period

$$= \Sigma L_1' = R\left\{\frac{X}{kM + X} + \frac{X}{kM + 2X} \cdots \text{ to } k \text{ terms}\right\}.$$

It is easy to see that, whatever the value of k, each successive term inside the bracket in this expression is less than the preceding term. It follows that

$$\Sigma L_1' < R\frac{X}{M + \dfrac{X}{k}}.$$

As k becomes indefinitely large, this last expression approximates to $R\dfrac{X}{M}$.

$$\therefore \; \Sigma \, L_1' < R\frac{X}{M}.$$

But
$$\Sigma \, L_1' = L_1$$

$$\therefore \; L_1 < R\frac{X}{M}.$$

That is to say, the maximum figure to which the real levy in the first circulating period can rise on any possible hypothesis is $R\dfrac{X}{M}$.

§ 9. To arrive at a corresponding minimum figure is less easy. The logical antithesis to instantaneous reaction is infinitely slow reaction (*i.e.* no reaction at all); but to postulate this is plainly ridiculous, and would lead to ridiculous results. We have, therefore, in this direction to look, not for the most extreme hypothesis which can be conceived, but for the most extreme which can sensibly be entertained. I suggest that the minimum speed of reaction which it is sensible to postulate is one conforming to the condition that the new money created in one atomic interval shall, in the next atomic interval, circulate at the same speed as the previously existing stock of money; in other words, that new money, after its first spending, shall be assimilated to the previously existing mass of money. It is easy to see that the figure for the real levy raised in the first circulating period, which conforms to this hypothesis, is

$$L_1 = R\left\{\frac{X}{kM + kX} + \frac{X}{kM + kX + X} + \frac{X}{kM + kX + 2X} \text{ to } k \text{ terms}\right\}.$$

This is obviously $> R\dfrac{X}{M + 2X}$.

That is to say, the minimum figure to which the real levy can fall on any sensible hypothesis is $R\dfrac{X}{M + 2X}$.

§ 10. The figure yielded by Mr. Robertson's formula $R\dfrac{X}{M + X}$ lies between these two extremes. Since the truth also must lie within these limits, his figure cannot be less than $\dfrac{M}{M+X}$ times the true figure, and cannot be greater

than $\dfrac{M+2X}{M+X}$ times the true figure.   It follows that, so long

as the amount of new money created during a circulating period is small relatively to the total stock of money, or, what comes to the same thing, so long as the new money created during a year is small relatively to the normal annual money income, Mr. Robertson's formula cannot err from the truth by more than a small percentage.   For example, if we suppose our normal stock of money to be £1800 millions and the monetary circulating period to be six months, his estimate of the real levy that would result from creating £150 millions of new money during six months can neither fall short of nor exceed the truth by more than $7\frac{9}{13}$ per cent.   The range of *probable* error is, of course, substantially smaller.   Similar reasoning is easily extended to other circulating periods beyond the first.   We may, therefore, I think, safely conclude that the formula set out in §. 3 is, for moderate creations of credit, an adequate one.

§ 11.   The preceding analysis, it has now to be recalled, was based on the assumption that other things are equal, *i.e.* that (1) the productivity of industry neither undergoes autonomous changes during the relevant period nor is affected at all by the act of credit creation, and (2) that the amount of real value which the public as a whole desire to hold in the form of money is unaltered.   In fact, of course, the act of credit creation is certain, through the extra industrial activity associated with it, to lead to some increase of productivity.   This will make the price level rise rather less than our formula indicates.   Hence, other things being equal, the amount of real levy carried by a given amount of credit creation will be rather larger than it indicates.   On the other hand, the act of credit creation, by making prices rise, may lead people to expect that they will rise still further ; may thus make them wish to get rid of money and buy things, which implies reducing the real value of their monetary holdings, or, in other words, shortening the circulating period.   This will make prices

rise more than our formula indicates.   Hence, other things
being equal, the amount of real levy commanded by a given
amount of credit creation will be smaller than it indicates.
This class of effect is extremely important when a number
of large credit creations are made at short intervals, as
happened in Germany, Austria and Russia after the War.
For ordinary industrial fluctuations it is less important,
but, nevertheless, may easily outweigh the converse effect
due to increased productivity.   On the whole, for the movements of an ordinary trade cycle, it seems probable that
the estimate of the gross real yield of credit creations
occurring in isolation, which our formula provides, is a
little, but only a little, in excess of the truth.   Of course,
in so far as, contrary to the assumptions set out in § 1,
credit creations are accompanied by other events not caused
by them, such as an independent increase of productivity
or an independent decision on the part of business men to
hold more real value in money form—events which force
prices down—the yield from a given sum of new credit will
be *pro tanto* augmented : in converse conditions it will be
pro tanto reduced.

CHAPTER XV

FACTORS DETERMINING PRICE CHANGES

§ 1. Up to this point we have been concerned with the direct effects of credit creations in modifying the volume of new capital available in different years (or months) to business men, and have had occasion to consider price changes only as incidents in this process. In the two chapters that follow we shall have to study the part played by these changes, however induced, as causal agents. It is, therefore, necessary to inquire more carefully than we have done hitherto how precisely they are brought about. Plainly one factor in evoking them consists in those variations in the amount of new credit creations, as between different years, which we have been examining. But this is certainly not the only factor at work : for, as was pointed out in Chapter XII., when business expectations improve — whether with or without warrant—increases in the volume of credit are accompanied, partly as concomitant effects of the improved expectations and partly, perhaps, as effects of a belief, generated by the credit creations themselves, that prices will presently rise higher, by diminutions in the amount of real value which business men, and so the public as a whole, of which they are a part, desire to hold in money form. They are also accompanied by increases in the productivity of industry. There are, thus, three factors present, connected together in highly complex ways. Our problem is to determine, so far as may be, the comparative parts which they severally play in causing the general level of prices to fluctuate.

§ 2. This question is most conveniently approached by

way of an interesting study of United States conditions recently made by Mr. Carl Snyder. He finds that, for the United States, there is no discoverable secular trend of change in the frequency with which monetary circulating media change hands during a year; that the short-period, or "cyclical", variations in this frequency are directly related to, and coincide closely, alike in times and in percentages, with short-period variations in the volume of trade; that these two sorts of variation cancel one another, so that neither of them is normally a factor of influence on the general price level; and that, therefore, changes in the quantity of circulating media constitute the sole unneutralised factor.[1] In this argument, it will be understood, volume of trade means real transactions which money accomplishes during a year. The above conclusion, which, if valid, is evidently very important, is also *a priori* surprising. We should expect, for example, that, whatever the average relation between variations in the frequency with which money changes hands and in the volume of trade might be, that relation would differ in detail in different circumstances. Thus it would seem that, when business men's optimistic expectations are correctly based —since A's optimism means the opinion that B will have more stuff to offer against his stuff — increasing volume of trade should balance increasing frequency of money transfers more nearly than when they are wrongly based. Thus a correct anticipation of a good harvest, or of an invention in some manufacturing industry, or of any analogous event should be followed by a smaller rise in general prices than an incorrect anticipation; and conversely with a correct anticipation of a bad harvest or analogous event. Again, in the later parts of trade cycles, when there is less scope for expansion in production above what is already attained than in earlier parts, we should expect given increases in the frequency with which money changes hands to be accompanied by smaller increases in the volume of trade than in the earlier parts of

[1] "New Measures in the Equation of Exchange", in *The American Economic Review*, December 1924, p. 698 *et seq.*

these cycles. It would, of course, be highly improper to set these *a priori* expectations against clearly demonstrated facts. But it is not improper, in the light of them, to scrutinise with especial care contentions which appear to conflict with them. It would be very imprudent for an Englishman to attempt to follow Mr. Snyder into the intricacies of his American study, the statistical basis of which, it should be observed, he himself frankly recognises to be less satisfactory than he would desire ; but an attempt may be made to test the issue for the United Kingdom.

§ 3. If things are as Mr. Snyder finds them, the rates at which the price level changes and the rates at which the volume of bank credit changes from year to year ought to be roughly similar after allowance has been made for trend. Are they in fact thus similar ? It happens that Sauerbeck's index number of wholesale prices stood at the same figure in 1881 and in 1914. The aggregate volume of bank credit, as measured by my credit index, multiplied itself during these thirty-four years a little more than three times, which implies an average increase in each year over the preceding year of about 3·4 per cent. The price level being the same at the end of our period as at the beginning, we may, therefore, infer that an increase in aggregate credits of 3·4 per cent per annum would roughly balance whatever trend of change there was in the volume of trade and in the frequency with which money changes hands. Since the argument is necessarily rough and there is nothing to be gained by an illusory appearance of precision, I have substituted in my calculations 3 per cent for the above 3·4 per cent. The accompanying chart has been constructed as follows. Curve I. shows the unemployment percentages inverted, so that the peaks represent minima of unemployment, built into a moving three - year average. Curve II. shows annual rates of price change, the price index of each year being divided by that of the preceding year, and the resulting numbers built into a moving three-year average. Curve III. shows annual rates of change in credit volume, the aggregate credits outstanding in each year being divided by the aggregate outstanding in the preceding year, 3 per cent being deducted from the figures thus obtained, and the resultant figures being built into a moving three-year average. It is immediately apparent that in times of good employment—industrial activity—the credit curve and the price curve both rise, and that in times of bad employment they both fall. But they do *not* rise and fall through equal ranges, as they should do if Mr. Snyder's proposition were valid for this country. On the contrary, the price curve swings in substantially larger measure, thus indicating that changes in the quantity of circulating media do not constitute the sole unneutralised factor in movements of the price level.

§ 4. The same result can be reached in a more direct way, but subject to a greater element of arbitrariness in eliminating trends, by means of the chart that follows. Curve I. shows Sauerbeck's annual index number, the index for 1900 being put at 100, and the trend thereafter eliminated by subtracting 1 from the number for 1895, 2 from that for 1894, 3 from that for 1893, and so on down to 1878 ; and also subtracting 1 from the number for 1897, 2 from that for 1898, 3 from that for 1899, and so on, down to 1914. The number for 1900 on this plan becomes, of course, 96. Curve II. shows my index number for aggregate credits outstanding, the index for 1900 being put at 100, 3 being subtracted from the number for 1899, 6 from that for 1898, 9 from that for 1897, and so on down to 1878 ; and 1 being subtracted from the number for 1901, 2 from that for 1902, 3 from that for 1903, and so on till 1914. This device removes the trend effectively down to the year 1909, after which it would seem that a steeper upward trend than before was initiated. The amplitude of the swings of the price curve is evidently much larger than that of the swings of the credits curve, a condition of things which would not come about if Mr. Snyder's thesis were applicable to British conditions.

§ 5. We may now turn from this critical study to something more positive. We know that, other things being equal, prices should vary (1) directly with the volume of

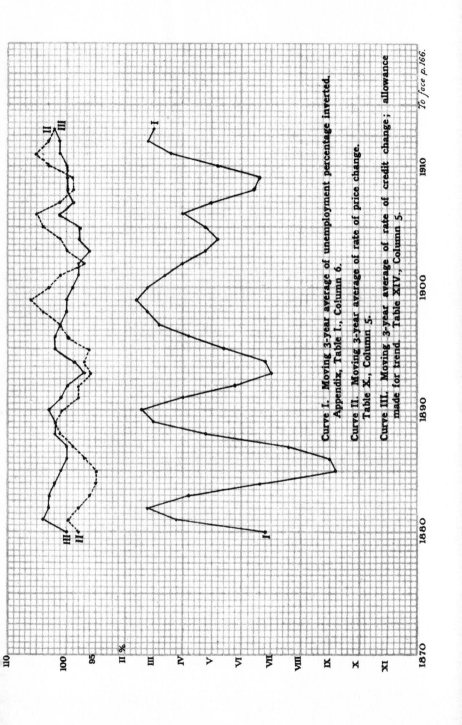

Curve I. Moving 3-year average of unemployment percentage inverted.
        Appendix, Table I., Column 6.

Curve II. Moving 3-year average of rate of price change.
        Table X., Column 5.

Curve III. Moving 3-year average of rate of credit change; allowance
        made for trend   Table XIV., Column 5.

To face p.166.

monetary circulating media, (2) inversely with real income or production, (3) inversely with the length of the monetary circulating period as defined in Chapter XIV. § 2. We should, therefore, wish, if it were feasible, to calculate separately for a succession of years the theoretic effects on the price level that " ought " to result from each of the three above factors, to add them together and to compare the results thus obtained with the price movements which have actually occurred. If the calculated movements agreed in a general way with the actual movements, we should have reason to believe that our calculations showed correctly the comparative parts played in determining price movements by these three factors. I proceed to discuss and, so far as may be, to make, these several calculations.

§ 6. A portion of the above programme can be carried out, not, of course, with accuracy, but by rough methods of approximation. The facts about price changes and about credit volume are set out in the preceding chart. A study of the two curves printed there suggests that, when trend is eliminated, the price level swings during a typical cycle through a range of some 10 per cent, and that the movement of credits is such as to induce a swing through about half that range, say 5 per cent. As regards variations in real income there are, as was pointed out in Chapter I., no adequate pre-war data. We must, therefore, fall back on employment statistics, postulating, in spite of what was said in Chapter I. § 3 that, allowance being made for trend, real income (production) varies in the same sense and in the same proportion as employment. When, that is to say, the percentage of unemployment falls from 6 per cent to 3 per cent, we presume that real income rises in the ratio $\frac{97}{94}$, and so on. Now a general view of the unemployment curve, as it has been several times printed (e.g. as frontispiece), suggests that, for a typical cycle, the range of variation covers some 5 per cent. The inference which this combination of facts suggests is that, as factors of cyclical price change, variations in credit volume and variations in real income roughly cancel out, being responsible for movements over a range of some 5 per cent in opposite directions, and that, therefore, changes in the period of monetary circulation—*i.e.* in the proportion of their real income which the public choose to hold as money [1] —being the sole unneutralised factor, must be responsible for the actual recorded price changes extending over a range of 10 per cent. This result, it will be observed, is precisely similar to Mr. Snyder's, except that, whereas, according to him, everything except changes in credit volume cancels out, according to my analysis everything except changes in the period of monetary circulation cancels out.

§ 7. At this stage we are naturally eager to obtain direct evidence as to what in fact happens during industrial cycles to the period of monetary circulation, so that the above result may be either clinched or overthrown; and at first sight it appears that such evidence is readily attainable. For it is natural to imagine that the period of monetary circulation, as defined in Chapter XIV. § 2, is the inverse of the velocity of monetary circulation as that term is used by Professor Irving Fisher, and that, therefore, changes in it can be discovered by dividing, for successive years, bank deposits into bank clearings, or by some analogous method. Unfortunately, however, this hope rests upon a confusion in language and ideas. The term velocity of money circulation has several senses.[2] In one sense it measures the number of times during which a representative unit of money appears as *income* during a year; that is to say, it is equal to the aggregate money income accruing to the community in a year divided by the aggregate stock of money. Let velocity in this sense—the income-velocity of monetary circulation—be called V_i. Then V_i is the inverse of the period of monetary circulation as defined in Chapter XIV. § 2. If this period is six months, $V_i = 2$; if it is three months, $V_i = 4$; and so on. In a second sense velocity of monetary circulation measures the number of times that a representative unit of money *changes hands* in a year against com-

---

[1] Cf. *ante*, Chapter XIV. § 2.

[2] My attention was called to the danger of ambiguity here by Mr. D. H. Robertson in a criticism made by him on a manuscript draft of this book.

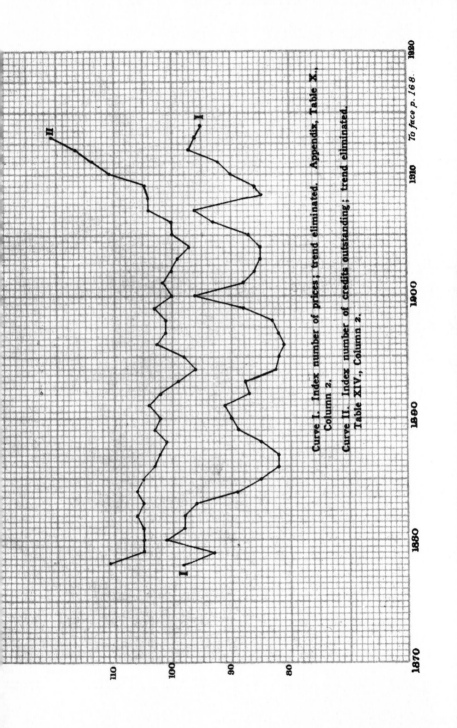

Curve I. Index number of prices; trend eliminated. Appendix, Table X., Column 2.

Curve II. Index number of credits outstanding; trend eliminated. Table XIV., Column 2.

To face p. 168.

modities and services coming into being during that year ; that is to say, it is equal to the money value of the annual *volume of trade in income goods, i.e.* goods produced during the year, divided by the stock of money. Let velocity in this sense—the trade-velocity of monetary circulation—be called V_t. If, then, h stands for the number of times that a representative unit of stuff and a representative unit of money change hands against one another during a year, $V_t = hV_i$. That is to say, the *trade-velocity of money* is equal to the *income-velocity of money* multiplied by the number of times during a year that a representative unit of income goods and a representative unit of money change hands against one another. Write Q for the real income (production) of the community during a year. Then obviously hQ measures the volume of trade in real terms, and $\dfrac{V_t}{h\text{Q}} = \dfrac{hV_i}{h\text{Q}} = \dfrac{V_i}{\text{Q}}$. If we knew the value of h, or, not knowing its value, if we knew that that value was always the same, we could infer the changes that occur in V_i from records of the changes in V_t. But it is to be expected that the number of times that representative units of income goods and of money change hands against one another will be larger in good times than in bad. Hence, during those periods when V_t is growing absolutely, it will also be growing relatively to V_i, and, during those periods when it is declining absolutely, it will also be declining relatively to V_i; and we have no means of discovering the magnitude of these relative movements. Hence not only are changes of V_t not equivalent to changes in V_i, but it is impossible to infer the latter set of changes from the former. Nor is this all. There is yet a third sense of velocity of circulation, namely, the number of times that a representative unit of money changes hands against anything whatever, whether income goods, real property or securities. This is the velocity of circulation in Professor Fisher's sense. Plainly it is different, not only from my V_i, but also from my V_t. In view of the large expansion of stock exchange speculation that takes place in booms, it probably fluctuates more widely than V_t does, and V_t cannot be deduced from it. But it is the only form of velocity of circulation which can be determined statistically by reference to bank deposits and clearing-house returns. The calculation by which it was desired to test the result tentatively reached in § 6 cannot, therefore, be made, and that result must remain provisional and insecure.

§ 8. Moreover, that result, if we are prepared to accept it as a rough approximation to the truth, must be interpreted with great care, lest fallacy ensue. There is some temptation to infer from it that, if, allowance being made for trend, variations in the volume of credit as between good times and bad were done away, the range of price fluctuations would be cut down from 10 per cent to 5 per cent. This inference is not warranted. First, if variations about the trend in the volume of credit were done away, some part of the associated variations in real income would be done away also as a consequence of this. So far as that happened, the range of price fluctuation would be cut down by less than 5 per cent. If, for example, the variations about the trend in real income were reduced by $1\frac{1}{2}$ per cent, this range would be cut down by only $3\frac{1}{2}$ per cent, namely, to $6\frac{1}{2}$ per cent. But secondly, and this is probably a much more important matter, the changes that take place in the income velocity of monetary circulation are not wholly independent of variations in the volume of credit. There is no doubt that extra credit creation itself causes, partly through the fact of price increases and partly through the expectation it engenders of further price increases, an expansion in the income velocity of monetary circulation. To eliminate variations about the trend in the volume of credit would, of course, imply the elimination of this part of the variations in the income velocity of monetary circulation. The aggregate effect in narrowing the range of price variations would, therefore, be greater than the direct effect. What this aggregate effect would amount to arithmetically we cannot determine, because we do not know how large a part of the variations in velocity is a result of variations in the volume of credit and how large a part is caused directly by variations in business expectations, nor yet how large the variations in real income would be if variations in the volume of credit and that part of variations in the income velocity of money that these cause, were removed. Complete price stabilisation would be achieved if the destruction of variations about the trend in the volume of credit caused so much destruction of variations in the income velocity of monetary circulation that the variations in this still remaining exactly balanced the variations in real income still remaining. It seems practically certain *a priori* that this exact balance will not be realised in fact. It is *possible* that to do away with variations about the trend in the volume of credit would destroy so large a part of the variations in the income velocity of money that not enough would be left to offset the surviving variations in real income. In that event, prices would fall in times of industrial activity, and rise in times of industrial depression. It is more likely, however, in my judgement, that the existing association of higher prices with good times and lower prices with bad times would continue, but that the price swings would be cut down to, say, a third of their present amplitude.

§ 9. An important further consideration remains. The movements in the general price level that are associated with trade cycles are not generated by the factors we have distinguished in a simple and direct manner. On the contrary, a highly complicated cumulative process is frequently involved. Thus suppose that the expectations of business men about *industrial* facts improve in a given measure, and that, in consequence of this improvement, they both induce the banks to create for them extra new credits and increase the income velocity of monetary circulation. Even though nothing further happens to *these* expectations on the part of business men, something further may easily happen to prices. For the fact that prices have risen may induce in the public mind a belief that they will continue to rise. If this happens, people will become anxious to get hold of things now rather than later on. To this end they will endeavour to raise still more credits from bankers and will shorten still further the period of monetary circulation—*i.e.* reduce the real value of their monetary holdings. These two proceedings on their part will make the price level rise further. This rise in turn will create, up to a point, belief in a further rise, and this again will call forces into play which bring that further rise about. Until some external event, such as the refusal of bankers to create any more credits, intervenes, there is no reason why this process should ever come to an end. The recent history of Germany, Austria and Russia afford examples of the great lengths to which it may be carried. Analogous considerations hold good of falling prices. The fact of fall may create belief in a further fall ; this will call into play forces that produce such a fall ; and this will create belief in another fall. Thus, when we say that changes in the volume of credit and changes in the income velocity of money cause associated changes in the price level, we must understand that the process of causation is often complex, involving the successive generation of price movements by changes in these factors, of further changes in these factors by price movements, and so on cumulatively.

§ 10. This analysis connects with that set out in § 6 of Chapter XII. It was there shown that the extra real resources, which business men secure in good times by drawing on their store of real value—increasing the income velocity of money—as a direct consequence of improvements in their expectations, is not an extra as against what they would have secured had there been no monetary and banking system. We now see that the extra real resources which they secure by increasing the income velocity of money, when they do this because, prices having risen, they expect them to rise further, *is* an extra in this sense ; for, with money and banking eliminated, there would have been no question of prices rising. This circumstance leads to an important practical consequence, to which attention will be called in Part II. Chapter III.

CHAPTER XVI

THE MODIFICATION OF THE TERMS OF PAST CONTRACTS

§ 1. In Chapters XIII. and XIV. we were concerned with the effects produced on the volume of new capital available to business men in good and bad times by variations in the quantity of new credit created for them by the banks. These effects were *not* due to the price changes associated with credit movements. On the contrary, the further prices rise when banks create a given volume of credit for business men, the smaller will be the contribution of real stuff which this credit carries with it. In the present chapter I turn to an effect which *is* produced through the changes that take place in the general level of prices. This effect arises out of the fact that price changes wrench the real terms of contracts for loans and wages away from what was intended when these contracts were made. Let us consider first contracts for loans. It is evident that, if these are made in terms of money, and if, after they have been made, the general level of prices alters in a way that was not allowed for when the contract was drawn up, borrowers will pay, and lenders will receive, a different real return (whether interest or principal) in terms of things than they originally contemplated. In so far as the change of prices which is going to take place is foreseen, it will, of course, be allowed for in the terms of contract. Thus suppose that the conditions of real demand and supply at the time the contract is made point to a 5 per cent real rate of interest for one year. If lenders and borrowers both expect prices to be unaltered at the end of the year, the contract will be made at the rate of 5 per cent. If both sides expect prices to have risen 10 per cent, it will be made at (approximately) 15 per cent. If one side expects prices to have risen 10 per cent, and the other expects them to have risen 5 per cent, it will be made at some rate intermediate between 10 per cent and 15 per cent, the exact rate depending on (1) which side expects the 10 per cent and which the 5 per cent rise, and (2) the elasticity of the demanders' demand for new capital in relation to the elasticity of the suppliers' supply of it. Correct foresight on both sides would necessarily lead to a money rate truly representing a 5 per cent real rate ; [1] and incorrect foresight on both sides, provided that one erred by excess and the other by defect, *might* do this. In actual fact, however, experience shows that the joint judgement of the market almost always under-estimates future price changes, and does not make sufficient allowance for them. Thus, supposing 5 per cent to be the real rate of interest at which contracts aim, when prices are rising they will almost always hit a real rate of less than 5 per cent, and, when prices are falling, a real rate of more than 5 per cent. The evidence which Professor Irving Fisher has collected leaves no doubt that this is so. Now the people in control of industry—dealers, manufacturers, and so on—are, in general, borrowers rather than lenders. It follows that, when prices are rising, they are relieved of a part of the real payment which they had contemplated making to debenture-holders and other lenders at fixed interest ; and, when prices are falling, they are compelled to make larger real payments than they had contemplated. Thus, in general, a rise in prices imposes a forced levy upon people who have lent at fixed interest to business men and transfers the proceeds of this levy to business men ; and a fall in prices has the opposite effect.

§ 2. This general statement must be brought into relation

[1] It should be observed, to obviate misapprehension, that the above statement is strictly accurate only if we assume that both parties to all contracts purchase different sorts of commodities and services in the exact proportions in which these enter into the national dividend. If they do not do this, a knowledge of the way in which the price of "commodities in general " is going to move will not carry to any one a knowledge of the way in which the price of the particular collection of commodities interesting to him is going to move. This, however, lies beside our main argument.

with certain popular arguments about dealers' stocks. If a dealer has £100,000 locked up in stock and prices fall 50 per cent, his stock is worth only half as much money as it was worth before. If this stock is a minimum requirement for the conduct of his business, like the mechanical equipment of a factory, there can be no question of his selling it except in so far as he is replacing it at the same time by equivalent purchases at the lower price level. Therefore he does not make any *realised* loss. If, on the other hand, part of his stock was surplus over his normal minimum requirements, bought, for example, in a false hope that prices would rise, he will, according to the common way of looking at things, make a realised loss when he sells this part. Thus, it is urged, when prices fall dealers must suffer some unrealised loss, which may be very large relatively to their aggregate capital ; and may also suffer a further large realised loss. This view of the matter is, however, misleading. Since we are dealing with changes in general prices, not in the price of a single particular thing, there will be no loss of any sort in real terms—only a nominal loss in money terms. Therefore the real position of the dealer is not affected at all on the positive side, *i.e.* in respect of the stuff that he holds. If his stock has been financed out of his own resources, he is not affected at all on any side. If, however, he has financed his stock by borrowing £100,000, he does suffer a heavy loss on the negative side, as it were, because the debt that he owes in terms of real things has, through the change in the price level, been doubled in amount. In like manner in the event of an undiscounted price rise he may secure a very large gain. What causes the loss and the gain in these cases is not, however, the fact that the stocks which dealers hold have altered in money value, but that the debt they contracted to finance these stocks has altered in real value. If the debt is repayable on demand or at a fixed date, they may be ruined because they are unable to meet it. If it is in the form of an unredeemable debenture debt, they cannot be called upon to repay the principal, but the real value of the annual interest they have to pay is doubled.

In either event, and this is the point I am concerned to stress, the damage that dealers suffer is not essentially due to the fact that they are dealers and hold stock, but to the fact that they have contracted loans in terms of sterling and that, subsequently, the real value of sterling has increased. Exactly analogous considerations hold of the relation between *falling* prices and dealers' stocks.

§ 3. At first sight it might be thought that, since, unlike many contracts for loans, contracts for wage-employment are nearly always on very short notice, nothing analogous to the transfers we have described above as between business men and rentiers could occur as between business men and wage-earners. This, however, is not so ; for, though the contract of engagement for individual workpeople is at short notice, rates of wages are often fixed by general agreements between associations of employers and workpeople. These are sometimes formally at fairly long notice, and, even if formally they are terminable quickly, in fact an alteration in their terms is apt to be a prolonged proceeding. Hence rising prices are apt to involve transfers to business men from wage-earners under what are in effect, if not in name, past contracts, and falling prices are apt to involve transfers in the opposite sense.[1]

§ 4. The transfers which I have been describing are, it must be clearly understood, transfers connected with past, not with future transactions. Being of this character, they carry with them no differential treatment between rival ways of employing resources ; and involve no promise of a bounty, or threat of a toll, in respect of future industrial spending. Hence, apart from indirect psychological reactions to which they may lead, and to which reference will be made presently, it is not at first sight clear that any effect will be produced on the amount of industrial

[1] The fact that in times of boom rising prices tend to transfer resources from wage-earners to business men is not inconsistent with the fact, to be noted later, that the upper halves of trade cycles have been associated in this country with higher rates of real wages and *a fortiori*, therefore, with higher aggregate real wages than the lower halves : for against the fall in the real supply schedule of labour in times of boom, consequent upon workpeoples' thinking in gold, there has to be set a rise in the real demand schedule for labour. Cf. *post*, Part II. Chap. I. § 3.

spending, or, what comes to the same thing, in the real demand for labour. Indeed, it may be argued that, leaving aside possible reduced demand on the part of the persons at whose expense the controllers of industry become better off, an increase in the resources of business men cannot affect their real demand for labour ; for in any event they can only offer to the nth worker the expected yield of his work, and that is not altered by the fact that an addition has been made to their resources. This argument would be valid if resources paid out to labour yielded their return instantly. But in fact they do not do this, and the argument is, therefore, not valid. Thus suppose that labour employed now takes one year to yield its fruit, and that hitherto business men have been ready to pay an nth man 100 units of stuff for work that will yield 105 units a year hence. When they have a large store of stuff at their disposal they will be content with a lower rate of interest, and so will be willing to pay the nth man more, say 101 units of stuff, for work that will yield 105 units a year hence. That is to say, the supply of new capital and, with it, the real demand for labour will be increased. We cannot tell by how much it will be increased ; but it is bound to be increased to some extent. It should be added, in accordance with the argument of Chapter XIII. § 10, that the net addition to new capital in any period that results from the trans-ference of resources from the general public to business men is likely to be less than the gross addition. For, if debenture-holders, and so on, are mulcted of a million units of stuff by enforced transfers, they will require more interest than before to induce them to make any given amount of new loans, and business men, having a million units more, will offer less interest. It is impossible to determine how much less than the gross addition the net addition will be. We may presume that it will be substantially less than this, but also itself a substantial quantity.

CHAPTER XVII

THE REFLEX INFLUENCE OF PRICE MOVEMENTS ON THE EXPECTATIONS OF BUSINESS MEN

§ 1. So far we have considered only part of the relation between monetary and banking mechanism and the amplitude of industrial fluctuations—namely, the effect which that mechanism has in rendering the supply of new capital more elastic in response to given fluctuations in business men's expectations of profit than it would otherwise be. We have now to observe that the price movements engendered by this mechanism also cause the expectations of business men to vary more than they would otherwise do, and thus in a second way augment the amplitude of industrial fluctuations. This reaction is twofold. On the one side the facts are altered, so that business men entertain with justification altered expectations. On the other side their attitude of mind is modified, so that they entertain improved or worsened expectations on the same basis of facts.

§ 2. The former sort of reaction depends on the circumstance that movements in general prices are not merely *imperfectly*, but are also *unequally*, foreseen. Imperfection of foresight by itself is not, for the present purpose, relevant. Suppose, for instance, that prices are really going to rise 10 per cent. If both borrowers and lenders think that they are going to rise 0 per cent or to fall 20 per cent or to rise 100 per cent,[1] both will agree to adjust the money

---

[1] It should be noted that it is only possible for both borrowers and lenders to expect prices to rise in a short time by a large percentage on condition that there are a number of other people who do *not* expect this.

rate of interest (and of wages) to the anticipated change, and business men will not expect either to reap benefit or to suffer loss from monetary movements. If, however, borrowers and lenders think different things, the fact of their difference—the inequality between their forecasts— gives ground for altered expectations of profit. This is so whatever the relation between the forecasts of the two sides are. Thus, if borrowers expect prices to rise $(x + 5)$ per cent and lenders x per cent, whatever the value of x, whether positive or negative, the effect is the same as though borrowers had expected a 5 per cent rise and lenders no rise at all. It will be as though the borrowers' demand schedule in money were pushed up throughout by 5 per cent and the lenders' left as before. Correspondingly, if lenders expect prices to fall $(x + 5)$ per cent and borrowers x per cent, whatever the value of x, whether positive or negative, may be, the effect is the same as though lenders had expected a 5 per cent fall and borrowers no fall at all. Now in fact the anticipations about price movements entertained respectively by business men and by those with whom they are accustomed to enter into contracts are unequal in a particular way. Experience shows that, in periods when there is a tendency for general prices to go up, business men are apt to expect a larger rise than either the lenders of capital or the providers of labour expect. Professor Cassel, having in mind, presumably, normal times, and not extraordinary conditions such as were recently current in Germany, goes so far as to say : " It seems quite certain that no investor of capital takes account of the possibility that his money may be worth less to him when he gets it back ".[1] Hence, when prices are rising, the business world's expectation of profit from investment is enhanced by the expectation of a bonus at the expense of capitalists and wage-earners ; when prices are falling, it is contracted

---

For, if " everybody " expects prices, which are now 100, to be 200 a month hence, this expectation will inevitably cause them (subject to a small allowance for interest) to become 200 now ; and the expectation will thus, so to speak, commit suicide at the moment of its birth.

[1] Cassel, *The Nature and Necessity of Interest*, p. 165.

by the expectation of a toll, which will have to be paid to capitalists and wage-earners. Thus, whereas imperfections of foresight would merely effect a transfer to or from business men after the event, inequality of foresight creates an expectation on their part of transfers to them in respect of each £ borrowed in times of rising prices, and a corresponding expectation of transfers from them in respect of each £ in times of falling prices.[1] The amplitude of industrial fluctuations is obviously enhanced by this consequence. of monetary and banking arrangements.[2]

§ 3. The other sort of reaction operates through psychology. When prices rise, business men become more prosperous on account of the transfer of resources described in the preceding chapter. Furthermore, besides the real change in their fortunes there is also an element of imagined change. For, when people have more or less money than usual, even though prices have changed in precise correspondence, the natural tendency to " think in gold " is apt to make them imagine themselves really richer or really poorer. But the judgements which people form are biased by their feelings. When they are, or believe that they are, enjoying good fortune, they are apt to look on the brighter side, and, when they are suffering bad fortune, on the darker side, of doubt. Consequently, anything which improves the fortunes of business men constitutes a spur to optimistic error, just as anything which worsens their fortunes constitutes a spur to pessimistic error. The fact of a transfer in their favour makes them more desirous of an active policy ; this sets up reactions which raise prices, and so indirectly

---

[1] Cf. Fisher, *The Rate of Interest*, p. 286.

[2] It is sometimes thought that there is a further element of bounty and toll present in so far as industry is organised by dealers who are different people from the manufacturers who supply them. For, it is said, if a dealer and his manufacturer both expect prices to go up 50 per cent, even though the manufacturer raises his price accordingly, the dealer, whose profit consists in a margin between his selling price and his buying price, will make an abnormal gain. There is, however, an arithmetical error in this argument. If the buying price has been £80 and the selling price £100, a 50 per cent price rise brings the buying price to £120 and the selling price to £150. This leaves a margin of £30, which, with prices 50 per cent higher, is exactly equivalent to the former margin of £20. There is thus no special bounty or toll here.

cause a further transfer in their favour; and so on cumula-tively. The fact of a transfer adverse to them has opposite consequences. Thus, alongside of the bounty or toll stimulus described in the preceding section, there is also operating a psychological stimulus. This completes the detailed study of those complex reactions of monetary and banking arrangements upon industrial fluctuations, which were roughly summarised in advance in Chapter XII.

CHAPTER XVIII

§ 1. In the two preceding chapters we have considered certain indirect effects, in stimulating or depressing industrial activity, which result from price movements induced either by changes in the volume of bank money, or by changes in the velocity of its circulation. We have now to inquire whether and how far these effects take place when upward or downward movements in the general price-level occur, as a result, not of any happenings on the side of money, but of enhancements or declines in the productivity (per head) of a country's industry.

§ 2. Let us consider first a fall in prices due to increased production, made possible by improvement in technique and the accumulation of capital equipment. As a result of such a fall rentiers and other creditors at fixed interest will receive increased real payments from the business men who have borrowed from them, precisely as they would have done had the falling prices been due to a contraction of the currency. Wage-earners will also in like manner receive increased real payments. None the less there is a vital difference between this case and that studied in Chapter XVI. Whereas there the gains of rentiers and wage-earners were associated with and were, in a sense, at the expense of the controllers of industry (including, of course, the ordinary shareholders of joint stock companies), here these persons are themselves in enjoyment of increased real receipts, out of which their enlarged payments can be made. Nor is this all. Not only do the enlarged receipts suffice to cover the enlarged payments, but they leave a substantial balance over. Thus suppose that throughout industry output is doubled in consequence of improved technique, while the quantity of labour employed remains unchanged. Rentiers and wage-earners will be paid (in real terms) twice as much as they used to be paid : but, since the total output of industry is doubled, controllers of industry will not merely be left with the same real incomes as before, but will themselves, just as their partners do, receive a net real income twice as large as before. It is still true, no doubt, that, if the same increase in productivity took place, but prices were nevertheless maintained at their old level by, say, the creation of new money, the controllers of industry, being relieved of a part of the extra payment to rentiers and wage-earners, would fare even better. But to admit this is in no way inconsistent with the view that a fall in prices due to increased productivity inflicts on them no handicap. Analogous considerations obviously hold good in the converse and practically much less important case of a rise of prices due to diminished productivity per head.

§ 3. The position of dealers and other intermediaries is in this matter somewhat different from that of industrialists, because the alteration in the flow of output does not take place, so to speak, in territory belonging to them. If, therefore, prices fall, there is no direct set-off to the extra real interest which they are forced to pay to their creditors : and, if prices rise, there is no direct set-off to the saving that they make in real interest. Even for dealers, however, there is an indirect set-off. For enlarged production will mean for them an enlarged turn-over, and so, presumably, bigger real earnings : while diminished production will mean a diminished turn-over and smaller real earnings.

§ 4. Since there is nothing that can properly be called a toll levied on industrialists when prices fall as a result of improved productivity, and nothing that can properly be called a bonus when they rise as a result of worsened productivity, there is obviously no ground for expectations of a toll or bonus, and consequently, reactions of the kind considered in Chapter XVII., § 2, will not arise. Nor will the further reactions operating through psychology, which were referred to in the section succeeding that just cited. Broadly speaking, therefore, we may conclude that, when general prices vary on account of changes in productivity per head, the secondary effects that follow from similar price movements brought about by monetary factors will not be set up.

CHAPTER XIX

FRICTIONAL INFLUENCES CONNECTED WITH THE NOTION OF SPOILING THE MARKET

§ 1. I PASS now to another and quite different set of conditions by which the scale of industrial fluctuations is in part determined. In every concern there are certain " overhead " charges, which remain roughly constant whether the concern is at full work or partial work, when once its plant and establishment have been built up. From the point of view of any given length of period we may distinguish between these charges, which may be called supplementary expenses, and the expenses more closely dependent on the amount of output that is being produced, which may be called prime expenses. The scale of the fixed capital equipment will be adjusted to the general run of anticipated demand, account being taken both of the probable average volume and of the probable variations of this. When the scale of capital equipment is given, the difference made to total prime expenses by the addition of an increment of output at any time will, after a point, be greater, the larger is the output. The conditions of equilibrium are : (1) that at all times the output shall be such that the selling price is equal to this difference in respect of the last increment (in logical, not temporal, order) that is produced, and (2) that the excess of the aggregate selling price over the sum of the prime expenses of all the units produced over good and bad times together is equal to what is required to cover supplementary expenses. With a given capital equipment and organisation, the curve representing the marginal prime expenses of successive quantities of output is the short-period supply curve of the commodity ; and, given free competition, we should expect *a priori* that in every industry, as the real demand for its products on the part of other people varied, its output (and, consequently, the quantity of labour employed by it) would fluctuate in such wise as always to equate this short-period supply price with the demand price. This arrangement may, therefore, reasonably be regarded as a sort of norm, or standard, from which the deviations occurring in real life can be measured.

§ 2. There are three influences, which, inactive in good times, tend in bad times to make business men restrict their output below the short-period norm, thus making industrial fluctuations larger than they would otherwise be. First among these is the well-known and widespread objection to " spoiling the market ". Spoiling the market means selling a thing in bad times at such a price, and, therefore, in such quantities, that in subsequent good times the market is already stocked and producers cannot benefit by the then good demand. This is a state of things which can only occur in connection with goods that are, in some measure, durable. As regards these goods, it will not, indeed, pay an individual manufacturer acting in isolation to restrict his output below the short-period norm, because only a very small part of the effect of his action in bettering future prices would accrue to his personal benefit. But it will pay the manufacturers in an industry, as a group, acting by tacit or open understanding, to do this. Thus the master cotton-spinners of Lancashire in periods of booming trade compete freely with one another, but in periods of depression enter into joint agreements to shut down for so many days per week :[1] and in many industries, it would seem, there are customs and traditions against excessive price-cutting, which involve restrictions of output in much the same way that these agreements do.

§ 3. A second influence is as follows. When the demand for anything falls off, there sometimes comes into play a

---

[1] But cf. Prof. Clay's statement : " It is commonly thought that it was the pre-war practice of the industry to meet deficiencies by organised short time. I believe this view is incorrect. Before the war the industry organised short time to meet a restriction, natural or artificial, in raw material supplies, but not to meet a falling off of demand, if cotton was plentiful and cheap " (*Manchester Guardian, Commercial,* July 12, 1928, p. 45).

species of psychological friction, which renders producers unwilling to maintain their output up to the limit of the short-period norm. While recognising that, when once resources have been definitely locked up in machinery, they are done with and no longer to be reckoned as costs of new production, people are much less ready to recognise this as regards stocks of materials. Mr. J. M. Clark puts the point very clearly thus. In filling an order at any time, " What the concern expends now is materials which it now has, not the money which it paid out for them some months ago, and the sacrifice now involved in putting these materials into a given order is really represented by what the concern could realise on these materials if it did not make them up and sell them to this particular customer. This sacrifice is measured by the market price of the materials and not by the original cost. The difference between the two is a loss due to holding goods whose price has fallen, and this loss should not be charged as a cost of making these materials into finished products. A firm has been known to lose numbers of contracts because it kept on figuring its bids on the basis of the original cost of materials after the market price had fallen heavily. They were refusing to make bids low enough to secure the orders, because these orders would not otherwise cover certain costs which they had incurred in the past. But such historical considerations have nothing to do with the question : What will our costs be next week if we take these orders, *compared to what they will be next week if we do not take them* ? It is more convenient to charge materials at their original cost, but it is possible to charge them at the market price prevailing at the time they are used, and thus to separate gains and losses arising out of the producing of goods from gains and losses due to changes in the value of materials in stock." [1]

§ 4. A third influence, which tends in present conditions to prevent price cuts in bad times from being carried down to the short-period norm, and output from being adjusted correspondingly, is as follows. The quantity of any commodity (of which it is possible to postpone the use) that is

[1] *The Economics of Overhead Costs*, p. 197.

demanded at any time does not depend solely upon the (real) price ruling at that time, but also on the (real) price that is expected to rule in the future. A cut in price may actually check demand, because buyers think it portends a further cut, for which they wish to wait ; and a raising of price may actually increase demand, because buyers think that it portends a further raising of price. Naturally the fear that this sort of result may follow makes producers hesitate to come down to the level of the short-period norm in bad times. It would seem, however, that the difficulty could be overcome by more intelligent action on the part of business men. Suppose that demand conditions have altered definitely in a given way, and that, apart from the above type of reflex action, the new demand schedule is established at a definite level. Then it is true that a cut in price, which is less than sufficient to equate the new demand with the short-period supply, is liable to cause demand to contract in expectation of a further price fall presently. But a cut in price that does equate the new demand with the short-period supply is the maximum possible cut and cannot lead, so far as people understand the facts, to the expectation of a further cut later on—apart, of course, from a further independent fall from the side of demand. Therefore, if this policy of cutting down to the short-period supply price were regularly followed and became an accepted part of business practice, it would not be liable to defeat itself in the manner described. This is probably the thought behind a recent American writer's condemnation of piecemeal reductions and his advocacy of large decisive cuts : " The practice of reducing prices by degrees has been shown to defeat its own purpose, because it gives the impression that prices will go lower still. It is not until they feel that the bottom has been reached and they expect prices to rise that buyers will come into the market. Sharp cutting and then maintaining the price stimulates buying, while several smaller cuts, which total as much or more than the decided reduction, fail to attract business." [1]

[1] S. E. Thompson, in *Business Cycles and Unemployment* (by Professor W. C. Mitchell and others), p. 167.

§ 5. A fourth and final influence is convenience—the joint convenience of producers and of purchasers. In some industries this influence is very important. A system, for example, under which railway rates continually varied and could not be foreseen would be intolerable. The policy pursued by the United States Steel Corporation for many years of keeping the price of their products, particularly of steel rails, absolutely constant in spite of large fluctuations of demand—which implies, of course, restricting output in bad times more than would otherwise be necessary—is defended by Messrs. Jenks and Clark principally upon the ground that it was convenient to the railway companies ; which are, indeed, said to have themselves first suggested the system.[1]

§ 6. These several influences restricting the cuts in price, and so augmenting the cuts in production that take place in bad times, play some part in industries ordinarily called competitive, in virtue of the tacit understandings against excessive price-cutting to which reference was made above. Plainly, however, they have widest scope where monopoly prevails and where, therefore, price policy is more completely under the control of the individual producer. There is, indeed, a complication here, since it will pay a monopolist to restrict output below what I have called the short-period norm in good times as well as in bad. From the point of view of industrial fluctuations this does not matter, because, in the absence of special knowledge, it is to be expected that monopolisation as such, *i.e.* the continuous full exercise of monopolistic power, would involve equal proportionate cuts in good and bad times,[2] so that the proportionate fluctuation in output would not be different from what it would have been under simple competition. In practice, however, monopolists often

---

[1] Cf. *The Trust Problem*, pp. 168 *et seq.* The policy was maintained for fifteen years, and only broke down in 1916 after nearly two years of war in Europe.

[2] On the assumption that the curves of demand and supply are straight lines, it is easily shown that the output proper to monopoly is always one-half of that proper to simple competition. If the curves are not straight lines conditions are possible in which the statement in the text is not even approximately correct.

decide, under the influence of the considerations discussed
in the preceding sections, to exercise their monopoly power
more fully in bad times than in good, thus augmenting
industrial fluctuations in the way in which they are augmented when normally competitive concerns tacitly or
openly agree not to spoil the market in bad times. For
example, according to the 1907 report of the British
Consul-General for Frankfort, "Syndicates prevented, during
the boom, the prices from rising to the level to which
they would otherwise have risen ; again, during the beginning of the set-back, they have made for stability ".[1]
Again, according to the same authority, "The Coal Syndicate
fixes its prices for a year, from April to April ; once such
base-prices have been fixed, they are only very exceptionally liable to modifications ".[2] Wherever this policy is
adopted output must vary more extensively than it would
do if monopolistic power were either exercised continuously
or not exercised at all. Of course, if in bad times prices are
only maintained at home and are allowed to fall abroad,
the variations of output will be smaller than they would
have been had the policy of price maintenance been adopted
in the foreign as well as in the home market; but they will
not, in general, be as small as they would have been if there
had been no price maintenance in either market.

§ 7. To the critical reader, perusing this summary of the
principal influences which hinder " appropriate " cuts in
price from being made in bad times, there may well have
occurred a somewhat perplexing difficulty. So long as we
are thinking of a single industry by itself, the adjustment,
which is required to conform to short-period equilibrium
when demand contracts, is naturally spoken of as an
appropriate cut in price. When, however, we are thinking
of industry as a whole this language will not serve. Under
a monetary system so arranged that general prices are
stabilised it is impossible that all prices should be cut :
while, under an ordinary monetary system, though this is
possible, it is, so far as the mutual trading of different

[1] *Report* (Cd. 3727—167), p. 64.
[2] *Ibid.* p. 75.

industrial groups is concerned, without effect upon the real terms of interchange, and so *prima facie* barren. From this circumstance there is some temptation to infer that frictional influences of the kind we are here contemplating, though relevant to fluctuations in the activity of particular industries, are somehow not relevant to general industrial fluctuations. This is a mistake. It is, of course, impossible for A to give a better price in apples for B's oranges and at the same time for B to give a better price in oranges for A's apples. But this does not prevent A from giving *better terms* to B at the same time that B is giving *better terms* to A. Both will be giving better terms—each will be altering his supply schedule in the other's favour— if, maintaining always an exchange rate of one apple against one orange, they exchange apples and oranges against one another to the number of 1500 instead of to the number of 1000. So soon as it is understood that adjustment means adjustment of terms in this wide sense, comprehending both rate of exchange and quantity offered, the difficulty we have been considering disappears. It becomes obvious that, when generality of statement is required, all that is needed is to translate, without change of meaning, what was said in preceding sections in the language of prices into a somewhat more cumbrous phraseology.

CHAPTER XX

§ 1. APART from the special reactions due to the deceptions of an unstable standard of value, which were discussed in § 2 of Chapter XVII., changes in the conditions of labour supply do not, it would seem, enter into the determination of industrial fluctuations. The various influences examined in preceding chapters focus themselves on, and come to action through, the real demand that employers make for labour. When, however, changes occur in this real demand, the amount of the effect which they produce—the size of the industrial fluctuations to which they lead—depends, not only on their own magnitude, but also on the elasticity of the response which labour makes to them, that is to say in technical terms, upon the elasticity of the supply of labour.[1] In studying this matter it is convenient to proceed by stages, and I shall begin with the case of varying demands for labour in a single industry supposed to be isolated from all the rest.

§ 2. At the outset attention must be called to an ambiguity in the concept elasticity of the supply of labour. A change in the quantity of labour at work, consequent upon a change in demand, may come about either through a change in the number of workpeople employed, or through a change

---

[1] The method of exposition which I have employed may, perhaps, unless a caution is given, suggest the inference that the aggregate real wages bill to be expended in any year or month is determined by the expectations of business men independently of the conditions of labour supply, these conditions merely deciding whether a high rate of wage shall be paid to a smaller number or a low rate to a larger number of men. This is not so. The expectations of profit entertained by business men help to determine the demand schedule for labour; this and the supply schedule together determine the wages bill.

in the amount of work done by each workman, or through changes in both these things. This fact does not merely indicate—a point already noticed in Chapter I.—that variations in the quantity of employment are a very inadequate measure of variations in the quantity of productive power at work. It shrouds in confusion the whole notion of elasticity as regards the short-period supply schedule of labour. It shows that, given the number of workpeople trained to any industry, the form of this short-period supply schedule will be one thing if custom permits, and another if it does not permit, variations in the length of the working day or of the intensity of effort put out by a man per hour. As noted in Chapter I. § 3, among coal miners the amount of work done is apt to *fall* when piece-wages are increased, because the men prefer extra leisure to extra income. Obviously this could not happen—the supply schedule of labour could not be of this sort—in conditions such that variations in the quantity of work done came about only through variations in the number of workpeople in employment. For our present purpose, however, this difficulty must be slurred over. We suppose—an untrue supposition, but one the falsity of which does not seriously falsify our results—that the quantity of labour supplied varies only by way of variations in the number of workpeople offering themselves for work. The elasticity of the supply of labour is then measured by a (small) proportionate change in this number divided by the associated (small) proportionate change in the real rate of wages. So conceived, it is evident that elastic supply signifies a determination on the part of workpeople to keep real wage-rates rigid in the face of changing demand, even though this involves large changes in employment ; and inelastic supply a readiness to allow real wage-rates to vary considerably or, in other words, to be fairly plastic.

§ 3. With these preliminaries, let us suppose the real demand schedule for labour on the part of employers in some industry to have been raised (or lowered) in a given degree : in such wise, for example, that, whereas, with the ruling rate of real wages, employers were formerly prepared to employ A workpeople, they are now prepared at the same rate of real wages to employ $(A \pm a)$, and at other rates to employ correspondingly larger (or smaller) numbers than they would have been prepared to employ before. It is easy to see that, given the form of the demand schedule for labour in the industry and given the extent to which it swings, the consequent change in the amount of labour at work will be greater, the more elastic is the supply of labour. If the supply of labour is perfectly inelastic, *i.e.* if the wage-rate is perfectly plastic, the alteration in the quantity of labour at work will be nil: if it is perfectly elastic, the alteration will be equal to a: if the elasticity of supply is neither perfectly inelastic nor perfectly elastic, the alteration will lie between nothing and a, approximating nearer towards a the more elastic is the supply.

§ 4. To this obvious proposition there is a subtler corollary. Still assuming the form of the demand schedule for labour in our industry and the extent of its swing to be given, we have to inquire upon what the *quantity of difference* made to employment fluctuations by a given difference in the elasticity of supply—rigidity of wage-rates—depends. It is easy to show that the quantity of difference made is less, the less elastic is the demand for labour. In the limiting case, when the demand is absolutely inelastic, the quantity of difference made is nil.[1] Suppose, for example, that it took 1000 dockers to unload 50 ships and 800 to unload 40 ships, and that in one week 50 ships came in and in the next only 40. Then, even though in the second week dockers offered to work for nothing at all, this would not prevent the numbers employed from falling from 1000 to 800. When, on the other hand, the demand for labour is highly elastic,

---

[1] This statement, as also the statements of § 3, can be elucidated by simple diagrams in the special case where the curves of demand and supply can be represented by straight lines. Let the original (real) wage-rate be represented by PM and the quantity of labour employed by OM. Let the demand curve swing to the right in such wise that, if this wage were retained, the quantity of labour employed would increase from OM to ON. Let the demand and supply curves be inclined to the vertical at angles ϕ and θ. Then it is easily shown that the addition actually made to employment, *i.e.*

$$MM' = MN \frac{\tan \theta}{\tan \theta + \tan \phi}.$$

Hence we obtain the following results (assuming that θ is $\geqq 0$). (1) If $\tan \phi = o$, that is to say if the demand is absolutely inelastic, the change

a small increase in the elasticity of the supply of labour will make a large difference to the effect produced on the number of men employed by a given swing in the demand schedule.

§ 5. In passing to concrete applications of this analysis we may usefully set up for ourselves a standard, or norm, of short-period adjustment analogous to that employed in a similar connection in Chapter XIX. Such a norm is given by that degree of elasticity of labour supply (more accurately, that shape of labour supply schedule) which would prevail in a world of pure competition free from any element of convention in the determination of wage-rates. Professor J. M. Clark suggests that, just as prime costs alone, and not supplementary costs, are relevant to the short-period supply price of commodities, so also prime costs alone are relevant to the short-period supply price of labour. On this basis the short-period supply price of any nth unit of labour in an isolated industry [1] is the money (or

---

in employment which takes place is determined wholly by the extent of the demand swing, and is the same whatever is the elasticity of supply. (2) If tan $\phi > 0$, the change in employment is greater, the greater is tan θ, *i.e.* the more elastic is the supply. (3) Whatever the value of tan θ (in excess of 0), *i.e.* whatever the elasticity of supply, the change in employment is greater, the smaller is tan ϕ, *i.e.* the less elastic is the demand. (4) The difference made to the quantity of employment by a shifting of tan θ from any given value h, to any given value $(h + k)$ is less, the smaller is tan ϕ. This last proposition follows from the fact that the quantity of employment rises in the ratio

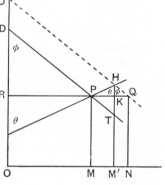

$$\frac{h^2 + hk + h \tan \phi + k \tan \phi}{h^2 + hk + h \tan \phi}.$$

Translated into language, the proposition asserts that, the less elastic is the demand for labour, the *less important it is, from the point of view of the effect on employment of changes in demand, whether the supply of labour is elastic or inelastic.* In the limit, when tan $\phi = 0$, no difference whatever is made by differences in the elasticity of supply.

[1] The assumption that the industry is isolated is, of course, necessary ; for, apart from that assumption, the elasticity of the labour supply in a particular industry will be chiefly dependent upon the opportunities open to workpeople for passing to and from employment in other industries.

commodity) representative of the extra dissatisfaction involved to a worker if that unit is produced, as against what would have been involved if it had not been produced. In normal times we must presume that this extra dissatisfaction will be roughly balanced by the normal rate of wage. Professor Clark suggests, however, that, when the demand for labour in any industry falls below the normal, the supply curve confronting the falling demand is practically a vertical straight line, because, as he argues, when a man has once been reared and trained to a particular industry, the real cost to him of working a reasonable number of hours, as against not working at all, or, still more, as against wandering the roads in search of employment, is practically nil.[1] On the assumption that changes in the supply of labour units can only come about through changes in the number of workpeople employed, this analysis appears to be valid. The standard or norm we have been seeking is a labour supply of extreme (short-period) inelasticity. There is not, it must be clearly understood, any implication that a wage policy on the part of workpeople conforming to the norm would be superior, from the standpoint of economic welfare, either to their actual policy or to a policy intermediate between that and one conforming to the norm. That issue, like the corresponding issue about " spoiling the market ", is deferred to Part II. The norm is here conceived as a basis for measurement, not as an ethical ideal.

§ 6. Supply conditions conforming closely to the norm might be expected to prevail in a community of intelligent peasant proprietors. The peasants would go on working in bad times at nearly full pressure, even though they knew that the resultant " wage " would be very much less than usual. They would not, of course, work, if, owing to deep snow, or some other cause, their efforts were certain to produce no result, because the actual process of work has in it, after a time, a certain unpleasantness. But their work would display, as against depressions of demand, a highly inelastic supply. In the bulk of modern industry,

[1] *The Economics of Overhead Costs*, pp. 20-1.

however, the status of the workpeople is fundamentally different from that of these hypothetical peasants. The difference leads to the adoption of policies embodying a much more elastic scheme of supply, or, which is the same thing in other words, a much more rigid wage system. To this end three factors are at work.

§ 7. First, peasants owning their own land receive the whole fruit, which their efforts, in conjunction with the fertility of the land, produce. Their aggregate receipts *must*, therefore, grow as their efforts increase. In wage industry, however, wage-earners receive an aggregate of wages equivalent to their marginal productivity multiplied by their numbers, the balance of the fruit of their efforts in conjunction with the equipment they use going to the owners of the equipment. If, therefore, the demand for their services is inelastic, a reduced amount of work may yield them a larger aggregate return, or, to put the same thing otherwise, a given proportionate drop in wage-rates may involve a less than proportionate expansion in the quantity of labour required. In bad times, therefore, when the demand for their services falls off, the workpeople in industries of inelastic demand may realise that a tacit or overt combination on their part to prevent their wage-rate from dropping will yield them, as a body, an absolute gain. It is true that this gain is, in general, available only to workpeople in certain industries, and in these largely at the expense of other workpeople. But that need not prevent it from acting as a real and powerful stimulus to the maintenance of rigid wage-rates. A second reason why workpeople often insist on rigidity is the fear that, if they once allow rates to fall, friction and the resistance of employers will make it extremely difficult to raise them again later on except at the cost of a strike. If they were sure that the issue really was between a wage fluctuating round a given mean and a constant wage at that mean, they might well be prepared to accept the fluctuating wage ; but, as things are, they fear that a fluctuating wage will, in fact, mean a lower wage on the whole. A third factor making for rigidity in workpeople's wage policy is the fact that the alternative to earning money in wages is, not merely not earning money in wages, but not earning money coupled with receiving money in the form of unemployment insurance, Poor Law relief, charitable help or otherwise. Naturally the knowledge that these alternatives are available lessens the extent to which men are willing to cut wage-rates in bad times.

§ 8. In any industry supposed isolated from all the others the *extent* of the difference made by rigidity in wage-rates to the amplitude of the employment fluctuations that result from given fluctuations in demand depends, as was shown in § 4, on whether the demand which fluctuates is (from a short-period point of view) elastic or inelastic. If this is highly inelastic, very much less difference will be made than if it is elastic ; because there will be much less scope for workpeople to retain employment, when demand falls off, by offering to accept a lower rate of wage. Now it is certain that in many occupations the demand for labour, from the point of view of a short period, is highly inelastic ; for in many of them labour cost is a very small part of total cost of production. It seems to follow that the unemployment consequent upon a depression of demand would only be very slightly smaller than it actually is if wage-earners were ready to adopt a plastic instead of a rigid system of wage-rates : and for this reason, more or less vaguely conceived, many popular writers hold that the hope of bettering employment in bad times in any substantial degree by wage reductions is illusory.

§ 9. Against this conclusion a retort, *prima facie* of great force, has lately been made by reference to certain British statistics. Since the end of the war there has been a strong *positive* correlation between rates of real wages and unemployment. Professor Rueff has calculated quarterly indices of real wages by dividing Bowley's index-number of money wages by the Board of Trade index-number of wholesale prices (each being put at 100 for 1913), and has compared the resultant figures with the Trade Union percentage of unemployment per quarter over the period

1919–25.[1] As the *Statist* writes : " It will be seen from the graphic representation of these data that an extraordinarily close correspondence between changes in the level of real wages and changes in the unemployment series exists. The principal increase in percentages of unemployed took place during the second half of 1920 and the first half of 1921. This was the period when wages, expressed in terms, not of sterling, but of purchasing power, were increasing most rapidly. The subsequent trends of the two curves show almost complete similarity. When prices fall more rapidly than money wages [*i.e.* when real wages rise], unemployment increases. When money wages tend to fall relatively to price movements [*i.e.* when real wages fall], the unemployment curve shows a corresponding fall." [2] The coefficient of correlation between the two series has been computed by Sir Josiah Stamp at the extremely high figure +·95 (complete direct correlation being statistically known as +1·0).[3] To calculate real wage-rates, as Professor Rueff has done, by dividing the index of money wages by the index of wholesale prices, is, indeed, an unsatisfactory proceeding. I have, therefore, obtained a real wage index-number by the more usual method of dividing the index of money wages by the Board of Trade *cost of living* index, and, besides continuing his tables up to the end of 1926, have added a third line to his chart embodying the resultant table.[4] The consilience of this new curve with the unemployment curve is, it will be seen, practically as close as that of Professor Rueff's original curve, so that no reason emerges for quarrelling with his method of presenting the facts. From the data thus brought together, one is strongly tempted to infer that the variations which have occurred in the unemployment percentage are directly caused by the congruent variations in the average rate of real wages—which implies, of course, that variations in rates of real wages are competent to affect the level of employment in a very important degree. This inference is not, however, really warranted. It is a matter of common

[1] *Revue politique et parlementaire*, December 1925, pp. 425 *et seq.*
[2] *Statist*, January 9, 1926, pp. 50-1.
[3] *Financial Times*, March 15, 1926, p. v.
[4] For the statistics on which the chart is based, cf. Table XVIII.

knowledge that the great slump of 1920–1 had its origin in
causes lying altogether outside wages, and was intimately
associated, whether, as some hold, as the direct effect of a
deliberate policy of monetary deflation, or, as others contend,
as a joint consequence of the bursting of a gigantic bubble of
unwarranted optimism, with a heavy fall in prices. In view
of the general tendency for rates of money wages to lag

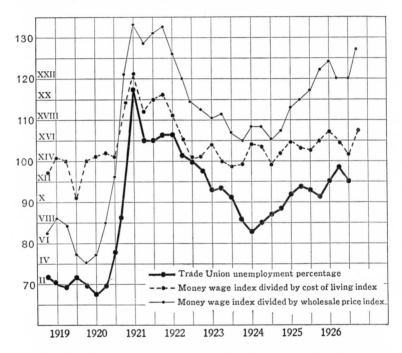

behind price movements, some rise in rates of real wages
could hardly fail, in such conditions, to come about. The
rise was predominantly an effect, just as the growth in unemployment was an effect, of the general causes lying behind
the slump. The second joint upward movement of unemployment and of rates of real wages, which began in 1924, was
also associated with a fall in prices. It may, therefore, fairly
be argued that, with these price movements and the causes
behind them in operation, the growth in unemployment
would on both occasions have been approximately as large

as it was, even though the rate of real wages had been prevented from rising in any degree. Though this contention is not necessarily correct, it is in no way inconsistent with the statistical facts, and cannot be refuted by reference to them. These correlations, therefore, interesting and suggestive as they are, must not be treated as an inductive disproof of the opinion referred to at the end of the preceding section. The case for scepticism is further strengthened by a study of the chart facing p. 238, which displays, for the period before the war, a distinct *negative* correlation between rates of real wages and quantities of unemployment.

§ 10. To meet the argument of § 8 we are, therefore, driven back, as so often happens in economic discussion, from facts to general analysis. In that argument, we now observe, the case is not stated quite fairly. In an industry where the demand for labour is highly inelastic because labour cost is a small part of the whole there must be employed a large volume of materials and machinery, into the making of which other labour enters. The aggregate effect on the quantity of labour demanded of a reduction of, say, 10 per cent in the wage-rate in one industry is, therefore, larger than the effect on the quantity of labour demanded in that industry : for account must also be taken of the effect on the quantity of labour demanded in the complementary industries. This point—and it is an important one—may be put thus. Suppose that ten groups of workpeople in ten occupations contribute in about equal proportions towards making some finished commodity. Suppose, further, that the elasticity of demand for the finished commodity is unity, *i.e.* such that a 1 per cent fall in price involves a 1 per cent increase in quantity demanded. Then a 10 per cent cut in the wages of one of the occupations will involve a 1 per cent fall in the price of the commodity and also a 1 per cent increase in the quantity of labour demanded in that occupation. But it will also involve a 1 per cent increase in the quantity of labour demanded in each of the other occupations. *Hence, although, if a single group accepts a 10 per cent wage-cut, employment in that group will expand only 1 per cent, should all the groups accept a 10 per cent wage-cut employment in all the groups collectively will expand 10 per cent.* Thus, if the workers in the magneto-making industry accepted a system of highly plastic wage-rates, *and nobody else did so*, the fluctuations taking place in their occupation would not be appreciably reduced, because a fall in the price of magnetos would involve so small a proportionate fall in the price of motor-cars that the stimulus to further sales of these would be negligible. But, if *all trades* relevant to the making of motor-cars accepted a plastic system, the fluctuations taking place in all of them collectively would be diminished in a much larger degree. So far I have been considering complementary industries. As regards industries which are not joint contributors to a common work, if the mutual demand for one another's products has an elasticity greater than unity, a reduction of costs in one will stimulate output in the others : so that here again the acceptance of a plastic wage system by ten of them will have a larger proportionate effect in promoting stability in these ten than a like acceptance by one of them would have in promoting stability in it.[1] Hence, we conclude, rigidity in the general system of wage-rates in any community has a more important bearing on industrial fluctuations than popular arguments, focussed on the circumstances of particular industries, suggest.

§ 11. It remains to inquire how far our results are affected when the assumption that different industries are isolated from one another is withdrawn. If labour can move with perfect freedom, and if there is one large occupation (*e.g.* agriculture) in which wage-rates are completely plastic, all the workpeople ejected in times of depression from other occupations may find a refuge there ; and, consequently, there need never be any unemployment at all. In these conditions the presence or absence of rigid wage-rates in the other occupations makes no difference to industrial fluctuations (measured by the employment index) as a whole. This imaginary picture is, of course, far from

---

[1] If the demands of the various industries have elasticities less than unity, this last argument is, of course, reversed. It is, therefore, important to observe that, in Mr. Robertson's view, in times of acute slump the public demand for (*a*) railway transport and (*b*) contractive goods is highly inelastic. (*Banking Policy and the Price Level*, p. 17.)

the facts of life. It suggests, however, a conclusion of practical significance. When labour is mobile, a rigid wage policy confined to some only of the industries in a community has a smaller effect in promoting industrial fluctuations than it would do if labour were not mobile : the difference being greater the narrower is the range over which rigidity prevails. Apart from this, what has been said about a community whose industries are isolated holds good also of one in which there is complete mobility, and *a fortiori* of one in which, as in the actual world, labour is in some degree, but not perfectly, mobile between different occupations.

CHAPTER XXI

THE PART PLAYED BY IMPERFECT MOBILITY OF LABOUR

§ 1. It was shown in Chapter I. that, when industry as a whole is expanding or contracting, the main body of individual industries are, as a rule, moving in the same direction. It is not, of course, suggested that there are no exceptions to this tendency. Such a state of things is *a priori* very improbable, and it certainly cannot be demonstrated by statistics. Indeed, as was pointed out in Chapter IX., there is reason to believe that depressions are sometimes started by contractions in *the rate of expansion* of consumption trades bringing about contractions in the *amount* of activity in instrumental trades. If this is so, there must be a period during which the demand for labour is still increasing in consumption trades but declining in instrumental trades. When, however, the upward and downward swings of demand manifested in the normal industrial cycle are looked at as wholes, discrepancies of this kind do not bulk very large. We may safely say that the fluctuations of demand in different industries are in very great measure consilient in direction. They are not, however, consilient in degree. The proportionate swings in demand in instrumental industries are very much larger than those in consumption industries, and there are also probably large divergencies within each of these two groups. In the light of these considerations it is necessary to inquire in what way imperfections in mobility influence industrial fluctuations.

§ 2. It is obvious that, if wage-rates were perfectly plastic—this implies the possibility of negative rates—there would be no unemployment in any event, and, therefore, it would not matter whether labour were absolutely mobile or absolutely immobile.   Hence, if our problem is to have a solution, we must make some assumption in regard to wage policy.   Let us suppose, as the evidence suggests, that a considerable degree of rigidity prevails.   In these circumstances swings of aggregate demand below its mean level may be associated with a little more unemployment if labour is not, than if it is, perfectly mobile.   For, in so far as demand is expanding in some industries, there may be vacancies there, which, with perfectly mobile labour, might be filled from among men now idle.   It is also *possible* that, when demand falls all round, the quantity of labour employed in industries in which it falls least may be *increased*, thus again providing jobs for idle men.   Professor Cassel has suggested that this happens to some extent in Sweden as between industry and agriculture.   " The capital-producing industries, which attract a good deal of outside labour during high conjunctures, reject it again during depressions, and so cause unemployment.   It is not necessary that these expelled workers become entirely without occupation, as it is conceivable that to some extent they will go back to agriculture, from which they came, and resume their activities there for a time.   In Sweden this is a fairly common practice.   The capital-producing industries may, to a great extent, take agricultural workers or members of peasant families direct from their occupation on the land.   This applies particularly to the timber industry, but also, in large measure, to the building trade.   When these workers can find no further employment in industry, they often go back to their former places." [1]   Plainly, however, in order that this kind of thing may happen, wage policy in the occupations where demand falls least must be considerably plastic—less rigid than it is likely in fact to be among the general body of consumption industries in such a country as England.   Hence we may conclude with some confidence that, in this country at all events, imperfections of mobility do not make the downward swings of employment, for which downward swings in aggregate demand are responsible,

---

[1] *The Theory of Social Economy*, vol. ii. p. 547

significantly different from what they would have been had
mobility been perfect.

§ 3. With swings of demand above the mean level the
case is different. Since general upward swings embrace
large proportionate rises in some occupations and small
proportionate rises in others, it may easily happen that in
occupations of the former class a good deal of labour is sought
for in excess of what can be provided by the men normally
attached to them; while a fair number of men attached to occupations of the latter class are not yet called up for employment
there. If this happens, imperfections of mobility may be
expected to make the upward swings of employment due to
upward swings in aggregate demand smaller in an appreciable
degree than they would have been with perfect mobility.

§ 4. Combining together the result of the two preceding
paragraphs, we conclude that imperfections of mobility in
times of depression leave the part of unemployment which
is associated with general downward swings of demand
practically untouched, but in times of boom render unemployment distinctly larger than it would have been
with perfect mobility. It follows that imperfections of
mobility lessen the difference between the unemployment
figures of bad times and of good times ; which means that
they *diminish* the amplitude of industrial fluctuations.
Prima facie this result seems paradoxical. But it only does
so because we are accustomed in a loose way to think that
reductions in the amplitude of fluctuations *must* be socially
advantageous, whereas what happens here is plainly a social
evil. The paradox is cleared up as soon as we realise the
precise nature of what is taking place : that the range of
difference between good times and bad is only narrowed
because the good times are made less good. The quantities
involved, however, are probably small, and the whole
matter is of academic rather than of practical interest.[1]

[1] It will, of course, be understood that this statement by no means
applies to the joint effect of rigid wage-rates, imperfect mobility and
variable *relative* demand in calling into existence a considerable *constant*
volume of unemployment. This matter was referred to in Chapter IV. § 12,
footnote ; but, since in this book we are concerned with fluctuations of
employment, it does not form part of our study.

CHAPTER XXII

THE COMPARATIVE IMPORTANCE OF VARIOUS FACTORS IN DETERMINING THE AMPLITUDE OF INDUSTRIAL FLUCTUATIONS

§ 1. In any serious study of industrial fluctuations it is plainly necessary to attempt some quantitative estimate of the comparative importance of the several factors that promote them. The term comparative importance is, however, ambiguous in this connection. For it is conceivable that, while factors (A, B, C . . .) are dominant in determining the amplitude of fluctuations in the sense of the difference in magnitude between maximum and minimum activity, another set of factors (X, Y, Z . . .) may be dominant in determining the time intervals between successive maxima and minima. In this chapter I shall consider comparative importance in the first of these two senses, plainly the more significant from the standpoint of social welfare, leaving over the other sense to Chapter XXIII.

§ 2. From our discussion hitherto the following broad results may be brought together. There are to be distinguished first certain initiating causes of industrial fluctuations capable of coming into play, as it were, spontaneously. The chief of these were set out in Chapter IV. as (1) harvest variations ; (2) inventions ; (3) industrial disputes ; (4) changes in fashion ; (5) wars ; and (6), partly overlapping some of the others, changes in foreign demand and foreign openings for investment. There are, secondly, errors of optimism and errors of pessimism, studied in Chapters VI. and VII. There are, thirdly, autonomous monetary movements, which constituted the subject-matter of Chapter VIII. These several causes, or originating impulses, of disturbance come into play in a world of complex organisation, the structure of which conditions the working of these impulses and, in great part, determines their effects. The most significant items in this organisation from the present point of view are the monetary and banking arrangements of the country, the policy of industrialists as regards spoiling the market, and the policy of workpeople as regards rigidity of wage-rates. The various factors involved are interdependent, so that the effect due to one element cannot be gauged absolutely, but only in reference to some given state of the other elements. For example, given such and such a degree of plasticity in wage policy, such and such changes in business sentiment will bring about a contraction of, say, 4 per cent in industrial activity. But, if wage policy was such that workpeople preferred any—even a negative—wage to unemployment, these changes would not bring about any contraction at all. Similarly, given certain variations in business sentiment, such and such a modification of wage policy will lead to such and such a modification in the movements of employment; but, if there are no variations in business sentiment (or other like factor), modifications of wage policy will produce no effect. Nor is this all. Several of the impulses, or causes, which are liable to come into play have the power of generating other impulses. Thus prosperity, whether due to a good harvest, to an invention, or to anything else, is liable to promote an error of optimism; and adversity an error of pessimism. This point was brought out very clearly by Jevons when he wrote : " Periodic collapses are really mental in their nature, depending upon variations of despondency, hopefulness, excitement, disappointment and panic. But it seems to be very probable that the moods of the commercial mind, while constituting the principal part of the phenomena, may be controlled by outward events, especially the condition of the harvests." [1] Again, with the monetary system as it is, the desire to exploit an invention leads to an expansion of bank credits and so to a rise of prices, and so sets the monetary factor to work. Yet, again,

---

[1] *Investigations in Currency and Finance*, p. 184.

an error of optimism, whether initiated by a good harvest or otherwise, starts processes that raise general prices, and an error of pessimism processes that lower them, thus invoking that factor from another side. Yet again, a rise of prices, however brought about, by creating some actual and some counterfeit prosperity for business men, is liable to promote an error of optimism, and a fall of prices an error of pessimism, and this mutual stimulation of errors and price movements may continue in a vicious spiral, until it is checked by some interference from outside. These considerations make it plain that the effects of the several groups of factors that we have distinguished in augmenting the amplitude of general industrial fluctuations cannot be treated as simply additive. The sum of their effects taken singly, each on the assumption that other things are unchanged, will, when added up, work out at something much bigger than the joint effect of all of them taken together.

§ 3. The practical importance of this analysis is very great. We see from it that a proof to the effect that the removal of factor A would reduce the amplitude of industrial fluctuations by three-quarters is not a proof that the removal of the other factors would not reduce it by more than one-quarter. It may be true both that, if the general price level were stabilised, industrial fluctuations would be so nearly eliminated that little advantage would be got from making harvests steadier or from governmental manipulation of stocks designed to mitigate the effects of variable harvests, and also that, if the general price level were not stabilised, large advantage would be got from those policies. Again, it may be true both that, if somehow errors of optimism and pessimism could be rendered impossible, little advantage would result from stabilising prices, and also that, while these errors are liable to occur, large advantage would follow from that policy. From these considerations there may result a great drama of reconciliation. Controversialists who have imagined themselves to hold incompatible opinions are not necessarily in conflict at all! One school of thought maintains that inequality in the harvest yields of different years is the dominant factor in industrial fluctuations ; another that errors of forecast among business men are dominant ; another that instability in the level of general prices is dominant.　Each of these schools holds that, if it is right, the other two must be wrong.　Our analysis shows that this is not so.　Each of the above factors may be dominant in the only sense that is intelligible, in the sense, namely, that if it, and therefore all the effects causally due to it, were removed, industrial fluctuations, as they exist to-day, would almost entirely disappear.　Of course, our analysis does not *compel* the members of these divergent schools to agree.　It is open to a member of the harvest school to hold that the stabilisation of prices by itself would accomplish nothing, and to a member of the stable money school to retort in kind.　But none of these schools is driven by the logic of its own opinions to deny the opinions of either of the others.　Harmony becomes at least *possible*, and a great deal of barren argument goes by the board.

§ 4.　Recognising then that a number of different factors may all be dominating determinants of the amplitude of industrial fluctuations, let us begin by considering the claim of the monetary factor ; which, as we have seen, plays a double rôle, acting sometimes as an initiating impulse to disturbance and sometimes as a condition upon which other initiating impulses impinge.　It is held by the upholders of this claim that, if other things remained the same, but currency arrangements were so modified as to keep the level of general prices substantially constant, the wave movements that now take place in industrial activity would altogether cease.　The condition that other things remain the same must not, of course, be taken to exclude changes which are results of changes in the level of general prices.　Thus the stabilisation of this level is understood to involve the elimination of such part of errors of optimism and pessimism as is induced by changes in this level.　It is further understood to include the prevention both of those fluctuations in the price level which arise from non-monetary causes (as studied in Chapters XII.-XVII.) and also of those which arise out of monetary causes, as discussed in Chapter VIII.　It is of stabilisation so conceived that Mr. Hawtrey is thinking when he asserts that the trade cycle is " purely a monetary phenomenon ".[1]   He and writers who agree with him do not merely mean that the monetary instrument could conceivably be so manipulated as to cancel out tendencies towards fluctuations set up otherwise than through its agency ; that, for instance, when a good harvest or an error of optimism is making for expansion, expansion could be prevented by so doctoring the currency as to make general prices fall.   They mean that, if the monetary (and banking) machine were remodelled in such a way that good harvests, errors of optimism and influxes of gold were prevented from causing prices to rise, and reverse movements were prevented from causing them to fall, the trade cycle would be abolished without the need of any further action.   Let us consider this claim.

§ 5. The more innocent among those who advocate it stress the undoubted fact that business men, in framing and carrying through their policies, think in terms of money, and regulate their conduct by reference to money profit, money loss and money prices.   Starting with the thesis that industrial fluctuations are the result of oscillations, partly warranted by the facts and partly not warranted, between optimism and pessimism among business men, they ask : What, after all, do business optimism and business pessimism essentially mean ?   Business optimism means an expectation that prices are going to rise or go on rising : business pessimism an expectation that they are going to fall or go on falling.   To stabilise prices, therefore, would be to destroy business optimism and business pessimism, and, hence, to abolish industrial fluctuations.   This line of reasoning will not stand analysis.   It depends on a confusion between *all* prices and *each* price.   Though, no doubt, in a period of optimism the typical business man will often expect that the general level of prices is going to rise, he will also often expect that the price of his own particular commodity is going to rise *relatively* to other commodities. A knowledge that the *general level of prices* must remain

. [1] *Economic Journal*, 1922, p. 298.

stable—and this is the utmost that any monetary or banking arrangements could secure—will not prevent him from entertaining this expectation. General prices may be absolutely stable, and everybody may be aware of the fact, and yet there is nothing to prevent A and B on occasions each thinking that the other is going to offer better real terms for his goods than he is in fact going to offer. A may think that the price of *his* stuff is going to rise, though he knows that prices in general cannot rise, and B may think the same thing about *his* stuff; and both of them, in consequence, may expand their output. The above argument, therefore, falls to the ground.

§ 6. The claim that the stabilisation of general prices would abolish the trade cycle is, however, sometimes defended by means of a more plausible line of reasoning. Whatever changes, it is said, whether warranted by facts or not so warranted, occur in the thoughts and intentions of business men, it is impossible for them, in a world that enjoys an organised currency and banking system, to produce such changes in conduct as will lead to the development of trade cycles, unless general prices are free to vary. In other words, these changes of thought and intention can only produce effects by way of the banking and currency mechanism ; and to restrain this mechanism from movement is to render them abortive, just as to chain up a man's limbs would render his desire for physical movement abortive. The argument runs thus. When business men, with or without warrant, become more optimistic than usual, they turn over their balances with exceptional rapidity and also borrow new balances from the bankers ; they employ their purchasing power to buy from stores materials and things that workpeople are accustomed to consume ; they use the materials in their industries and pay out the other articles as wages to set more workpeople to work in these industries. When they become more pessimistic than usual, they act in the opposite sense. But to stabilise prices implies preventing them from doing these things, and, therefore, preventing them from taking practical action in accordance with their changed sentiments. In examining this argument we need to recall the analysis of Chapter XII. It was there pointed out that business men are able to swell the volume of new capital available for them in any (say) month when their expectations of profit improve, not only by turning over their balances more quickly and by borrowing from the banks but also by borrowing direct from the public by the issue of new securities. This latter process, since it merely alters the distribution of the money stream without changing its volume, does not tend to push up prices, and, therefore, could not be obstructed by price stabilisation. It was also pointed out in Chapter XIII. that rentiers and others have it in their power to augment their contribution towards the aforesaid volume through the mediation of banks, even when they have no private currency holdings and no bank debts. If, under the stimulus of high interest rates, they refrain from spending their balances, leaving them instead on deposit account, they make it possible for the banks to create a corresponding quantity of new credit in favour of business men without causing the price level to rise. Here, again, it is evident that a policy of price stabilisation could exercise no restrictive influence. This argument, therefore, like the preceding one, appears to be invalid.

§ 7. The third argument to be considered is statistical in character. In its simplest form it is based upon a direct comparison of movements in industrial activity and movements in the general level of prices, as illustrated in the chart facing p. 134. Attention has already been called to the close general parallelism between the two curves shown in that chart. So soon, however, as the chart is examined in detail, it becomes apparent that we cannot argue from it that the elimination of price movements would estop industrial fluctuations. For, on the whole, the turns in the unemployment curve *precede* the corresponding turns in the price curve. Unemployment turned down and prices up together in the same year in both curves in 1852, 1858, 1879, 1886 and 1908 : in 1868, 1893 and 1903 employment began to improve before prices began to rise. In 1864 prices turned downward before employment fell off, and the same thing happened in 1881 : but in 1853, 1856,

1872, 1890, 1899 and 1906 employment began to worsen while prices were still rising. The normal course of events appears to be as follows. When depression is passing into revival the employment index usually begins to mount *some months before* the wholesale price index turns. Then, during the earlier stages of revival, after the price index has turned, the employment index improves at a fairly rapid rate as compared with the price index : but in the later stages, practically all employable persons having already found work, the employment index scarcely improves at all, while the price index continues to mount steeply. In general terms we may say, of the upward half of the cycle, that at first there is no price rise at all, then a price rise which becomes greater in proportion to the rise of employment, until employment stops rising altogether while prices continue to mount because employers (whom bankers finance) bid against one another to secure labour and materials, the supply of which it is no longer possible to increase.[1] When revival culminates and the turn down to depression takes place, a fall in employment in like manner usually *precedes* the fall in prices. For example, in the post-war crisis in the United Kingdom unemployment began to increase in May 1920, wholesale prices (Board of Trade) turned down in June 1920, and retail prices (Ministry of Labour) in November 1920.[2]

[1] Thus Mr. Bellerby, *Control of Credit*, pp. 77-9, writes : " From an examination of the periods preceding the years 1891, 1900, 1907 and 1913, it will be seen that employment rose to within 1½ per cent of the maximum for the period about eighteen months or two years before the peak of the boom—that is to say, before prices began to show a marked rise. Thus in 1889 employment had reached 97·9 per cent, this being the maximum yearly average for the period, in spite of the boom continuing until 1891. In 1898 employment stood at 97·2 per cent, the maximum for the period being 98·0 and the boom continuing until 1900. In 1905 the employment percentage was 95·0, the maximum being 96·4 in 1906, and the rise of prices continuing until 1907. The percentage reached in 1911 was 97·0, the maximum being 97·9 in the culminating year of the boom, 1913. It would seem to follow that the period of most rapidly rising prices can only add, at the most, about 1½ per cent to the forces of labour employed, and in some cases has even shown a fall in employment."

[2] For the delay in the price movement Professor Mitchell offers the following explanation : " The effect of a depression in reducing the costs of doing business has already been pointed out as among the factors which favour resumption of activity. But it does not favour an advance in the

§ 8. There is, however, available a much more effective form of statistical argument. The accompanying chart brings the unemployment figures (inverted) into relation in each year with the quotient obtained by dividing the Sauerbeck index for that year by the corresponding index for the preceding year, *i.e.* with an index of the *rate* at which general prices are rising or falling. The correspondence between these two curves is very close. There is no tendency for the turns in the employment curve to precede the turns in the price curve. Nor is there anything mysterious about the relation thus displayed. In view of the analysis of Chapter XIII. it is to be expected ; for variations in the annual amount of new credit creations, which we there saw to be closely associated with variations in industrial activity, are direct determinants, not of contemporaneous positions of the price level, but of contemporaneous changes of position. The suggestion that a causal influence may be at work from the side of changes in rates of price change is emphasised by a study of the next chart. In this there are set out three-year moving averages of the annual additions made to the aggregate bank credit outstanding and, alongside of these, a curve, also fashioned out of three-year moving averages, to represent annual increases in the aggregate wages bill. This chart is constructed from figures published by Dr. Bowley down to 1901 and continued from that date on the basis of his wage index

---

price level. On the contrary, it means that profits can be made without restoring prices to the level which prevailed before the depression set in. Secondly, at this stage of the business cycle business enterprises are anxiously soliciting orders. The advantage in strategic position as bargainers is on the side of the buyers—much more so than later when factories, railways and shops already have all the business they can readily handle. Third, a prolonged period of depression often wracks to pieces certain combinations to maintain prices, and leaves the field over which free competition rules wider at its close than at its beginning. Fourth, every increase in the volume of business obtained in the early stages of revival makes a more than proportionate addition to profits, even though it be taken at unchanged prices. For, until the existing equipment of standard efficiency for handling business is already busy, new orders can be filled without an increase in prime costs and at a reduction of supplementary costs per unit of output. These conditions explain why prices often fail to rise promptly at the beginning of the trade revival, and why in other cases the initial rise is slow." (*Business Cycles*, p. 458.)

numbers with allowances for changes in the occupied population. I have assumed, in the light of the 1900 and 1910 census figures, that this population increased in each year to the extent of $\frac{1}{100}$th part of what it was in 1900. It will be seen that, apart from a peculiar movement in the wages-bill curve about 1899, due, no doubt, to the South African war, the two curves moved throughout in intimate connection, the credit index curve lagging a little behind the other in the earlier years. The agreement of direction is, of course, to be expected, and tells us nothing more than we already knew from the chart facing p. 144. But, besides the agreement of direction, this chart also displays a very remarkable agreement in the scale of the associated movements. The aggregate wages bill seems to vary in terms of money by an amount very nearly equivalent to the amount by which the volume of bank credit varies. In other words, the fluctuations which take place over a trade cycle in the aggregate wages bill seem to be provided, not merely in some measure but *in the main*, out of fluctuations in the amount of credit created for industrialists by the banks.

§ 9. The above results agree in a striking manner with certain conclusions which Professor Irving Fisher has recently published for the United States. Over the period 1915–23, he found a correlation, as he puts it, of 77 per cent between changes in the *rate of change* in wholesale prices and changes in the *amount* of basic materials produced *seven months later*.[1] Carrying his investigations further, he has more recently found that, if we assume the lag of production behind price change to be, not a single uniform lag for all sorts of commodities, but a lag distributed in accordance with the principles of probability over different lengths of time for different things, there is a correlation of 94 per cent, the mean lag being reckoned at $9\frac{1}{2}$ months. To test these results he has examined also the periods 1877–99 and 1903–15, and has found in them also a correlation, which, though not so high as that of the

---

[1] *The Business Cycle largely a Dance of the Dollar.* (Journal of the American Statistical Association, December 1923.)

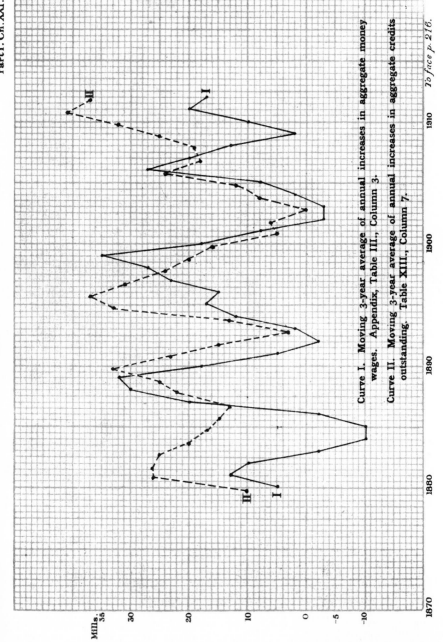

Curve I. Moving 3-year average of annual increases in aggregate money
wages. Appendix, Table III, Column 3.

Curve II. Moving 3-year average of annual increases in aggregate credits
outstanding. Table XIII, Column 7.

To face p. 216.

war period—when the price factor was obviously of exceptional importance—is still very high.[1] The presence of a time lag in these correlations, to which there is nothing analogous in my chart, may, perhaps, be explained by the fact that Professor Fisher is relating rate of price change to quantity of production, while I am relating it to quantity of employment: for it is to be expected that changes in production will lag somewhat behind changes in employment. When account is taken of this circumstance, my results and Professor Fisher's are in close accord.

§ 10. Evidently these assembled facts give a much better ground for holding that the trade cycle is " largely a dance of the dollar ", capable of being estopped by ending that dance, than the facts cited in § 7: for here there is no longer the objection that the alleged causal factor is subsequent to the alleged effect. Indeed, Professor Fisher's contention, with its imposing mathematical façade, is, at first sight, exceedingly persuasive. It is necessary, however, to bear in mind the fundamental distinction between *causes* and *channels* along which causes act. In modern mountaineering there is an almost perfect correlation between the possession of an ice-axe and the ascent of snow mountains. Practically nobody ever ascends a snow mountain who has not previously bought an axe. The previous purchase of an axe is thus intimately associated with the ascent of snow mountains ; but this does not prove that, if the purchase of ice-axes was prohibited by law, snow mountains would no longer be ascended. It does not even prove that the existence of ice-axes substantially increases the number of ascents that are made. Our correlations, in short, throw no light on the question how far people use ice-axes as implements in doing something that they would have done anyhow, and how far they are induced by their existence to do something which otherwise they would not have done. This question still remains open in spite of Professor Fisher's mathematics, and can only be answered by judgement and guess-work. The point may be pushed home by an historical parallel. In the

---

[1] *Our Unstable Dollar and the so-called Business Cycle.* (Journal of the American Statistical Association, January 1925.)

earlier part of the nineteenth century there was an intimate statistical association between the note issues of country banks and industrial fluctuations. Anybody arguing along Professor Fisher's lines would have been tempted to claim that the fixation of these issues would put an end to the fluctuations. History proves that he would have been wrong. The issues, though, no doubt, in part causes, were in the main only channels of action. In like manner, it may well be that, while expanded confidence, with existing monetary and banking arrangements, acts on industry through credit creations and price movements, if that channel were shut off, it would simply seek some other channel. The statistical facts are in no way inconsistent with this supposition.

§ 11. The thesis that the monetary factor is dominant in determining industrial fluctuations, in the sense that, if, through the control of bank credits, general prices were stabilised, these fluctuations would be almost wholly eliminated, is thus not proved. Can it be *disproved* ? It is sometimes imagined that the correlation established in Chapter IV. between changes in crop yields and industrial fluctuations disproves it, for this correlation demonstrates—or rather makes probable—the existence of a transitive causal nexus of considerable strength from crops to industry. Since, however, as we have seen, the influence of crops may act indirectly through psychology by modifying business confidence, which in turns modifies prices, and so on cumulatively, the correlation is not incompatible with the thesis that, if price movements were eliminated, industry would be rendered practically stable even though crop changes continued. This supposed disproof of the monetary school's contention, therefore, breaks down. Nor, in my opinion, is there available any other argument capable of disproving that thesis in a strict mathematical sense. There is available, however, a line of reasoning by which the mind can be turned very strongly towards a denial of it. Consider the great war of 1914–18. The enormous industrial expansion with which that war was associated was, in fact, financed in the United Kingdom, and indeed, in all other countries, in a manner that involved a great rise in prices. But will anybody seriously contend that, if we had insisted on so controlling bank credit and currency as to keep the average level of general prices steady, there would have been no industrial expansion ? Plainly, the fundamental fact was the enormously enhanced desire of the community for soldiers' services and munitions of all kinds, a desire to satisfy which we were ready to pay heavily alike in work and in promises. With prices stabilised, this desire could still have achieved a large part of its objective through the machinery of taxes and loans raised from the public (not bankers) at very high interest. No doubt, it would not have been politically feasible to bring about by these means alone an industrial expansion so large as was actually brought about. But to suggest that no industrial expansion whatever, or only a trifling expansion, would have occurred, is to propound a paradox from which common sense recoils. It may be answered that the advocates of the thesis I am discussing are not contemplating wars, which are exceptional events, but only the normal process of what is called the trade cycle. This, of course, is true. But, after all, the enormous enhancement of desire for munitions in a war is different only in degree—it is not different in kind—from the enhancement of desire for labour and the materials of construction, which is experienced by the business world when favourable harvests or an epoch-making invention offer good prospects of profit from the use of these things. It is not possible to obtain any precise quantitative result from this type of analysis. In the last resort we have no guide but common-sense judgement and more or less well-informed guess-work. In the light of the preceding discussion, negative and positive, my personal judgement is adverse to the full claims of the monetary school. I hold that, if a policy of price stabilisation were successfully carried through, the amplitude of industrial fluctuations would be substantially reduced—it might be cut down to half of what it is at present—but considerable fluctuations would still remain.

§ 12. The psychological school attributes a dominant influence, in the sense defined above, in causing industrial fluctuations to errors, now on the side of undue optimism, now on that of undue pessimism in the forecasts of business men, and maintains that, if these errors and their *sequelae* (including, of course, the price movements to which they give rise) could somehow be eliminated, industrial fluctuations would practically disappear. The logical position of this thesis is very similar to that of the thesis just discussed. We know that harvest variations and so on produce their effects in part by inducing errors, just as they produce them in part by inducing price movements : and, further, that errors and price movements mutually generate one another. We know also that, if a large and widespread error of forecast took place, and everything else, other than things directly caused by it, remained the same, a substantial industrial fluctuation would result. Here again our estimate of quantities must rest on judgement and guess-work. I suggest that the importance of the error factor is of the same order as that of the monetary factor : that, if all errors were eliminated, the normal range of industrial fluctuations would be reduced substantially, perhaps to the extent of one-half ; but that considerable industrial fluctuations would still remain.

§ 13. The harvest school bases its case upon the correlation displayed in Chapter IV. between changes in the yield of crops per acre and industrial fluctuations. On the strength of this it claims that, if crop yields were somehow rendered steady, industrial fluctuations would, not indeed entirely but in very large measure, disappear. It would be a mistake to dismiss this argument from any general suspicion of arguments from correlation induced by our previous criticism of such arguments. For this argument is of stronger texture than the others. As has already been indicated, if there is any causal nexus between yield of crops per acre and industrial activity, it cannot well be other than a transitive nexus operated from the side of crops. For it seems very unlikely that the correlated changes are both effects of a common cause, and more unlikely still that the changes in yield per acre are an effect of changes in industrial activity. Nor is it to the point

here, as it was in § 2, to observe that harvest changes
may produce a main part of their effect on industry,
not directly, but indirectly through business psychology.
This does not matter : for, if the initiating changes
were removed, their indirect, as well as their direct, effects
would be removed with them.   I conclude, therefore, with
the harvest school, that crop changes are an *important*
factor in determining industrial fluctuations.   But the
correlations on which this school rely are very far from
perfect correlations.   They cannot, therefore, rightly claim
that these changes are a *dominant* factor in the sense in
which I am using that word.

§ 14. In seeking to gauge *how* important a part they
play we are confronted with considerations, which, if they
do not enable us to answer our question directly, at least
help us to compare the part played by harvest variations
now and in the past.

First, it is obvious that the proportionate effect produced
on industrial activity by a given proportionate change in
harvest yield will be smaller, the smaller is the part of the
product of industry that is normally exchanged against
agricultural commodities.   Now, as man's powers increase
—and particularly as agricultural machinery and improved
methods of tillage are developed—the proportion of them
that he needs to expend in obtaining Nature's raw products
tends steadily to diminish.   As a result, a greater proportion
of the community's total expenditure is devoted to non-
agricultural goods than was so devoted in earlier times.
The proportionate reaction on industrial activity due to
given proportionate harvest changes is likely, therefore, to
be smaller now than it used to be.

Secondly, there have been at work several factors
tending to make the size of the proportionate harvest
changes that occur smaller.   Thus, as civilisation advances,
mankind tends to substitute less variable kinds of produce
for more variable kinds.   The introduction of a type of
wheat immune to the disease of rust is an instance in point.
Again, the range of action of natural forces outside human
control, which promote variability, is itself, in some

degree, subject to human control. As wealth increases, people are able to afford more expenditure to buy off irregularity and uncertainty, and so tend to introduce machines to undertake tasks that were formerly left to Nature. In India, for example, the development of irrigation works has done much to mitigate the effect of the vagaries of the seasons in rendering the crops variable.[1] Again, the development of the means of communication tends to diminish the variability of agricultural production as a whole, because, as intercourse is opened up, different crops come to be so distributed among different countries that each country becomes the producer of that one which in it is relatively invariable. Moreover, there is a general tendency for harvest variations, which occur independently in different parts of the world, partially to compensate one another —a tendency which is stronger the more numerous are the different independent sources of supply. Nor is it only in this quasi-mathematical way that improvements in communication make for stabilisation. As was well pointed out by the *Economist* some years before the war : " Sowing is taking place in every month of the year, and a shortage of European harvests is apparent early enough to influence the acreage put under wheat in the southern hemisphere, in Australia and Argentina. The effect of this system on prices has been that, whereas, prior to 1898, they showed big fluctuations, since that date they have been remarkably steady, though with a slight upward tendency." [2] The great practical importance of these influences in combination is illustrated by the fact that, whereas in the ten-year period 1898–1907 the wheat crop of the British Empire had a variability of 15 per cent, the variability of the crop of the whole world was only $5\frac{1}{2}$ per cent.[3]

A third factor remains. The thing relevant to the activity of industry is not merely, as we have so far tacitly

[1] Cf. Morison, *The Industrial Organisation of an Indian Province*, pp. 155-61.

[2] *Economist*, April 17, 1909, p. 811.

[3] *Economist*, April 24, 1909, p. 861. The details are given in the following table :

assumed, the size of harvest variations, but the size of the
variations in the volume of crops offered for sale. These
two things, with immediately perishable goods, are identical.
But with goods capable of being stored the latter variations
are the smaller of the two ; for the surpluses of good years
may be held in stock and afterwards be offered for sale in
years of shortage. Modern developments have strengthened
this stabilising factor in two ways. In the first place, the
invention of refrigerating and other preserving processes
has rendered a number of agricultural commodities much
more durable than they used to be. The Committee on
Hops, for instance, wrote in 1908 : " At the time of the
previous inquiry in the year 1886 attention was called to
the fact that ' the deterioration which hops suffer when
kept prevents the superabundance of one year from
adequately supplying the deficiencies of another.' The
advent of cold storage has effected an adjustment between
years of plethora and years of scarcity." [1] In the next place,
organised speculative markets have been established at least
for wheat and cotton. In these markets persons specialised
in the art of making forecasts come together and by their
action affect, first prices, and, through prices, the stocks

	World's Crop.	Per cent Increase or Decrease compared with Previous Year.	Crop of British Empire.	Per cent Increase or Decrease compared with Previous Year.
	Million bushels.		Million bushels.	
1898	2948	..	453	..
1899	2765	− 6·2	377	− 16·8
1900	2610	− 5·6	428	+ 13·5
1901	2898	+ 11·0	411	− 4·0
1902	3104	+ 7·1	471	+ 14·6
1903	3190	+ 2·7	572	+ 21·6
1904	3152	− 1·2	458	− 19·9
1905	3321	+ 5·3	565	+ 23·3
1906	3435	+ 3·4	565	..
1907	3109	− 9·5	412	− 27·1

The greater variability of the Empire imperial crop was not, of course, due
merely to the relatively small area of growth. It so happens that, owing to
climatic conditions, India and Australia are liable to almost complete crop
failures, while the Canadian harvest is also extremely variable.

[1] *Report*, p. x.

held back in stores and shops.   No doubt a speculative market may, on some occasions, be manipulated, and, on other occasions, may make mistakes.   On the whole, however, the modern wheat pit and cotton exchange tend to bring about the holding of larger stocks in anticipation of shortages and of smaller stocks in anticipation of bumper crops.   They must, therefore, lessen the percentage variations in the *supplies* of agricultural products offered to industrialists in consequence of given variations in the *yield* of these products.

The general effect of these considerations is to suggest that harvest variations as a factor determining, whether by direct or by indirect process, fluctuations in industrial activity, are substantially less important than they used to be fifty or a hundred years ago.   It is not, unfortunately, possible to step from this comparative result to a positive one.   Once more, we must fall back on informed guesswork.   My guess is that, if the world yield of crops per acre were rendered stable, and if everything else, other than things causally due to crop changes, remained the same, the amplitude of the representative trade cycle in this country would be cut down, to a less extent, indeed, than it would be if prices were stabilised or if errors of forecast were eliminated, but still to a considerable extent,—say, by something like one-quarter.

§ 15. The other principal impulses to disturbance, which were referred to in the course of Chapter IV., may be dealt with in a more summary fashion ; for nobody has claimed for any of them that it is dominant in the sense in which the term is here used.   We have already seen in that chapter itself that stoppages of work due to industrial disputes probably contribute very little towards industrial fluctuations. Big industrial inventions may sometimes be important, but it is the *decision to exploit* inventions that is the active cause of disturbance, and the time and intensity of exploitations are largely determined by the state of business confidence. As a rule, therefore, inventions are guides to the route which industrial expansion shall follow, rather than causes of these expansions.   No large place need, therefore, be assigned to them. Big wars, on the other hand, produce tremendous effects, and to prevent their occurrence would obviate large industrial movements. Fortunately, however, such wars are not merely sporadic, but also very rare, events, and are not, therefore, relevant to the ordinary run of industrial cycles.

§ 16. There remains for consideration the three environing conditions, considered in Chapters XIX.-XXI., upon which the various impulses to disturbance which we have been studying impinge. These are the policy of business men as regards cuts of price towards prime cost in bad times, the wage policy of workpeople and the degree of mobility which labour enjoys. It is possible to conceive a state of affairs in which, when demand falls off, business men would cut their prices, or workpeople would cut their wages, to such an extent that no unemployment whatever would occur. In order to secure this result, however, it would be necessary, on occasions, for prices in the one case and wages in the other to be cut, not merely below the short-period supply price, but below zero! Clearly no interest attaches to a study of such cuts as these. It is, however, of interest to inquire how far the difference as regards (1) price-rigidity and (2) wage-rigidity between actual policies and such more plastic policies as may fairly be considered within the region of practical politics contributes, other things being taken as given, towards actual industrial fluctuations. Again our answer can be nothing but a more or less intelligent guess. I suggest that in both cases the contribution made is appreciable, but not large ; say of the orders of one-sixteenth and one-eighth respectively. The peculiar reactions of our third condition, the state of labour mobility, were studied in Chapter XXI., and it was argued that, from the standpoint of general industrial fluctuations, they have very little significance.

§ 17. What has been said in the course of this chapter will have made it clear that the effect of introducing a " remedy " for industrial fluctuations in the form of an attack upon any one of the principal factors which we have distinguished will be one thing if that remedy is applied alone, and something different and smaller if it is applied in conjunction with other remedies. For example, if a stabilising price policy were adopted, much less would be gained by eliminating business men's liability to error or by rendering the yield of crops stable than would be gained by these reforms if currency and banking arrangements remained as they are now. This circumstance will have to be borne in mind throughout the discussion upon which we shall enter in Part II.

CHAPTER XXIII

RHYTHM OR PERIODICITY

§ 1. I now pass to the last problem proper to this Part. Up to this point we have studied, with such references to quantity as have been open to us, the various factors that may be supposed to underlie and jointly to promote industrial fluctuations. For all that was said in the last chapter it might be supposed that these fluctuations occur in a purely sporadic and haphazard manner. In fact, however, as statistical records show, there is, not, indeed, uniformity in respect either of period or of amplitude among successive industrial movements, but a distinct approach to regularity. This rhythm may be " accidental " in the sense defined in Chapter II. On the other hand, it may be susceptible of explanation by reference to one or more large causes which it is possible to disentangle. *Prima facie*, there are two broadly distinguished ways in which the recorded rhythmic, or quasi-rhythmic, movements might come about. First, they might result from the operation of causes which are sporadic in their nature, and do not recur rhythmically, but which, once they have come into play, instead of exhausting themselves in a single effect, start wave movements after the manner described in Chapter VII. Secondly, they might result from a succession of disturbing influences that themselves recur with the periodicity of actual industrial movements. Several factors of either of these two types, or of both types, might, of course, be present together. I shall follow, in my discussion, the lines suggested by this logical scheme.

§ 2. It is sometimes sought to include under the former of the above types, and indeed to stress as an important "explanation" of the facts, a movement or process that does not properly belong there. It is observed that, after a point, as "prosperity" grows, costs of production gradually catch up with selling prices, thus closing the door to the special profits that were obtained in the earlier stages of advance. Businesses, having passed the optimum scale of output, find that increasing production no longer yields falling real costs. Inferior workpeople have to be taken on, overtime worked, rates of wages raised, higher interest paid on loans. In this way the tendency to further expansion is checked; raised demand comes up against a heightened supply price; and the stimulus to further expansion is removed. Now, this kind of reaction obviously limits the extent to which production expands in response to a given rise of demand : and, since the whole process takes time, it is natural that we should find expansions carried forward continuously up to a point, and then stopped. But there is nothing here to set going any sort of rhythm, because there is nothing to cause the upward swing of demand to be followed by a downward swing. The factors referred to merely set limits to the size of industrial expansions (and analogous reasoning applies to contractions) initiated by given movements of demand. They are concerned with the adjustment of supply to changes of demand, and are not determinants of these changes.[1]

§ 3. Leaving mere negations, I shall next consider in turn several processes which do fall within the former of the two types of cause distinguished in § 1. First, there is the tendency of human constructions to wear out after a certain interval—their limited length of life. A boom, as was shown in Chapter IX., is always characterised by an abnormal mass of constructional work and of work upon the manufacture of machines and other instrumental goods. When the boom is over, the mere fact that it has occurred and has led to an extensive provision of instruments makes further provision unnecessary. It is known, of course, that the durable things

---

[1] The distinction drawn in the text is on the lines of the familiar distinction between movements of the exchange index *along* a demand curve and movements *of* a demand curve.

which have been called into being will eventually wear out and will have to be replaced, and it is possible, therefore, that some production may be undertaken in anticipation of that event. As a rule, however, this will not happen extensively, partly because of the loss of interest involved in it, and partly because technical improvements are likely to be invented that will make machines and so forth, which are manufactured now, obsolete before renewal becomes necessary. The result is that the group engaged in making these things for a time works less hard. The period of quiescence passes away when the life of the things made in the first boom draws to an end. Of course, different things have lives of different lengths. Houses, for example, last much longer than delicate tools. But there is reason to believe that many different sorts of machinery enjoy the same sort of length of life. Ten years seems to be, not merely the average, but also the markedly predominant length. This, at all events, is the view of the Director of the British Census of Production.[1] At some such interval as this, therefore, we should look for a secondary boom : to be repeated again and again after equal intervals. In this process, it would seem, there is a true cause making for rhythmic movement. In view, however, of the large obstructive influence exercised by friction, it can hardly be a very important cause. As Professor Irving Fisher writes : " The twig, once deflected and then left to itself, soon stops swaying. So also a rocking chair, left to itself, will soon stop rocking ; so also will a pendulum in a clock which has run down. Friction brings them to rest. To keep them going some outside force must be applied. So, in business we must assume that the effect of any initial disturbance would soon wear off, after a very few oscillations of rapidly diminishing amplitude. The resultant business cycle would speedily cease altogether if dependent only on its own reactions. To keep it up there must be applied some outside force." [2]

§ 4. Turn, secondly, to the alternation of optimistic and

---

[1] Cf. *Report* (1907), pp. 35-6.
[2] Cf. Fisher, *Our Unstable Dollar and the so-called Business Cycle.* (American Statistical Association, January 1925, p. 193.)

pessimistic errors among the controllers of industry. The interval here depends, not on the length of life of the commodities affected, but rather on their " period of gestation " ; for it is when production and marketing are finished that errors stand revealed. Plainly this will be different for different things, and we cannot suppose that there is any predominant period of gestation corresponding to the predominant ten years' length of life of capital instruments. On the other hand, the effect in stimulating and depressing industry of oscillations between errors of optimism and pessimism seems likely to be much greater than that exerted by the wearing out of limited groups of instruments. Therefore, in the absence of definite evidence to the contrary, it is reasonable to conclude that a significant part in building up the recorded rhythm of industry is played by the mutual generation of errors of pessimism and errors of optimism.

§ 5. Lastly, under this head, attention may be called to a process on the side of money. It was implicit in the analysis of Chapter XIII. that, when the annual (or monthly) rate at which new credit is being created on behalf of business men diminishes, the annual (or monthly) volume of new capital flowing into their control will, other things being equal, be diminished. But, since every fresh creation of credit extends the banks more and more, in the sense of increasing the proportion which the aggregate liabilities of the banking system bear to the ultimate reserve in the Central Bank, the rate at which fresh credit is being created *must*, after a time, diminish. For, first, the banks other than the Bank of England, in order to prevent their " cash and balances " at the Bank of England from falling unduly relatively to their liabilities, will borrow or buy with securities more balances at the Bank of England, thus causing the Bank's deposits to increase. Secondly, in consequence of the associated rise in general prices, the public will draw out extra currency from the Bank's reserve in order to cover the extra sums they have to pay for retail purchases or for the hire of labour.[1] Thirdly, again

---

[1] The process of the internal drain is well described in a recent report of the United States Federal Reserve Board : " In the earlier stages of a

as a consequence of the rise in general prices, in countries with a full-value metallic money—and the same thing, in substance, happens under a gold exchange standard—the reserve will be subjected to an external drain to pay for the extra imports which higher prices induce. In view of these movements the Central Bank must force up discount charges, and the rate at which fresh credit is being created must, after a time, diminish. As soon as this happens, even though the absolute sum of created credit continues to increase, the flow of new capital to business men will fall off, and so industrial activity will, not merely cease to expand, but will definitely contract. Thus industrial expansion, so far as it is assisted by credit creations, carries within itself the seeds of its own reversal, and, when once reversal has taken place, this of itself tends to shift men's minds towards pessimism, and so to start a cumulative process making for industrial depression. This analysis is, of course, rough, and qualifying considerations have been omitted. But the general drift is, I think, right. If it be so, we have here another factor that should make for some sort of rhythm. But how far the period of this theoretical rhythm corresponds to the actual period of recorded industrial cycles, and how far, therefore, it contributes towards building up that period, there are, so far as I can see, no means of deciding. For, though, as has been shown, turns in the *rate* of new credit

---

period of banking expansion there is usually a roughly parallel upward movement of the loans and deposits of the banks. Later on, however, the situation changes. There comes a time when the increase of business activity and the fuller employment of labour and increased pay rolls call for an increase of actual pocket money to support the increased wage disbursements and the increased volume of purchases at retail. At this stage the rough parallelism between the growth of loans and deposits of the banks gives way to a divergent movement between these items. Loans may continue to increase while deposits will remain either stationary or show a decline. When the point is reached in a forward movement of business where manufacturers and dealers need more currency for pay roll and other purposes, they draw down their deposits at the banks. What in the first instance was the creation of bank credit in the convenient form of a checking account has now become a demand for cash. In other words, the customer's demand for book money (deposits) at the bank becomes converted into a demand for pocket money. This change is reflected in the altered position of the banks. The ratio of loans to deposits rises with an increased demand for currency " (*Annual Report of the Federal Reserve Board*, 1923, p. 25).

creation synchronise with turns in the *amount* of industrial activity, this affords no proof that the turns are the expression of internal banking stresses—in which case it would be proper to regard them as causal agents—and not effects of external impulses, to which they and the turns in industry are jointly due.

§ 6. Under the second type of factor distinguished in § 1—causes which, it is claimed, are themselves rhythmically recurrent—it is only necessary to consider one, namely, harvest variations. Several important writers have attempted to show that the rhythm found in industry is generated exclusively—if the solecism may be permitted— by a concordant underlying rhythm in harvest yields—a rhythm which in turn, according to some of them, is due to meteorological changes set up by variations in the condition of sun-spots, or to the machinations of the planet Venus, or, it may be, to some still more obscure and *prima facie* irrelevant physical cause. The discussion of this matter has resulted in wide differences of opinion as to what the underlying rhythm of harvest yields in fact is. Dr. Shaw's inquiry into " An apparent periodicity in the yield of wheat in Eastern England " appears to reveal the existence of an eleven-year period. Professor Moore's study of the central grain district of the United States suggests an eight-year crop period, closely correlated with an eight-year rainfall period.[1] Mr. P. G. Wright disputes Professor Moore's analysis of the rainfall period, insisting that he has paid inadequate attention to the relation between average annual rainfall and rainfall in the critical portion of the year, but he does not quarrel about the crop period.[2] Professor Jevons claims to have established a three-and-a-half-year period for the world's harvests, connected with a three-and-a-half-year solar period of varying average barometric pressure ; [3] and Mr. Robertson doubts whether any periodicity is really demonstrated by his figures.[4] I shall not enter into this controversy. Whether, and if so what, period can be found

---

[1] Cf. *Economic Cycles*, chaps. ii. and iii.
[2] Cf. *Quarterly Journal of Economics*, May 1915, p. 631 *et seq.*
[3] *The Sun's Heat and Trade Activity*, p. 6.
[4] *A Study of Industrial Fluctuations*, p. 147.

underlying harvest variations is, from the present point of view, a secondary issue. Our problem is : given the facts as to industrial fluctuations, can the rough rhythm that they display be traced, in whole or in part, to the effects of harvest changes ?   That there is *some* sort of causal sequence here is suggested by the statistical correlations displayed in Chapter IV. Those correlations are, however, very imperfect. They do not warrant the opinion that crop variations are the sole, or even the main, determinants of such periodicity as there is in industrial fluctuations.

§ 7. In summary, then, we may conclude that some part in determining the recorded rhythm of industry may well be played by each of the several factors which have been considered in §§ 3-6 of this chapter. Sometimes supporting, sometimes partly cancelling one another, they, in association, no doubt, with a number of sporadic accidents of greater or less importance, jointly determine the duration of successive industrial cycles. This compromise view does not really conflict with the opinion of competent writers who have laid special stress upon harvests. Thus Professor Jevons, while he claims that bumper crops occur at intervals of from three to four years and give *some* impulse to industry each time they occur, admits that they only give an *effective* impulse at intervals of seven or ten and a half years, when other conditions are ripe.[1] It is, indeed, evident that such things, among others, as wars and the inflation of currency by or for governments unable to balance their budgets— witness recent experience in Germany—must sometimes lengthen and sometimes shorten the intervals that would otherwise have elapsed between successive booms and successive depressions. To attribute the actual rhythm of industry, such as it is, exclusively to an underlying rhythm of harvests is extravagant ; but to recognise that harvest variations, whether or not they are truly " periodic ", play a significant part is concordant both with the evidence and with *a priori* probability.

[1] *The Sun's Heat and Trade Activity,* p. 8.

PART II
REMEDIES

CHAPTER I

§ 1. It is the practice of popular writers to assume at the outset that industrial fluctuations must, in the nature of things, be evil, and ought, therefore, to be "remedied", provided only that a remedy can be found which does not involve too great a cost, *i.e.* does not reduce average production or the mean rate of progress in production by too much. Our first task is to show that this assumption is not correct. It is easy to imagine a community in which industrial fluctuations occur because, and only because, for physiological or other reasons, people's aversion from work, or desire for the fruits of work, undergoes periodic changes. This kind of thing in fact happens over short periods, as between day-time wakefulness and night-time sleep; and there would be nothing to surprise us if similar periodic changes occurred over longer intervals, three or four years of exceptional physical and mental energy being followed by three or four years of comparative quiescence. In a community so affected it would not be proper to regard the industrial fluctuations experienced by it as evils. Given the present constitution of human nature, we obtain more welfare from alternations of complete wakefulness and sound sleep than we should enjoy if these fluctuations were "remedied" by governmental action designed to promote a continuous intermediate state of semi-somnolence. If the matter is pushed further and it is asked whether we should be better off with a physical and psychical make-up so transformed that continuous semi-somnolence came to us "naturally", it seems at first sight that no answer is possible. In fact, however, it can be shown that, other

things being equal, to substitute for a variable level of
aversions and desires an intermediate level, *in the sense of the
arithmetic mean between the actual levels,* would diminish
the sum of economic welfare.[1] The popular notion that
industrial fluctuations as such *must* be social evils is thus
definitely disproved.

§ 2. This result, however, though important for accurate
thought, has little practical bearing. For the actual industrial cycles in which we are interested are not in fact generated
in the above manner. If variations in aversion to work were
fundamental, booms would be associated with the offer by
workpeople to accept lower rates of wages, and depressions
with demands on their part for higher rates. In fact, as the
accompanying chart shows, the upper halves of trade cycles
have, on the whole, been associated with higher rates of real
wages than the lower halves.[2] If the secular trend were

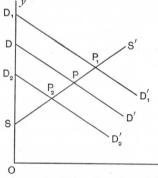

[1] The proof of this as regards variations in net desire for commodities
requires the assumption that fluctua-
tions of desire are foreseen, so that
production can be adjusted to them.
On this assumption let SS' be the
supply curve of work, and D_1D_1', and
D_2D_2', two demand curves, of which
DD' represents the arithmetical mean;
(*i.e.* each point on DD' bisects a
vertical line between D_1D_1' and
D_2D_2'). It is then apparent that the
sum of the areas D_1P_1S and D_2P_2S is
greater than twice the area DPS.
The explanation is, of course, that a
heightening of demand adds consumers' surplus in respect of more
units of output than the number in
respect of which a lowering of demand subtracts consumers' surplus. An
analogous proof holds of variations in aversion from work.

[2] It should be understood that, in view of the tendency of higher
prices, which are associated with booms, to lead to a fall in the real supply
schedule of labour (cf. *ante*, p. 176), there is no *a priori* necessity about this
relationship. Thus, had prices in Germany been stabilised, and the boom
due to post-war inflation thereby stopped, it is *probable* that the rates of
real wages in Germany would have been higher and not lower than they
were. If, however, we suppose the real demand for labour to have an
elasticity greater than unity, from the point of view of a cycle period,
there *is* an *a priori* necessity about the effect of price stabilisation on the
aggregate amount of real wages. It must—the proposition is self-evident
on inspection of an appropriately drawn diagram—make this sum more
steady than it would otherwise have been.

eliminated from the wages-curve, this would appear still more plainly.[1] Moreover, the proof that variations in aversion from work are not fundamental is really stronger than the chart suggests at first sight, because, as was shown in Part I. Chapter XVI., workpeople, being accustomed to think in gold, do not make enough allowance for price movements, and, therefore, accept lower rates of wages in booms and demand higher rates in depressions than they would do if they fully realised all the facts. If net variations in desire for commodities in general were fundamental, we should expect to find stocks depleted in booms and expanded in depressions—the opposite to what, if the argument of Part I. Chapter III. can be trusted, usually takes place. Of what the causes at work in promoting industrial fluctuations actually are, an elaborate account has been given in the preceding pages. Everybody will agree that fluctuations produced by the operation of these causes are, *prima facie*, social evils, in the sense that, if they could be mitigated without cost, economic welfare would be increased. For, given people's attitude towards work on the one hand and towards consumption on the other, less satisfaction—this follows from the law of diminishing utility—is obtained out of a variable real income than out of a constant real income of equal aggregate amount.[2]

[1] It must be recognised, however, that Mr. Rowe's valuable study of *Wages in Practice and Theory* (1928), Part I., throws grave doubt on the reliability of available index numbers of general wage-rates, and so on the significance of my chart.

[2] That is to say, a real income varying from $(A + a)$ to $(A - a)$ yields less satisfaction than one constant at A, the arithmetic average of these two magnitudes.

The following points may be added :

First, if the curve of demand is a rectangular hyperbola, *i.e.* if the elasticity of demand is equal to unity for all quantities purchased, the consumers' surplus from an output varying from $(A + a)$ to $(A - a)$ is equal to that from an output constant at $\sqrt{A^2 - a^2}$, the *geometric* mean of the two varying outputs.

Secondly, whatever the conditions of demand, when a fluctuation in productivity (through climatic changes and so on) is foreseen, adjustments will be made to it, and the social evil resulting from it will be lessened. Consequently, less good is done by eliminating a foreseen than an unforeseen fluctuation in productivity. The only exception to this occurs when the demand curve is a rectangular hyperbola ; for then the amount of investment made will be the same whatever productivity per unit is expected.

§ 3. This *prima facie* conclusion is strengthened by more detailed analysis. Variations in the real income of a rich man probably involve but little loss of satisfaction to him ; for, in the first place, they are likely to work themselves out chiefly in variations in new investments, so that his consumption remains nearly constant; and, in the second place, a given *percentage* variation in the consumption of a rich man almost certainly hurts less than an equal percentage variation in the consumption of a poor man.[1] The relation between industrial fluctuations and the real incomes of the wage-earning class is, therefore, a dominant factor in determining their social significance. It has already been shown that, in general, good times are associated with higher, and bad times with lower, rates of real wages ; and from this it follows *a fortiori* that the former go with higher, the latter with lower, *aggregate amounts* of real wages. It is true that the aggregate consumption of wage-earners is rendered by various devices, temporary borrowings from shop-keepers in bad times, the use of accumulated reserves of purchasing power, systems of national insurance against unemployment, Poor Law Relief, and so on, substantially less variable than their aggregate real income. To test the range of this qualification I have printed a chart, in which unemployment percentages (inverted) are brought into conjunction with certain indices of consumption. Statistics of consumption are notoriously unsatisfactory. I have set out figures for beer and for meat, the sources of which are indicated in Table VI. of the Appendix, and I have added to them a tentative index of consumption in general printed by Mr. H. G. Wood in the *Journal of the Royal Statistical Society* of December 1899. A study of this chart shows that there is a rough concordance between the movements of the three consumption curves and of the employment curve. Good

---

[1] This proposition, it should be noted, does *not* follow from the law of diminishing utility. This law states that, if x be the amount of consumption and $F(x)$ the marginal satisfaction derived from it, $F'(x)$ is negative. The proposition in the text involves the further condition that $F''(x)$ is negative, *i.e.* that the curve representing the successive increments of satisfaction derived from successive increments of consumption by a man of representative constitution is convex when looked at from that origin.

employment (represented by peaks on the curve) is associated with larger consumption of beer and meat and with a better state of the general consumption index than bad employment. This evidence is not, indeed, conclusive, but it makes highly probable the conclusion that, when every allowance has been made for the qualifications to which attention has been called, variations of real income are associated with important variations in consumption.

§ 4. Moreover, figures of aggregate consumption give an inadequate idea of the social evil involved in fluctuations, because they take no account of the way in which the cuts of consumption necessitated by depressions are distributed among different individuals in the wage-earning class. Cuts are not made in equal proportions by everybody, but are, in great part, concentrated on the unfortunate few. That the aggregate suffering they involve must be rendered greater by this fact follows from the law of diminishing utility, and is obvious to common sense. Of course, here again unemployment insurance and the other influences referred to in the previous section cause the individual variations in consumption that accompany industrial fluctuations to be much less scattered than individual variations in earnings. There is good reason to believe, however, that the scattering of consumption variations is considerable, and the consequent damage to economic welfare grave.

§ 5. Again, besides the consumption aspect, it is proper to consider also the work aspect of industrial fluctuations. A given aggregate of work distributed unevenly in time and adjusted between different people in such wise that some of them suffer much greater variations than others involves more dissatisfaction than an equal aggregate distributed evenly. Nor is it only in the dissatisfaction directly associated with work that injury is done. Irregularity of work reacts upon the quality of the workpeople affected by it. Considerable spells of unemployment may damage a man's technical capacity and, what is much more important, the general make-up of his character. The habit of regular work may be lost and self-respect and self-confidence destroyed, so that, when opportunity for work does come, the man,

once merely unemployed, is found to have become unemployable. The Royal Commissioners on the Poor Laws
have in evidence : " The enforced idleness on completion of
a job naturally throws the men upon their own resources,
which is, in nine cases out of ten, the nearest public-house.
The frequent change from strenuous hard work to absolute
indolence to men of this character naturally tends to gradual
moral and physical degeneration, and ultimately the individuals become unfit for work, even when opportunity
offers." [1] A large employer of labour is reported to have
said : " Between 5 and 6 per cent of my skilled men are out
of work just now. During the long spell of idleness any one
of these men invariably deteriorates. In some cases the
deterioration is very marked. The man becomes less
proficient and less capable, and the universal experience of
us all who have to do with large numbers of working men is
that nothing has a worse effect upon the calibre of such men
than long spells of idleness." [2] The Transvaal Indigency
Commission report : " Unemployment is one of the most
fruitful causes of indigency of a permanent and hopeless
kind. However skilled a man may be, he is bound to
deteriorate during a long period of unemployment. His
hand loses some of its cunning and he acquires the habit of
idleness. The tendency is for the unemployed to sink to the
level of the unemployable." [3] Reference may also be made
to the results of a recent American inquiry : " If a period of
enforced idleness were a season of recuperation and rest,
there would be a good side to lack of employment. But
enforced idleness does not bring recuperation and rest.
The search for labour is much more fatiguing than labour
itself. An applicant, sitting in one of the charity offices
waiting for the arrival of the agent, related his experiences
while trying to get work. He would rise at 5 o'clock in the
morning and walk three or four miles to some distant point,
where he had heard work could be had. He went early so
as to be ahead of others, and he walked because he could not

---

[1] Quoted in the Minority Report, p. 1138.
[2] Alden, *The Unemployed, a National Question*, p. 6.
[3] *Report of the Transvaal Indigency Commission*, p. 120.

afford to pay car fare. Disappointed in securing a job at the first place, he would tramp to another place miles away, only to meet with disappointment again. . . . As the man told his story, he drove home the truth that lack of employment means far more than simply a loss in dollars and cents; it means a drain upon the vital forces that cannot be measured in terms of money." [1] Moreover, the evil consequences of lean months are not balanced by good consequences in fat months. Indeed it may well be that, when, as often happens, the fat months imply long hours of overtime, they will not yield any good effects to set against the evil effects of the lean months, but will themselves add further evil effects.

§ 6. Yet another element of evil remains. Unemployment varies in amount from time to time in ways that are uncertain, in the sense that they cannot be foretold, and the uncertainty that attaches to unemployment in the aggregate attaches, of course, in still stronger measure to its incidence in respect of particular individuals. There necessarily results, among those persons whose reserve fund is small, a haunting sense of insecurity and danger, which is in itself a serious evil. Sir H. Llewellyn Smith sums up the matter thus : " It is, I think, a definite induction from history and observation that, when a risk falls outside certain limits as regards magnitude and calculability, when, in short, it becomes what I may call a gambler's risk, exposure thereto not only ceases to act as a bracing tonic, but produces evil effects of a very serious kind ".[2] In the same spirit Leroy Beaulieu declares, and is surely right in declaring : " It is not the insufficiency of pay which constitutes, in general and apart from exceptional cases, the social malady of to-day, but the precariousness of employment ".[3]

§ 7. What has been said should be sufficient to show that industrial fluctuations, as they actually occur in the modern world, involve a substantial loss of economic welfare

[1] *United States Bulletin of the Bureau of Labour*, No. 79, pp. 906-7.
[2] *Economic Journal*, 1910, p. 518.
[3] *La Répartition des richesses*, p. 612.

as against what would have been won from an equal aggregate quantity of income and work distributed evenly through
time. In putting the issue thus, however, we have greatly
understated the case. For it can be shown that the complex
forces, which cause industrial activity to fluctuate, also cause
the aggregate amount of it and the associated aggregate
amount of real income to be substantially less than they
would have been under stable conditions. The argument,
which is somewhat complicated, runs as follows : As was
pointed out in Part I. Chapter XX., wage-rates in modern
conditions are held more or less rigidly at conventional
levels higher in bad times than is warranted by the conditions
of short-period supply. The consequence of this is that in
bad times a considerable volume of labour is thrown out of
employment because it refuses to accept the wage that it
is then worth, in spite of the fact that that rate would more
than compensate the direct prime cost of its effort. We
cannot, indeed, step at once from this to the inference that,
if the demand for labour were somehow made even through
time, this loss would be done away with. For the elimination
of industrial fluctuations implies, not only increasing the
demand for labour in bad times, but also diminishing it in
good. In these circumstances, if we suppose the wage-rate
to be absolutely rigid at 30s., both for abnormally large and
abnormally small demands, to transfer £100,000 of demand
from good times to bad would involve a contraction of work
in good times exactly equal to the addition to work in bad
times. Thus the only effect, say, of putting 1000 men to
work in bad times to erect a town building, which would
normally have been erected in good times, would be to
transfer these men's idleness from bad times to good—a
change that yields little or no benefit.[1] This pessimistic
conclusion, however, depends upon the assumption that the
wage-rate is held absolutely rigid at 30s. for all levels
of demand and in all circumstances. This assumption does
not tally with the facts. First, in most industries con-

---

[1] Cf. *Report of Royal Commission on the Poor Laws*, p. 383. " Carrying
out ordinary work at an earlier period than is necessary is directly calculated to have the effect of causing at a future date a reduction in the
number of men regularly employed."

vention allows a certain amount of fluctuation in wage-rates above the rate appropriate to normal times, and only enforces rigidity in an absolute manner at a level somewhat lower than this. Thus in good times the wage may grow from 30s. to 32s. along the line of the short-period supply curve : but it will not go below 30s. in bad times. The consequence of this is somewhat as follows. To withdraw £100,000 worth of demand from good times, when a million pounds would normally be spent, involves lowering the rate of wages, say, from 32s. to 30s. ; so that the, say, £900,000 worth of demand that is left employs 600,000 men, as against the 625,000 men formerly employed. In bad times we suppose that £800,000 used to be expended at 30s. per man and employed 533,333 men. The addition of a further £100,000 to the wage investment now, leaving, as we may suppose it will, the rate at 30s., adds 66,666 men; that is to say, it increases the numbers employed from 533,333 to 600,000. Therefore, whereas, with the untransposed demand, we had in bad and good times respectively 533,000 and 625,000 men, i.e. a total of 1,158,000 men employed, when the demand is transposed we have 600,000 men and 600,000 men, i.e. a total of 1,200,000 men. This evidently implies a larger aggregate of production. There is, however, a second and more important point. The assumption cited above implies that the same rigid minimum wage-rate would be held to if demand were stabilised as is held to now. In fact it is much more probable that, if, in any industry, or series of industries, demand were stable, the wage-rate would settle down at the level required to give employment to the whole available supply of able-bodied labour. It is only because demand fluctuates that convention in wage-rates acts as it does : the rate is adapted to the conditions of normal times : convention holds it near that level when times cease to be normal : if all times were normal, there would be no scope for such action. Hence we may properly conclude that, in actual life, industrial fluctuations are responsible for contracting substantially the aggregate volume of production over good times and bad together. Moreover, there is a further consideration available in support of this conclusion. It is well known that upward movements in demand are often associated with attempts on the part of workpeople to force wages up, and downward fluctuations with attempts on the part of employers to force them down : and that these attempts lead to strikes and lock-outs, which inflict injury both directly and indirectly upon production. With steadier demand there is good reason to believe that stoppages of work consequent upon industrial disputes would be less frequent and less extensive than they are under present conditions. No doubt, it may be argued on the other side that this increased steadiness, by making life easier for business men, would remove a part of the stimulus that they now have to counter difficulty by technical improvement, and would enable the less competent among them to hold their own against the more competent for rather longer than they can do now ; and that in these ways the productive power of the country would be indirectly weakened.[1] To balance this, however, we may set the increased efficiency of workpeople and of their children, which should follow their relief from the distresses of unemployment and the strain of booms : and our conclusions remain intact.

§ 8. We proceed then to the next stage of the argument. To show that industrial fluctuations, as they actually exist, are a social evil, is not to show that governments should attempt to "remedy" them. For it may be that everything which can be done in this direction, without causing more harm in other ways than of good in this way, has been done already. There is, indeed, a preliminary presumption in this sense bred of the old doctrine of the economic harmonies. This doctrine taught that, in general, the pursuit by individuals of their private self-interest will make the sum of economic satisfaction a maximum, subject to the proviso that the surrounding facts are what they are. This does not mean, of course, that the community obtains as much economic satisfaction as it would do if the surrounding facts were different : but that, given these facts, the

[1] Cf. *ante*, Part I. Chap. I. § 3.

free play of self-interest causes people to accommodate themselves to them in such wise that any further adjustment would yield a return in satisfaction smaller than its cost. In other words, whatever causes and conditions of industrial fluctuations may be in play, such reactions to them as are worth their cost will already have taken place, as it were automatically, and, therefore, there is no room for anything further. Just as people, if left to themselves, may be expected to distribute their demand among different occupations to the best advantage that the circumstances permit, so also they may be expected to distribute their demand among different times to the best advantage. Thus consider the analogy of a co-operative family of peasants working on the land when the seasons are variable. Such a group, after having devoted activity to rendering the seasons less variable up to the point at which the marginal return to this activity balances the marginal cost, will distribute their labour in reaping and sowing crops between different years on the same principle : and, on the same principle again, they will store up part of the surplus of good years against the needs of bad years. Any modification of their action, however philanthropic its intent, would disturb what, in the conditions, is the *optimum* arrangement and would do more harm than good. On similar lines it may be argued that attempts to remedy the industrial fluctuations of the actual world in the interest of general economic welfare must, on the whole, do more harm than good.

§ 9. This rigid doctrine, which is merely a particular application of the more general doctrine of maximum satisfaction, is now known, like that more general doctrine itself, to be subject to large qualifications. The heart of the matter is that industrial fluctuations involve evil consequences of such a kind that, if an individual takes certain sorts of action to remove or lessen them, the social gain resulting from his action will not enter at full value into his private profit. In the following chapters we shall be engaged in disentangling several types of remedy for industrial fluctuations, of which this statement holds good, and in studying in detail possible methods of applying them. We shall distinguish : (1) remedies directed to eliminate or mitigate one or other of the factors responsible for industrial fluctuations, thus attacking the fluctuations indirectly through their causes : (2) remedies aimed directly at the fluctuations themselves, without reference to their causation, by, for example, transferring to bad times a part of the demand for labour, which, in the ordinary course of things, would have been exercised in good times. In both cases we have to inquire whether, and why, the relevant remedies have not already been carried as far as is desirable, and, if this has not been done, to formulate plans by which a further advance can usefully be made.

§ 10. Even in an ideally intelligent community, much more in the actual world, it is certain that neither of the above two sorts of remedy will be carried so far as to abolish industrial fluctuations altogether. Consequently, some fluctuations must remain, and, with them, some periods in which a number of workpeople find it difficult to obtain employment. The evils that result from this, along with parallel evils due to those seasonal variations of employment that we have excluded from our study, have led to the devising of further remedies—palliatives of the effects of the disease rather than specifics against the disease itself. The chief of these are relief works, systems or organised short time and insurance against unemployment. They will be studied in turn in the three concluding chapters of this volume.

CHAPTER II

REMEDIES FOR THE SEVERAL NON-MONETARY IMPULSES
TO INDUSTRIAL FLUCTUATIONS

§ 1. THE natural order of procedure in this Part is to consider separately, from the point of view of possible remedies, each of the principal causes and conditions tending to promote industrial fluctuations which were examined in Part I. In the present chapter I shall refer to the causes examined in Chapters IV., VI. and VII. For reasons that will appear as we proceed, the discussion here will be very brief.

§ 2. In Chapter XXII. of Part I. some account was given of several ways in which, with the progress of civilisation, the significance of harvest variations as a cause of industrial fluctuations has been reduced. Clearly there may yet be available new measures of a kind which it would pay no individual to introduce, but the net effect of which in limiting the range of harvest changes would more than repay their cost. Scientific work devoted to the development of new types of cereals—on the pattern of rustless wheat—or to the treatment of the soil, or possibly even to controlling the incidence of the rainfall, are instances in point. Nothing, however, can usefully be said upon matters of this kind by one who is not an expert agriculturalist.

§ 3. Attacks upon inventions, or, more accurately, upon changes in the rate at which inventions are made, as causes of industrial fluctuations need not detain us. It would, of course, be *possible* for the community, by collective action, to prevent inventions from being made, or, at all events, from being embodied in material forms. But nobody seriously advocates such a policy, because whatever benefit might be secured in this way through diminishing industrial fluctuations would almost certainly be outweighed by the permanent loss of that economic power which inventions produce. It might, indeed, be suggested that, while no attempt should be made to check the progress of invention, some collective control should be exercised over the times at which new inventions are exploited. Very brief reflection, however, is enough to show that nothing of this kind is practicable.

§ 4. Attacks upon the influences that make for industrial disputes and international war may be dismissed for a different—indeed an opposite reason. It is evident without argument that improvements in organisation that reduced the frequency of wars and of industrial disputes would almost certainly pay for their cost many times over, apart altogether from their indirect effect in diminishing industrial fluctuations. The problem of preventing international war is a political problem to which much thought is being devoted at the present time. That of preventing, or rather rendering less frequent, industrial war is partly a political, partly an economic problem ; I have discussed it at some length in my *Economics of Welfare.* Both problems are urgent and important, but to canvass them here would carry us too far afield.

§ 5. There remain the very important causes studied in Chapters VI.-VII. of Part I. under the title of Psychological Causes. I do not propose to examine remedies for them in this place, because all that I have to say has already been said by implication in the course of the chapters cited. The practical problem throughout is to balance, at the margin, the cost of various devices for preventing errors—the official collection and publication of statistics and so on—against the resultant gain in diminished industrial fluctuations : it being always borne in mind that this gain will be smaller if successful attacks have, than if they have not, been made against the companion causes of disturbance, harvest variations and monetary instability.[1]

[1] Cf. *ante,* Part I. Chap. XXII. § 17.

CHAPTER III

§ 1. IN the course of Part I. it was shown that, when industrial fluctuations are initiated by non-monetary causes, monetary and banking conditions augment the amplitude of the fluctuations in four ways. First, the banks increase in good times, and decrease in bad times, the forced levies which, by means of credit creation, they make for industrialists at the expense of the rest of the community. Secondly, the rise of prices in good and the fall in bad times, to which this credit policy, together with the associated changes in the income-velocity of monetary circulation, leads, doctors the terms of past contracts in ways not fully foreseen when the contracts were made, thus benefiting industrialists in good times and injuring them in bad times at the expense of lenders at fixed interest and, in a less degree, of wage-earners. Thirdly, the price movements which actually occur cause an expectation of their continuance, and business men, realising that they can allow for these changes better than other people, reckon upon a bounty in good times and a toll in bad times, as against these other people, in the terms of future contracts. Fourthly, the price movements and the doctoring of contracts associated with them react on business psychology, causing people to look more optimistically upon given facts when prices are rising than when they are falling. When industrial fluctuations are initiated by monetary causes, as described in Part I. Chapter VIII., the processes involved are similar. Hence, whether the origin of a fluctuation is monetary or non-monetary, there are to be distinguished, as factors magnifying its scope : (1) the action of the banks in respect of credit creation ; and (2) movements in the general price level. The monetary and banking influences which at present augment the range of industrial fluctuations will be eliminated if *both* the banks refrained from interference by way of forced levies with the normal flow of new capital to industry *and* the general price level were kept constant.

§ 2. Even if this twofold ideal were attained, nobody outside the school of writers which regards industrial fluctuations as " purely monetary phenomena " [1] believes that fluctuations of industry and employment, in the face of variations (whether warranted or not) in the expectations of business men, would be entirely prevented. It is recognised that, if these men's forecasts of profit improve, they will borrow more new capital, either directly from the public or indirectly from them through the mediation of the banks in ways that do not raise prices ; [2] and that, if their expectations of profit are worsened, they will act in the opposite sense. In order, therefore, to stabilise industry through the action of banks, we should need, in periods of business optimism, to make prices fall below the average, and, in periods of business pessimism, to make them rise above the average. The recent experience of Germany has shown that currency inflation, by conferring a continuing bounty upon business men at the expense of rentiers and wage-earners, can keep an industrial boom alive long after, in the ordinary course, reaction would have set in ; and, as some would hold, the experience of the United States shortly after the war and the experience of the United Kingdom since 1921 have shown that currency deflation can render an industrial depression much deeper in extent and much more prolonged than it would have been if deflation had not been attempted. Thus it need not be doubted that, if the Government could accurately adjust to the desired end a policy of making prices rise in depressions and fall in booms, the level of industrial activity in depressions would be raised, and in booms lowered, in such wise that a fairly close approximation to industrial stability would be attained. There is nothing inherently impossible about such a policy. Moreover, economists will

[1] Cf. *ante*, p. 211.   [2] Cf. *ante*, p. 213.

perceive that it is in essence much the same as the device —to be discussed later—of imposing taxes on production in good times and using the proceeds to accord bounties to production in bad times. To practical men, however, this policy has an appearance so violently paradoxical that there is no chance of it being adopted. In any case it is not the policy that I propose to discuss. That policy is the less ambitious one of preventing monetary and banking factors from making the range of industrial fluctuations wider than it would be in a moneyless and bankless world.

§ 3. Since, as was pointed out in § 1, monetary and banking factors act upon industry along two separate routes, an essential preliminary to formulating any remedial policy is to ascertain whether it is possible to block both routes at once or whether the blocking of one of them implies leaving the other in some measure open. The key fact, brought out in Part I. Chapter XIII., is this. Additions to the volume of bank credit available to industrialists, which keep prices steady in the face of reductions in the income-velocity of monetary circulation brought about by the action of persons other than industrialists, do not involve the making of forced levies by the banks for industry : all other additions to the volume of bank credit available to industrialists do involve this.[1] Hence, in order to obviate forced levies by the banks and their inverse, credit must be so controlled that prices are kept stable in the face of alterations in the income-velocity of money initiated by non-industrialists, but not in the face of alterations in this income-velocity initiated by industrialists, nor yet in the face of alterations in the size of the community's real income. Hence avoidance of forced levies and forced anti-levies for industry by the banks is compatible with price stabilisation if, and only if, either (1) no changes in the income-velocity of money initiated by industrialists and no changes in the real income of the community take place ; or (2) such changes in these respects as do take place are so related in magnitude and direction that their effects upon the price level exactly cancel out.

§ 4. From the analysis of Part I. Chapter XV. it can be

[1] Cf. ante, p. 148, footnote 1.

inferred that credit control so exercised as to eliminate forced levies and anti-levies for industry by the banks would reduce substantially the range of price fluctuations over a representative trade cycle, but would probably still allow prices to rise slightly in booms and fall slightly in depressions. Of course, what we may call accidental changes in the price level, due to such things as labour disputes or a sudden influx of dumped imports, would not be corrected at all. But accidents of this sort are not likely often to be sufficiently large or widespread to affect seriously the general level of prices. Hence, so long as we ignore the existence of trends of change in the magnitude of the community's real income, we may conclude that the form of credit control required to eliminate forced levies and anti-levies would nearly succeed in stabilising general prices ; though, for complete success in this, it would probably be necessary to make small forced levies in depressions and small forced anti-levies in booms ; which implies that bankers must cut their loans when high interest is offered below what they are when the interest rate is low. To ignore the existence of trends of change in real income is, however, to depart violently from the facts of life. For, broadly speaking, it is a characteristic of modern communities that their real incomes trend steadily upwards on account both of increasing population and of increasing productivity per head. In these conditions it is practically easier to achieve price stability than it would be if real income did not trend upwards ; because the volume of credit need not now be less absolutely in good times than in bad, but only less relatively to the trend. But this is a minor point. The vital fact is that, when the community's aggregate real income is growing because real income *per head* is trending upwards, though not when it is growing because population is growing, the policy of eliminating forced levies and anti-levies and the policy of stabilising general prices are fundamentally incompatible with one another. The former policy implies a price level which is not stable but trends downward in a proportion inverse to that in which real income per head increases : the latter implies that bankers make a continuing series of forced levies from the public ; [1] and, though they may hand some of them back again to consumers by heavily financing such things as instalment selling, in this country at all events it is certain that the bulk of them would be passed to industrialists.

§ 5. It follows from this analysis that, in a community where real income per head is subject to an upward trend, an important practical issue must be faced. Provided that the trend movement in productivity is a steady one, it does

---

[1] At first sight it appears that the disharmony, which exists when real income per head is growing, must also exist when aggregate income is increasing because population is growing, while real income per head remains constant. Mr. Robertson has shown, however, that this is not so, but that in these conditions, provided that population is increasing at a constant rate, the policy that obviates forced levies and anti-levies by the banks will also keep the price level stable. (Cf. *Banking Policy and the Price Level*, pp. 55-7, and *Money*, second edition, pp. 97-9.) The explanation of this apparent paradox is as follows. When aggregate real income expands because real income per head expands, if the banks do nothing the price level will fall in inverse proportion, and the real value of existing money balances will expand in direct proportion to the variation in aggregate real income. The public, therefore, will have no call to make new savings in order to conform their real balances to their enlarged real income. The income-velocity of monetary circulation being thus unaltered, there is nothing for the banks to cancel. If, however, population increases, the new population having the same real income per head as the old, the newcomers will presumably need real balances on the same scale as the old population. They must buy the money that embodies these by work, the fruit of which they save and hand over to others, of equivalent real value. In order that the savings which they make may not be dissipated in increased consumption, but may materialise in new capital, the banks must create and hand to business men such amount of new credits as is necessary to convey to them the intended savings.

Let $\phi(t)$ be the stock of credits at time t; $f(t)$ the population; k the real income per head; and C the period of monetary circulation.

Then, if P be the price level, $P = \dfrac{1}{C} \cdot \dfrac{\phi(t)}{kf(t)}$.

Each new increment of population desires to save and transfer to capital new real balances per head equal to the real balances per head of the existing population, and the banks, we suppose, create sufficient credits for this.

$$\therefore \quad \frac{\phi'(t)}{f'(t)} \cdot \frac{1}{P} = \frac{\phi(t)}{f(t)} \cdot \frac{1}{P},$$

$$\therefore \quad \frac{\phi'(t)}{f'(t)} - \frac{\phi(t)}{f(t)} = 0.$$

But this is the condition that $\dfrac{d}{dt}\left\{\dfrac{1}{C} \cdot \dfrac{\phi(t)}{kf(t)}\right\}$, namely, $\dfrac{dP}{dt} = 0$.

$$\therefore \text{ P is constant.}$$

This proof, it will be noticed, is general, and does not require that the rate at which population grows shall be constant.

not, indeed, greatly matter, from the standpoint of industrial fluctuations, whether the banks aim at stabilising the price level in an absolute sense or at stabilising it relatively to a trend adjusted to the rising trend of real income per head. For, while, of course, these policies will operate on industrial activity quite differently, the difference will be about the same at all stages of an industrial wave movement. The waves will move up and down from different initial levels, but their form and scale will not thereby be altered. Though, however, this is so, the issue is not, therefore, unimportant; for it is most unlikely that the two policies will be equally advantageous to the *general* interest of the community. On the one side we have no forced levies and a price level falling in inverse proportion to the upward trend of real income per head; on the other side continuous forced levies and a constant price level. Forced levies—provided that, as is customary, their proceeds are turned over to industrialists—are *prima facie* objectionable, because they imply an artificial stimulation of investment beyond what would " naturally " come about : but those who hold that "Nature" normally causes too little of our resources to be devoted to future uses will regard a moderate measure of this stimulation as a social benefit. A continuously falling price level when productivity per head is stationary—aggregate output growing only because population is growing—obstructs industry in the manner described in Part I. Chapters XVI.-XVII. and also modifies distribution to the advantage of interest receivers in a way that it is difficult to justify. In Part I. Chapter XVIII., however, it was shown that when prices fall as a result of and in correspondence with increasing productivity per head, industrial activity is *not* handicapped. Moreover, in this case the distributional advantage conferred on interest receivers is not wholly without warrant; for it only enables their incomes to move parallel with other people's—not to step in front of them. On the whole, therefore, it would seem that, in a progressive community, the goal at which credit regulation can most usefully aim is not price stabilisation in an absolute sense, but price stabilisation adjusted to the trend of real income per head ;

that is to say, a state of things in which prices fall in inverse proportion to the upward trend of *average* real income.

§ 6. A word must be said in conclusion about the practical implications of this policy. If the trend of real income per head is foreknown, the approximate trend of prices will, of course, also be foreknown. Thus, if real income per head trends upwards at the rate of 2 per cent per annum, relative stabilisation means a price level falling at the rate of approximately 2 per cent per annum. But in practice the trend of real income per head is generally not foreknown. In these circumstances it is sometimes suggested that what is required can be accomplished by stabilising in an absolute sense the money price of labour ; on the ground that the value of labour in terms of commodities will vary in the same proportion as real income (*i.e.* production) per head varies. This, however, is not necessarily so. For the relation between the change in output per head and the associated change in the commodity value of labour will depend on how the increased productivity has been brought about—whether by a mere increase in capital or by capital-saving inventions or by labour-saving inventions—and upon the elasticity of the respective demands of capital and labour for one another's services. Thus our ideal, when set out in concrete terms, is not very clear-cut. Some practical guidance may perhaps be gained from the following consideration. With real income (production) per head constant, stability of prices, when the price level is measured by reference to wholesale prices, may be expected to imply approximate stability in terms of retail prices also. With real income per head expanding, there is, however, a presumption, since the real wages of labour are likely to be increased, that the prices of handling and service and, therefore, retail prices, will rise relatively to wholesale prices. If a retail price index number, or some other index number that gives large weight to labour, be selected as the thing to stabilise, we shall come nearer to our ideal than we should do by employing a wholesale price index number.[1]

---

[1] Cf. Robertson, *Money* (second edition), pp. 137-8.

CHAPTER IV

A TABULAR STANDARD FOR LONG CONTRACTS

§ 1. BEFORE we embark on a study of the process of credit control designed to promote price stabilisation, it will be convenient to interpose a brief discussion of a more modest plan for mitigating the tendency of current monetary and banking arrangements to expand the range of industrial fluctuations. This plan, while leaving credit and price policy untouched, seeks to obviate some of the disturbing effects to which movements in the general price level at present lead. It is, broadly, that a tabular standard of value, based upon a considerable number of commodities, should be promulgated authoritatively, and that people should be encouraged to make contracts for loans and, where these cover periods of any length, for wages, in terms of this standard.

§ 2. The idea is explained with great lucidity by Marshall as follows : " Let us suppose that (as was suggested long ago by Joseph Lowe, Poulett Scrope and others) a Government Department extends to all commodities the action taken by the Commissioners of Tithes with regard to wheat, barley and oats. As they, having ascertained the average prices of grain at any time, state how much money is required to purchase as much wheat, barley and oats as would have cost £100 at certain standard prices, so this Department, having ascertained the prices of all important commodities, would publish from time to time the amount of money required to give the same general purchasing power as, say, £1 had at the beginning of 1887. The prices used by it would be the latest attainable ; not, as in the case of tithes, the mean of the prices for the last seven years. This standard unit of purchasing power might be called for shortness simply THE UNIT.

" From time to time, at the beginning of each year or oftener, the Department would declare how much of the currency had the same purchasing power as £1 had at the beginning of 1887. If, for instance, it declared in 1890 that 18s. had this purchasing power, then a contract to pay a unit in 1890 would be discharged by paying 18s. If it declared in 1892 that 23s. had only the same purchasing power as £1 had in 1887, or 18s. in 1890, then any contract to pay a unit in 1892 would require for its settlement the delivery of 23s.

" When a loan was made, it could, at the option of those concerned, be made in terms of currency, or in terms of units. In the latter case the lender would know that, whatever change there might be in the value of money, he would receive, when the debt was repaid, just the same amount of real wealth, just the same command over the necessaries, comforts and luxuries of life, as he had lent away. If he bargained for 5 per cent interest, he would each year receive money equal in value to one-twentieth of the units which he had lent ; and, however prices might have changed, these would contribute a certain and definite amount to his real means of expenditure. The borrower would not be at one time impatient to start ill-considered enterprises in order to gain by the expected rise in general prices, and at another afraid of borrowing for legitimate business for fear of being caught by a general fall in prices.

" Of course every trade would still have its own dangers due to causes peculiar to itself ; but by the use of the unit it might avoid those heavy risks which are caused by a rise or fall in general prices. Salaries and wages, where not determined by special sliding scales, could be fixed in units, their real value would then no longer fluctuate constantly in the wrong direction, tending upwards just when, if it changed at all, it should fall, and tending downwards just when, if it changed at all, it should rise.

" Ground-rents also should be fixed in general units, though for agricultural rents it would be best to have a special unit based chiefly on the prices of farm produce. The reckoning of mortgages and marriage settlements in terms of units of purchasing power, instead of gold, would remove one great source of uncertainty from the affairs of private life, while a similar change as to debentures and Government bonds would give the holders of them what they want—a really constant income. The ordinary shareholders in a public company would no longer be led to take an over-sanguine estimate of their position by a period of prosperity, which, besides enriching them directly, diminished the real payments which they have to make to debenture holders and, perhaps, to preference stock holders. And, on the other hand, they would not be oppressed by the extra weight of having to pay more than their real value on account of these fixed charges when prices were low and business drooping.

" The standard unit of purchasing power being published, the Law Courts should, I think, give every facility to contracts, wills and other documents, made in terms of the unit ; and Government itself might gradually feel its way towards assessing rates and taxes (except, of course, such things as payments for postage stamps) in terms of the unit, and also towards reckoning the salaries, pensions, and, when possible, the wages of its employees at so many units instead of so much currency. It should, I think, begin by offering, as soon as the unit was made, to pay for each £100 of consols a really uniform interest of three units, instead of a nominally uniform but really fluctuating interest of £3. The public, though at first regarding the new notion as uncanny, would, I believe, take to it rapidly as soon as they got to see its substantial advantages. Their dislike of it even at first would be less than was their dislike of coal fires, of railways and of gas. Ere long the currency would, I believe, be restricted to the functions for which it is well fitted, of measuring and settling transactions that are completed shortly after they are begun. I think we ought, without delay, to set about preparing for voluntary use an authoritative unit ; being voluntary, it would be introduced tentatively, and would be a powerful remedy for a great evil. This plan would not cause any forced disturbance of existing contracts. It would give a better standard for deferred payments than could possibly be given by a currency (as ordinarily understood), and, therefore, would diminish the temptation to hurry on impetuously a change of our currency with the object of making its value a little more stable ; and it could be worked equally well with any currency." [1]

§ 3. Marshall's "unit" is, of course, stable in an absolute sense as defined in the preceding chapter. But it would be easy to construct a unit stable in the other sense : and it would be a matter for debate which kind should be preferred. Perhaps one would be better for some types of contract, and the other for other types. For our present purpose the issue is not an important one ; and the advantages, from the standpoint of industrial fluctuations, which a tabular standard offers, as compared with the wider policy of price control, can be canvassed in a general way without reference to it. Marshall's plan has great attractions. There is, however, one very serious objection to it as against its more ambitious rival. This is that, though the Government can construct and publish a tabular standard and can endeavour in one way and another to encourage people to make use of it, it cannot compel them to make use of it. It cannot even put severe pressure upon them to make use of it, in the way that, by its control over public clocks, it can put severe pressure upon people to adopt daylight saving. Hence, as a matter of practice, what is open to us, along this line of remedy, is not a thorough-going resort to a tabular standard, but a very partial and imperfect resort to it. Even, therefore, if we believed, which we do not, that a thorough-going use of such a standard would accomplish practically as much towards steadying industry as price stabilisation, and would be free from difficulties and objections to which that policy is exposed, we ought not to reject the wider policy out of hand. Its rival would cost less, but, since it cannot be applied thoroughly, it would also accomplish less. There need,

---

[1] *Memorials* of Alfred Marshall, pp. 197-9, reprinted from an article in the *Contemporary Review* of March 1887.

however, be no difference of opinion upon one point. Unless and until the wider policy is adopted, there is everything to be said for pursuing the narrower one. Under the Dawes scheme, provision has been made for varying Germany's reparation obligations in terms of gold in the event of gold itself altering seriously in terms of things. To encourage private borrowers and lenders to follow this example would injure no one and would certainly diminish industrial fluctuations in some degree.[1]

---

[1] A practical instance of the type of loan contemplated is afforded by an issue of bonds recently made by the Rand Kardex Company in the State of Delaware, U.S.A. The bonds are described as " seven per cent thirty year stabilised debenture bonds, registered and safeguarded as to purchasing power of both principal and interest " : and their nature is explained in the following extract from the terms stated on the face of the bonds.

"Rand Kardex Company, Inc., a Delaware Corporation, hereinafter termed the 'company', for value received, hereby promises to pay to the registered holder hereof on the first day of July 1955, at the principal office of the Buffalo Trust Company, in the City of Buffalo, State of New York, such sum of money as shall possess the present purchasing power of One thousand dollars ($1,000.00) with interest thereon at the rate of seven per cent. per annum, payable quarterly on January first, April first, July first and October first, in such sums as shall, at the respective times of payment, equal in purchasing power One and seventy-five one hundredths per cent. (1.75 %) of said purchasing power of One thousand dollars ($1,000.00), all to be based upon an index number of the prices of commodities defined and fixed in accordance with the amplified statement below.

" . . . The index number of the prices of commodities employed hereunder shall be the well-known index number of wholesale prices of the United States Bureau of Labor Statistics as published each month, subject to such modifications and amplifications and changes of method in making and computing the same as shall, or may be, made by said bureau from time to time.

" If, as of any due date, the index number of the prices of commodities shall remain at approximately the present level, that is to say, if it does not rise or fall as much as one-tenth part of the level fixed as of July 1, 1925, i.e. 157.5, then the amount to be paid as principal shall be One thousand dollars ($1,000.00) ; and the amount to be paid as interest on any quarterly interest date shall be Seventeen dollars and fifty cents ($17.50).

" In case the index number as of any due date shall be found to be more or less than that fixed for July 1, 1925, by as much as one-tenth part of said index number of July 1, 1925, then for every full one-tenth rise or fall of said index number, there shall be added or subtracted respectively one-tenth of the payment then due, said one-tenth being $1.75 for any quarterly payment of interest and $100·00 for the principal sum.

" The index number measuring the present price level as of July 1, 1925, shall be the average of said index numbers for the three calendar months preceding July 1, 1925, which have been published on or before July 1, 1925, namely, the index numbers for March, April and May of 1925, which average is 157.5 on the basis of 100 as representing the 1913 price level.

" The index number measuring the price level as of July 1st of any other year hereunder shall be the average of the said index numbers for March, April and May of such other year, and the index number as of October 1st in any year shall be in like manner the average of the said index numbers for the preceding June, July and August, and the index number as of January 1st in any year shall be in like manner the average of the said index numbers for the preceding September, October and November, and the index number as of April 1st in any year, shall be in like manner the average of the said index numbers for the preceding December, January and February. . . .

" In case the United States Bureau of Labor statistics should discontinue the computation and publication of its said monthly index number of wholesale prices, or the publication thereof should be delayed so as to prevent its use hereunder, there shall be substituted therefor by the Trustee, as specified more fully in said indenture, such other index number or method of ascertaining changes in the price level as resembles in the opinion of the Trustee most closely the index number and method of arriving thereat of said Bureau."

CHAPTER V

CREDIT CONTROL AND PRICE STABILISATION

§ 1. In the present and two following chapters I shall study the policy of controlling bank credit with a view to stabilising, whether absolutely or about a moving trend, the general level of prices. At first sight we may be inclined to suppose that, if a Government so chooses, it can, without difficulty, by administrative orders, fix the sum of bank credit outstanding at a constant amount, or—in a progressive society —at an amount increasing at a constant rate, or in any other way that may seem good to it. In real life, however, the banking system is divided into a number of separate banks—of which, of course, in this country the Big Five are much the most important—confronting different groups of customers. In these circumstances it is not feasible to regulate the aggregate amount of credit outstanding from the banking system as a whole by fixing limits for individual banks ; any more than it is feasible in this direct way to regulate the aggregate amount of butter sold by retail shops in the United Kingdom. The only practicable method is to wait for signs that the desired aggregate is being exceeded or is not being attained, and thereupon to apply, as the case may be, a brake or a stimulant.

§ 2. It is important to notice that brakes and stimulants alike have a double action. On the one side they act directly on the quantity of bank credit that is forthcoming in the face of given conditions of demand on the part of the industrial community. On the other side they modify the conditions of demand. As was explained in Part I. Chapter XVII., an upward swing of prices creates an expectation of its own continuance, and the profit that business men foresee for themselves in this causes them, apart from any other reason that they may have for doing so, to employ their balances more actively and to seek further balances : and this pushes prices up further. If it is known that, as soon as prices show signs of rising, the banks will take steps to contract their loans and stop the rise, these reactions on the demand of business men will not take place. A corresponding consideration applies to falling prices. It follows that, in order to achieve stability or to reduce instability in any given measure, considerably less violent action on the part of the banks to modify the volume of bank loans is necessary in fact than would appear to be necessary if the direct consequences of their action were alone taken into consideration. The banks' action on the supply side calls out an ally working to the same end on the demand side.

§ 3. There are two forms of brake and stimulant available to the banking system, the method of rationing and the method of discount control, coupled, if necessary, with open-market operations. The range of both methods is limited, in that neither of them can touch loans already contracted for, but only new or renewed borrowings. It follows that different classes of business people will be affected in different degrees. Thus suppose that there are two men of equal ability, each reckoning to get roughly the same return, say £10,000, for his efforts. One is a manufacturer with a factory worth £90,000 financed by debentures and a working capital of £10,000 financed by short loans : the other is a merchant with a plant worth £10,000 financed by debentures and a working capital of £90,000 financed by short loans. The former of these two men can only be affected by a change in discount rates, or a cut in the ration allowed, in respect of £10,000 ; the latter can be affected in respect of £90,000. Plainly in this second case—and it is typical of the merchant's position as compared with the manufacturer's—the effect on the volume of borrowing is likely to be much larger than in the first. In both cases, however, there will be *some* effect. Nor is this all. The check or stimulus administered to merchants is reflected

after a little while in a further indirect check or stimulus
to the borrowings of manufacturers.   For, if money becomes
dearer or becomes scarcer, merchants will not wish to hold
such large stocks of goods, and will cut down their orders.
If manufacturers are booked up well ahead, this will not,
indeed, affect their activity immediately.   After a little
while, however, as the earlier orders are worked off, they
will find themselves with less to do and will contract their
purchases of raw material and their aggregate payments to
workpeople.   Thus, as an indirect result of the check
imposed on merchants, they will be led to make a second
cut, additional to the first cut directly imposed on them,
into their borrowings from banks.   In the converse case
of lowered discounts or expanded loans, analogous results
will follow.

§ 4. For downward adjustments the discount method
and the rationing method could both, theoretically at
least, be pushed so far that all bank loans would
be swept out of existence and the volume of bank
deposits cut down to the volume of currency that had
been actually deposited, in the sense of physically handed
over into the charge of bankers.   Under rationing this
result could be achieved by refusals to grant any new loan
or to carry forward any old one as it fell due for repayment :
under discount control it could be achieved by fixing the
rate of discount at a million per cent.   In practice, of
course, extreme measures of this sort would wreck society,
and are not to be contemplated.   Moreover, in some circumstances, *e.g.* when the Government is in the market
borrowing for an urgent purpose, such as the conduct of a
war, even milder applications of them are not possible.
Direct rationing of the Government's demands would be
out of the question, and the imposition of high discount
rates, since the Government *must* borrow at whatever cost,
would be ineffective.   Still, within reasonable limits it
remains true that, in respect of downward adjustments,
either rationing or discount control can be used to achieve
whatever effect on the sum of bank credits the banks may
desire.

§ 5. With regard to upward adjustments, however, both weapons are somewhat blunted. Of course, up to a point, the volume of loans can be increased by a readiness on the part of the banks to make loans on conditions, or on a type of security, that they have hitherto refused to entertain ; and they can also be increased by a drop in the discount rate, for this, in general, will tempt additional borrowing. But in times of depression on neither plan can borrowing be expanded beyond a point. People do not want to borrow on any terms, and the banks cannot force them to do so. In any strict sense of rationing, since this is essentially a negative process—a refusal of loans to some persons, who, at current prices, would like to take them— it is obvious that rationing cannot *in any degree* increase the volume of loans in depressions. Discount regulation is in somewhat better case, but not in much better. As Mr. Hawtrey puts it : " Even lending money without interest would not help if borrowers anticipated a loss on every conceivable use that they could make of the money ".[1] No doubt, if we are prepared to contemplate indefinitely large negative rates of money discount—it will be recollected, of course, that, when prices are expected to fall 12 per cent in a year, a money rate of minus 5 per cent implies a real rate of approximately plus 7 per cent—this limitation on the power of bankers to regulate the borrowing of loans in an upward direction would be removed. But negative rates of discount need not be considered here ; for they are not practical politics.

§ 6. This restriction upon the power of bankers seems at first sight exceedingly important. There are, however, mitigating considerations. While, as we have seen, industrial fluctuations are in part due to harvest variations and other such things, they are also in part due to swings of business confidence between excessive optimism and excessive pessimism ; and these antithetical swings do not as a rule arise independently, but are, as it were, generated the one from the other. If errors of optimism can be prevented from arising, the disappointment to which they lead and

---

[1] *Economic Journal*, 1922, p. 299.

the consequent reaction towards errors of pessimism will also be prevented from arising. In so far, therefore, as errors of optimism result from the fact that, when confidence begins to expand, general prices move upwards, a policy that prevented this upward movement would not only do away with errors of optimism, but would do away with errors of pessimism also. A successful attack on upward price swings would thus check both parts of those swings of confidence for which credit and price swings are responsible. If, therefore, we are satisfied that bankers wield weapons adequate for a successful direct attack on upward price swings, our doubt of their ability to defeat downward swings by direct action need not greatly trouble us. On the strength, then, of what has been said in this chapter, in conjunction with the analysis of Part I., we conclude that, if the banking system chose, or was compelled, to adjust the volume of its loans, from one time to another, either by rationing or through discount policy, with a view to restricting the swings of credit, and so of prices, that accompany swings of business activity, it would eliminate a factor which now contributes in an important degree to swell the amplitude of industrial fluctuations.

CHAPTER VI

CREDIT RATIONING *VERSUS* DISCOUNT POLICY

§ 1. A FUNDAMENTAL distinction between loan control through rationing and loan control through discount policy is that under rationing bankers have actively to select for rejection certain claimants for loans : under the discount method they cause certain claimants to select themselves. Until quite recently the latter method was practically universal and the former practically unknown, alike in the money market and in the market for ordinary commodities. People who could give adequate security were free to buy as large an amount of loans from bankers as, at the ruling rate for money, they wished to buy : just as they were free to buy as large an amount of wheat as, at the ruling price, they wished to buy. In the money market demand and supply were adjusted through the rate for money, just as in the wheat market they were adjusted through the price of wheat : and there was no question of the sellers interfering, through any other means, with the quantity that the buyers chose to take. Clearly, however, it is *possible* for sellers, in the money market and the wheat market alike, to fix a price adapted to find buyers up to such and such a quantity, and then to ration the buyers to a smaller quantity than this. In the Great War this practice was adopted for a number of important articles of food : and in the period of boom following the war resort was had to it in some degree for bankers' loans. What, from a broad social point of view, are the merits of this policy as compared with those of its rival ? Since, as was shown in the last chapter, rationing, being essentially a negative policy, is only available to check loans in times of boom, not to expand them in times of depression, attention may be confined to times of boom.

§ 2. In one respect it is evident that selection by rationing is at a disadvantage. Resort to it implies that in times of boom sellers of the rationed article accept an artificially low price ; otherwise there would be no surplus demand to which the rationing could be applied. Hence the production of the article—in this case not merely credit creations by banks but also voluntary savings by the public—will be reduced below what it would be in a free market, and, therefore we may presume, below what is socially desirable. This objection is on all fours with the corresponding objection to fixing a maximum price, lower than the " natural " price, for wheat, and distributing supplies by rationing. The stimulus to farmers to grow wheat would necessarily be weakened, and the presumption is that less wheat would be grown than it is socially desirable should be grown.

§ 3. From the point of view of distribution the issue appears at first sight less clear. Whether a distribution accomplished by selective rationing will be socially better or worse than a distribution resulting from the free working of demand and supply in a community composed of people of very different degrees of wealth cannot be determined until we know how skilful the rationer is and what principles of policy he adopts. In the way of distribution by rationing, as a regular policy in normal times, whether for loans or for anything else, there is, however, an overwhelming practical difficulty. There is no recognised or easily formulated basis in accordance with which rationing can be regulated. For the rationing of food during the war a basis was available in the fact that different people's physiological needs are not very far from equal, and, therefore, subject to a limited number of exceptions, equal rationing could be adopted. In the rationing of materials, again, there was a feasible basis in the pre-war requirements of different firms. Even here, of course, there were bound to be many hard cases and much difficulty. But for rationing credit in times of peace the difficulty of finding an acceptable basis would be enormously greater. Equal rationing would be absurd, and rationing based on past requirements would ignore the fact that in booms the needs of different borrowers expand in very different degrees. In the early post-war period an attempt was made to ration in accordance with the purposes for which different people needed loans. But this plan not only involves a kind of inquisition for which bankers, at all events in England, are ill equipped, but also requires them to decide what is the relative importance, from the standpoint of peace-time needs, of a multitude of competing purposes. Moreover, there could hardly fail to be serious friction and discontent among potential borrowers. These borrowers would also be made to suffer from a new sense of insecurity, since they could never know for certain how far they might rely on obtaining accommodation from the banks, even though they had good security to offer.

§ 4. A further very important consideration is as follows. If the volume of loans is to be controlled, in a country organised as England is the rationing would have to be worked by the various joint-stock and private banks other than the Bank of England : for it is these banks that are responsible for the main part of the loans made to the public. But these banks are independent of one another. It is not to the interest of any of them to ration in a restrictive sense its financially sound customers. Each bank would prefer that such rationing as has to be done should be done by its rivals : and, unless some common understanding is arrived at, each will fear that, if it adopts a policy of rationing, customers to whom it refuses accommodation may merely go and find it elsewhere. Hence, if the policy of rationing is to be effectively adopted and carried through as a corrective of excessive loans in boom periods, it is essential that the chief members of the national banking system shall co-operate on definite and agreed lines. Plainly, it would be very difficult to secure and keep unimpaired this type of co-operation on a voluntary basis. Nor is it easy to see how in this matter it is possible for anybody to enforce co-operation from outside.

§ 5. The method of loan control through discount is free from this difficulty. For though the Central Bank does not, when it alters its discount rate, by that very fact compel the market to follow—indeed in some circumstances a rise in its rate, by encouraging the importation of gold for delivery to the other banks, may actually make for a lowering of the market rate—it has means at its command by which it can do this whenever it so desires. If it wishes to lower discount generally from 5 per cent to 4 per cent, and a lowering of its own rate to 4 per cent does not accomplish this, it has only to purchase securities in the market, thus increasing the " cash " holdings of the other banks and enabling them to follow it in reducing rates. *Per contra*, if it wishes to raise discounts generally from 5 per cent to 6 per cent, and the raising of its own rate does not accomplish this, it has only to sell securities in the market, thus draining the market of money and forcing the market rate to follow its own rate ; for the joint-stock banks will not be willing to allow their cash and balances at the Bank of England to fall much below the proportion (say 1 to 9) in which these usually stand to their liabilities. The need for this subsidiary action exists, not merely in England, where it is contrary to tradition for the other banks to rediscount bills at the Central Bank, but also in the United States, where rediscounting with the Federal Reserve Banks is a regular practice : for, if the other banks are in funds, they may be able to meet the demands on them for loans without rediscounting, and, in that case, they will not be forced to raise their rates by a mere raising of the Reserve Bank's rate unaccompanied by supporting operations on the part of that Bank in the market. A valuable account of the recent practice of the Federal Reserve System in this matter is given in the evidence— particularly that of Governor Strong and Professor Commons —taken before the Committee on Banking and Currency of the House of Representatives (1927) and printed in the Report entitled *Stabilisation*. It is especially interesting to observe that, in order to prevent violent disturbances, the Reserve Banks, when desiring to put a brake on credit expansion, have been accustomed first to " prepare the market " by selling securities, thus drawing money from it, and then, when the member banks are, by this action, forced to borrow from them, to raise the rediscount rates.

Thus the money rates in the market go up *before* the re-discount rates of the Reserve Banks, so that anybody looking at discount movements alone and neglecting the associated open-market operations might easily be tempted to argue that the causes initiating credit restrictions must lie in the market, and not in the Reserve Banks![1] For our present purpose, however, the detailed nature of the machinery employed is of secondary importance. The essential fact is that, so long as a Central Bank, desiring to adopt any form of stabilising discount policy, holds a substantial amount of readily saleable securities,[2] it always has the power to engage in these supporting operations.[3] When therefore,

---

[1] Cf. *Stabilisation.* Evidence of Governor Strong, p. 307 ; and evidence of Professor Commons, p. 1087.

[2] This qualifying clause indicates that a point may come beyond which it is impossible for a Central Bank to neutralise the tendency of gold imports to raise prices. The other banks selling the gold to the Central Bank *pro tanto* increase their reserves. The Central Bank can only counter-act this process so long as it has securities to sell to the banks or their customers.

[3] In present conditions this statement needs to be qualified in one respect. As is well known, there is in England now a large mass of short-dated Treasury Bills continually due for renewal. If the Bank of England, desiring to raise discount generally, put up its rate and began selling securities in the market, the Treasury *could*, if it so desired, defeat the Bank's purpose. If it refused to raise the Treasury Bill rate and main-tained it at, say, 2½ per cent below the Bank of England discount rate, people (including banks) could get a better return by putting money on deposit with other banks or with the Bank of England than by taking up Treasury Bills. Therefore, many of these bills would fail to be renewed, and the Treasury would perforce fall back on Ways and Means Advances from the Bank of England, which, even in these conditions of conflict, that institution could not refuse, since refusal would involve a national default. The employment by the Treasury of these Ways and Means Advances to pay off Treasury Bills would, however, create a corre-sponding volume of new balances at the Bank of England to the credit of the joint-stock banks. These new balances would constitute an inflow to their "cash and balances at the Bank of England" in contra-distinction to the outflow which the Bank of England was trying to set up by selling securities in the market, and might enable the market to maintain low rates in spite of the Bank of England's action. Though it is not, of course, to be supposed that the Treasury and the Bank of England would ever allow themselves to come into open conflict in the way imagined above, it is not inconceivable that the Treasury, being possessed of the power that I have been describing, might use it as an unuttered threat to prevent the Bank from endeavouring to force discount rates up on occasions when the Government wished them to remain low.

One further point in this connection should be mentioned. It is often

I speak of the method of loan control through discount I include under that concept the use of these methods. I conceive it as a part of discount policy, not as something additional to it. In the discount method of loan control thus understood no complicated set of agreements and undertakings among persons whose interests are really in conflict is involved. The decision is always the decision of a single institution. This consideration, in conjunction with those advanced in earlier sections, makes it evident that, as an instrument of control over bankers' loans in the world as it is to-day, the regulation of discount rates is greatly to be preferred to the method of rationing credits.

---

argued that the funding of Treasury Bills would have a deflating effect, because Treasury Bonds are taken up to a greater extent by private persons (as compared with the banks) than Treasury Bills are. This view seems, however, to be incorrect. If I buy a £1000 Treasury Bond out of my balance at the Westminster Bank and the Government therewith pays off a £1000 Treasury Bill held by the Westminster Bank, that bank has the same " cash and balance at the Bank of England " as before, but £1000 less liabilities. Therefore it is in a position to lend a new £1000 without hurting its " proportion ". If it does not do this, the reason is, not that it cannot do it, but that people do not want to have so much money for trading as hitherto. Had there been no conversion of Treasury Bills the bank's liabilities would still have fallen. The connection which exists between the funding of the Treasury Bills and the contraction of bank liabilities can be accounted for by the fact that the times when there is not much competition for borrowing in industry are the times most suitable for funding operations. This reasoning is, however, subject to the qualification that some bankers may regard Treasury Bills as akin to " cash and balances at the Bank of England " when they are thinking of their " proportion ", so that, if commercial bills took the place of Treasury Bills in their portfolios, they would need, for ease of mind, a rather bigger " proportion " than before.

CHAPTER VII

A DISCOUNT POLICY DIRECTED TOWARDS PRICE
STABILISATION

§ 1. BEFORE the main subject-matter of this chapter is attacked it is desirable to deal with a preliminary difficulty. The rate of discount is tied up to the rate of interest—money rate—on long loans; this rate, it is argued, is determined by the general conditions of demand and supply of real capital; these lie outside the Central or any other bank's control; and, therefore, though, no doubt, on occasions for a little while a strong Central Bank could hold its discount rate above or below the rate for long loans (with due allowance for differences of risk), attempts to do this for any length of time must lead to a transfer of borrowings between the long and the short loan markets, and so defeat itself. Hence, it is argued, the Central Bank, despite its apparent autonomy, is in fact merely a medium through which forces wholly external to it work their will. Though, that is to say, in determining the discount rate, the voice is the voice of the Bank, the hands are not its hands.

§ 2. This reasoning is not valid. Let us start from a state of equilibrium, in which the real rate on capital, the money rate on long loans and the discount rate on short loans are all, appropriate allowances being made for differences in the risks involved, 5 per cent. There is no iron law that, other things remaining the same, bankers must retain the discount rate at 5 per cent and cannot, on their own initiative, shift it for any length of time to 2 per cent or 10 per cent. The only iron law is that, *if* they do either of these things, certain consequential adjustments must

275

take place in the prices of long-term securities and of commodities. If the discount rate is dropped to 2 per cent, fixed interest securities will rise in value and the money yield of interest on long loans will be dropped to correspond with the drop in discount. The drop in yield will not, of course, be equal to the drop in discount unless this drop is expected to be permanent. A drop in discount from 5 per cent to 2 per cent, expected to last for one year, should involve, as an arithmetical equivalent, a drop in the money rate of long loans, as represented, *e.g.*, by the yield on consols, to 4·85 . . . per cent. Correspondingly, a rise of discount from 5 per cent to 10 per cent, expected to last for one year, should involve a rise in the yield on consols to 5·24 . . . per cent. So much for the adjustment in the prices of securities.[1] The adjustment in the prices of commodities is in this wise. So far as the facts of the situation are known and their consequences foreseen, prices must change at once in whatever degree is required to make the money rate of 2 per cent representative of a real rate of 5 per cent, or, more exactly, of that real rate slightly different from 5 per cent, to which the forced levies described in Part I. Chapter XIII. have changed the 5 per cent real rate. If we ignore this qualification, the arithmetic will be as follows. Prices must rise at once to such a point that £100 now will buy $\frac{100}{105}$ times as much stuff as £102 are expected to buy a year hence : that is to say, they must rise at once in a

---

[1] Lavington, in a study of the comparative yields on long and short loans, has shown that in times of boom the capital value of consols has tended to fall so far that the yield on consols is pushed up relatively to the yield on bills (*i.e.* the discount rate) more than it " ought to be ". The explanation he suggests is that, when high discount has led to a fall in the capital value of consols, holders are apt to fear a further fall and so to throw consols on the market " until the prospective profitableness of investment in consols exceeds that of investment in bills by an amount which compensates the investor for the possibility of a further fall in their capital value " (*Economica*, November 1924, p. 300). Professor Cassel explains the low rate for short loans, which prevailed, together with a high rate for long loans, in England towards the end of 1922, by suggesting that " the market more or less consciously feels that a rise in the bank rate must come, and keeps back the long investments in expectation of the fall of securities which is then bound to take place " (" The Restoration of the Gold Standard ", *Economica*, November 1923, p. 181).

certain definite measure above the level at which they are
expected to stand a year hence. If the rate of discount
were raised to 10 per cent instead of being dropped to 2 per
cent, there would be a converse type of adjustment. These
details are, of course, merely illustrative. The essential
fact, for our present purpose, is that there is no iron law,
imposed, as it were, from outside, limiting the choice of
a Central Bank in the matter of discount rates : though,
of course, in any given set of external conditions, the choice
is limited internally by the Bank's knowledge of, and regard
for, the probable effect of different policies on its own
economic interest and on the wider interest of the nation
as a whole.

§ 3. It may, indeed, be replied that in this answer the real
point has been evaded. Nobody, it may be said, seriously
supposes that it is beyond the power of a Central Bank, on
its own initiative, to modify the money rate of discount.
The position taken is that, if the money rate of discount
is altered at the volition of the banks, just those associated
changes which have been described in the preceding section
must take place, and must be carried to the point at which
the real rate of discount is equated (with the proper allowances) to the real rate of interest on long loans ; this real
rate being throughout determined by conditions outside the
bankers' control. Hence, the argument runs, it is only in
so far as people fail to understand what is happening that
the bankers' action in altering nominal discount rates
can make any real difference to industry. A perusal of
Chapter XIII. of Part I. should, however, make it clear
that this analysis is incorrect. When bankers create more
credit for business men, they make, in their interest,
subject to the explanations given in that chapter, a forced
levy of real things from the public, thus increasing the
stream of new capital available for them, and causing a
fall in the real rate of interest on long and short loans
alike. It is true, in short, that the bankers' rate for money
is bound by a mechanical tie to the real rate of interest
on long loans: but it is not true that this real rate is determined by conditions wholly outside bankers' control. This

preliminary objection to the use of discount rates as an instrument of stabilisation may, therefore, be dismissed.

§ 4. We have next to observe that the Central Banks have for a long time been accustomed to control the volume of credit by means of this instrument. It is quite legitimate to speak of the gold standard, when operated in a country in which paper money (*e.g.* Bank of England notes) as well as gold is in circulation, as a paper standard regulated by the Central Bank in such wise as to keep the monetary unit at parity with gold.[1] When, therefore, it is proposed that the discount rate should be employed to stabilise prices, whether absolutely or relatively to a moving trend, by controlling credit, the change contemplated, as against current practice, is not in the weapon to be used but in the end towards which it is directed. The task of the present chapter is to show in what ways present practice, or, more accurately, pre-war practice,[2] needs to be modified in order to attain the new end.

§ 5. The key fact determining the practice of the Bank of England, as of other Central Banks, is that it is bound by law to meet instantly with legal money or gold bars any (sufficient value) of its own notes—and it must provide notes against valid cheques upon its customers' balances—that may be presented to it for payment. In view of this fact it is vital to it in all circumstances to keep a reserve sufficiently large in proportion to its liabilities to make it absolutely secure against any danger of default. But, on the other hand, it will not wish to keep a reserve larger than is necessary to achieve this purpose, because every £ that it keeps locked up in reserve means a potential profit sacrificed. Consequently, self-interest should, in theory at least, bring about a continuous balancing on the part of the Central Bank of the advantage of a little extra security to be got by enlarging its reserve proportion and the advantage of a little extra profit to be got

---

[1] Cf. Cassel, *Fundamental Thoughts in Economics*, p. 134.
[2] This qualification is inserted in order to take note of the fact that the Federal Reserve Board and, since the restoration of the gold standard, the Bank of England have recently, it would seem, adopted in some considerable degree, a policy directed towards price stabilisation.

by contracting it. In times of " prosperity ", when people are ready to pay higher interest on a given volume of loans and when the risk of bad debts is, because of prosperity, diminished, both the profit from a given increase in loans relatively to reserve is greater than in normal times and the risk involved is less. Thus self-interest points to a diminution in the proportion of reserve to liabilities in times of prosperity when prices are rising ; and, conversely, it points to an increase in the proportion in times of depression when prices are falling. But it also sets limits to these variations in the proportion ; so that, when the proportion contracts, which means when prices rise, the rate of discount is put up to restrain the rise ; and, conversely, when the proportion expands the rate of discount is put down. Of course, Central Banks, whether technically private concerns, like the Bank of England, or connected by some legal tie with Government, do not regulate their policy merely with regard to their private interests. None the less, their policy—it may for convenience be called the reserve discount policy—has, at all events until quite recently, accorded broadly with the foregoing description. There are only two respects in which, so long as we ignore disturbances initiated on the side of currency supply, a stabilising discount policy can diverge from this reserve discount policy : namely, (1) in the timing and (2) in the magnitude of the changes that are made in the discount rate. It will, of course, be understood that, in speaking of changes in this rate, we intend to include whatever subsidiary action may be required in order to render the changes " effective " in the market.

§ 6. It is sometimes held that a reserve discount policy could be converted into a stabilising discount policy if the signal for action were looked for in price movements instead of in movements of the reserve proportion ; for in that event the required correction would be applied at a much earlier stage. Thus Mr. Hawtrey writes : " So long as credit is regulated with reference to reserve proportions, the trade cycle is bound to recur. The flow of legal tender money into circulation and back is one of the very tardiest consequences of credit expansion or contraction. If the Central Bank waits for the flow to affect its reserves, and sits passively looking on at an expansion or contraction gathering impetus for years before it takes any decisive action, we cannot escape from the alternations of feverish activity with depression and unemployment. If the Central Bank watches, not the reserve proportion, but the aberrations of the flow of purchasing power (as measured by prices subject to the necessary allowances) from a perfectly even course, early action will become the rule, the expansion will be checked in time and the contraction will be avoided." [1]   This thesis is exceedingly plausible *a priori*. It is, however, inconsistent with the facts. For. the United States, Mr. L. W. Hall has carried through a careful and elaborate investigation of the cyclical fluctuations occurring in the national bank system during the years 1903 to 1921. He concludes as follows : "Deposits, on careful inspection of the charts, seem to show a persistent three to six months' fluctuation in advance of prices. At times the fluctuations are nine months in advance of prices." [2]   Also : "There seems to be a tendency for cash in vaults to precede prices in fluctuations by about nine months to a year. This seems to be well marked in periods approaching a price fall, but not so marked in periods of a price rise." [3]   I have set out in the accompanying chart annual (not monthly) figures giving the relation between price movements (as represented in Sauerbeck's index numbers), and the proportion of reserve to liabilities in the Bank of England over the period 1860–1910. From this chart it appears that the years of clear price maxima, 1857, 1864, and 1889, are also years of proportion minima : and that the other three clear price maxima occurring in 1873, 1900, and 1907 lag a year behind the corresponding proportion minima. The year of clear price minimum, 1858, is the year of proportion maximum : the price minimum of 1870 precedes a proportion maximum in 1871 : the relation in 1887 and 1902 is ambiguous ; and

[1] *Monetary Reconstruction*, pp. 144-5.
[2] *A Study of the Cyclical Fluctuations occurring in the National Bank System during the Years 1903 to 1921*, p. 44.
[3] *Ibid.* p. 47.

the price minimum of 1896 lags two years behind the corresponding proportion maximum. Thus these annual figures
do not warrant the view that price changes in general precede proportion changes ; but, on balance, suggest that the
price changes lag a little behind. It would be instructive
to test this result by a detailed study of the monthly
figures, if a satisfactory device could be found for dealing
with seasonal movements. I shall not, however, attack
that problem here. What has already been said is sufficient
to show that Mr. Hawtrey's argument against the use of
proportion changes as a signal for the application of corrective discount is invalid.

§ 7. Though, however, it is not true that, to convert a
reserve discount policy into a stabilising discount policy,
price movements should be substituted for proportion
movements as the signal for action, it is true that action
would need to be taken considerably earlier than has
hitherto been customary. A good deal could be done
in this sense without seeking any new signal for action.
For, under a reserve discount policy, though the Bank
looks to the reserve proportion, it does not alter the
discount rate immediately that signal has moved, but
waits until the proportion has undergone a substantial
change and a clear tendency to expansion or decline has
become manifest. Thus, although, as we have seen, the
proportion moves before prices, and discount is regulated by
the proportion, the changes in discount lag behind changes
in the price level. In the United States there appears to
be a time-lag of some four months in short money rates
behind prices.[1] For the United Kingdom Mr. Williams made
in 1912 an elaborate study of the relation between rates of
discount for three months' bank-bills and the movements of
Sauerbeck's index number over the period 1845–1911. He
summarises his conclusions as follows : " The result of this
investigation shows that for every maximum rate of discount
there is a corresponding maximum of prices ; the few
exceptions when complete information is at hand can be
explained by reference to price levels in other countries.

[1] *Review of Economic Statistics*, 1922, pp. 169-70.

Out of fourteen pairs of maxima twelve pairs have both maxima during the same year, and in the other two the maximum prices come in the year preceding the year of maximum discounts. Again, in the years 1900 and 1907, although both maxima come in the same year, yet the price maximum precedes the maximum discount by about six months. The same may be said of several other pairs ; for example in 1873, 1882 and 1890 ; in each of these years there are statistics available which give an indication of the time when prices began to fall. Of the earlier years, 1851 has been mentioned as one in which the price maximum came late in 1850, or early in 1851, and where the price maximum precedes the rate of discount. In the years 1847 and 1857 the bank rate was higher in the autumn of both, and this favours the supposition that the price maximum came first. Out of the fourteen pairs two price maxima came in the year preceding the discount maximum, five came during the same year but in earlier months, three have certain evidence to show that they probably came first, and four, for which there are no statistics, may or may not have come first. Hence we may conclude that generally the price maximum precedes the maximum rate of discount by a few months. The minima for prices and the rate of discount are not as clearly shown as the maxima."[1]   It is clear from this that market discount movements lag somewhat behind price movements. This lag could be wiped out if the Bank of England were to take action to change its rate, and to force the market to follow it, immediately prices began to move. It could be more than wiped out if the Bank took this action immediately the *proportion* began to move.

§ 8. Apart, however, from the serious practical difficulty of determining whether the first beginnings of a proportion change are really significant or are a mere momentary flutter, we have now to observe that the requirements of a stabilising discount policy would not be fully met by making changes in the discount rate coincide with turns in the proportion. The rates should be changed earlier than this.

[1] T. T. Williams, " The Rate of Discount and the Price of Consols ", *Journal of the Royal Statistical Society*, March 1912, p. 390.

For this there are two reasons. First, it may easily happen
that the sum of bank credits created for industrialists turns
upward or downward some little while before the Central
Bank's proportion is affected. For, though the ordinary
banks tend in a general way to work to a definite proportion
between their deposits and their cash and balances at the
Bank of England—a proportion which, since the war, has
been about 1 : 9 [1]—this proportion is not rigid, but elastic.
In booms the joint-stock banks, feeling optimistic like everybody else, may be willing to cut down their proportion, and
in depressions, being pessimistic, may wish to expand it.[2]
Thus it has been written of the United States : " When
business is active the banks are led to utilise their own
resources, and are put in a position of dependence on the
rediscounting agency. In a period of depression, however,
they have unused resources of their own, and are in a position
to take care of a considerable increase in customers' demands
without borrowing." [3] Secondly, the seeds of expansions
and contractions are sown some little while before the movements in credit occur, and it is the sowing of the seeds, and
not their sprouting, if they have been sown, that discount
policy is chiefly able to influence. In respect of contracts
that are already entered into and constructions that are

[1] Cf. Keynes, *A Tract on Monetary Reform*, p. 179.

[2] The suggestion, that the extra provision of money in booms comes, in
the first instance, from the joint-stock banks, and that the Bank of England
is only called in later, fits in with evidence which Mr. Silberling has recently
brought together concerning the first quarter of the nineteenth century.
From his figures it appears " that important cyclical movements of the
volume of discounting at the Bank regularly *followed* those of the price
barometer ", but that cyclical movements .in the volume of notes issued
by country banks " were simultaneous with, or preceded, prices " (*Review
of Economic Statistics* : Supplement, October 1923, pp. 241 and 243).

[3] Hardy, *Risk and Risk-Bearing*, pp. 100-1. Developing his thesis
with special reference to American conditions, Mr. Hardy continues :
" No matter how low the rate, they will not rediscount so long as their
own funds are lying idle. Hence a lowering of the rediscount rate is like
an importation of gold in times when reserves are already superabundant,
or an immigration of labor in times when our own labor forces are largely
unemployed, or the opening of new land for settlement in a pioneer country
where there is already good free land. It has no immediate, direct effect;
it only gives assurance that there are larger resources to be drawn upon
in case of need." In England the other banks do not borrow from the
Bank of England directly, but, by calling in their own loans to bill-brokers,
cause it to lend more to these persons.

already on the way to completion a rise of discount can have little effect. Whatever money is wanted to finance these things will still be wanted in spite of enhanced rates. Thus in the report of the Federal Reserve Bank for 1923 we read : " Business transactions which are already under way will ordinarily be carried through to completion, quite irrespective of changes that have supervened in credit conditions and money rates. The rise in discount rates is not intended to interrupt or interfere with antecedent commitments that are in process of completion, but rather to induce a more prudent attitude on the part of borrowers with regard to new commitments. It requires, therefore, some time for a rate change to show its effects in the altered lending operations of the banks." [1] From these two considerations it follows that under a really effective stabilising discount policy discount rates must move considerably before the signal set by the Central Bank's proportion is affected. It seems, therefore, that we must seek for a more sensitive signal.

§ 9. Recent American investigations help us here : for they have thrown light on the order of events in the typical trade cycle. Thus it has been established by the Harvard Bureau of Economic Research that an early reaction of improved business expectations is on the values of speculative stocks. In the United Kingdom a study of the period 1903–14 suggested that the prices of variable-interest securities tend to move upward at the turn of the tide some nine months before the prices of commodities do so. [2] There is reason to believe, though unfortunately detailed statistics are not here available, that at about this time, or perhaps a little later, dealers in commodities, upheld by the same optimism that is sending up the prices of speculative stocks, increase their orders to manufacturers of goods, so that the stocks of goods in their (the dealers') hands begin soon to go up. The signal for action might thus be found in movements in the prices of speculative securities, or, if statistics were available, in the volume of new orders given

[1] *Loc. cit.* pp. 4-5.
[2] *The Review of Economic Statistics*, 1922, p. 168.

per month in important industries, or in the stocks of finished goods in dealers' hands, or, possibly, in the percentage of workpeople out of employment. The use of any of these things as a signal—due allowance being made for seasonal changes and for the effect of "accidents" irrelevant to the main movement—would enable corrective discount to be brought into play at an early period when the seeds of future booms and depressions are being sown.

§ 10. If a discount policy directed towards price stabilisation were adopted under conditions such that it was not possible to set the corrective discount changes to work at an earlier stage than that at which they are set to work under a reserve discount policy, it is evident that the discount changes, to be effective, would have to be much larger than they have usually been under the reserve discount policy. Granted, however, that the correctives are applied at an earlier stage, it is not certain that they would have to be larger than the actual changes that occur now. For a small change applied in good time may well prove a stronger stabiliser than a large change applied later on when the forces tending to push prices up or down have gathered way.

§ 11. If we continue to ignore price movements initiated otherwise than in industrial fluctuations at home, it will appear from what has been said that a stabilising discount policy could be introduced by modifying to only a small extent reserve discount policy as practised hitherto ; and, as has already been implied, it is immaterial here whether the stabilisation aimed at is absolute or relative to a trend. Reserve discount policy, since it has prevailed for a long time, is, we may presume, broadly in accordance with the interests of Central Banks as private institutions. In so far, therefore, as a stabilising discount policy differs from a reserve discount policy, its adoption would involve some sacrifice by the officers of Central Banks of the private interests of their shareholders to the public good. Already, as is indicated in § 5, the Bank of England, private institution though it is, regards itself in large measure as an organ of public service. The sacrifice required of it would probably be greater than it at present makes, but, the changes required being small, the extra sacrifice also would probably be small. We have no right then to assume that, if the public interest in price stabilisation were clearly demonstrated and understood, the Bank would decline, on the ground of private interest, to do its part to promote it. Should it do so, however, it is not a law of nature that the Central Bank shall be a private institution. There is nothing to prevent its being compelled by charter to accept a certain measure of Treasury control or even from being converted into a Department of Government. I do not now raise the question whether changes of this kind are, on the whole, desirable : they are referred to merely to make it clear that, *apart from price changes initiated on the side of money supply*, the consideration of which has been excluded from this chapter, such incompatibility as there may be between a stabilising discount policy and the private interest of the Central Bank can in no circumstances prove an insuperable obstacle to the adoption of that policy.

CHAPTER VIII

THE SUPPLY OF CURRENCY AND A RESERVE DISCOUNT POLICY

§ 1. When the discount rate of the Central Bank is regulated and the volume of credit controlled with an eye, not to stabilising prices in any sense, but to the state of the reserve, industrial fluctuations may be initiated, as was pointed out in Part I. Chapter VIII., by autonomous deviations away from its line of trend in the supply of currency : for these carry with them changes in the volume of credit, and so also in the price level. In this chapter I shall inquire, assuming that a reserve discount policy continues to be pursued : (1) how far it is practicable to safeguard industry from disturbance in spite of movements of this sort in the quantity of currency in the reserve ; (2) how far it is practicable to prevent these movements from occurring. For the purposes of the first of these inquiries it will be convenient to narrow our subject - matter by postulating the existence of a gold standard.

§ 2. It has frequently been pointed out that given drains upon, and given influxes into, a country's gold reserve will normally have a smaller proportionate effect upon the volume of credit, and so upon the level of prices, the larger that reserve is. Thus one way of mitigating the disturbances to industry due to autonomous changes in the supply to it of gold is for the banking system to hold large normal reserves of gold relatively to its liabilities. A like effect is produced if, given the size of the reserves, the whole of them are concentrated in a single Central Bank instead of being scattered as they are under a many-reserve banking system. Moreover, the possession by the Central Bank of instruments, which, while not themselves gold, are capable of being turned with ease and certainty into gold obtained from abroad, comes, for many purposes, to nearly the same thing as large gold reserves. Examples are large net holdings of foreign gold bills approaching maturity, large holdings of first-class securities with an international market and great undocumented power to borrow abroad.[1] Other things being equal, by strengthening the reserve position through any of these means, we can lessen the scale of industrial fluctuations that are brought about by given inflows or outflows of gold that result from happenings outside our country. It has to be observed, indeed, that such a policy, adopted by itself in a community where the banks act upon what I have called a reserve discount policy, will prove double-edged, in that it will *increase* the scale of industrial fluctuations initiated by non-monetary causes. For, the stronger is the reserve position, the more largely the banking system will be prepared to grant increased credits in response to any given increase in the demands of industrialists. If, however, the policy of large reserves is adopted in conjunction with a stabilising discount policy, it will strengthen the hands of the banking system to carry through that policy in the face of changes initiated on the side of money.

§ 3. The apparently obvious thesis that, the larger the reserve of gold held in normal times by the Central Bank, the smaller will be the effect on the volume of bank credit outstanding, and so on the level of prices, of given inflows or outflows of gold, needs now to be qualified. If there is fixed by law a minimum reserve, which must be *always* maintained

[1] The United Kingdom, before the war, was, it may be observed, strong in all the above respects. Not only were we large lenders both in the short and the long loan market, but also it was very much against the interest of foreigners to allow a monetary crisis to develop here. As the late Lord Goschen well observed, when the Bank of France provided three millions to tide us over the Baring crisis: "Paris was interested in saving the situation, let there be no mistake about that"—*Essays and Addresses,* p. 109. At the present time, in so far as we occupy a less important position as short-time lenders to foreigners and in so far as the gold in the outside world is more closely locked up and less accessible to us, the defences that stand before our reserve are less powerful than they were.

either absolutely or subject to a penalty, the *available* reserve
in times of stress is not the whole of the actual reserve, but
only the excess of the actual reserve above the legal minimum ;
and, of course, it is the *available* reserve that is relevant to
the present argument. It follows that the legal establishment of a minimum reserve will only strengthen the reserve
position in the sense defined in the preceding section if it
causes the actual normal reserve to exceed what it would
have been in the absence of any law by more than the
amount of the legal minimum.

§ 4. In this country, of course, the reserve to be held
against the *aggregate liabilities* of the Central Bank has
never been regulated by law ; but since 1844 the State has
considered it necessary to make stringent rules as regards
that part of the Bank of England's liabilities that consists
in bank notes. The Bank may issue as many notes as it
pleases against an equivalent backing of gold : but the
amount which it may issue against securities (the fiduciary
issue) must not exceed a defined maximum. If then the notes
in circulation (*i.e.* in the hands of the public and in bankers'
tills) normally amount to £x, and the maximum fiduciary
issue to £a, £ $(x - a)$ out of the Bank's actual gold reserve in
normal times is locked up, and is not *available* to meet drains.
In 1914 the total gold reserve of the Bank of England
was about 40 millions, the fiduciary issue 18 millions, the
notes in circulation 30 millions, and the locked-up portion
of the reserve 12 millions—leaving about 28 millions available. At the present time, under the Act for amalgamating
Treasury notes and Bank of England notes, the total gold
reserve is about 160 millions, the fiduciary issue 260 millions,
the circulation some 370 millions, the lock-up some 110
millions, and the available reserve, therefore, some 50 millions
out of a total reserve of 160 millions. Critics of the new
Act have urged that the limit of the fiduciary issue should
have been set at 300 millions instead of at 260 millions, thus
setting free from the lock-up, and making available, 40
millions more of the total gold reserve. This arrangement,
it has been argued, would have enabled the Bank to leave
the discount rate, and so, indirectly, the volume of bank

credit, unaltered in the face of much larger gold movements than it can now face with equanimity. This reasoning is valid upon the assumption that the Bank of England would have so regulated its policy as to maintain the same normal gold reserve with the higher fiduciary maximum that it in fact maintains with the lower one. With a higher fiduciary maximum, however, it would have been open to the Bank, had it so chosen, to treat the extra 40 millions of fiduciary notes as equivalent to gold, and to keep money cheap until the total gold reserve had been reduced by that amount. In that case, the lock-up and the total reserve being reduced by equal amounts, the normal *available* reserve would be the same with the 300 million as with the 260 million fiduciary limit. The new Act contains provisions under which, with the assent of the Treasury, the fiduciary limit may be temporarily raised at the Bank's request. These provisions, if resort is had to them, not merely in times of panic,[1] but also to meet large temporary withdrawals of gold by foreigners, will, in effect, release gold from the lock-up when there is need for it, without tending so strongly as an enlargement of the fiduciary maximum would do to bring about a reduction in the normal total reserve. Thus a 260 million fiduciary maximum together with these provisions *may* make the *available* reserve in times of stress larger than a 300 million reserve without these provisions would have done. Whether it *will* do this depends, of course, on the policy which the Bank of England and the Treasury elect to pursue.

§ 5. In passing to our second question—how far it is practicable to prevent autonomous deviations from the trend in the currency supply from occurring—we note first that a substance may be chosen to serve as currency which is less liable than gold to disturbance on the side of supply. Thus, if the money unit were made out of a mixture of several different sorts of commodities, it would probably be subject to smaller changes in annual output than one made out of a single sort of commodity, because variations in the supply conditions of some of the several commodities might be expected more or

---

[1] Cf. *post*, Chap. IX. § 5.

less to cancel variations in those of others. This is the conception underlying Marshall's suggestion of symmetalism; and, of course, it would be possible to make up the currency unit out of more than two metals, or commodities other than metals. In principle, there can be no doubt that such an arrangement would yield a currency unit more stable in annual output and, therefore, in total supply (both absolutely and relatively to any given trend) than a gold standard is likely to do.

§ 6. A much more far-reaching solution is provided by what is commonly known as the Fisher standard. The root idea embodied in that standard is that the currency, whether made of paper or of gold or of anything else, should be so constructed that the material in a unit of it is worth very much less as material than it is when turned into currency. A government department should publish month by month an index number showing the variations in the purchasing power of a unit of currency. The Mint, or some corresponding agency, should always be prepared to exchange currency into or out of gold bullion. The quantity of currency given or taken in exchange for a given weight of bullion would not, however, on Professor Fisher's plan, be a fixed quantity, but would be increased or diminished according as the index number of general prices showed a tendency to fall or to rise. When general prices began to fall, the Mint would offer to sell currency for bullion at a reduced rate in the market; and when prices began to rise, the Mint would offer to buy currency at an increased rate in the market. In this way the volume of currency available for the reserve of the Central Bank would be automatically increased whenever prices fell and automatically diminished when they rose; [1] and the volume of credit would be altered correspondingly. These processes would be controlled with a view to main-

---

[1] Of course, if the currency were made of gold, the whole purpose of this plan would be upset were the government to *deposit* the coined gold, which it buys in order to reduce reserves, with the banks : it must withdraw it altogether from the money-providing machine. The Philippine law establishing a gold exchange standard sets a bad example in this respect, in that it allows a certain proportion of the gold standard fund to be held on deposit in Manila banks. (Cf. Kemmerer, *Modern Currency Reforms*, pp. 375-7.)

taining the currency at " a par, not with a fixed weight of gold (as under the gold exchange standard), but with such weight of gold as should have a fixed purchasing power ".[1]

§ 7. It is not necessary for my purpose to examine the Fisher plan in detail from the point of view of currency technique. There are, however, four matters falling under this head to which it is desirable to direct attention.

First, as was made plain in Chapter VII. of the preceding Part, it is of the utmost importance in times of panic that the banks should lend freely. It might be thought that Professor Fisher's plan would prevent them from doing this. That is a delusion. In ordinary times, of course, large bank loans mean large expenditure and, therefore, a rise in prices ; and, when this happens, the plan attacks the reserve and so checks lending. But in times of panic people want money, not to spend, but to discharge debts and to hold against the danger of failure. To this end they offer, as in times of boom, a high rate of discount, but they also offer, at a greatly reduced rate, their holdings of commodities. In other words, the loans which business men seek when confidence collapses, unlike those which they seek when it expands, are associated with a fall of prices.[2] In these circumstances, the plan, so far from making it more difficult for banks to lend freely to check the panic, would, by creating new reserves, make it easier for them to do this. Thus this objection is without substance.

Secondly, if the supply of gold greatly expands, so that commodity prices in terms of gold bullion rise rapidly, the quantity of gold bullion, which the Mint or Treasury would need to pay in order to withdraw any given quantity of currency from circulation, will largely increase. This means that a much larger bullion reserve than was thought necessary at first will need to be established, and the Treasury will, therefore, have to buy or borrow in the market a large extra quantity of bullion. This circumstance, though not of first-class importance, threatens a certain amount of awkwardness

[1] Fisher, *The Purchasing Power of Money*, p. 342.
[2] Cf. Kemmerer, " A large demand for call money sometimes is a sign of low confidence and represents liquidation, and sometimes is a sign of high confidence and represents good opportunities for new investment " (*Money and Prices*, p. 124).

and expense.[1] It will be noticed, however, that, though the quantity of bullion which the Treasury will need to hold is bound to increase, the aggregate value of it in terms of things in general is not so bound.

Thirdly, should the supply of gold fail to expand, in such wise that commodity prices in terms of gold bullion fall, then, if the currency has been constructed of token gold coins, it may happen that these coins will cease to be tokens, as in fact the Indian rupee did as a result of the war, and even that, in order to carry out Professor Fisher's plan, the Mint will have to give a greater weight of coined gold in return for a given weight of uncoined gold.[2] This it obviously cannot do except at great cost. Consequently, in order that the plan should continue in operation, it would be necessary to reduce the weight of gold in the token coin ; and this would almost certainly involve a considerable shock to business confidence. We should, in short, be compelled, as the government of the Philippines was compelled for this very reason in 1906, to recoin the whole of the currency into coins containing a smaller amount of bullion. The danger that this might become necessary would, however, be very small if the original coins contained very little bullion, or, in other words, were issued at a high seigniorage. If the currency were made up, not of coins at all, but of those paper notes of low denominations with which the war has made everybody familiar, it would be done away with altogether.

The fourth point concerns the cost of the scheme. In order to carry it out in practice, the Board of Control, which it would be necessary to set up in any country operating it, would, of course, need to retain in store a large quantity of gold. The real annual cost of the scheme *to that country* would be measured by the interest which it had to sacrifice through the retention of such part, if any, of this gold as was not formerly locked up in its own currency and bank reserves. It would be exactly analogous to the real annual

---

[1] Cf. J. M. Clark, *American Economic Review*, September 1913, p. 577 *et seq.*

[2] Cf. Patterson, *American Economic Review*, December 1913, p. 864.

cost to the people of India of the exchange funds of gold and rupees, which they hold in London and Calcutta for the purpose of keeping the relative value of gold and rupees constant. The real annual cost of the scheme *to the world* would be somewhat less than its cost to the country adopting it, because, in so far as the gold fund needed was taken from the monetary machines of other countries, its withdrawal would not diminish the efficiency of those machines.

§ 8. In conclusion a word may be said of the relation between a stabilising discount policy and a reserve discount policy coupled with the Fisher standard. The purpose of that standard is to stabilise prices against all classes of disturbance by operating on the currency reserves of the banking system, it being tacitly assumed that the Central Bank will continue to regulate its credit in accordance with a reserve discount policy. With such a standard what is sought by a stabilising discount policy is very nearly attained without the introduction of that policy. But it is not quite attained ; because action is not taken to modify the reserve until after prices have moved. If, therefore, a stabilising discount policy, instead of a reserve discount policy, were superimposed on the Fisher plan, its effectiveness as a price stabiliser would be somewhat increased. It should be added, however, that the Fisher plan *could* be so modified that, under it, the banks, though following a reserve discount policy, would alter their rates in the exact way required by a stabilising discount policy. This would happen if the signal for operating on the ratio at which the Mint exchanges currency and bullion against one another consisted, not in movements of the price index number, but in movements of one or more of those "forecasters" referred to in the last chapter. It must be confessed, however, that, if anything other than accomplished price movements were taken as the signal for action, it would scarcely be possible to make the response to the signal a purely mechanical one. Some discretion in interpreting the movements of the forecasters would have to be allowed, or paradoxical results would, on occasions, follow. So soon, however, as an element of discretionary choice is introduced, the contention, on which Professor Fisher lays great stress, that his scheme, being mechanical, is, therefore, fool-proof, disappears. Room is made for stupidity and perversity on the part of governing persons, and, therewith, serious dangers are introduced.

CHAPTER IX

PRICE STABILISATION POLICY AND A PAPER STANDARD

§ 1. IF a stabilising discount policy is adopted in a whole-hearted manner, the logical sequel as regards currency is neither the gold standard plan nor a plan on the Fisher model. It is a paper currency, the volume of which is not regulated by law, but is free to vary in response to whatever changes in the demand for it the stabilising discount policy allows. For, when once it is decided that the Central Bank shall regulate discount, regardless of anything else, in the interest of price stabilisation, a breakdown cannot occur through an excess of currency ; it can only occur, if at all, through a deficiency. Thus a currency system so constituted that the Central Bank is free to create and issue as much legal tender money as it requires to do from time to time is the natural associate of this form of discount policy. In so far as that policy is loyally adhered to, this freedom can lead to no excess, while it may obviate the danger of a shortage. In contrast with what happens under the gold standard *plus* a reserve discount policy, the currency position is always a consequence of the discount policy, and not sometimes a cause of it. No regulation of the currency position is required, for it will regulate itself.

§ 2. This assumes, however, that the stabilising discount policy will in fact be loyally adhered to and that safeguards against human frailty are not required. A Central Bank, whether a private concern or an agent of the executive government, that is free to create legal tender money without limit, has it in its power, if it does depart from the stabilising discount policy, to make an enormous levy from the public by expanding circulation. A government in difficulties will be sorely tempted to use this weapon, or, if the Central Bank is a private institution, to make the Bank use it in its behalf. The main purpose of legislative enactments limiting the note issue is to provide a safeguard against this: and the main argument in favour of a gold standard, as against a paper standard, is that, whereas Governments and banks can create paper money at will, they can only obtain gold money by buying it. To leave the Bank or the Government a free hand in currency manufacture, without any obligation to convert notes into gold and without any legal limit to the quantity of notes that may be created, is to open the door to grave abuse. Moreover, even if grave abuse does not in fact take place, the fear that it may take place and the suspicion that it will are likely to weaken the general sense of security, which is an important factor in industrial progress.

§ 3. It is often maintained that the conduct of Governments and Central Banks during and immediately after the Great War affords conclusive evidence of the dangers inherent in all paper currencies not strictly tied to gold, and of the unwisdom of allowing them to continue. This contention is not, however, legitimate. The outbreak of the war found the principal belligerents in the possession of thoroughgoing gold standard currencies, not of so-called " managed currencies ". What the experience of the war proves is that, in the presence of a sufficiently great catastrophe, any currency system will break down and nothing will prevent Governments from financing themselves by means of currency inflation. It is admitted that, if circumstances similar to those of the late war arose, a paper currency of the type here contemplated would break down. But this is no argument against such a currency, because we now know by direct experience that even a gold standard currency, firmly based and deeply rooted in tradition, will also break down. The real question is whether a managed paper currency, in association with a stabilising discount policy, is likely to be perverted to the uses of inflation when the conditions are such that a more rigidly constituted currency system would stand firm.

§ 4. It may be argued that, with such a currency, the danger is greater than under a legally regulated standard—gold standard, Fisher plan or another—because inflation can be resorted to without any alteration of the law, whereas under the other type of plan the passage of an Act of Parliament is required. This argument has considerable weight. It suggests that it might be advantageous to provide by statute that the aggregate issue of legal tender money shall not exceed some defined maximum except with Parliamentary sanction. If, with the growth of population and industry, it were found after a time that the successful operation of a stabilising discount policy required a circulation in excess of this maximum, there need be no difficulty about changing the law and fixing a new maximum. But, if the Bank, either on its own account or under Government pressure, were disloyal to the stabilising policy, and increased currency were needed to sustain an inflation of credit, the fact that a halt must be called or issue be definitely joined in Parliament might prove a restraining influence. Nor is it necessary that legal regulation should take the simple form of a mere maximum provision. It would be possible to enact, for example, that, if prices rose by more than, say, 10 per cent above the " proper " level, no further issue of money from the Bank could take place except with Parliamentary sanction. The presence of this danger-post would be a warning to the Bank against allowing itself to drift away from stabilisation into a policy of inflation.

§ 5. There is, however, a difficulty to be faced here. In ordinary conditions, under a monetary system aiming at price stabilisation, as, indeed, under any other monetary system, we may expect that fluctuations in the volume of bank credits and fluctuations in the volume of currency in people's pockets required to support them will be more or less proportionate to one another, the fractions of their resources that people choose to keep in the form of bank money and of currency respectively being more or less constant. In these circumstances, the variations in the volume of currency that are needed—even if stabilisation in an absolute sense is aimed at [1]—will not be large or rapid, and it will be possible, if so desired, to fix from time to time a legal maximum at a level that will be an effective safeguard against inflationist policies and yet no obstacle to normal progress. On certain occasions, however, people wish to hold a larger proportion than usual of their pur- chasing power in actual currency instead of in bank balances. When this happens, though the total amount of credit provided by banks is unchanged, the reserve of currency at the Central Bank is diminished by the amount of the extra currency that the public hold in their pockets. As a rule the drain on the reserve brought about in this way, for example, at the holiday season in England and at the period of crop movements in the United States, is small, and need not put the Central Bank in a difficulty. On rare occasions, however, there arise financial panics of such severity that a great number of people, while still feeling confidence in currency, come to doubt the security of bank deposits. A panic of this kind took place in the United States after the failure of the Knickerbocker Trust in 1907, and in this country after the Overend and Gurney smash in 1866. The essence of it is fear that bankers have not enough currency to meet their obligations, and consequent urgency on the part of each depositor to draw out and hoard what is due to him, before it is absorbed by other depositors.[2] In a panic of this type the quantity of currency that is required, relatively to the volume of bank credit outstanding, expands enormously and may easily exceed the whole of the normal currency reserve of the Central Bank. Any legislative limit to the permitted issue of currency, that is based upon the conditions of ordinary times and has any practical efficacy as a protection against inflationist policies, will, if it is adhered to then, involve an enormous slump in prices and have other consequences of a disastrous kind. As was argued in Chapter VII. of Part I., the only way to meet public

---

[1] Cf. *ante*, Part II. Chap. III. §§ 4-6.

[2] A very similar effect is produced when the general public is not in fact running on the banks, but when bankers are afraid that they will do so, and, consequently, as in August 1914, themselves demand currency for their tills as a safeguard.

distrust in the ability of banks to cash cheques with currency
is to provide them with ample currency for this purpose.
To that end the volume of currency normally in existence
must be for a time greatly exceeded. Hence, even though
it is desirable on the whole to fix by law a maximum for
the issue of currency, in times of panic the note-issuing
authority must somehow or other be given power to overstep
this limit. Upon this there would be general agreement.

§ 6. As to the form in which the power to make excess
issues in emergencies should be given, there may, however,
well be differences of opinion. This matter has often been de-
bated in connection with the limitation of the fiduciary issue
of convertible notes under a gold standard. The problem is
nearly the same there as here : how to get rid on special
occasions of a limitation which it is desired in general to
maintain. In pre-war England the method adopted was
to suspend the Bank Charter Act by emergency action,
which was technically illegal, on the part of the Cabinet.
The Currency and Bank Notes Act of 1928 gives authority
to the Treasury, on the request of the Bank of England, to
suspend the limit for defined periods. In pre-war Belgium
technical illegality was avoided, under a law which permitted
the Finance Minister to set aside, at his discretion, the
National Bank's obligation to keep specie in hand equal to
one-third of the combined amount of its bank-note circulation and other sight obligations. In pre-war Germany and
in the United States under the Federal Reserve Act extra
issues of notes beyond the normal provisional maximum
are permitted on condition that a tax is paid on the excess.
In criticism of the pre-war English system it was widely
argued that, when a crisis had actually begun, doubt as to
whether or not the Bank Act would be suspended in time
terrified the market and intensified panic. Under an automatic arrangement permitting excess issue on conditions
defined beforehand — the payment, as in Germany and
the United States, of a tax on the excess, the establishment
of a high discount rate, the prevalence of an adverse exchange
—this unfavourable reaction could not, it was held, be set
up. It was replied that the very rigidity of our system,

and the solemnity of the step—a definite breach of the law—which was needed to release extra fiduciary notes, fortified the Bank of England in a policy of caution and conservatism towards the discount rate and the reserve, well calculated to check at an early stage speculation that might otherwise have led to severe crises. Moreover, any automatic plan is faced with the formidable difficulty of so defining the conditions of excess issue that such issue shall always be permitted when required to check a panic and never permitted when not so required. The German system, with its elastic limit, did not accomplish this, because, under it, it might pay the Reichsbank to issue notes while a boom was still under way, thus intensifying both the boom itself and the collapse to which it leads.[1] Plainly, from our present point of view, the choice between rival methods of getting rid, at need, of a limit, which it is only just worth while to set up at all, is not very important.

[1] It should be noted that the case for an elastic limit is considerably stronger in countries where the cheque system is little developed and bank loans are made chiefly in the form of notes than it is in countries where these loans are usually made by crediting borrowers with new deposits.

CHAPTER X

PRICE STABILISATION AND A GOLD STANDARD

§ 1. APART from its negative quality of guarding against anti-social currency manipulation by Government, the chief merit of a gold standard or gold exchange standard is that under it a country's exchange with other gold standard or gold exchange standard countries cannot fluctuate outside the narrow limits set by the import and export specie points. This smooths the road for foreign trade. For, if the exchanges are not stable, it may happen that, after a sale has been made in terms of a foreign currency and before payment has been received, the value of the foreign currency in terms of native currency (and, it may be, in terms of native goods also) undergoes a considerable change. To exclude this risk is plainly an advantage, and it is often thought to be a great advantage. It must, indeed, be observed that, where the risk is not excluded, as with the eastern exchanges before the war, it can always be shifted by traders, at a price, to the shoulders of exchange banks, which will contract to buy from exporters their prospective foreign currency three months hence at a definite rate in native currency. In so far as the banks are able to hedge, by contracting at the same time to sell to importers the foreign currency which they expect to need three months hence at the same definite rate in native currency, the risk is not merely shifted, but is actually destroyed.[1] Thus the exchange difficulty is less serious than it is sometimes supposed to be. But it is, none the less, so far as it goes, a real difficulty ; for, of course, insurance

[1] Cf. Kemmerer, *Modern Currency Reforms*, p. 297.

is not effected without expense. In so far, therefore, as policies designed to promote stability of prices promote at the same time instability of exchange rates, that fact has to be set against such other advantages as may be claimed for them.

§ 2. Had this country in the period before the war abandoned gold and adopted instead a paper money system regulated with a view to price stabilisation—whether absolute or relative to a trend,—there can be no doubt that its exchanges as a whole would have been rendered much less stable than they were; for at that time most of the important commercial countries were on a gold or gold exchange standard. In the quinquennium following the war all those countries except the United States were off the gold standard, and many of them possessed paper currencies regulated on no fixed principles. It is not certain that the adoption by us then of a paper standard aiming at stable prices would have rendered our exchanges with these countries any less stable than the adoption of a gold standard would have done. Now, however, the move back to gold has become definite and general: and it is certain that a paper standard of the kind contemplated must be less favourable to steadiness in the foreign exchanges than a gold standard or a gold exchange standard. Policies of price stabilisation and exchange stabilisation are once again definitely opposed to one another. It is not open to any country acting by itself to secure both a water-tight system of stable prices and a water-tight system of stable exchanges.

§ 3. If the value of gold in the world market, while varying from time to time, is not subject to any upward or downward trend, it is, indeed, possible for a country that desires to do so to keep one foot in either camp. For, if a Central Bank has a sufficiently large holding of gold or of foreign exchange, it may refuse to allow its credit policy to be affected by moderate influxes into or effluxes out of its reserve. The Federal Reserve system of the United States since the early 1920's and the Bank of England since the restoration of the gold standard appear to have acted in this way. Such action, indeed, implies an artificial stimulus to the export trades when the external value of gold is below the internal value, and an artificial discouragement when this condition is reversed. But a country which sets high value on stable exchanges—and one in whose economic life foreign trade plays a large part is especially likely to do this —may be ready to pay that price.

§ 4. If, however, the value of gold in the world market trends upward or downward for a considerable period, it is not possible for any country upon a gold standard, no matter how large its normal reserve may be, to maintain stable prices either absolutely, or, unless the desired trend happens to conform to the trend of world gold prices—which is extremely improbable—relatively to a specified trend. For suppose, first, that in the world outside this country the value of gold trends downward, or, in other words, that world gold prices go on rising, for many years. Exports from this country will be stimulated, and foreign balances, liquidated ultimately by gold, will accrue to it : and this process will continue so long as the discrepancy between external and internal gold prices continues. The Central Bank in our country, in pursuit of its stabilisation policy, must sell securities in the market to offset the credits it has to give in purchase of the inflowing gold, thus preventing that gold from serving as a basis of further loans from the banks. But this policy cannot in prac-tice be continued indefinitely, since the Banks' stock of securities available for sale must ultimately become ex-hausted. Moreover, even if this does not happen, no country will consent for long to pour out ever-growing floods of exports and receive in exchange something of which no use whatever is made. The difficulty is still greater if, in the world outside this country, the value of gold trends upward, i.e. gold prices fall, for many years. Then imports are stimulated and gold flows out to pay for them. The Central Bank, to prevent prices here from falling, must reduce its discount rate and create more and more credits on the basis of a steadily diminishing gold reserve. Obviously it cannot carry on this policy for long :

if it presses it too far, it may find itself without sufficient legal tender to meet its customers' cheques, and collapse in ignominy. If, therefore, we decide to operate a discount policy that will stabilise prices, not merely in the face of our own internally caused industrial fluctuations, but in general, if we wish to make that policy watertight, and if we act alone, we shall be compelled to abandon the gold standard.

§ 5. Though, however, for one country acting alone there is here no middle path, for the community of nations a synthesis of opposites is possible. The principal commercial countries may agree to retain a gold standard or gold exchange standard, and then, by concerted action among their Central Banks in the matter of gold reserves, associated, perhaps, with some control over the sources of gold supply, may aim at stabilising, either absolutely or relatively to a defined trend, the value of gold itself throughout the world. This is the method of attack contemplated in the resolutions of the Genoa Conference of 1922. To make a choice between that policy and the other various policies that are open to us is a task that cannot be attempted in a work of this kind. Economic analysis can provide data for statesmen; but the attitude of public opinion and the current political and diplomatic situation are dominant factors in determining what, on the whole, it is best to do; and these lie beyond our range.

CHAPTER XI

§ 1. In Chapters XIX. and XX. of the preceding Part the tendency of industrialists to hold up prices in bad times and the tendency of workpeople to hold up wages were set side by side as factors of a like character among those that enhance the amplitude of industrial fluctuations. Since, however, the former tendency is less widespread and less marked than the latter, it probably exercises a smaller influence. Moreover, such damage as it does inflict on economic welfare by promoting industrial fluctuations is in part offset by gain. For, where an industry is largely financed by debentures, failure to pay interest on which means foreclosure, a policy of refusing to " spoil the market " in bad times may, if the demand for their commodity is inelastic, enable firms to survive which must otherwise have crashed, with highly injurious effects on future production in the industry primarily affected and highly disturbing effects on industries in general. This is, perhaps, the reason why Marshall refuses to condemn the policy as necessarily anti-social.[2] Again, where, as with railways,

---

[1] For a lengthy discussion, from a different angle, of the subject-matter of this chapter, cf. *The Economics of Welfare*, Part iii. chap. xx.

[2] Cf. *Principles of Economics*, p. 375. On similar lines it is possible to defend Government action to restrict output in bad times in industries where the process of production is spread over a long period. " The produce continues to come forward in quantities which the market is unable to absorb, and, if nothing is done about it, the price falls to a level which means a ruinous loss and perhaps bankruptcy, not only to the inferior producers, but to the main body of producers. If this process is allowed to work itself out, forces will be set in operation which will mean in course of time a curtailment of output much greater than is required, with a corresponding rebound of prices at a later date to a level which is as

steadiness, which implies ˜ertainty, of price yields great convenience, the evil involved in the associated unsteadiness
of industry is in considerable measure—in some circumstances perhaps completely — compensated. Partly for
these reasons I shall not attempt to review possible improvements in the current price policy of industrialists, but
shall concentrate attention upon the larger and more widely
discussed issues that arise in connection with wage policy.

§ 2. When it is proposed, as a means of lessening the
amplitude of industrial fluctuations, that real wage rates
should be made somewhat more plastic in the face of changes
in demand than they are now, it is not, of course, intended
that they should be made more plastic only in a downward
sense. That arrangement would imply a reduction in the
average rate of wages over good and bad times together, and
no such reduction is contemplated. On the contrary, to
offset the increased cuts in wages that are asked for in bad
times, increased additions to them are asked for in good
times, the mean level over good and bad times together
being left pretty much as it is. As things are at present,
employers frequently obtain the extra labour that they need
in good times, not by raising the general rate of wages, but by
taking on new and inferior workpeople at the wage per hour
then ruling for their present workpeople, and, therefore, at
a higher wage per unit of capacity than these workpeople
are enjoying. Under the more plastic wage-system that is
here in view employers would raise their general rate of
wages sooner and more largely when they have need of
increased supplies of labour, to offset the earlier and larger
reductions that they would make in times of depression.
It is important that this should be understood ; for otherwise the issue between plastic and rigid wage-rates is liable
to be confused by irrelevant assertions that the former policy
is a veiled device for exploiting wage-earners in the interests
of the employing class.

---

excessive as the former price was insufficient. In the long run this
violent oscillation in price and in supply will be as injurious to the consumer
as to the producer. Obviously the world will be better off on the whole
if it can be prevented " (J. M. Keynes, *The Nation*, June 12, 1926, p. 268).

§ 3. With this preliminary I turn to a fact noticed in Part I. Chapter XVII., namely, that the tendency of work-people to "think in gold" leads them to resist reductions in money wages when prices are falling and to acquiesce in refusals to raise money wages when prices are rising, thus in effect demanding an increase in the rate of real wages in times of depression and assenting to a decrease in times of prosperity. It is clear that, in so far as rigidity in wage policy involves this, it and the enlarged fluctuations of employment to which it leads are anti-social, and ought to be done away with ; for, whatever case there may be for constancy in real wage-rates in the face of changing demand, there can be none at all for variations in real wages *inverse* to associated variations in demand. With the large and rapid alterations that took place in the value of money during and after the Great War the popular tendency to think in gold has been greatly weakened, and it is now common for wage agreements to provide, over the period of the agreement, for money rates to vary in accord with such changes as may take place in "the cost of living". In July 1925 it was estimated by the Ministry of Labour that the wages of rather more than 2½ million workpeople were subject to adjustments under sliding-scales of this type.[1] In view of this we may take it that the policy of holding blindly to rigid money rates of wages, irrespective of what these rates mean in real terms, is rapidly losing ground. The remedy for industrial fluctuations, which consists in abandoning that policy, is accepted everywhere in theory and is already applied widely in practice.

§ 4. The very fact, however, that the general public has come to think in terms of the cost of living instead of in terms of gold has tended to make wage policy, as regards *real* wages, somewhat more rigid than it used to be. Having discovered that the cost of living is *a* relevant factor in determining the relation which ought to subsist between the money rates of wages at two periods, many people have jumped to the conclusion that it is *the only* relevant factor, at all events when proposals to reduce money wages are in

[1] *Labour Gazette,* July 1925, p. 228.

question. Thus in some industries the real wages that prevailed in 1913 (or some other year) have come to be looked upon as a sacrosanct standard, any attack upon which must, whatever the circumstances, be resisted to the death. In view of this tendency of popular thought, it is the more important to study on their merits the comparative social advantages of rigid and plastic systems of real wages.

§ 5. If we can bring ourselves to tolerate the conception of negative wages, it is possible to imagine a wage policy that would ensure full employment in all industries continuously, whatever changes demand might undergo. Even in pure theory, however, this state of affairs can only be admitted on the assumption that wage-earners possess stores of goods, out of which they can make payments to employers (negative wages) for the privilege of being allowed to work ; and that assumption is inconsistent with the facts. To the practical man, moreover, the whole notion of negative (or zero) rates of wages seems fantastic. In this the practical man's instinct is right ; for to adopt a wage policy of that degree of plasticity, even though it should abolish fluctuations of employment, would not be to the advantage of society. The utmost degree of plasticity that, even *prima facie*, has any claim to promote social welfare is a plasticity conforming to the conditions of true short-period supply, as described in Chapter XX. § 5 of Part I.—a plasticity which, it may be remarked, would *not* suffice to prevent some unemployment from occurring when demand was severely depressed. Moreover, if we look below *prima facie* appearance, we soon perceive that even this degree of plasticity is, from the point of view of social welfare, excessive ; it would purchase a measure of industrial stability at a cost beyond its worth. It is not, indeed, true that a highly variable rate of wages in any group necessarily implies highly variable aggregate earnings to the group as a whole. On the contrary, given the fluctuations that take place in the demand for labour, a highly variable wage will yield more stable aggregate earnings than a comparatively steady wage, provided that the demand for the services of the group concerned has an elasticity greater than unity. But a wage system plastic in the degree we are here contemplating would, on occasions, involve rates of wages per man so low as to be out of harmony with the moral sense of the time and incompatible with our social structure ; rates of wages, for example, below the rate of benefit paid from the Unemployment Insurance Fund to workpeople wholly unemployed. Plainly, as things are, a system permitting wage-cuts of that magnitude must be ruled out of court as, in a broad sense, anti-social. Hence, when we inquire whether any remedy for industrial fluctuations can properly be looked for in modifications of current wage policy, the only modifications which it is practically worth while to study are modifications on a comparatively small scale— nothing in the least resembling the introduction of a wage system conforming to the conditions of what I have called "true short-period supply". It was this sort of modification that I had in view when I suggested, in Part I. Chapter XXII., that wage policy as it actually is, contrasted with wage policy as it might be, is responsible for adding something of the order of one-eighth to the amplitude of industrial fluctuations.

§ 6. There can be no doubt that at the present time real rates of wages are held very rigid in a number of industries, because employers fear that, if they allow them to rise in good times, they will be unable to secure reductions in subsequent bad times, while workpeople fear that, if they allow reductions in bad times, they will not be able to secure a cancelling of these reductions in subsequent good times. So far as rigidity is due to this cause, it is plain that, if the mutual fears responsible for it could be removed, the resultant increase of plasticity would not merely—as it must— in some measure reduce the amplitude of industrial fluctuations, but would make a net contribution towards economic welfare as a whole. Hence remedies that are directed to making wages more plastic by removing these fears are safe remedies, and, though their effect in promoting industrial stability may not be large, such advantage as they do yield in this respect is not offset by any cancelling disadvantage. A brief discussion of them is, therefore, appropriate in this place.

§ 7. In the iron and steel and some allied industries agreements have often been entered into by employers and employed, under which wage-rates vary in a determinate manner with the price of certain products—subject, as a rule, to the condition that the wage-rate shall in no case fall below a certain defined minimum.[1] In these sliding-scale agreements the employer in effect pledges himself, for the period of the agreement, not to resist upward adjustments of wages in prosperity, on condition that the workpeople will not resist downward adjustments in depressions ; and the workpeople pledge themselves in a corresponding fashion. Thus the agreements at once eliminate the mutual fears which militate against plasticity in wage-rates and directly organise that plasticity. It seems at first sight, therefore, that in this form of sliding-scale we have ready to hand an ideal remedy for undue rigidity in wage-rates, the use of which can and should be extended over the main body of industry. There are, however, serious difficulties in the way of that policy.

§ 8. The first of these is technical. The fundamental assumption of a price-wage sliding-scale is, of course, that variations in the price of the selected commodity are indications of variations in the demand for labour, so that, when wages move up and down in accordance with the formula by which they are bound to the price of this commodity, they are responding in an appropriate manner to upward and downward movements of demand. Now, in industries in which the cost of materials plays a small part it may be possible to find a price, changes in which indicate correctly changes in the demand for labour over short periods ; and, even where materials of variable cost play a large part, it may be possible to construct a fairly good index of demand variations by subtracting from the price of a unit of finished product the sum of the prices of appropriate quantities of the

---

[1] An account of the principal agreements of this type in existence in this country in 1925 is given in the *Labour Gazette* for August 1925, pp. 269-72.

principal materials that are employed in making it. This, however, assumes that the industry in question is a fairly simple one. In an industry engaged in making a number of different articles, particularly if the quality and nature of these varies from time to time—ships, for example, or ladies' hats—the technical difficulty of finding any price, or combination of prices, that will correctly indicate variations in the demand for labour is very great ; and when, in addition, the industry is one in which methods of production are frequently changed by the introduction of improvements and new processes, it becomes, for practical purposes, insuperable. Hence the range over which the remedy of sliding-scales can be applied is restricted somewhat narrowly by purely technical incidents.

§ 9. There is, however, a more fundamental difficulty. Before it is possible for employers and workpeople in any industry to bind themselves to a formula for adjusting wages to fluctuations in the demand for labour, they must be agreed as to what rate of wages is proper under " normal ", or " standard ", or " average " conditions of demand. Unless they are so agreed, what employers regard as a temporary rise of wages warranted by exceptional prosperity, to be withdrawn when that prosperity ends, workpeople will regard as a tardy raising of the normal standard of wages to a " proper " level, and *vice versa*. Thus in recent discussions as to the wages of railwaymen, to the employers' contention that these wages have, since the war, risen much more largely than the wages of other classes of labour, the workpeople have replied that before the war railway wages were abnormally low. Moreover, even when the two sides are agreed that such and such a wage does, at a given time, fairly conform to normal conditions of demand, they cannot possibly be agreed that that same wage will always so conform. Both must contemplate the possibility of large-scale industrial changes which will make a much higher—or, less probably, a much lower—wage the appropriate standard for normal conditions of demand. In these circumstances it would be unreasonable to expect either side to bind itself to any mechanical formula for wage adjustments to cover more than

a short period.   In fact, agreements are rarely made for a
period of more than two years at the start, and are, as a
rule, subject thereafter to a few months' notice.   Since trade
cycles extend over periods of from five to ten years, sliding-
scales so limited cannot contribute much towards the wage
adjustments that these cycles make necessary.

§ 10. This does not mean, however, that there is no way
in which the fear of mutual intransigence entertained by employers and employed can be modified in such wise as to allow
wage-rates to become effectively plastic.   Machinery for collective bargaining may be set up, and, partly as cause, partly
as effect of this, a spirit of goodwill and accommodation
may be engendered.   In representative meetings of employers
and employed not only mechanical indices of prices and so
on, but all considerations relevant to wages, may be periodic-
ally reviewed in a whole-hearted effort to secure a reasonable settlement.   Where arrangements of this kind exist each
side will be ready to make concessions if the conditions seem
to call for them, confident that the other side, in converse
circumstances, will do likewise.   Wage-rates will be rendered
less rigid, the amplitude of industrial fluctuations associated
with given variations in demand will be *pro tanto* reduced,
and economic welfare correspondingly augmented.

CHAPTER XII

§ 1. Up to this point we have been concerned with remedial policies designed to modify causes and conditions that promote industrial fluctuations. We now suppose that these causes and conditions, whether modified or not by the above policies, are given, and we turn to the second class of remedy distinguished in Chapter I. § 10 of this Part, namely, those aimed, not at the causes of industrial fluctuations, but directly at the fluctuations themselves. Is it feasible for the purchasers of goods, actuated by private philanthropy or impelled by State suasion, to lessen industrial fluctuations in a way conducive to economic welfare by creating new demand for commodities in bad times, or by transferring to bad times a part of the demand which they normally exercise in good times, thereby inducing the people in control of industry to transfer in like manner a part of their demand for labour ? In this chapter we shall leave aside altogether questions of method and technique and consider only fundamental issues.

§ 2. At the outset it is necessary to conceive clearly the relation between the two policies of (1) creating new demand in bad times and (2) transferring demand to bad times from good times. At first sight it seems that, while the two agree in that both diminish industrial fluctuations, they differ in the important respect that, whereas the former does, the latter does not increase aggregate demand, and so aggregate activity and production, over good and bad times together. A consideration of what was said in Part II. Chapter I. § 8, shows, however, that this distinction is illusory. It is evident that the creation of demand for durable objects in bad times directly involves the destruction of a roughly equivalent amount of similar demand in good times. For example, if more ships are ordered in bad times, the supply of ships in succeeding good times will be so much larger, and the demand for further new ships then will be correspondingly reduced. It is evident, too, that, if a man decides to spend extra money on dinners or on machinery in bad times, he will have so much less to spend in good times. There is, however, something more fundamental than this. If the fluctuations of demand between good and bad times are reduced, whether through the creation of demand in bad times or through the transfer of demand to bad times, the fact of steadiness causes the aggregate mass of activity and output over good and bad times together to expand. The process has been described in the section cited above. It follows that there is, in essence, very little difference between a policy of transferring demand from good times to bad and a policy of creating demand in bad times. The main effect of both policies, assuming them to be applied successfully, is that more work is done—by people who wish to do it—in bad times without any corresponding contraction of work in good times. Under a policy of transference, instead of 1500 men working at occupation A in good times and 500 working, while 1000 stand idle, at that occupation in bad times, 1000 work at occupation A in both good times and bad, and 500 at occupation B in both good times and bad. Under a policy of making work, 1500 work at occupation A in good times, while in bad times 500 work at occupation A and 1000 at occupation B. Thus the two arrangements come to much the same thing.

§ 3. We have next to inquire whether the creation of additional new demand in bad times, either directly or as one side of a process of transfer, is possible. Nobody denies, of course, that it is possible for a private philanthropist, or a public department, if it so chooses, to add in bad times to the demand for a particular sort of commodity and to cause the demand for the labour engaged in producing that commodity to expand. It is sometimes maintained, however, that increases so brought about in the demand for labour in one industry are always and necessarily cancelled by equivalent decreases in the demand for it in other industries. In the words of the Transvaal Indigency Commission : "Wealth is the only source from which wages are paid, and the State must levy taxation (or raise loans) in order to pay wages to its workmen. When, therefore, a Government gives work to the unemployed, it is simply transferring wage-giving power from the individual to itself. It is diminishing employment with one hand while it increases it with the other. It takes work from people employed by private individuals, and gives it to people selected by the State." [1] Evidently this argument, if valid at all, holds good, not merely of direct employment by Government, but of any attempt to increase the real demand for labour in bad times. But the contention is not valid. The dividend of consumable products, that comes at any time into the hands of the people in control of industry, is devoted to three purposes, *i.e.* immediate consumption by entrepreneurs and capitalists, storage, and the purchase of labour engaged to produce goods for the future. The labour purchase fund (in terms of real things), which is available at any time, is, therefore, not rigidly fixed, but can be enlarged or contracted by the transference of resources between it and the two funds designed respectively for consumption by entrepreneurs and capitalists and for storage. Such transference may be effected in times of depression without it being necessary for any transference to be made in the aggregate, if resources are borrowed by the persons who expand their labour purchase in bad times and repaid with interest in good times. It is, no doubt, true that a part of the resources borrowed in bad times would be taken from funds which would normally have been devoted by private persons to investment involving the purchase of labour. Another part, however, would be taken from funds which would normally have been stored and from funds which would normally have been consumed by the relatively well-to-do. Consequently, though the net alteration in the aggregate resources devoted to labour purchase will be less

[1] *Report of the Transvaal Indigency Commission,* p. 129.

than the alteration in the resources devoted to this use by the persons we are considering, there will always be some, and there will often be a considerable, net alteration in these aggregate resources.[1] Nor is this all. In civilised countries at the present time there is, as was pointed out in Part I. Chapter XI., a further source—wholly ignored by the Transvaal Commissioners—from which a substantial part of the requisite resources could be drawn without diminishing in any degree the quantity of investment in labour purchase by private entrepreneurs. This source consists in the large sums annually devoted, through unemployment insurance, charity and the Poor Law, to the relief of persons who have been brought low through the effects of intermittent employment. In so far as an expansion of labour demand in bad times checked unemployment, the expenses involved in it would be balanced by a reduction in the expenses incurred by these agencies. Finally, when we are considering the circumstances of a particular country, and not of the whole world, we must take account of the fact that real resources for the payment of wages can be obtained by importation from abroad in exchange for gold or securities or promises of future repayment. For these reasons the thesis we have been discussing falls to the ground.

§ 4. The foregoing argument and the answer to it were stated in a form applicable to a community in which transactions and contracts are made in kind and in which money and banking do not exist. It is sometimes held that, where money and banking do exist but are organised in such a way as to keep the general level of prices stable, the argument of the Transvaal Indigency Commissioners can be restated in a new form, which *is* valid. This new contention is as follows. Broadly speaking, if any group of persons who employ labour decide, or are induced, to employ a larger quantity of labour in bad times, they can, in general, only accomplish their object by borrowing money from banks. As things are at present, the rate of interest would, thereupon, be raised

---

[1] The mathematically minded reader will perceive that the quantitative problems involved here can be attacked by a method analogous to that followed in the footnote on pp. 325-6.

and the borrowings of other employers of labour would be checked, but, it is admitted, not checked so far as those of the original borrowers are expanded. If, however, a stabilising discount policy is being practised, the discount rate will have to be raised so far that the net volume of borrowings from banks is prevented from expanding. Does not this imply that the real resources available to other employers for the hiring of labour are cut down to an extent equal to that by which those available to our particular employers are expanded? This argument—which is in substance that adopted by Mr. Hawtrey [1]—appears at first sight to be plausible. It neglects the fact, however, that higher interest rates stimulate the public to transfer balances to business men against new issues of securities, thus increasing the stream of resources available to business men, while leaving the price level unaltered. It also neglects the fact that the raising of the discount rate stimulates lending (on deposit) to the banks. But, as was explained in Part I. Chapter XIII. § 9, when a rentier decides to add £100 to his balance instead of spending it, the banks are thereby enabled to create a new £100 of credit for business men without causing prices to rise. In these ways, despite the stabilising discount policy, there is an increase in the balances of those people who want to employ labour. Hence this narrower contention, like the preceding wider one, is found to be invalid. Even when there is in play a stabilising discount policy, an " artificially " induced enhancement in the real labour demand of one employer does not cancel itself through a consequent contraction in the real wage-fund available for other employers. There is some cancelling effect, but not full cancellation. Indeed, a brief reflection

[1] Cf. *Economica*, March 1925, pp. 38 *et seq*. This is the logical basis of Mr. Hawtrey's further contention that the creation of new demand by municipalities, and so on, in bad times is only effective in so far as it is financed through the creation of new bank credits, and is, therefore, a " mere piece of ritual " (p. 44). If it were true that the creation of new demand is only effective in this way, the conclusion would follow. For the creation of new bank credits can be brought about by a reduction in the Central Bank's discount rate, by Government borrowing from the Bank to meet a deficit due to the remission of taxes, or in a number of other ways that do not involve any deliberate transfer of demand from good times to bad. But, as is argued in the text, the proposition required as a premise for Mr. Hawtrey's inference is not true.

shows that the position here is really identical with that
contemplated in the preceding section.   With a money of
constant value everything happens, so far as fluctuations are
concerned, in precisely the same way as it would happen in
a world of barter.   The monetary mechanism is a passive
channel and not an active cause.   Hence, apart, of course,
from the fact that money, by lubricating business, enables
everything to be on a larger scale, the same amount of
cancellation will take place in a community of the type
considered in this section as with the barter community
of § 3.

§ 5. When a stabilising discount policy is not in vogue,
the situation is more complicated, and a further factor must
be taken into account.   In a country organised as England
is at present the expansion of activity brought about in bad
times by " artificial " creations of demand is likely to be
financed in part by the creation of new credit by the banks,
over and above what is required to enable the savings
that rentiers are trying to make through the banks to
realise themselves.   In so far as this happens, streams of
real resources are diverted from rentiers and others to
business men in the manner described in Chapter XIII. of
Part I. and general prices rise.   In this way secondary
influences are set to work that further enlarge the aggregate real demand for labour.   This is a very important
matter.   Suppose that in bad times the volume of resources used in the purchase of labour is less than normal
by some ten million bushels of wheat per month.   At
first sight it appears that, in order to " remedy " this
state of affairs, it would be necessary for whatever agency
is endeavouring to intervene to call into play " artificially "
at least as much resources for wage-payment as this, and
probably, in order to neutralise various cancelling influences,
substantially more than this.   We now perceive that the
contraction of ten million bushels of wheat in the real
wage-fund of any period is made up of two parts, a
primary part of, say, x million bushels and a secondary
part, the outcome of reactions set up through the monetary
mechanism, of $(10 - x)$ millions.   But our artificially stimu-

lated demand will also carry with it secondary effects of the
same character as those carried by the primary part of the
contraction with which we are confronted. Hence, if x should
turn out to be large—unfortunately, we do not know at all
how large x is—it may be found that an artificial calling into
play of a new wage-fund much less than equivalent to 10
million bushels would be adequate to cancel the contraction.
This assumes, of course, that the artificially stimulated production is financed in the same way as normal production.
If it is financed by a contemporary levy of taxes, so that no
creation of bank credit is involved, the remedial action of a
given amount of artificially stimulated investment will be
smaller than this : if, on the other hand, it is financed by
Ways and Means advances from the Bank of England, the
use of which automatically improves the " proportion " of
the other banks and so enables them to provide cheap loans,
it will be larger than this.

§ 6. We have thus found that the creation of demand in
bad times, and, therefore, also the transfer of demand from
good times to bad, in such wise as to lessen the amplitude of
industrial fluctuations, is possible. We have now to consider the suggestion that whatever transfer is sociably
desirable, in the sense that the gain in steadying industry
exceeds the cost, will already have been made under the
influence of private self-regarding motives. It can easily be
shown that this suggestion is incorrect. For consider the
position of any body of purchasers, a manufacturing concern,
a private person or group of persons, a municipal council, or
anything we choose. Such a body of purchasers, we suppose,
requires from time to time building, engineering or printing
work to be done for it ; or it needs to buy stores to be used
in its service. It has to decide whether to make its purchases
in good times, when presumably the real prices of capital and
labour are relatively high, or in bad times when they are
relatively low. It knows that, if it postpones its building
plans from a boom or antedates them to a depression, it will
get its work carried out cheaper ; and, so far as its foresight
allows, it takes account of this fact in settling its policy. If
it decides, nevertheless, to build in the boom period, we may

presume that it finds an advantage in building then that more than outweighs the extra cost.   For instance, suppose that it is a question of building a structure which will not be required for use till three years hence, and to build which now would cost £90,000, but then £100,000.   The saving in price will not make good the loss of interest involved in building at the early date if the present value of £100,000 three years hence is less than £90,000.   Though, however, purchasers, in distributing their orders between good times and bad, take account of the fact that it is cheaper to buy in bad times, they do not take account, in any significant degree, of the effect of steady demand (1) in reducing the aggregate volume of unemployment and so increasing production, and (2) in lessening the period during which capital equipments, adjusted to the peak of the load, are only partially occupied, and so diminishing the average net cost of production per unit.   For any one debating whether or not to transfer a part of his demand from good times to bad cannot reckon to reap for himself the equivalent of more than a very small part of the social benefit that this involves.   Such action as he takes to steady aggregate demand will, no doubt, cause the things he purchases to fall a little in real price, because labour, being employed more regularly, will be content with a smaller day-wage.   But his purchases will only constitute a trifling proportion of the whole, and the bulk of the gain will go elsewhere.   In other words, the marginal private net product of individual efforts to stabilise demand is substantially less than the marginal social net product ; and, therefore, when self-interest alone is at work, these efforts are pushed less far than the general interest of society demands.   It follows that, even if fluctuations of industry were wholly due to real causes, and not at all to errors or monetary abnormalities, some transference of demand from good times to bad in excess of what self-interest left to itself tends to bring about would promote economic welfare.   Moreover, as a matter of practice, it is certain that other remedies for industrial fluctuations will not be carried to the point of eliminating altogether errors of forecast and bounties and tolls engineered through money.   The case for creating demand in bad times or transferring demand from good times to bad is, therefore, stronger than our argument hitherto has suggested. How much creation or transfer is sociably desirable depends, in each individual case, all the surrounding conditions being taken into account, on a balancing at the margin of gain against cost; but the presumption in favour of *some* creation or transfer beyond what comes about " naturally " is very strong.

CHAPTER XIII

VOLUNTARY ACTION BY PRIVATE PRODUCERS AND CONSUMERS

§ 1. THE initiative in transferring demand for labour from good times to bad may be taken either by employers of labour themselves or by purchasers of their products. In the former case the transfer of demand for labour is brought about directly, in the latter indirectly through an alteration in the comparative profit yielded to the controllers of industry by employing labour in the two types of period. When an employer of labour is also the ultimate consumer of what he produces, *e.g.* when a municipality erects a public building without the mediation of a contractor, this distinction disappears, and the matter may be treated equally well under either of the above heads. This, however, is exceptional. I proceed to consider the two sorts of initiative in turn. For either sort it will be understood, in accordance with the argument of the preceding chapter, that, where extra new capital is called for in one occupation, the cost of it will be raised and the amount of it used in other occupations will be, in some measure, reduced. In the sections which follow nothing further will be said about *that* sort of cancelling reaction.

§ 2. If a manufacturer or other employer of labour is to shift any part of the production that he would normally have undertaken in good times to bad times, he must either offer more of his stuff on the market in bad times (and correspondingly less later) or he must make more for stock in bad times and dispose of the stock in the good times that follow. Let us take first the device of additional manufacture for stock. A manufacturer who adopts this "remedy" against industrial fluctuations does not damage the market for other producers in bad times, and does not therefore—apart from the above-mentioned reactions on capital supply—impel them to produce less, thus cancelling in part the addition to his own production. There are, however, only a limited number of industries in which any large amount of manufacturing for stock is feasible. Obviously producers who make goods to the specification of their customers cannot make for stock. Nor in practice can those who manufacture goods which are liable to rapid changes of fashion ; for the risk of loss would be too great. Nor, again, can those who manufacture goods which are either quickly perishable or are so bulky that the cost of storing them is very large relatively to their value. The opportunity for applying this remedy against industrial fluctuations is, therefore, confined to producers of staple goods which are at once durable and fairly cheap to store ; and there are not very many of these. It is possible, however, that more goods may fall into this class as the practice of national standardisation of important articles is extended.[1]

§ 3. There remains the other plan. Public-spirited producers can, if they choose, deliberately maintain in bad times a larger output than their private interests suggest, and throw it upon the market. There are records of some firms which have contrived to do this without appreciable injury to themselves by spending more money on advertising and salesmanship in bad times than in good, thus deliberately moulding the market to suit their needs.[2] This device, however, is only open to makers of specialities. For the main body of producers the only way in which sales can be pushed in bad times is by a reduction in price. But a single manufacturer among a number of others, who forces a market by cutting prices, cannot accomplish much towards general stabilisation unless his product is one for which the demand is very elastic ; because the reduction in price will make

---

[1] Cf. *Factors in Industrial and Commercial Efficiency*, by the Balfour Committee, p. 292.

[2] Cf. Mitchell and others, *Business Cycles and Unemployment*, p. 126.

other manufacturers contract their output almost as much as their public-spirited colleague has expanded his.[1] Thus

[1] The extent to which one producer's action is cancelled in this way, and the extent to which, in corresponding conditions, one consumer's action is cancelled, can be determined mathematically as follows:

Let there be n producers, each normally producing x units, with an elasticity of supply e; and let there be n consumers each normally purchasing x units with an elasticity of demand $-\eta$.

Then, if one supplier increases the quantity he supplies from x to $(x + hx)$ units, thus adding hx units to his supply, the addition to the supply of all the suppliers together is approximately

$$hx\frac{-n\eta}{-n\eta + (n-1)e}.$$

Correspondingly, if one demander increases the quantity he purchases from x to $(x + hx)$ units, thus adding hx units to his purchases, the addition to the purchases of all the demanders together is approximately

$$hx\frac{ne}{ne - (n-1)\eta}.$$

Write $-\eta = er$. Then the aggregate addition to supply, due to an addition of hx to the supply of one supplier

$$= hx\frac{nr}{nr + n - 1}$$

$$= hx\frac{1}{1 + \dfrac{1}{r} - \dfrac{1}{r}.\dfrac{1}{n}}.$$

Correspondingly, the aggregate addition to demand due to an addition of hx to the demand of one demander

$$= hx\frac{n}{nr + n - r}$$

$$= hx\frac{1}{1 + r - r.\dfrac{1}{n}}.$$

Whatever the value of r, both these expressions become equal to hx when $n = 1$; when n is small, say anything less than 4, they are substantially nearer to hx than when n is large; and, so soon as n has become large, they are approximately the same whether it is moderately large or very large.

The above formula shows further that, when the acting supplier or demander contributes only a small part of the whole market, an increase in the output of this supplier by hx leads to an aggregate increase of

$$hx\frac{-\eta}{-\eta + e},$$

and an increase in the consumption of this demander by hx to an aggregate increase of

$$hx\frac{e}{-\eta + e}.$$

Therefore, a supplier's increase of supply is only cancelled to a slight extent when the demand is very elastic; and a demander's increase of

" convincing testimony was given on behalf of the Firewood Trade Association that the adoption of wood-chopping as the task at the Labour Homes of the Church Army, as well as in many workhouses, had definitely resulted in ruining independent wood-chopping firms, in throwing many men out of employment and in reducing some actually to pauperism ".[1] Thus, again, the action of those philanthropic ladies who in August 1914 started workrooms to give employment, in making garments for sale, to women thrown out of work by the war, probably did little more than divert work from the ordinary channels of trade.[2] If, however, the main body of manufacturers engaged in some industry, and not merely one or two of them, were to undertake jointly this policy, their efforts would not be open to this sort of cancelling and would, therefore, be proportionately more effective. As regards luxury and semi-luxury consumption goods, for which the demand is fairly elastic, a good deal might be done in this way to stabilise production at no great cost to the producers. But for those important instrumental goods, the production of which is in fact liable to vary most largely, the demand, from a short-period point of view, is likely to be highly inelastic ; and this means that sales could not be pushed much in bad times except at the cost of a very large fall in prices, and, therefore, of a very heavy loss to manufacturers.

§ 4. I now pass to the opportunities for promoting industrial stability which are open to public-spirited consumers. Let us imagine a group of consumers who are accustomed to purchase some given commodity, say clothes. Suppose that, instead of buying clothes, as they do now, at the times when they specially want them or can most conveniently afford to pay for them, they decide, in the interest of society at large, to shift a substantial part of their purchases away from periods of prosperity to periods of depression. What, in detail, will be the effect of their action ?

demand is only cancelled to a slight extent when the supply is very elastic. If the two elasticities are equal, either kind of increase is cancelled to the extent of (approximately) one-half.

[1] *Royal Commission on the Poor Laws*, Minority Report, p. 1099.

[2] Cf. *The War, Women and Unemployment*, Fabian Tract No. 178, p. 11.

Since these consumers demand more clothes in bad times and less in good, the price of clothes in bad times will be higher, and in good times lower, than it would otherwise have been. Consequently, other consumers will buy less in bad times and more in good times than they would have done. In this way the net addition to the quantity of clothes bought in bad times and the net subtraction from the quantity bought in good times will be smaller than the addition and subtraction for which the public-spirited consumers are personally responsible. The extent to which the effect of their action is cancelled depends upon two things, (1) the proportionate part of the total demand for clothes that their demand constitutes, and (2) the degree of elasticity in the demand of other buyers of clothes. The larger the proportionate part played by their demand and the less elastic the demand of the others, the smaller the proportion of cancellation will be. In any event, however, *some* net shift-over in the monetary demand for clothes, as between good and bad times, takes place. Hence the stores of these things in shops are correspondingly affected, and the demand of shopkeepers upon manufacturers for new stock is made smaller in good times and larger in bad times than it would otherwise have been. This means, in turn, that manufacturers set less labour to work in making clothes in good times and more in bad times than they would otherwise have done.

§ 5. An important point, relevant to both the two sorts of initiative which have been distinguished, remains to be considered. Under both heads it has been seen that the proportion in which the primary effect of stabilising action is cancelled by secondary effects is smaller the larger is the scale of action taken. If 100 employers act, the net effect of their action is more than ten times as great as the net effect of the action of ten employers; and similarly with purchasers. But—so it appears at first sight—the aggregate cost of stabilising action to the stabilisers will be directly proportionate to the number of people who take it : if, for example, 100 similar men decide, in the public interest, to paint their houses this year rather than next, the sacrifice they collectively undergo must be 100 times the sacrifice that a single man so acting would undergo. With that premiss it follows that the proportion of benefit to cost must always be greater when action aiming at industrial stability is taken on a large scale than when it is taken on a small one ; and, therefore, that it is sometimes desirable for a number of people, if they can agree, to take this action, and yet not desirable, in ·lack of such agreement, for a single individual (unless, of course, his position is such that other people are likely to imitate his action) to do so. The premiss of this argument is not, indeed, completely water-tight, because, if, for example, 100 men decide to paint their houses this year instead of next, the price of painting may be raised slightly, whereas, if only one man did this, the price could not be appreciably affected. Thus the sacrifice incurred by the 100 men acting collectively will be slightly more than 100 times that incurred by the one man acting alone. Against this has to be set the fact that the men who paint their houses next year will have the advantage of greater cheapness then. On the whole, it seems fairly certain that the rate at which sacrifice grows as the numbers acting are increased will, in general, be much smaller than the rate at which benefit grows. Therefore the conclusion suggested above holds good. Adjustment of production or of purchases in the interests of stability, which it would not be worth while for a small group of persons to undertake, because the benefit to the community would not exceed the cost to the group, may be worth while for a large group to undertake.

CHAPTER XIV

THE ADJUSTMENT OF ORDERS BY PUBLIC AUTHORITIES

§ 1. ATTEMPTS on the part of private persons, whether producers or consumers, to promote industrial stability on the lines discussed in the preceding chapter have never been, and there is little prospect that they ever will be, on a large enough scale to produce significant effects. Public authorities, central and local, are, however, differently placed. Many of them are accustomed from time to time to give large orders for goods, which imply large orders on the part of the manufacturers of these goods for labour wherewith to make them. From the present point of view it does not matter whether the orders are given to private concerns or to productive establishments belonging to the Government departments that give the orders. In either case equally there is scope for a transfer of orders from good times to bad, and a consequential corresponding transfer of demand for labour. Boards of Guardians order so much stores, the Board of Admiralty so many ships, municipalities so many school and other buildings and so much repair work on roads ; and there is no rigid compulsion on them to order these things at a particular instant. In actual fact it usually happens that, when industry in general is depressed —and at such times most individual industries are depressed too — the demand of public authorities is low, and in converse circumstances high. " The reasons for this are easy to tell. Public revenue faithfully follows the fluctuations in the economic activity of the country ; in times of crisis it tends to diminish. In order to meet the resultant deficit, the Administration, for prudential reasons, cuts down expenditure as far as possible, and, consequently, postpones all work that does not seem absolutely indispensable. With the resumption of business, the execution of many orders, which it had been thought could be postponed without inconvenience, becomes urgent. Economic equipment, which had seemed sufficient for the needs of commerce and industry in a period of calm, proves inadequate, and the deficiency must be remedied with all speed. On the other hand, the surplus values obtained at the same time in receipts encourage the administrative authorities to set going less urgent works."[1] It is not necessary, however, that the orders of public authorities should be operated in this way. A policy of precisely opposite tendency, designed in the interest of industrial stability, can, if desired, be adopted.

§ 2. Such a policy was embodied in a circular concerning the Organisation of the Provision of Employment, issued by the Prussian Minister of Commerce in 1904, and quoted in Schloss's report on foreign methods of dealing with the unemployed. The circular runs : " We further request you to have the goodness to direct your attention to those measures which are calculated to prevent the occurrence of want of work on a wide scale or to mitigate its effects when it is unavoidable. Not only the State, but also the provinces, districts and communes, in their capacity as employers, are bound to do their utmost to counteract the evil in question by paying general and methodical attention to the suitable distribution and regulation of the works to be carried out for their account. In almost every industrial establishment of importance there are tasks which do not absolutely need to be performed at a fixed time ; just so in every state and communal administration there are works for the allotment of which the time may, within certain limits, be freely chosen according to circumstances. If all public administrations, in making their arrangements, would take timely care to choose for such works times in which want of employment is to be expected— if, especially, works in which unemployed people of all kinds,

---

[1] R. Viviani, quoted in the *Report of the International Labour Office on Remedies for Unemployment*, 1922, p. 117.

including, in particular, unskilled labourers, can be made
use of, were reserved for such times of threatening want of
employment as have almost regularly recurred of late in
winter in the larger towns and industrial centres—the real
occurrence of widespread want of employment could certainly
be prevented in many cases and serious distress warded
off." [1] The same policy is embodied in the proposal of the
majority of the Poor Law Commission concerning irregular
municipal work. They write : " So far as it may be
inevitable to employ occasionally other than their own
regular workers, or to place contracts, we think that it may
be desirable for public authorities to arrange such irregular
work so that, if possible, it comes upon the labour market
at a time when ordinary regular work is slack. This point
has been well put by Professor Chapman, who suggests that,
so far as the public authorities' demand for labour fluctuates,
it is desirable to liberate such demand from the influences
of good and bad trade and seasonality, and then deliberately
to attempt to make it vary inversely with the demand in
the open market." [2] A policy on similar lines won the
approval of the Royal Commissioners on Afforestation.
They were concerned to satisfy themselves that " that part
of sylvicultural work which requires most labour, namely,
the establishment of the forest, is of a sufficiently flexible
character to be capable of being pushed on when labour is
abundant, and suspended when labour is scarce " ; [3] and
they advised that it should in fact be pushed on, and suspended, on these principles.

§ 3. The same point of view, in respect of a much more
extended field, is adopted by the minority of the Royal
Commissioners on the Poor Law. They write : " We think
that there can be no doubt that, out of the 150 millions
sterling annually expended by the National and Local
Authorities on works and services, it would be possible to
earmark at least four millions a year, as not to be undertaken

---

[1] *Report on Agencies and Methods for Dealing with Unemployment in
Foreign Countries*, p. 103.

[2] *Report of the Royal Commissioners on the Poor Law*, p. 41.

[3] *Report of Royal Commission on Coast Erosion and Afforestation*,
vol. ii. p. 13.

equally, year by year, as a matter of course ; but to be
undertaken, out of loans, on a ten years' programme, at
unequal annual rates, to the extent even of ten or fifteen
millions in a single year, at those periods when the National
Labour Exchange reported that the number of able-bodied
applicants, for whom no places could be found anywhere
within the United Kingdom, was rising above the normal
level. When this report was made by the Minister responsible for the National Labour Exchange—whenever, for
instance, the Percentage Unemployment Index, as now
calculated, rose above four—the various Government departments would recur to their ten years' programme of capital
outlay ; the Admiralty would put in hand a special battle-
ship and augment its stock of guns and projectiles ; the
War Office would give orders for some of the additional
barracks that are always being needed, and would further
replenish its multifarious stores ; the Office of Works would
get on more quickly with its perpetual task of erecting new
post offices and other Government buildings and of renewing
the worn-out furniture ; the Post Office would proceed at
three or four times its accustomed rate with the extension
of the telegraph and telephone to every village in the kingdom ; even the Stationery Office would get on two or three
times as fast as usual with the printing of the volumes of
the Historical Manuscripts Commission and the publication
of the national archives. But much more could be done.
It is plain that many millions have to be spent in the next
few decades in rebuilding the worst of the elementary
schools, greatly adding to the number of the secondary
schools, multiplying the technical institutes and training
colleges, and doubling and trebling the accommodation and
equipment of our fifteen universities. All this building
and furnishing work, on which alone we might usefully
spend the forty millions per decade that are in question, is
not in fact, and need not be for efficiency, done in equal
annual instalments. There might well be a ten years'
programme of capital grants-in-aid of the local expenditure
on educational buildings and equipment. It requires only
the stimulus of these grants-in-aid, made at the periods

when the Minister in charge of the National Labour Exchange reports that the index number of unemployment has reached the warning point, for these works to be put in hand by the local Education Authorities all over the kingdom to exactly the extent that the situation demands. At the same time the Local Authorities could be incited to undertake their ordinary municipal undertakings of a capital nature, whether tramways or waterworks, public baths or electric power stations, artisans' dwellings or town halls, drainage works or street improvements, to a greater extent in the years of slackness than in the years of good trade. This, indeed, they are already tending to do ; and to the great development of municipal enterprise in this direction, setting up a small ebb and flow of its own to some extent counteracting the flow and ebb of private industry, we are inclined to attribute the fact that the cyclical depressions of the last twenty years have been less severely felt in the United Kingdom than were those of 1878-9 and of 1839-42."[1] An estimate of the scale of adjustment needed has been made by Dr. Bowley as follows : " The wages bill for 1911 was computed to be about £800 million. A typical cycle may be thus represented, the first year being one of maximum employment :

TEN SUCCESSIVE YEARS.

Unemployed (per cent)	2½	3½	4½	5½	6½	7½	6½	5½	4½	3½
Relation to average (per cent) . . .	-2½	-1½	-½	+½	+1½	+2½	+1½	+½	-½	-1½
Variation of wage bill (million sterling)	+20	+12	+4	-4	-12	-20	-12	-4	+4	+12

In public expenditure we may perhaps take wages to be 80 per cent of the whole cost. On these figures the wave of unemployment would be levelled to a uniform 5 per cent if a total of £36 million wages (£45 million expenditure) were held over during the first three years, the average period of postponement being four years ; and if a total of £16 million wages (£20 million expenditure) were advanced in the seventh and eighth years ; the average period of advancement being two and a half years. . . . At present the

---

[1] *Royal Commission on the Poor Laws*, Minority Report, p. 1196.

employable population is about 8 per cent more than in 1911, and weekly wage rates about 70 per cent more. The expenditure to be postponed in the first three years would now be £81 million, and that advanced in the seventh and eighth year £37 million."[1] It will be noticed that Dr. Bowley takes no account of the secondary effects discussed in § 5 of the last chapter but one.

§ 4. In a country organised as England is, the dominant part of those sorts of public expenditure that might be made available for transfer from good times to bad is in the hands of *local* authorities. Such authorities, with their system of committees in control of different departments of work, with their frequent changes and the constant fear of the ratepayers before them—all of which things make a well-thought-out general financial policy very difficult—have seldom of themselves the power or the will to undertake a compensating policy in employment. Hence we may conclude, with Dr. Bowley, " that the only possible way of influencing the amount of employment provided by local authorities, without whose co-operation the policy of regularisation can only be partly successful, is by exercise by the Central Government of its powers of compulsion, of making or withholding grants, of granting or refusing power to borrow and, above all, of providing capital on easy terms at times when it is desirable on national grounds that public works should be set in hand".[2] During the difficult period of the post-war slump the Central Government exercised its power of stimulus through grants-in-aid in very considerable measure.[3] An arrangement looking to regular and continuous action on these lines had already, in 1909, been embodied in the Development and Road Fund Act, where it is provided that parliamentary grants to local authorities " must be expended, bearing in mind the general state and prospects of employment ".

§ 5. In this connection, however, it is important to introduce a qualifying consideration. Costs apart, social advantage must result from action by a public authority that steadies

---

[1] *Is Unemployment Inevitable*, 1924, pp. 367-8.

[2] *Ibid.* p. 376.

[3] For a summary of what was done cf. Morley, *Unemployment Relief in Great Britain*, pp. 189-91.

the aggregate demand for labour and also steadies the demand for labour in the centre on which the public authority is operating : and social advantage may result, while social damage cannot result, from action by a public authority designed to fit the peaks of its own demand into the depressions of general demand and *vice versa*, while leaving the peaks and depressions of its own demand unaltered in size. But social damage *may* result from action by a public authority that steadies aggregate demand at the expense of making its own demand less steady. If, indeed, between the public authority and other centres of industry labour is perfectly mobile, this cannot happen. But if, on the other hand, labour is perfectly immobile, it not only can, but it must happen. Thus let us suppose that between a particular industry and others labour is absolutely immobile. If the demand in this industry, which has been stable at 5000 men, is made to vary from 1000 men in times when other industries are prosperous to 9000 men in times when they are depressed, in order to compensate the fluctuations of these other industries, all that happens is that 8000 men in our particular industry are rendered idle at a time when they might have been working ; and against this loss there is nothing whatever to set. The aggregate amount of work and of production over good and bad times taken together will be diminished and not increased. Moreover, the earnings and activity of the representative man in the industry in which demand has been manipulated will be rendered more variable than before : and no compensation for this will be obtained in other industries. Thus there is bound to result social loss and not social gain. It must be conceded, of course, that this extreme illustration does not fairly represent the facts. In practice we have to do neither with complete mobility nor with complete immobility, but with something between the two. In these circumstances the question whether—costs aside—a steadying of aggregate demand at the expense of unsteadying the demand of a particular industry is socially advantageous cannot be determined in a general way. The answer depends in each separate case upon the degree of mobility that exists among the workpeople affected. The greater the mobility, the greater is the chance that advantage will result : the smaller the mobility, the less is this chance. Thus, when a municipal enterprise controls the demand for only a part of the services of a particular class of workpeople, production and economic welfare generally are fairly certain to be increased—for the present we ignore any costs that may be involved—if the demand of the municipal enterprise, which might have been constant, is made to fluctuate inversely with that of the other establishments *employing this class of labour in the neighbourhood.* On the other hand, it is not unlikely that production and economic welfare would be damaged if the demand for labour upon State forests, which might have been constant, was made to fluctuate inversely with that of city businesses employing artisans and mechanics.[1] Anything, such as the development of a national system of employment exchanges or the growth of jobs common to many industries, which makes for improved mobility, whether between places or between trades, increases the probability that policies designed to steady the demand for the whole of labour by introducing compensating fluctuations into the demand for a part will yield social advantage. This probability will be still further enhanced if the authorities entrusted with the management of national and local spending do not take account merely of the general percentage of unemployment, but look to the detailed figures of separate industries, and distribute their expenditure among them in proportion to the extent of the depressions from which they are severally suffering.

§ 6. Subject to the above qualification, we are left with the result that some social advantage is likely to result from attempts on the part of public authorities to regulate the incidence of their demand in the interest of industrial stability. It must not be inferred, however, that such attempts can with advantage be pushed indefinitely. For, besides the gain, they also involve a cost. The margin at which gain and cost balance constitutes a limit beyond which it cannot

---

[1] The experience of Belgium seems to show that forest work is well adapted to give winter employment to *unskilled* workmen engaged in the building trade during the rest of the year. (Cf. Rowntree, *Land and Labour*, p. 507.)

pay society to carry them. Where that limit lies varies, of course, from case to case. In some conditions the time incidence of the public authorities' demand can only be altered at very great cost. A particular town, for example, may be quite uncertain now whether it will want more school buildings five years hence : and, five years hence, when it does want them, it cannot conveniently postpone the satisfaction of its needs. The Central Government, again, cannot foresee exactly its future need for ships and guns : it will not care to anticipate these needs for fear of finding itself saddled with obsolete types; and, when the need becomes urgent, it will not dare to delay. Yet again, when a war threatens there can be no question of allowing care for steadiness of industry to affect the time at which the fighting services order necessary materials. In other conditions it makes very little difference either to the public convenience or to the public purse at what time, within a year or two, the requirements of governmental authorities are satisfied, and in these conditions the cost of transferring demand from good times to bad is small.

§ 7. It may be observed in conclusion that the policy discussed in this chapter is logically on a par with a policy under which public authorities should seek to promote industrial stability by purchasing commodities for stock at times when the general demand is low and selling them from stock at times when that demand is high. That policy is out of the question as regards goods which are perishable or subject to sudden changes of fashion, but it is *prima facie* defensible as regards other sorts of goods. Owing to the long period covered by cyclical industrial fluctuations, it must, however, always prove very expensive. Apart from anything else, with interest at 5 per cent, to hold anything for four years involves a cost of $21\frac{1}{2}$ per cent—is equivalent, that is to say, to selling immediately at a reduction of that amount. Moreover, in a period of that length " styles will change and specifications alter, so that few goods are durable in the sense of holding their economic value through the changing phases of boom and depression ".[1]

---

[1] J. M. Clark, *The Economics of Overhead Costs.* p. 164.

This is, of course, especially true in a period of rapid mechanical improvement and invention. Nor do these considerations exhaust the case. There remains a very important practical consideration. For public authorities to regulate the time at which they give orders for things which they *must* order at some time, all that is needed is a decision as to method in a field they already occupy. But for these authorities to buy commodities in bad times and to sell them to the public in subsequent good times involves their entering into an entirely new field—the field of commercial speculation. To any such action on their part violent objection would be taken by all the dealers who already occupy part of that field. This would make successful action difficult. But, apart from this, even those who agree that public authorities are adequately equipped to operate productive enterprises may well hesitate about the fitness of the Central Government—and no public authority except the Central Government could act here—for speculative commerce. The achievements of the various official purchasing authorities during the war throw no light upon this matter : for the conditions prevailing then were entirely different from those that rule in normal times. The burden of proof clearly lies with those who advocate, rather than with those who resist, proposals to place this new and difficult task upon the shoulders of the Government.

CHAPTER XV

§ 1. WHEN public authorities are not themselves important purchasers of the product of an industry, the method of attack described in the first six sections of the last chapter is not open to them. In all circumstances, however, there are available to them indirect methods. They can encourage activity in any industry at any time by favours and discourage activity by obstructions. Nor is it, as a rule, essential to the end desired that both favours and obstructions should be employed. In industries engaged in making durable goods a favour that calls out increased production in bad times will, because of the extra supply that is left over in succeeding good times, cause diminished production to be forthcoming then : and, conversely, an obstruction that impedes production in good times will cause increased production to be forthcoming in succeeding bad times. As a matter of fact, one-sided action, and not two-sided action, is found in current practice.

§ 2. One form of such action consists in offers to selected sorts of private enterprise in bad times of a Government guarantee. This method was embodied in the British Trade Facilities Act of 1921. That act " empowered the Treasury, after consultation with an advisory committee, to guarantee the payment of interest and principal, or of either, of loans raised by governments, public authorities, corporations, or other persons, on condition that the proceeds of the loan were utilised in carrying out capital undertakings, or in the purchase of articles manufactured in the United Kingdom for the purpose of such undertakings, which are calculated to

promote employment in the United Kingdom.   The duration
of the act was twelve months, and the limit to the amount
that might be guaranteed was £25,000,000." [1]   This Act
(subsequently renewed and enlarged), as an emergency measure
in the unprecedented post-war slump, does not seem to have
accomplished much, but the idea underlying it, carefully
developed and worked out in advance, might, none the less,
prove a valuable means of combating normal cyclical trade
depressions.[2]   The Export Credit scheme, also initiated in
1921, provides in a similar manner for a State guarantee to
persons exporting goods in certain conditions to certain
markets.

§ 3. A second form of action on the same general lines
consists in the offer of bounties to selected industries in bad
times.   This has been advocated for industries engaged in
works of construction.   In 1923–24 the Unemployment
Grants Committee made grants of Government money to
private enterprises willing to commence revenue-producing
works of a public utility character, such as gas, water,
electricity, tramways, docks, harbours and canals, which
would otherwise have been postponed.[3]   Similar grants have
been advocated, *e.g.* by Lord Balfour, for certain export
industries.   Differential favours in the form of direct money
payments by the Government to particular industries are,
however, likely to be resented very strongly by other industries not similarly favoured :   and, when it is an export
industry that receives such subsidy, there is the further
objection that foreign purchasers of its product are likely
to receive, at least in part, what British tax-payers have
provided.   The former of these difficulties would, of course,
be met if the Government were to adopt a two-sided policy,
coupling with special bounties in good times special taxes in
bad.   But the inconvenience and administrative difficulty of
imposing duties on production in particular industries for
short periods of time and then removing them are too great
to permit of this.

---

[1] *The Third Winter of Unemployment*, p. 54.
[2] Cf. *ibid.* p. 86.
[3] Cf. Morley, *Unemployment Relief in Great Britain*, p. 191.

§ 4. In the (probably rare) cases where the bounty method is employed it is a matter of some interest to determine in what quantitative relation the sum expended in the bounty stands to the total addition which it causes to the purchasing price expended in the bounty-fed industry. A simple mathematical analysis shows that, if the demand for the product of that industry has an elasticity equal to unity, the aggregate expenditure on its product will be increased exactly by the amount of the bounty : if the demand has an elasticity less than unity, by less than the amount of the bounty ; and if it has an elasticity greater than unity, by more than the amount of the bounty. In an industry, the demand for whose product is very elastic, a very small sum devoted to the provision of a bounty would lead to a very large increase of aggregate expenditure. Other things being equal, therefore, since certain indirect costs are likely to be involved in raising the funds out of which bounties are provided, and these will be larger the larger is the sum which has to be raised, the case for applying the bounty method is specially strong in industries of highly elastic demand.

§ 5. A peculiar and ingenious form of bounty was suggested by Lord Melchett in a pamphlet published in 1925.[1] In substance the suggestion was that any four workmen who chose could hand over to the State their insurance benefit money (23s. a week each), that the State would then pay this money over to an employer on condition that he set to work at trade union rates, in addition to the existing staff, these four men together with one other. The root ideas here are, first, that the only money used for the bounty should be money which otherwise would have been paid in insurance benefits, so that no extra funds would have to be raised for it; secondly, that the bounty should be paid, not in respect of the whole of a firm's work, but only of additions made to its work. If we suppose the standard wage to be 40s., the plan, from the employer's point of view, amounts to an offer on the part of men out of employment to work at a wage of $21\frac{3}{5}$ shillings, the remainder of the

[1] *The Remedy for Unemployment.*

standard wage being paid out of the insurance fund. There can be no doubt that an arrangement of this sort would lead to increased employment in bad times, if the bounty could be confined to the excess of staff that employers do engage over what they would have engaged apart from the bounty. Except, however, in conditions so bad that immediate improvement is despaired of, the staff that would be engaged apart from the bounty cannot be treated as equivalent to the staff that was engaged just before the bounty. When what is desired is a heroic remedy for a single emergency by means of a special *ad hoc* law, this difficulty need not be fatal. Plainly, however, any plan on Lord Melchett's lines could not be made a regular standard means of dealing with industrial depressions ; for, if it were, individual employers, when they saw a depression coming, would be tempted to dismiss workpeople in the hope of re-engaging them immediately on terms that would throw a large part of their wages bill upon the shoulders of other people.[1]

§ 6. One-sided action of a type converse to the above, namely, the setting up of obstructions to activity in good times, is illustrated by rules imposing a legal limitation upon systematic overtime : for such rules, though nominally applicable to all periods, would only operate in any important degree in periods of boom. So operating, they would affect the preceding bad times by anticipation, causing increased making for stock and increased purchases by consumers in preparation for future needs. The latter point is well illustrated by the following passage from the Minority Report of the Royal Commission on the Poor Laws : " The variations in the consumer's pressure can be made much less extreme by means of a legal limitation of the hours of labour. When the hours of cotton-operatives were settled by the individual mill-owner, cotton-spinning and weaving were extreme instances of seasonal trades ; and the manufacturer was unable to resist the customer's insistence on instant delivery. Now that the maximum hours are legally

[1] Cf. *Report of the Blanesburgh Committee on Unemployment Insurance*, 1927, pp. 79-80.

fixed, the buyer has learnt to be more regular in his demands. The extreme seasonal irregularity of the London dressmaking trade would undoubtedly be mitigated if dressmakers were absolutely prevented from working more than a fixed maximum day. Customers would simply not be able to insist on delivery in an unreasonably short time."[1] It is true that these illustrations refer to seasonal, and not to cyclical, fluctuations, but the principle involved is clearly the same.

§ 7. There is, however, a consideration to be set against this, which is not present when fiscal inducements or deterrents are being employed. The limitation of overtime, besides leading to the reactions just indicated, would have the effect of tempting employers in the industry affected to raise their wage-rate in order to attach to their industry a larger number of hands. The resource of overtime, by which periods of booming trade could formerly be met, being restricted, they would be driven back on the alternative resource of more men. This, however, implies more unemployment in bad times, and, therefore, a larger volume of unemployment on the whole. It is probable that, in some cases, this influence would outweigh, and that, in other cases, it would be outweighed by, those other influences of restriction upon overtime which tend to lessen unemployment. The more perfect is the mobility of labour and the greater is the extent to which the fluctuations of demand in the different parts of the industry affected tend to cancel one another, the greater is the likelihood that the volume of unemployment would, on the whole, be reduced.

[1] *Report of the Royal Commission on the Poor Laws*, Minority Report, p. 1185.

CHAPTER XVI

§ 1. WE saw in Chapter XII. that, in principle, the systematic transfer of demand from good times to bad and the systematic creation of demand in bad times come to much the same thing. Under the transfer system, instead of 1500 men working at A in good times and 500 working there while 1000 stand idle in bad times, 1000 work at A continuously and 500 work at B continuously ; under the rival system 1500 work at A in good times and 500 in bad times, while in bad times the remaining 1000 work at B. It is possible in theory to operate the second plan in such a way that its social consequences should be indistinguishable from those of the first. In practice, however, the second plan is almost certain to be less favourable to economic welfare. For under the method of transfer the men set free from A are, presumably, scattered over the margin of many occupations—B is not here a single definite occupation —so that each of them confronts a demand almost as keen as that which he has left ; whereas under the rival method the men set free from A are concentrated on jobs especially invented to absorb them, and, therefore, probably of relatively small social utility. Of course it may be possible on occasions to find tasks to carry out in bad times, the social value of which is very high, but which it would, nevertheless, not pay private industrialists to undertake. But it is not really relevant to cite tasks of this kind, because it would have been the part of wisdom to undertake them in the ordinary course, even though there were no call to find occupation for the unemployed. Hence the method of

344

making work in bad times, even when the work to be made is well selected, is likely to prove a somewhat less advantageous method of counteracting industrial fluctuations than the method of transferring work from good times to bad.

§ 2. The issue just discussed, though it is concerned with what may perhaps without impropriety be called *relief works for unemployment,* is not concerned with what are ordinarily known in England as *relief works for the unemployed. Relief works for unemployment* in bad times are designed to increase the general demand for labour over the whole field, or, at all events, over that part of it which is occupied by works of construction, without primary reference to particular unemployed persons. *Relief works for the unemployed* are designed to provide work for these particular persons. This type of relief works, operated through municipalities, originated in this country with a circular issued by the Local Government Board in 1886, and was more elaborately organised under the Unemployed Workmen's Act of 1905. The intention underlying the circular and the Act alike was to enable workmen, normally in regular employment but thrown out of work in some period of exceptional depression, to be assisted without incurring the stigma of pauperism. Mr. Gerald Balfour, in his evidence before the Royal Commission on the Poor Laws, said : " The unemployed for whom the Bill was intended were respectable workmen settled in a locality, hitherto accustomed to regular work, but temporarily out of employment through circumstances beyond their control, capable workmen with hope of return to regular work after tiding over a period of temporary distress ".[1] The Act, however, contains no definition that could confine employment on relief works to this type of workmen ; while the spirit of it excludes at once normal methods of hiring and disciplinary dismissal.

§ 3. In practice the difference between the policy thus illustrated and the policy of stabilising demand by transferences from good times to bad is very great. Under the latter

---

[1] *Royal Commission on the Poor Laws,* Majority Report, p. 386.

policy the pools of labour attached to industries hitherto
fluctuating are partly drained, and the workers set free are
absorbed into regular properly organised industries with no
friction and no waste. Under a policy of relief work for
the unemployed in bad times a miscellaneous collection of
relatively inefficient people are set to work at some task for
which many of them are in no way trained, with no proper
organisation and under conditions such that effective dis-
cipline is impracticable. However carefully we insist that
the work which is " made " shall be work of " actual and
substantial utility ", and not obviously futile work, such as
the digging of trenches to be afterwards filled up again, the
economic waste involved is bound to be very great. There
is risk too that workmen of a high grade may suffer permanent damage from association with casual and chronically
unemployed persons of low industrial character, for whom
the relief works were not intended, but who cannot practically
be excluded from them. On some occasions, no doubt, it
may be necessary to face this risk, because there may be no
other way of maintaining the morale of a large population
thrown out of work on account of some catastrophe that has
not been provided against. But, as a policy designed to
meet the more or less regular effects of cyclical industrial
movements, relief works for the unemployed stand con-
demned at once by analysis and by experience.

CHAPTER XVII

SHORT TIME *VERSUS* UNEMPLOYMENT

§ 1. WE have now to suppose that whatever it is decided to
do in the matter of mitigating cyclical fluctuations in the demand for labour has been done.[1] It is certain in the world of
real life that considerable fluctuations will still remain. The
social consequences of these do not depend entirely on their
size, but partly also on the way in which the shortage of
work and, consequently, of wages, that occurs from time to
time, is distributed among workpeople. There are available
two methods of spreading these shortages among a large
number of men and one method of concentrating them upon
a small number. The methods of spreading are (1) working
short time and putting the whole staff to work during the
whole of the working period and (2) working full time and
retaining the full staff, but rotating employment so that
only a proportion (say two-thirds) are actually at work at
any one time. The method of concentration is working full
time and dismissing a part of the staff. We have now to
consider by what influences the choice between these two
methods is normally determined.[2]

§ 2. As between the short-time plan and both the others
the relevant influences are primarily technical. Resort to
the short-time plan is easiest where conditions are such

---

[1] Of course the fact that attention is here confined to the relation of
general industrial fluctuations to employment must not be taken to imply
that, with industrial stabilisation, neither unemployment nor short time
could ever occur. Industrial stabilisation in our sense does not exclude
relative movements as between different industries, set up by sporadic
causes independently of the trade cycle.

[2] What follows is in part taken from Part III. chap. xi. of the *Economics
of Welfare*.

that an appreciable advantage can be gained by cutting down the most expensive *hours* of work, those, for example, that involve extra charges for lighting and heating. But one or other of the rival plans is favoured where much expensive machinery is employed and it is practicable, by spreading labour more sparsely, to keep the whole of this going with a reduced staff.

§ 3. As between the dismissal plan and both the others, the issue depends to a large extent upon how important it is to an employer to maintain a lien upon the services of the people who have so far been working for him. When the work to be done is skilled and specialised, it is often very important for him to do this.[1] Workpeople possessed of special aptitudes practically always acquire special value to the particular firms which have employed them for any length of time. This is partly because the detailed methods of different factories are different, and, therefore, workmen who have become accustomed to any given factory, particularly if the work they have to do in it is of an all-round kind, are more useful there than other similar workmen would be. It is partly also because skilled workmen often handle expensive materials or delicate machinery, and employers naturally prefer to trust these things to men of whose qualities they have had continuing experience. Finally, among firms making certain proprietary articles, it is partly because workmen may be expected, after a time, to get an inkling of their firm's manufacturing secrets, and the firm is, therefore, unwilling to let them enter the service of its rivals.[2] Thus, " among goldsmiths and jewellers the masters share work among a permanent staff, since there are many secret and special patterns, and adjust production by overtime for short periods ".[3] In like manner, employers are keenly anxious to retain a lien on the services of engine-drivers, domestic servants and specialised agricultural workers.[4] Even when

---

[1] It is to be expected, therefore, that the turnover of labour will, in general, be lower for skilled than for unskilled workers. For evidence that this is so in the United States cf. Schlichter, *The Labour Turnover*, pp. 57-64. But cf. also *ibid.* p. 73.

[2] Cf. Fay, *Co-partnership in Industry*, p. 90.

[3] Webb, *Seasonal Trades*, p. 43.   [4] Cf. *ibid.* p. 23.

the work to be done is of such a sort that a man who has been employed before with a particular firm is not appreciably more valuable to that firm than one who has not, an employer in bad times, who knows, or hopes, that things will improve, will like to keep in touch with more men than he needs at the moment, so as to make sure that enough will be available later on. This consideration is especially likely to influence employers in industries where the fluctuations are known to be seasonal ; for in these industries there is practical certainty that a full staff will be needed again shortly. It has been suggested that seasonality of this kind is partly responsible for the prevalence of the short-time method in coal-mining and in agriculture.

§ 4. In this choice between the dismissal plan and the other two another very important factor is the degree of accuracy with which wages are adjusted to efficiency. When the payment normally made to inferior workers is higher, relatively to their efficiency, than that made to better workers, there is a strong inducement to employers to meet bad times by dispensing with the least profitable part of their staff. It is thus natural to find that the dismissal method is relatively dominant in time-wage industries as compared with piece-wage industries. In like manner, it is natural to find that in Germany, where, before the war, trade unions were relatively weak, and where, partly as a consequence of this, a rigid standard rate in time-wage industries was much less effectively enforced than it was in this country, the practice of meeting slack periods by working short time, rather than by a reduction of staff, was considerably more general. " Some of the German authorities declare that the practice of short time in some industries reduces earnings by as much as one-fourth or one-third in the course of a year. It is certain that, though certain British industries, notably coal-mining and the cotton industry, resort to the system of short time, the extent to which this system operates to lower the figure of unemployed workmen in the United Kingdom is much less than in the German Empire."[1] I do not wish to stress these facts unduly. They seem, however, to

[1] *Report on the Cost of Living in German Towns* [Cd. 4032], p. 522.

illustrate the general tendency set out at the beginning of this section.

§ 5. As between rotation of hands and the two other plans, the dominant fact is that the rotation method is troublesome to arrange and involves a good deal of organisation and collaboration with the workpeople. It appears to prevail among " the riverside corn porters working regularly at the Surrey docks " ;[1] it has been practised to some extent among the iron-workers of the north of England ; and it was tried, alongside of the short-time plan, in the cotton industry during a part of 1918. Yet again, as a result of negotiations with the Tailors' Trade Union, the Master Tailors' Association announced : " We fully recognise that the work ought to be fairly shared during the slack seasons (subject to certain explanations), and we urge upon our members throughout the country to carry these principles into effect ".[2] But, broadly speaking, the inconvenience of this method has not permitted it to be adopted at all widely.

§ 6. The general result is that, in the main part of industry, depressions are met either by the short-time method or by the dismissal method, or by a mixture of the two. Sir Sydney Chapman gives some interesting figures to illustrate the varying degrees in which different textile industries, all employing the same (namely, the piece-wage) form of wage payment, have adopted the two methods respectively. Between November 1907 and November 1908 it appears that in the cotton industry, among the firms investigated, a 13·3 per cent contraction of output was met, to the extent of 5 per cent by reduction of staff, and to the extent of 8·3 per cent by short time ; whereas in the silk industry an 8·1 per cent contraction of output led to a 6·2 per cent reduction of staff and 2·1 per cent short time.[3] As is well known, the

---

[1] *Report of the Royal Commission on the Poor Law*, p. 1156, footnote.

[2] *Report on Collective Agreements*, 1910, p. xxviii.

[3] Cf. Chapman, *Unemployment in Lancashire*, p. 51. When a firm employs both factory workers and home workers, it is, of course, to its interest in bad times to withdraw work from home workers rather than to reduce factory work and home work equally, because it is thus enabled to keep its machinery going. It may be added that the power to treat home workers in this way indirectly checks employers from superseding home work altogether by factory work, since it enables them to face the prospect

method of short time is dominant in coal-mining, where it is carried out by a reduction, in times of depression, in the number of shifts worked per week ; and the method of dismissal in the building, shipbuilding and engineering trades.[1]

§ 7. Apart from indirect effects, it is evident that the dismissal method, involving, as it does, concentration of worklessness and wagelessness on a small number of men —for naturally the least competent will always be selected for dismissal—involves more social damage than the other methods. For, however well unemployment insurance and other palliative devices are arranged, it must mean that the cuts in consumption, which have to be made in bad times, are not distributed evenly. Moreover, the dismissal method indirectly checks production. For under it workpeople tend to " spin out their jobs unduly ", being rendered by the fear of unemployment less anxious to exert themselves. Yet again, the dismissal method, involving, as it does, long periods of unemployment to particular men, threatens grave damage to their industrial quality and morale in the ways described in Chapter I. of this Part.

§ 8. If we had to do with a single industry only, or with a world of various industries between which labour was absolutely mobile, these indirect evil consequences of the dismissal method would stand alone, with nothing to set against them. In the actual world, however, there are also in certain circumstances indirect evil consequences associated with the rival method of short time. If in a factory (or industry) employing 100 men the demand so falls that, at the current rate of wages—which we assume to be maintained —$\frac{1}{100}$th part less work than before is required, this state of

of periodic expansions without the need of erecting factories too large for the demand of ordinary times. (Cf. Vessilitsky, *The Home Worker*, p. 3.)

[1] Of course it is not meant that in these trades no short time is known. On the contrary, even when the dismissal method is adopted for contractions of work from below the normal, what is, in effect, the short-time method is always adopted to some extent for contractions from above the normal. Thus in the engineering trade, whereas the average amount of formal short time is very small, overtime used to add on the average 3¾ per cent to the normal man's working time (Cd. 2337, p. 100); and, as against overtime working, normal hours are, of course, really short time.

things may be met either by short time all round to the extent of $\frac{1}{100}$th part of normal time or by the dismissal of one man. It is plainly in the interest of production that one man should move elsewhere if the cost of movement, translated into terms of daily payment, is less than the whole of the daily wage. If the method of dismissal rules, one man—the one who has been dismissed—will, in fact, given that he has the necessary knowledge, move elsewhere when this condition is fulfilled. But, if the method of short time (or rotation of work) rules, nobody will move unless the cost of moving, translated as above, is less than $\frac{1}{100}$th part of the daily wage. On this side, therefore, the method of short time is likely to be more injurious to production than the method of dismissal. When the costs of movement are so large (*e.g.* when it is a question of moving from one skilled industry to another), or when the depression of demand is only expected to last for so short a time, that movement would not take place on either plan, there is, indeed, nothing in this. But, when conditions are such that movement would have taken place on the dismissal plan, but does not take place on the short-time plan, production so far suffers. This is more likely to happen if a single firm adopts short time to meet a depression peculiar to itself, while there is a good demand for work in other parts of the industry, than if it adopts it to meet a depression shared by other firms ; for the costs obstructing movement between firms are less than those obstructing movement between industries. The above objection to the short-time plan deserves more attention than is usually paid to it. It is interesting to observe that an objection on exactly the same lines lay against the cotton industry's war policy of rotating such work as there was among all the work-people and providing out-of-work pay for those " playing " from a special levy upon such employers as were working more than the normal proportion of their machinery.[1] The

---

[1] For an account of the work of the Cotton Control Board during the war, cf. H. D. Henderson, *The Cotton Control Board*. In August 1918, the rota system, which had been established in September 1917, was abolished, and it was decided that the proceeds of the special levy should henceforward only be used for giving out-of-work pay to men played off definitely and continuously.

objection, it need hardly be said, is not decisive. The difference made to movement will generally be small, while, on the other hand, many men will be saved from the grave injury which unemployment, if no provision has been made against it, may inflict. In the very peculiar conditions of 1921–24 in the United Kingdom, when, as it appears, the engineering and shipbuilding industries were overcrowded as a result of movements into them during the war and the general interest required a substantial shifting of men out of them, it was important. As a rule, however, it does not amount to very much. For, while it is true that movements between one firm in the same industry and another might easily occur under the dismissal method and be obstructed under the other methods, as a matter of fact, when short time is extensively adopted as a means of meeting depressions, it is more apt to take the form of organised short time throughout a whole industry—as in the cotton industry of Lancashire—than that of independent short time at isolated centres ; and, therefore, there is little scope for obstruction of movement between firms. As between a whole industry and other occupations, on the other hand, temporary movements of workmen can rarely take place in any event to an appreciable extent; and, therefore, the fact that short time somewhat obstructs such movements makes no significant difference. Consequently, though it must be admitted that in certain special cases the short time method may, from this side, inflict an injury on production of comparable weight with the evils attributed in § 7 to the dismissal method, this will happen but rarely. As regards indirect social consequences the short-time method has, as a rule, a substantial balance in its favour.

§ 9. On the line of reasoning followed in Part II. Chapter XII. § 6, it is easily seen that only a small part of the indirect social consequences of the choice they make between the method of short time (or rotation of hands) and the method of dismissal enters into the marginal return of those who control industry. It results from what has been said that, if left to themselves, they are likely to have more resort to the dismissal method and less resort to the other methods

than it is desirable that they should have.   Hence, except
when conditions are such that the objections of the
preceding section have special force, there is a strong case
for external intervention in favour of the methods of short
time or rotation of work.   Such intervention may be
attempted by trade unions, which sometimes put pressure
on employers to meet depressions by short time or rotation.   The arrangement between the Tailors' Trade Union
and the Master Tailors' Association cited in § 5 illustrates
this sort of action.   Intervention by governmental authorities is a more difficult matter, since the detailed conditions of different industries vary greatly and no general
rule is likely to be appropriate to all of them.   Still,
note should be taken of the interesting proposal made in
the Italian Parliament in 1921 that, " in the event of the
necessary reduction of the staff (in any concern), before
dismissing hands the hours of work must be reduced to a
minimum of thirty-six hours a week with a proportionate
reduction of wages ".[1]

[1] *Economic Review of the Foreign Press,* 1921, p. 20.

CHAPTER XVIII

INSURANCE AGAINST UNEMPLOYMENT

§ 1. THOUGH in the logical sequence of our argument we are concerned only with the part of unemployment which results from general industrial fluctuations, it is not practicable, for the purpose of this final chapter, to separate that part from other parts. We suppose, then, that, statesmen and private philanthropists having done what they can, the volume of unemployment and the way in which it is distributed among workpeople are given. The bulk of those affected are certain to be affected in different degrees at different times. As a necessary consequence, their wage-incomes must fluctuate. But a fluctuating income carries with it a fluctuating consumption ; and this involves an element of evil, from which a consumption of equal average amount that did not fluctuate would be free.[1] This implies that, when the volume and the distribution of unemployment are both given, it will be to the advantage of those concerned to accept a certain diminution in their average consumption, if, by so doing, they can separate, by some form of buffer, fluctuations in consumption from fluctuations in income. It will pay them, in short, to consume somewhat less, in order to consume more regularly. There follow two inferences. The first is that the evil consequences resulting from

[1] Of course, if an individual's needs vary—they are likely to be greater when he has a family to support than either before he marries or after his children have become self-supporting—welfare will be greater, the more closely variations in consumption are adjusted to variations in needs. This consideration, however, though very important in its place, is not relevant to variations of consumption due to industrial fluctuations, which are obviously not adjusted in this way.

a given volume of unemployment will be less, the more efficient and economical are the arrangements to which work-people are able to resort for the purpose of steadying their consumption ; the second, that these evil consequences will be less, the more closely the amount of resources actually devoted by workpeople to the above purpose approximates to the amount that a full understanding of their true interests would dictate. The business of the present chapter is to work out the practical bearing of these two inferences.

§ 2. If the fortunes of all wage-earners varied in exactly the same manner, the only way in which, by their own action without help from outside, they could secure steadiness in their consumption would be by accumulating savings in the good times against the needs of the bad times. It makes no essential difference whether saving takes place after the bad times, to pay back debts contracted in them, or before the bad times, to provide a fund that will be drawn upon in them. In either event the steadying cause is saving and nothing else. Plainly, if this device were carried sufficiently far, it would reduce the variability of the representative working-man's consumption to zero. A less complete resort to it acts *pro tanto* in the same way. It reduces the variability of the representative working-man's consumption to some extent below the variability of his income. In real life the fortunes of different workmen vary differently. This circumstance opens the way for a second device for steadying the consumption of the representative worker. This is a mutual pledge that those who are fortunate at any time shall hand over part of their income to those who at that time are unfortunate. This device taken by itself is imperfect, because it makes no provision against the danger of common misfortunes affecting a large proportion of the workpeople at the same time. But, when it is combined with the device of saving, this imperfection is removed. The advantage, however, remains. While the device of saving, taken alone, *can* reduce the variability of workpeople's consumption to zero, it can only do this at the cost of withholding a very large quantity of resources from consumption. Each person needs to retain, on the average, a reserve large enough to make good the variations that occur in his individual income. In any group of persons, however, whose individual circumstances result from partially independent causes, the sum of the variations from the average of individual incomes in any year will be much larger than the variation from the average of the sum of individual incomes. It follows that, by saving collectively instead of individually, a group of people can greatly lessen the amount of saving that is required in order to reduce the variability of the representative man's consumption in any given degree. Hence arises that combination of the device of "mutuality" and the device of saving which is commonly known as insurance. This method is a cheaper way than saving alone of producing a given increment of stability. Consequently, among the poorer classes, to whom cheapness is of vital importance, attempts to foster it have been successful, where—witness the subsidies given under the Ghent system to provision made individually against unemployment—attempts to foster individual saving have failed.[1]

§ 3. The contribution which insurance can make towards steadying consumption is greater or less, according as the machinery embodying it can overcome, with greater or less success, certain practical difficulties. Of these the most fundamental is the tendency of insurance arrangements to tempt people to simulate, or, it may be, deliberately to bring about the insurable event. Unless this tendency can be held in reasonable control, insurance is impracticable. It is, therefore, essential that some study be made of the methods by which, in the special case of insurance against unemployment, the tendency can be combated. For our present purpose unemployment may be defined as want of work on the part of a workman desiring to obtain work at the ruling rate of wages appropriate to his

[1] " The supplementary provision made at Ghent and elsewhere for unorganised workmen has been either a total failure or a not altogether gratifying success. At Strassburg, and in most of the French towns, it has been omitted, and the benefits of the municipal subvention have been confined to members of trade unions, in spite of the objections raised on social and political grounds to thus forcing workmen to join such associations " (*Report of the Royal Commission on the Poor Laws*, Appendix, vol. ix. p. 737).

occupation.[1] This is the insurable event in regard to which the dangers of voluntary creation and of simulation have to be examined. Our task is, in some measure, simplified by the fact that the notion of involuntariness is embraced in the definition of unemployment. With such an insurable event as sickness, it is at least possible, however improbable in practice, thát people may make themselves ill on purpose. If unemployment had been defined simply as lack of work—an event not unpleasant in itself, but only in its effect on income—a system of insurance, which in part cancelled this effect, would, very probably, lead people to become unemployed on purpose. Since, however, we have defined unemployment as the state of being out of work *involuntarily*, it is impossible, in the nature of things, for anybody to bring it about on purpose. Consequently, the danger of the deliberate creation of this insurable event is non-existent, and the whole of our attention may be concentrated upon the danger of simulation. With such an insurable event as death or—where a proper system of birth registration exists—as old age, simulation is practically impossible. When the event is unemployment, as defined above, one conceivable form of simulation is almost equally out of the question. If a man is really at work, he can scarcely pretend not to be and escape detection. A simple rule, such as that often enacted by trade unions and adopted in the administration of the British Unemployment Insurance Law, requiring men in receipt of out-of-work benefit to sign the vacant book daily at some time that falls within normal working hours, affords a complete safeguard. The possibility of simulation of this kind is, therefore, a matter of no practical importance. Until

---

[1] When insurance is effected in a trade union, the wage named is, of course, the standard rate of the union. In wider systems of unemployment insurance the determination of this wage presents, however, some difficulties. The English National Insurance Act 1911 determines it as not lower than that at which the man concerned habitually works, or, in the event of an offer of work in another district, than the rate current there. Strictly, it would seem that this latter concession is right when the lower rate in another district is due to the prevalence of a lower cost of living, but wrong when it is due to the existence there of a lower average of capacity among workpeople.

recently, however, the case was very different with that form of simulation which consists in being out of work on purpose and pretending to be out of work involuntarily. It was easy to abandon a job on plausible grounds and to be unenthusiastic in the search for a new one ; and it was hard for anybody to prove that a man was shirking in this way. This circumstance, more than any other, was responsible for the fact that all the early systems of insurance against unemployment, which had any measure of success, were worked through trade unions of workpeople engaged in the same industry and working together in groups. For, though to guard against the kind of simulation we have been discussing is always hard, it is least hard when benefit is arranged in such a way as to make a man's neighbours and comrades in work interested inspectors of his conduct. Of late years the development of an organised system of Employment Exchanges in the more advanced industrial countries has changed the situation. In former times the workman's task included, not only doing his work, but also finding it ; and, though his trade union might, by collecting information, greatly help him in the search, it made no pretence of undertaking the search for him. The modern Employment Exchange, however, when it is developed so far as to constitute, not merely a bureau of information, but an actual centre of engagement, itself in a sense takes over the task of searching for work. The individual workman, no longer having to perform that task, cannot be made slack about it by his knowledge that unemployment benefit exists. It is no longer possible for anybody to pretend to be out of work involuntarily, when he is really out of work on purpose. If he is out of work in spite of an offer of work from the Employment Exchange, then he is certainly out of work on purpose ; if he is out of work because the Employment Exchange is unable to make him an offer, he is certainly unemployed in the strict sense. The importance of this point is recognised in the great emphasis which, in European countries, is almost always laid upon the need of associating schemes of subsidised insurance against unemployment with some form of Employment

Exchange. " In Cologne and Berne the Insurance Fund and the public Labour Exchange are practically amalgamated. In Strassburg, Milan and Antwerp receipt of subvention by an unemployed person under the ' Ghent system ' is conditional upon his registration at the Labour Exchange. . . . The State subvention to unemployed benefit in France can only be claimed by unions having an organised method of finding employment for their members." [1] In like manner, Part II. of the National Insurance Act of the United Kingdom, 1911—the Part, that is, which deals with unemployment — and the extending Act of 1920 have throughout been administered through the agency of the national system of Employment Exchanges. No doubt, the practice of engaging workpeople at the Exchanges as yet prevails only over a limited field. The task of searching for work has not been transferred to these institutions in a sufficient measure to destroy altogether the danger that insurance against involuntary failures to find work may lead to failures which pretend to be involuntary but are really deliberate. Furthermore, it must be remembered that the struggle to find work may include such things as the learning of a subsidiary trade, as well as mere search for work at a man's present trade, and that Employment Exchanges provide no protection against a slackening of effort in this direction. Nevertheless, we may rightly hold that, with the development of these Exchanges, the danger that simulation of unemployment will be brought about by insurance against it has been very much reduced.

§ 4. The bearing of this discussion upon the question how far in practice insurance can help to steady consumption at a low cost is plain. When the conditions are such that an insurable event can be simulated easily, it is necessary to make the inducement to simulation small. This implies, in the first instance, that the benefit paid to unemployed persons must amount to substantially less than the wage they would have earned had they continued to work. Thus, before the war, the British engineers, who are among the aristocracy of labour, provided, in respect of

[1] [Cd. 5068], p. 737.

a man who had belonged to the union for ten years, a benefit of 10s. a week for the first 14 weeks' unemployment ; 7s. for the next 30 weeks, and 6s. for further unemployment. The benefit provided under the compulsory clauses of the British National Insurance Act of 1911 was 7s. a week, commencing after the first week's unemployment, and extending for a maximum period of 15 weeks in any 12 months. Even now (under the 1927 Act) the benefit is only 15s. for a man and 12s. for a woman, with other additional allowances for dependents. The device of making benefits small, introduced in order to prevent simulation, cannot fail also to limit the efficacy of insurance against unemployment as a means of steadying consumption. For, although a certain limited measure of steadiness can be brought about by it at a smaller cost than would otherwise have been necessary, the cost of evolving steadiness in excess of this limited measure is not affected at all. If we are content to prevent a man's consumption from falling in times of unemployment by more than, say, a third of its normal amount, the instrument of insurance enables us to do this fairly cheaply. But, if we wish to prevent his consumption from falling by more than, say, a twentieth, that instrument cannot at present be employed. As Employment Exchanges come to play a more important part, it will, however, become applicable to larger tasks.

§ 5. Another technical obstacle to insurance is the fact that the liability to unemployment of different people engaged in the same occupation is different, and that, therefore, unless a highly elaborate system of adjusted premiums is introduced, insurance implies a subsidy from those less liable to the risk for the benefit of those more liable. The difficulty is not, it should be clearly understood, that *after the event* some insured persons find their premiums paid over to other people. Provided that, *before the event*, when the bargain is entered into, it is not known who the fortunate and who the unfortunate are going to be, this does not matter. In virtue of the law of diminishing utility, a chance of one in a thousand that I shall lose £10,000 is more burdensome to me than the actuarial value of the chance, namely, £10, and I am willing, therefore, to pay a premium of more than £10 to guard myself against this chance. Hence, if there are enough people in a similar position to myself to make a mutual insurance arrangement fairly secure on the basis of a premium of not much more than £10, it will pay all of us to contribute the required premiums into a fund, from which those who, in fact, suffer losses may be compensated. Furthermore, it will pay all of us to do this, even though the adjustment between the premiums paid and the risks carried by different members is imperfect. Within limits workmen less liable to unemployment will gain by combining for insurance on an equal footing with workmen more liable to this evil. Moreover, the limits are further extended when persons not likely to draw much benefit from insurance schemes come into them in the hope of inducing less fortunate fellow-members to adopt a line of conduct which the more fortunate believe to be advantageous to themselves. This class of consideration is largely responsible for the willingness of good workmen to allow bad workmen to associate with them in the enjoyment of the unemployment benefit provided by trade unions. Bad workmen are, indeed, partially excluded from trade unions by an initial test on admission, by limitation of the period during which benefits are paid (a long period one year meaning a shorter period in the following year) and by the refusal of benefit till premiums have been regularly paid for some time. This practice of exclusion is, however, generally exercised in a very lenient manner. The reason is that the event insured against is, not simply failure to find work, but failure to find it in the man's ordinary trade at the rate which the trade union considers a proper rate for that trade. Better workmen, being interested to prevent inferior workmen from cutting into the standard rate, are prepared to include many of them in their fund, though they know that, by doing so, they suffer a direct loss. They have an indirect gain to look to, for which they are willing to pay. Hence voluntary insurance against unemployment, worked through a trade society, will tend to embrace, at the same premium, men of more divergent capacities than at first sight seems to be probable.[1] The fact, that "practically one set of men continually pay more than they receive, and another (smaller) number of men as continually receive more than they pay",[2] is not fatal to the voluntary continuance of the arrangement by both sets of men. But—and this is the point—though it is not a conclusive obstacle, it is a very serious one. Though the limits, within which advantage may be derived from an insurance scheme by the less vulnerable among any group of insurers, are wider than might perhaps be expected, they are still narrow. The ratio between the premiums charged and the actuarial value of the different risks, with which they are connected, must not differ widely. We shall not, for instance, find a voluntary unsubsidised [3] insurance fund, paying a uniform benefit for accident or for sickness, that includes among its members, at the same premium, workers in safe or healthy trades and also workers in dangerous or unhealthy trades. Nor shall we find voluntary life insurance associations accepting obviously healthy persons and obvious invalids on equal terms. In like manner we shall not find voluntary unsubsidised schemes of insurance against unemployment dealing in this way with workers in the railway industry and also with workers in the highly fluctuating building and engineering trades. Of course the theoretical solution of this difficulty is plain, namely, to build up an insurance scheme on a basis of premiums carefully adjusted to the varying risks included under it. But in actual life misunderstanding and friction may easily make this plan impracticable. The technical difficulty of constructing a

[1] For example : " The Cigar Makers' Union spends a great deal of money on out-of-work benefit, and the managers of this fund inform us that a large number of the recipients of this relief are infirm persons who cannot earn the average wages, and that many of these are advanced in years " (Henderson, *Industrial Insurance in the United States,* p. 92). It should be noticed that the danger to *competent* men from the acceptance of low wages by *incompetent* men is generally much exaggerated in popular thought.

[2] *Third Report of the Committee on Distress from Unemployment,* Mr. Booth's Evidence, Q. 10,519.

[3] Where there is a subsidy the better workmen need not, of course, be tempted to hold off ; for they may reckon to receive from the State more than they have to pay to the worse workmen.

system that will include these adjustments considerably restricts the effective range of voluntary unsubsidised insurance.

§ 6. This completes what it is necessary to say in connection with the first of the two inferences distinguished at the beginning of this chapter. It was there laid down that the evil consequences of unemployment are likely to vary in extent with the efficiency and economy of the arrangements which are available for enabling people to make their consumption steady in the face of a fluctuating wage income. These arrangements have now been examined. The second inference was to the effect that, given these arrangements, the evil consequences are likely to be less, the more closely the amount of resources actually devoted by workpeople to the task of promoting steadiness approximates to the amount that a full understanding of their true interests would dictate. We now turn to the practical implications of this proposition. If everybody was perfectly intelligent and self-controlled, there would, indeed, be nothing to discuss. The workpeople concerned would understand their interests fully and would expend their resources in the best possible way. In real life, however, perfect intelligence and self-control are in all classes somewhat lacking, and in the wage-earning class not less than in others. Experience has shown that, as a matter of fact, there is a tendency to let the future take care of itself, and not to make such preparations in good times as a dispassionate review of the probabilities would show to be desirable. This is partly due to the difficulty of grasping the reality of a distant prospect, to which all persons, and particularly those who are imperfectly educated, are liable, and partly to that essential vanity of human nature, through which a man, while fully recognising the risks of a given venture to the average person, secretly assumes that he himself is somehow superior to the average. Be the causes, however, what they may, of the fact there is little doubt. In view of this fact there is *prima facie* ground for holding that the evil consequences of unemployment might be substantially reduced by legal enactments designed to induce workpeople to devote a larger proportion of their resources than they naturally tend to do to the work of rendering their consumption more steady.

§ 7. Before this conclusion is finally accepted it is, however, necessary to envisage certain indirect ill-effects, also not likely to be taken into account by those persons who guide practice, to which insurance against unemployment (and systematic short time) may lead. First, the fact of insurance being available may, on occasions, prevent workpeople from permitting reductions in wage-rates in bad times of a sort that would really benefit both themselves and society at large. Secondly, the fact of unemployment insurance being arranged, as in practice it always is, with the proviso that benefit is payable if an insured person is unable to obtain work in his accustomed trade may, on occasions, injure production by checking the movement of workpeople in decaying trades away to others. This evil is probably of small importance in ordinary times. In the Great War regard for it caused the official out-of-work pay provided in the jute industry for workpeople who lost their jobs through the enforced closing down of machinery, to be withheld from persons who refused reasonable offers of other kinds of work.[1] A similar condition was made in a plan adopted in Germany at about the same time for compensating workpeople whose work was stopped through a shortage of coal.[2] In the British Insurance (amending) Act of 1927 it is provided that, after the lapse of a reasonable interval, employment of a kind other than the claimant's usual employment may be regarded as suitable, subject to certain safeguards. In Denmark the hindrance to mobility towards jobs outside a man's own trade is partly met by an arrangement allowing the unemployment fund to pay, to any one accepting work at a lower-paid job, the difference between the wage on that job and the maximum of unemployed benefit.[3] The above indirect ill-consequences of insurance against unemployment must be borne in mind.

---

[1] Cf. *Labour Gazette*, 1918, p. 138.
[2] Cf. *ibid.* p. 141.
[3] Cf. Schloss, *Insurance Against Unemployment*, p. 61.

On balance, however, nobody would contend that they count for much against the direct benefit of steadier consumption.

§ 8. Broadly speaking, two forms of encouragement to insurance are possible—namely, bounties and compulsion. Both of these may appear in various forms and degrees. Thus bounties may merely consist in the supply, at the cost of the State, of statistical material and tariffs of risks. They may include the free provision of an institution through which insurance can be effected, thus affording to insurers a guarantee against fraud or insolvency. Again, they may include a small subsidy in money, such as that accorded in England to life insurance by the rule exempting the premiums paid on such insurance from income-tax. Yet again, they may include a considerable subsidy, such as is accorded to Trade Union insurance against unemployment in those places on the Continent of Europe where the so-called " Ghent system " has been adopted. These subsidies have, in some cases, amounted to as much as 50 per cent of the benefits paid. In like manner, encouragement by compulsion, if such a phrase is permissible, may assume various forms, according as the compulsion is conditional or unconditional, operated through localities or through trades, limited or unlimited in its range. The most important instance of this method is contained in the British National Insurance Act.

§ 9. If it be granted, on the strength of what has been said in earlier paragraphs, that some form of encouragement to insurance against unemployment is likely to diminish the evils associated with unemployment and is, therefore, socially desirable, it becomes necessary to decide which of the two forms of encouragement just distinguished is to be preferred. In order that this discussion may be conducted fairly, we must be careful to set in contrast with compulsion, not current examples of the method of bounties, but examples of a superior kind. For current examples are, all of them, so arranged that the amount of subsidy accorded is dependent on the expenditure which the subsidised societies make upon unemployment benefit. Under the Ghent plan the subsidy is some fixed proportion of this expenditure, and under the (now obsolete) sections of the British National Insurance

Act (1911) providing for State aid to voluntary insurance against unemployment it was also a fixed proportion—in this case limited to one-sixth. Arrangements of this kind are open to two serious objections. The first and most obvious of these is that, other things being equal, larger benefit is likely to be paid by richer groups of working men, and that, therefore, the system involves State aid to different groups varying more or less *inversely* with their need. This is the exact contrary of what is socially desirable ; for clearly, if any discrimination is allowed, State aid should vary directly, and not inversely, with need. The second objection is that, other things being equal, highly fluctuating industries are likely to have a larger expenditure upon unemployment benefit than steady industries. Bounties proportioned to expenditure will, therefore, confer upon them a differential advantage similar to that which would be conferred upon dangerous industries if the State were to contribute to all industries in proportion to the number of accidents occurring in them. But such differential encouragement of particular industries—unless, indeed, the particular industries are specially selected for encouragement on the ground that too little of the nation's resources is normally invested in them—is almost certain to involve economic waste and, therewith, social injury. Consequently, so far as encouragement by bounties involves differentiation of this kind, a strong ground for condemning it is revealed. It is, however, possible to devise a system of bounties that is not open to either of the above two objections. After the pattern of the State contribution towards sickness benefit in Germany, subsidies to unemployment benefit might be made proportional to the number of persons attached to any insurance fund, on condition that a certain minimum benefit was provided to men out of employment. It is this ideal form of encouragement by bounty, rather than current forms, that ought to be compared with encouragement by compulsion.

It is easily seen, however, that even this form suffers from two serious disadvantages. The first is that, in practice, bounties on insurance against unemployment can hardly (apart from compulsion) be given with effect in any industry except through a trade union. In all countries, however, even in those where unions are strong, large numbers of workpeople are to be found outside the unions. Consequently, unless the bounty is to be discriminating in its incidence, a rule must be made compelling these societies to allow outsiders, who will not become regular members, nevertheless to become members in respect of the fund subsidised by the State. A rule of this sort prevails in Denmark and also in Norway, but it is obviously unsatisfactory and likely to lead—as, indeed, in Norway it has led —to considerable friction. A compulsory scheme is free from this difficulty. The second disadvantage of the method of bounties is that, as a means of inducing people to insure, it is immensely less effective than compulsion ; and this in spite of the fact that a bounty enables workmen less liable to unemployment to enter, without fear of loss, into a common scheme with workmen much more liable to it. Even the large bounties frequently offered under the Ghent system, though they extended the range of insurance operated by unions already in existence, had practically no effect in building up trade union insurance among classes of workpeople hitherto innocent of it. " The great bulk of those claiming the public subvention are drawn from highly skilled and organised trades—such as printing, cigar-making, diamond working. The unskilled and semi-skilled occupations—in which the bulk of distress through unemployment is found in the United Kingdom—do not appear as yet to be touched by the Ghent system anywhere. In Strassburg the hope of reaching these classes in this way is expressly abandoned and annual relief works are contemplated as the only resource for the seasonal labourers." [1] In this respect compulsory insurance is obviously a more powerful instrument. It does not, indeed, imply, as popular opinion supposes it to do, universal insurance. For, since in all systems, so far as they are concerned with unemployment, benefits lapse after a time, highly inefficient men must often become uninsured in spite of compulsion. The English National Insurance Act, for example, as amended in 1927, makes it a condition for

[1] [Cd. 5068], p. 732.

the receipt of benefit that at least 30 contributions have been paid in the two years preceding the date of claim. Still, it is plain that, though compulsion does not mean insurance for all workpeople covered by the compulsion, it must, in general, approach much more nearly towards this goal than any system of bounties. We are not, indeed, entitled, on the strength of the above considerations, to infer, without reserve, that compulsion is, in this matter, necessarily superior to bounties. What people *think* good in such a case goes a long way towards determining what *is* good. In a country where the idea of State compulsion was violently unpopular, that fact might turn the scale in favour of the less efficient method of bounties. In fact, however, the unpopularity of compulsion appears to be imaginary rather than real, at all events among the workpeople of Western Europe. The device of combining with compulsion a certain element of State aid has apparently sufficed to render it reasonably palatable.

§ 10. If, on the basis of the foregoing discussion, it is decided to adopt in any country a national system of compulsory insurance against unemployment (and corresponding losses through short time), we are faced with the issue between a general flat-rate scheme, with uniform premiums and benefits, and a scheme in which premiums or benefits or both differ for different groups of wage-earners.

Two forms of differentiating scheme may be advocated. First, it may be urged, premiums should be set higher, or benefits lower, in industries subject to large than in those subject to small fluctuations. For, as was pointed out in § 9, the risks of unemployment being much more serious in highly fluctuating industries, such as engineering and shipbuilding, than in comparatively stable industries, such as railway service, a general flat-rate scheme will favour industries of the former class and will tend to push an unduly large number of persons into them. The kind of adjustment required would be obtained if equal premiums were collected from all industries and were used to provide whatever benefits they were actually good for in the several industries, and if, on the top of this, extra variable premiums were collected from the less stable industries, so adjusted as to allow the final benefits everywhere to be equal. Unless this is done the payment of equal benefits *must* involve a socially injurious form of favouritism.[1] This disadvantage has to be balanced against the evident advantage in administrative simplicity that is enjoyed by a system of flat-rate premiums and bounties. The British Act of 1920, which extended compulsory insurance to all occupations except domestic service and agriculture, attempted a compromise. It set up a general level-premium scheme, but permitted particular industries to contract out of it and to set up special schemes for themselves—the presumption, of course, being that the industries least exposed to unemployment would do this. Since, however, they could only contract out at the cost of sacrificing 70 per cent of the normal Treasury grant, they did not, by doing this, altogether escape adverse differentiation. Special schemes under that rule have been set up in the banking and insurance industries. The Act of 1927, while preserving these, does not permit any further special schemes to be formed. The same idea is embodied in those forms of the policy of insurance by industries in which it is proposed that the State should make an equal contribution per head towards the insurance fund of each industry. All schemes of insurance by industries are, however, faced with two great practical difficulties. On the one hand, in the same industry there are always men of many trades belonging to many trade unions. On the other hand, the border-line between different industries is often obscure.[2]

Secondly, it may be urged, as between occupations subject to similar degrees of fluctuation, both premiums and benefits should be set higher in well-paid than in badly-paid

---

[1] A clear perception of this point is shown in the Swiss accident compensation law. This law distinguishes between occupational and non-occupational accidents, throwing the whole of the compensation costs of the former upon the employer, while the workman and the State jointly provide against the latter (*Labour Gazette*, May 1912).

[2] For a discussion of the technical and administrative difficulties in the way of these schemes cf. Cohen, *Insurance by Industries Examined* (1923).

occupations. For, under a uniform flat-rate scheme, the rate of benefit *must* be put too low to provide any near approach to stability in the consumption of the better-to-do workpeople. If it were put high enough to achieve that, the worst-to-do workpeople would be receiving, when unemployed, more money than the wage they normally get when in full work. This would be an unworkable arrangement,. even though insurance premiums were provided by the State, so that the poorer workers, who were not unemployed, did not find themselves mulcted of impossible sums. On the other side, however, there is once more the fact that a single flat-rate scheme is enormously simpler to administer, avoiding, as it does, the complications which, on the other plan, inevitably arise in connection with people on the border-line of two occupations and liable to pass from one to the other. The generally accepted view appears to be that compulsory schemes should be flat-rate ones with relatively low benefits, the better paid workpeople being left free to provide for themselves supplementary benefits with supplementary premiums if they desire to do so.

§ 11. A further difficult question is whether benefits should be equal for all workpeople or whether they should be larger for those who have than for those who have not a dependent wife and dependent children to support. Plainly, from a distributional point of view, the latter plan is superior. Moreover, since young unmarried men are subject to the " risk " of having a wife and children later on, it does not involve any tax upon them as a class, though it does involve such a tax upon older unmarried men and older men with small families. A technical difficulty in the way of the plan is that, under it, unless the normal benefit is put low relatively to the normal wage, a man with a large number of children might be actually better off when unemployed than when employed. Under the English Act of 1921–22 the amount of the premiums was increased, and dependents' benefits now (1927) amounting to 7s. in respect of a wife (or dependent husband) and 1s. (now 2s.) in respect of each child were added to the normal benefits ; but, even so, hardly anybody in this country can expect actually to gain by being unemployed. There are, however, some fundamental difficulties. First, this plan involves *pro tanto* a bounty on child-bearing, about the wisdom of which opinions are likely to differ. Secondly, if bachelors, or the public in general, are required to contribute towards the expenses of men with families, it is paradoxical that they should do so only when these men are unemployed.[1] The logical proceeding would be to provide children's benefit continuously whatever is happening to the parents; and in this case these benefits would lie outwith the scope of unemployment insurance.

§ 12. There remains the issue between State provision and private provision of the money required to constitute the insurance fund. There are three parties on whom, jointly or severally, the costs can be thrown, namely, the insured persons themselves, their employers and the State.

To collect premiums from the insured persons themselves and to collect them from their employers comes to very much the same thing. From the point of view of a short period, this is, of course, not so. For a considerable time after the initiation of any new scheme employers would really bear that part of the cost of insurance that is put upon them and workpeople the part that is put upon them. As Mr. Rubineau well remarks : " No shifting takes place automatically without meeting opposition and without losing some part of its momentum. It is much easier for the working class to resist the employers' effort to shift the cost upon them than to try to shift the cost upon the employers." [2] But the final incidence of insurance charges as between employers and workpeople is not determined by the accident of who actually makes the payment. Ultimately, just as with taxes and rates, the incidence is determined by general causes, and is the same whichever party is made the immediate subject of it. For the employers' demand for labour

---

[1] Most extant forms of "family wage" are guilty of the still more violent paradox of providing children's benefit only when the parents are at work—and the benefits, therefore, presumably least needed. As Mr. Cohen points out, this is a strong reason for preferring to them what he calls "family income insurance" (*Family Income Insurance*, p. 3).

[2] *Social Insurance*, p. 493.

varies with the burden directly put upon them, in such wise
that, when they are called upon to provide premiums, wages
tend to be less by the amount of these premiums than they
would have been if workpeople had provided them.   Thus,
rules about the distribution of insurance costs between workpeople and employers have only a secondary importance.[1]

If the costs of insurance are thrown on the tax-payer
and if the benefits paid in all industries are the same,
differentiation in favour of fluctuating industries, as described
in § 9, is present.   In a comparison between this system
and compulsory insurance with premiums provided by the
parties and adjusted to risks, this is a very important matter.
But in a comparison between it and compulsory insurance
with premiums so provided but not adjusted to risks, it is
not relevant, because that system also involves differentiation.   It is with this comparison that we are now concerned.
We need not inquire in detail how far, under a compulsory

---

[1] A sharp distinction must, however, be drawn between these rules
and rules which, whether they operate upon the employers or the workmen's contribution, differentiate between firms within the same industry
according as their methods tend to mitigate or enhance the risks against
which insurance is made.   Such differentiation encourages the adoption
of arrangements calculated to minimise unemployment ; whereas, if
there is no differentiation, good firms are, in effect, taxed to provide a
subsidy for bad firms.   This consideration has been applied in practice to
accidents.   In Germany each mutual association under the law providing
for insurance against accidents " determines for itself the danger class to
which each of the contributory establishments belongs, and is authorised to
levy a premium according to hazard.   It is also empowered to enforce rules
and regulations " (Frankel and Dawson, *Working Men's Insurance in
Europe*, p. 96).   Employers neglecting the rules may be put into a higher
danger class (*ibid.* p. 115).   In Austria " it is to the interest of each
employer to cut down the number of accidents in his establishment, as
his annual contribution may then be apportioned on the basis of a lower
danger coefficient.   This is the chief factor in the campaign of accident
prevention in Austria, insurance institutions not being permitted to make
preventive regulations, as is the case in the trade associations of Germany "
(*ibid.* p. 120).   A device on the same lines, designed to encourage preventive
measures against unemployment, is found in the English National Insurance
Act (1911).   A clause (now repealed) in this Act in effect imposed a
reduced rate on employers, so far as they engaged men for long terms and
so far as they met periods of depression by working " short time ".   A
similar principle is embodied in a Bill of the Wisconsin legislature, which
would vary the employers' contribution to unemployment insurance according to their success in stabilising employment and avoiding discharges,
i.e. in maintaining a low rate of labour turn-over (*Labour Overseas*, January
1921, p. 11).

system without State aid, the cost of insurance premiums is ultimately borne by others than workpeople,[1] because it is obvious that workpeople themselves must bear at least a large part. The assumption of the cost by the State means, therefore, transferring a large part of the burden of supporting those workpeople who happen to become unemployed from the shoulders of other workpeople who do not happen to become unemployed to the general body of tax-payers.

An important argument often urged against this policy is that it is bound to cause a serious contraction in the savings which workpeople would otherwise have contributed to the national capital, because it will discourage them from making provision against bad times for themselves. The force of this objection is, however, considerably mitigated when account is taken of the precise way in which, under insurance, provision against bad times is made. Suppose that a group of persons, *prima facie* with similar prospects, agree to subscribe annually for the needs of any of their number who may suffer misfortune in the course of the year. Being ignorant as to which of them will so suffer, it is worth while for all of them to enter into the contract. It is plain, however, that income paid over in fulfilment of it is simply income transferred for consumption by other people, and does not imply any addition to income saved. Of course, the insurance arrangements of real life are not fashioned in this simple way. Since, in all insurance societies, the annual outgoings in benefits are, within limits, variable and uncertain, *some* capital funds must be put by to guard against exceptionally bad years, and these funds must be greater, relatively to the turn-over, the smaller is the range the society covers and the more interdependent are the risks it assumes. In fire insurance, for example, provision must be made against the danger of heavy drains through widespread conflagrations. This, however, is not the main point. Unemployment, like most of the other risks insured against by the wage-earning classes, is a thing to which a man becomes more liable with advancing years.

---

[1] It will be noticed that the analysis of the preceding paragraph did *not* answer that question.

But it is not convenient to set up a system of insurance involving steadily increasing premiums. Such systems have, indeed, been tried in other branches of insurance, but, in practice, they cannot compete in attractiveness with systems based on uniform annual subscriptions. If, however, a level-rate system is to be solvent, in the sense of being competent at any time to fulfil the contracts outstanding against it, even though the influx of new members were to cease, the annual or weekly premium must be fixed at a rate exceeding the actuarial value of the annual or weekly risk involved in the insurance of the younger among the insurers. This means, in effect, that the insurance society must hold as reserve, and, therefore, presumably invest, a sum of money equal to the present value of the obligations which it has contracted in favour of its existing members, *minus* the present value of the probable future premiums to be paid by those members.[1] So much is necessary to maintain technical solvency. Under schemes of compulsory insurance of guaranteed permanence the certainty that the inflow of young members will not be checked makes it safe to keep the reserve at a level much below this. In some compulsory systems advantage is taken of this fact. Thus in the German law of accident insurance " provision is made only for payment of the benefits falling due during the current year, leaving payments of sums falling due in subsequent years to be met out of the receipts of such years ".[2] In other schemes, *e.g.* in the Norwegian law for compulsory insurance against accidents, it is provided that the finance shall be based on " capitalised values ", which means that reserves adequate to technical solvency have to be built up. But, even under voluntary schemes and compulsory schemes of this latter type, the point made above in regard to simple assessment societies still holds good in great measure. The reserve required for solvency is neces-

---

[1] For a good discussion of this matter cf. Gephart, *Principles of Insurance*, chap. viii.

[2] Frankel and Dawson, *Working Men's Insurance in Europe*, p. 112. " Employers prefer this arrangement because they can thus retain the money in their business, which sums would otherwise have been collected by the associations and accumulated in the capitalised values " (*ibid.*).

sarily much less than the sum which would yield interest sufficient to pay the benefits as they fall due, because, for purposes of solvency, the accumulated capital must itself be regarded as a distributable fund.[1] In the most completely solvent society, therefore, the money paid over in benefits in any year will include, besides income derived from invested funds, a large slice of the subscriptions received during that year ; and in societies that are not completely solvent the slice will be still larger. We conclude, therefore, that the provision which workpeople would make for themselves in the form of insurance against unemployment—or, indeed, against anything else—is not, in the main, income correlated with a large net contribution of real savings. Consequently, for the State, by providing for insurance, to discourage people from making provision for private insurance, will not involve a large injury to capital accumulation. It will, of course, involve *some* injury, because as explained above, a part of the insurance premiums are turned into real savings. The injurious effect is not, however, likely to be very important.

On the other side, in favour of the policy of free State-provided insurance, appeal is made to its greater simplicity and cheapness in administration. Mr. Sidney Webb once wrote : " Regarded as a method of raising revenue, compulsory insurance of all the wage-earning population, with its elaborate paraphernalia of weekly deductions, its array of cards and stamps, its gigantic membership catalogue, its inevitable machinery of identification and protection against fraud, involving not only a vast and perpetual trouble to

---

[1] If i be the rate of interest and a a given annuity, to begin next year and last for n years, the sum required to yield that annuity at interest without exhausting the principal is $\frac{a}{i}$, but, if the principal also may be called upon, the sum required, even without allowing for the future subscriptions of present members, is only $\frac{a}{i}\left\{1-\frac{1}{(1+i)^n}\right\}$; and, when allowance is made for these subscriptions, it is smaller than that. It is, indeed, necessary that, besides the reserve just described, an insurance society should keep a further reserve to guard against the occurrence in any year of a quantity of claims in excess of the " probable " annual amount. In large societies, however, the reserve needed for this purpose is, in general, small, relatively to their turn-over.

every employer, but also the appointment of an extra-ordinarily extensive civil service staff—is, compared with all our other taxes, almost ludicrously costly and cumbersome to all concerned."[1]   At the present time, however, the administrative costs of compulsory contributory insurance do not appear to be very great.   The main appeal on this side, therefore, must be a more general one—to the gain in economic welfare that results from transferring resources from the relatively rich to the relatively poor, wherever this can be accomplished without causing serious injury to production.   This appeal raises issues too large for discussion here.   Some study of them has been attempted in Part IV. of *The Economics of Welfare*.

[1] *The Prevention of Destitution*, p. 170.

APPENDIX

STATISTICAL TABLES

APPENDIX

TABLE I

MEAN ANNUAL PERCENTAGES OF WORKPEOPLE UNEMPLOYED

Columns I.-V. are taken from *British and Foreign Trade and Industry* (Second Series) [Cd. 2337], pp. 89-92, and from the "17th Abstract of Labour Statistics", p. 2.—Persons on strike or locked out, sick or superannuated are excluded.

Year.	I. General Percentage of Unemployment.	II. Engineering, Shipbuilding, and Metal.	III. Building (*i.e.* Carpenters and Joiners only).	IV. Wood-working and Furnishing.	V. Printing and Book-binding.	VI. Moving 3-Year Averages of General Percentages. The Figure is placed against the Middle Year in each case.
1851	3·9	3·9	..	..	..	..
1852	6·0	6·0	..	..	..	3·9
1853	1·7	1·7	..	..	..	3·5
1854	2·9	2·9	..	..	..	3·3
1855	5·4	5·4	..	..	..	4·3
1856	4·7	4·9	..	..	1·6	5·4
1857	6·0	6·1	..	..	2·3	7·5
1858	11·9	12 2	..	..	2·5	7·2
1859	3·8	3·9	..	..	1·4	5·9
1860	1·9	1·9	0·2	..	2·1	3·6
1861	5·2	5·5	1·8	..	3·1	5·2
1862	8·4	9·0	1·8	..	3·5	6·5
1863	6·0	6·7	1·2	..	3·2	5·7
1864	2·7	3·0	0·4	..	1·3	3·6
1865	2·1	2·4	0·3	..	2·0	2·7
1866	3·3	3·9	1·1	..	1·8	4·3
1867	7·4	9·1	3·0	4·8	2·7	6·2
1868	7·9	10·0	2·9	5·0	2·5	7·3
1869	6·7	8·9	3·6	4·5	2·8	6·2
1870	3·9	4·4	3·7	4·8	3·5	4·0
1871	1·6	1·3	2·5	3·5	2·0	2·1
1872	0·9	0·9	1·2	2·4	1·5	1·2
1873	1·2	1·4	0·9	1·8	1 3	1·3
1874	1·7	2·3	0·8	2·1	1·6	1·8
1875	2·4	3·5	0·6	2·0	1·6	2·6

TABLE I (*continued*)

Year.	I. General Percentage of Un-employment.	II. Engineering, Shipbuilding, and Metal.	III. Building (*i.e.* Carpenters and Joiners only).	IV. Wood-working and Furnishing.	V. Printing and Book-binding.	VI. Moving 3-Year Averages of General Percentages. The Figure is placed against the Middle Year in each case.
1876	3·7	5·2	0·7	2·4	2·4	3·6
1877	4·7	6·3	1·2	3·5	2·6	5·1
1878	6·8	9·0	3·5	4·4	3·2	7·6
1879	11·4	15·3	8·2	8·3	4·0	7·9
1880	5·5	6·7	6·1	3·2	3·2	6·8
1881	3·5	3·8	5·2	2·7	2·8	3·8
1882	2·3	2·3	3·5	2·5	2·4	2·8
1883	2·6	2·7	3·6	2·5	2·2	4·3
1884	8·1	10·8	4·7	3·0	2·1	6·7
1885	9·3	12·9	7·1	4·1	2·5	9·2
1886	10·2	13·5	8·2	4·7	2·6	9·0
1887	7·6	10·4	6·5	3·6	2·2	7·6
1888	4·9	6·0	5·7	3·1	2·4	4·9
1889	2·1	2·3	3·0	2·4	2·5	3·0
1890	2·1	2·2	2·2	2·5	2·2	2·6
1891	3·5	4·1	1·9	2·1	4·0	4·0
1892	6·3	7·7	3·1	3·8	4·3	5·8
1893	7·5	11·4	3·1	4·1	4·1	6·9
1894	6·9	11·2	4·3	4·4	5·7	6·7
1895	5·8	8·2	4·4	3·6	4·9	5·3
1896	3·3	4·2	1·3	2·0	4·3	4·1
1897	3·3	4·8	1·2	2·2	3·9	3·1
1898	2·8	4·0	0·9	2·3	3·7	2·7
1899	2·0	2·4	1·2	2·1	3·9	2·4
1900	2·5	2·6	2·6	2·8	4·2	2·6
1901	3·3	3·8	3·9	3·7	4·5	3·3
1902	4·0	5·5	4·0	4·1	4·6	4·0
1903	4·7	6·6	4·4	4·7	4·4	4·9
1904	6·0	8·4	7·3	6·8	4·7	5·2
1905	5·0	6·6	8·0	5·8	5·1	4·9
1906	3·6	4·1	6·9	4·8	4·5	4·1
1907	3·7	4·9	7·3	4·6	4·3	5·0
1908	7·8	12·5	11·6	8·3	5·5	6·4
1909	7·7	13·0	11·7	7·6	5·6	6·7
1910	4·7	6·8	8·3	5·4	4·9	5·1
1911	3·0	3·4	4·2	3·3	5·1	3·6
1912	3·2	3·6	3·7	3·1	5·2	2·8
1913	2·1	2·2	3·3	2·4	4·0	2·9
1914	3·3	3·3	3·3	4·1	4·5	..

TABLE II

Aggregate Duration in Working Days of Industrial Disputes

From the " 17th Abstract of Labour Statistics," p. 189.

Year.	Millions.	Year.	Millions.
1899	2·51	1907	2·16
1900	3·15	1908	10·83
1901	4·14	1909	2·77
1902	3·47	1910	9·89
1903	2·33	1911	10·31
1904	1·48	1912	40·91
1905	2·47	1913	11·63
1906	3·02		

TABLE III

Aggregate Money Wages Bill in the United Kingdom

Column I. down to the year 1901 is taken from Dr. Bowley's article, " Tests of National Progress ", in the *Economic Journal*, Sept. 1904, p. 459. From 1901 onwards I have made estimates based on Dr. Bowley's figures for rates of wages and on estimates of variations in the numbers of the wage-earning population.

Year.	Column I. Aggregate Money Wages.	Column II. Excess over Preceding Year.	Moving 3-Year Averages of Preceding Column.
	Million £.	Million £.	
1860	300	..	..
1861	300	0	..
1862	300	0	3
1863	310	10	7
1864	320	10	13
1865	340	20	13
1866	350	10	10
1867	350	0	0
1868	340	− 10	0
1869	350	10	5
1870	365	15	17
1871	390	25	30
1872	440	50	40
1873	485	45	27
1874	470	− 15	8
1875	465	− 5	− 8

TABLE III (*continued*)

Year.	Column I. Aggregate Money Wages.	Column II. Excess over Preceding Year.	Moving 3-Year Averages of Preceding Column.
	Million £.	Million £	
1876	460	− 5	− 3
1877	460	0	− 8
1878	440	− 20	− 10
1879	430	− 10	− 7
1880	440	10	5
1881	455	15	13
1882	470	15	10
1883	470	0	− 2
1884	450	− 20	− 10
1885	440	− 10	− 10
1886	440	0	2
1887	455	15	20
1888	500	45	30
1889	530	30	32
1890	550	20	18
1891	555	5	5
1892	545	− 10	− 2
1893	545	0	2
1894	560	15	12
1895	580	20	17
1896	595	15	15
1897	605	10	23
1898	650	45	27
1899	675	25	35
1900	710	35	18
1901	705	− 5	8
1902	700	− 5	− 3
1903	700	0	− 3
1904	695	− 5	2
1905	705	10	8
1906	725	20	27
1907	775	50	20
1908	765	− 10	13
1909	765	0	2
1910	780	15	10
1911	795	15	20
1912	825	30	17
1913	830	5	..

TABLE IV

ESTIMATED RATE OF REAL WAGES OF PERSONS IN FULL WORK IN THE UNITED KINGDOM [1]

1850 = 100

Year	Value	Year	Value
1850	100	1882	135
1851	102	1883	139
1852	102	1884	144
1853	105	1885	148
1854	96	1886	151
1855	95	1887	155
1856	96	1888	157
1857	96	1889	159
1858	102	1890	166
1859	104	1891	164
1860	103	1892	163
1861	100	1893	167
1862	105	1894	170
1863	109	1895	174
1864	117	1896	176
1865	117	1897	176
1866	116	1898	174
1867	109	1899	180
1868	110	1900	183
1869	115	1901	181
1870	118	1902	177
1871	121	1903	172
1872	122	1904	170
1873	128	1905	172
1874	133	1906	174
1875	135	1907	176
1876	137	1908	172
1877	133	1909	170
1878	132	1910	169
1879	137	1911	..
1880	134	1912	..
1881	136	1913	..

[1] From W. T. Layton, *An Introduction to the Study of Prices*, p. 184.

TABLE V

PIG-IRON CONSUMPTION IN THE UNITED KINGDOM IN MILLIONS OF TONS

Year	Value	Year	Value
1850	..	1882	6·9
1851	..	1883	7·0
1852	..	1884	6·6
1853	..	1885	6·5
1854	2·8	1886	6·0
1855	2·9	1887	6·5
1856	3·2	1888	7·0
1857	3·3	1889	7·2
1858	3·1	1890	6·8
1859	3·4	1891	6·6
1860	3·5	1892	6·0
1861	3·3	1893	6·2
1862	3·5	1894	6·6
1863	4·0	1895	6·9
1864	4·4	1896	7·7
1865	4·3	1897	7·7
1866	4·0	1898	7·7
1867	4·3	1899	8·2
1868	4·5	1900	7·7
1869	4·7	1901	7·3
1870	5·3	1902	7·8
1871	5·6	1903	8·0
1872	5·5	1904	8·0
1873	5·6	1905	8·7
1874	5·3	1906	8·6
1875	5·5	1907	8·3
1876	5·7	1908	7·8
1877	5·8	1909	8·5
1878	5·5	1910	9·0
1879	4·8	1911	8·5
1880	6·2	1912	7·7
1881	6·7	1913	9·3

From [Cd. 2145], pp. 24-5, and the " 17th Abstract of Labour Statistics,"
p. 44.

TABLE VI

Consumption of certain Commodities in the United Kingdom

Column I. is taken for 1856–80 from Beveridge's *Unemployment*, p. 42 ; subsequently from [Cd. 2145], p. 15, and from the "17th Abstract of Labour Statistics", p. 15.

Column II., Table A, is taken from the "13th Abstract of Labour Statistics", p. 42 ; Table B from the 17th Abstract, p. 46.

Column III. is taken from Mr. H. G. Wood's paper, entitled "Some Statistics relating to Working-class Progress since 1860", in the *Journal of the Royal Statistical Society* for Dec. 1899, pp. 655-6. The commodities included in his index are wheat, cocoa, coffee, cotton, currants and raisins, meat, rice, sugar, tea, tobacco, wool, wine, spirits and beer.

Year.	I. Beer per Head.	II. Meat per Head.		III. Index of General Consumption.
	Gallons.	Lbs.	Lbs.	Aggregate.
1850 . .	..	..	..	..
1851 . .	..	..	..	..
1852 . .	..	..	..	..
1853 . .	..	..	..	..
1854 . .	..	..	..	..
1855 . .	..	..	..	..
1856 . .	22·6	..	..	..
1857 . .	22·6	..	..	..
1858 . .	23·6	..	..	..
1859 . .	24·8	..	..	..
1860 . .	23·8	..	..	..
1861 . .	24·3	..	..	..
1862 . .	24·1	..	..	..
1863 . .	25·4	..	..	..
1864 . .	26·7	..	..	80·2
1865 . .	29·8	..	..	78·2
1866 . .	29·4	..	..	81·7
1867 . .	28·1	..	..	81·7
1868 . .	28·2	..	..	87·8
1869 . .	29·1	..	..	90·0
1870 . .	30·2	..	..	91·4
1871 . .	29·3	..	..	93·0
1872 . .	32·2	..	..	96·4
1873 . .	33·5	..	..	102·4
1874 . .	34·0	..	..	102·0
1875 . .	33·3	..	..	104·0
1876 . .	33·7	..	..	105·0
1877 . .	32·3	..	..	103·3
1878 . .	32·2	..	..	101·6
1879 . .	28·0	..	..	98·8
1880 . .	27·0	..	..	101·8
1881 . .	27·8	..	..	103·8

TABLE VI (*continued*)

Year.	I. Beer per Head.	II. Meat per Head.		III. Index of General Consumption.
	Gallons.	Lbs.	Lbs.	Aggregate.
1882 . .	27·6	..	..	105·3
1883 . .	27·2	..	..	105·0
1884 . .	27·8	..	..	104·5
1885 . .	27·1	..	..	101·5
1886 . .	26·9	..	..	101·5
1887 . .	27·3	..	..	104·0
1888 . .	27·2	..	..	104·5
1889 . .	28·9	A.	..	108·7
1890 . .	30·0	106·1	..	110·8
1891 . .	30·2	117·2	..	114·9
1892 . .	29·8	114·3	..	111·4
1893 . .	29·6	111·4	..	108·3
1894 . .	29·5	109·6	..	111·5
1895 . .	29·6	113·1	..	114·9
1896 . .	30·8	121·1	..	115·5
1897 . .	31·3	120·5	..	..
1898 . .	31·8	119·0	..	..
1899 . .	32·5	126·7	..	..
1900 . .	31·6	125·0	B.	..
1901 . .	30·8	122·5	136·2	..
1902 . .	30·3	114·7	135·1	..
1903 . .	29·8	119·6	129·4	..
1904 . .	28·9	121·4	131·9	..
1905 . .	27·8	120·5	132·6	..
1906 . .	28·2	117·9	132·6	..
1907 . .	27·8	118·4	130·6	..
1908 . .	26·9	..	131·4	..
1909 . .	26·1	..	130·1	..
1910 . .	26·3	..	125·5	..
1911 . .	27·2	..	127·2	..
1912 . .	26·7	..	131·2	..
1913 . .	27·3	..	127·6	..

TABLE VII
INDEX OF VOLUME OF MANUFACTURED IMPORTS GIVEN FOR A UNIFORM
QUANTITY OF FOOD IMPORTS INTO THE UNITED KINGDOM[1]

(1910 = 100)

Year	Index	Year	Index
1881	132	1898	111
1882	130	1899	105
1883	128	1900	93
1884	120	1901	95
1885	114	1902	100
1886	117	1903	100
1887	116	1904	96
1888	114	1905	99
1889	116	1906	92
1890	107	1907	92
1891	106	1908	98
1892	112	1909	104
1893	112	1910	100
1894	107	1911	98
1895	104	1912	102
1896	106	1913	97
1897	110	1914	105

[1] Reproduced from a table printed by Mr. J. M. Keynes in the *Economic Journal*, Dec. 1923, pp. 477-80, which was based on earlier calculations made by Dr. Bowley.

TABLE VIII
ADJUSTED INDEX OF PHYSICAL PRODUCTION OF (1) AGRICULTURE (TWELVE CROPS) IN THE U.S.A., (2) PIG-IRON IN THE U.S.A., WITH SECULAR TRENDS ELIMINATED [1]

Ordinates of the secular trend = 100

Year.	Agriculture.	Pig-iron.	Year.	Agriculture.	Pig-iron.
1879	106·2	85·0	1900	100·3	96·0
1880	110·8	107·0	1901	88·5	102·2
1881	86·8	105·1	1902	108·0	106·6
1882	107·1	107·6	1903	97·5	100·6
1883	102·0	98·7	1904	105·6	86·5
1884	106·7	81·7	1905	104·8	113·4
1885	104·5	75·3	1906	109·1	118·0
1886	96 8	99·3	1907	96·5	113·9
1887	91·6	105·4	1908	100·2	66·9
1888	101·5	100·7	1909	97·8	103·2
1889	103·5	111·8	1910	100·1	104·3
1890	89·0	128·6	1911	94·0	86·4
1891	108·4	110·2	1912	108·3	104·1
1892	90·5	116·3	1913	94·2	104·1
1893	90·0	86·6	1914	102·6	75·5
1894	87·9	77·6	1915	106·3	93·2
1895	99·1	105·7	1916	92·3	118·6
1896	103·4	92·7	1917	98·6	112·1
1897	102·7	89·4	1918	96·1	109·6
1898	109·0	98·2	1919	98·2	84·2
1899	102·2	103·5	1920	100·3	..

[1] From "An Index of the Physical Volume of Production", by Prof. E. E. Day, *Review of Economic Statistics*, 1920, pp. 259 and 297.

TABLE IX

PRODUCTION OF AGRICULTURE AND MINING IN THE UNITED STATES

Year	Index of Yield per Acre of Nine Principal Crops in the U.S.A.[1] Moving 3-Year Averages.	Adjusted Index of Physical Production for Mining in the U.S.A. with Secular Trend eliminated.[2] Ordinate to Secular Trend = 100. Moving 3-Year Averages.
1880	99·7	103·7
1881	96·0	104·8
1882	93·0	105·2
1883	99·3	103·1
1884	98·7	96·2
1885	97·3	92·6
1886	93·3	92·8
1887	94·0	97·1
1888	97·7	99·5
1889	97·7	103·6
1890	100·3	105·8
1891	99·3	109·0
1892	99·3	104·7
1893	93·3	98·7
1894	94·7	96·0
1895	98·0	96·4
1896	102·0	101·4
1897	105·0	100·7
1898	106·0	101·6
1899	106·7	99·5
1900	99·3	98·7
1901	102·3	97·5
1902	103·3	98·2
1903	111·7	97·2
1904	112·3	99·8
1905	116·3	101·1
1906	113·7	106·0
1907	111·3	100·0
1908	107·7	99·1
1909	108·7	96·9
1910	105·3	99·6

[1] Compiled from an annual table printed by Prof. H. L. Moore in *Economic Cycles*, p. 130.

[2] Compiled from an annual table printed by Prof. E. E. Day in *The Review of Economic Statistics*, 1920, p. 298.

TABLE X

PRICES IN THE UNITED KINGDOM

Column I. Jevons' index number from 1850–60 and Sauerbeck's index number, to base 1867–77, from 1860 onwards; the number for each year being reduced in the proportion required to make that for 1900 = 100; reproduced from Layton, *Introduction to the Study of Prices*, p. 150.

Column II. The figures of Column I. are corrected for trend by subtracting 1 from that for 1895, 2 from that for 1894, and so on till 1872: prior to which date 24 is subtracted from the figure for each year; and by subtracting 1 from the figure for 1897, 2 from that for 1898, and so on to 1914.

Column III. gives moving 3-year averages of the figures in the preceding column, the moving average being written against the middle year throughout.

Column IV. is obtained by dividing for each year the index number for that year, as given in Column I. by the index number of the preceding year and multiplying by 100.

Column V. gives moving 3-year averages of the figures in Column IV.

Year.	I. Index of General Prices in the United Kingdom.	II. Index of Prices with Trend eliminated.	III. Moving 3-Year Averages of Column II.	IV. Index of Rates of Price Change.	V. Moving 3-Year Average of Column IV.
1845	..	..	..	..	..
1846	..	..	..	..	..
1847	..	..	..	..	..
1848	..	..	..	..	..
1849	..	..	..	..	..
1850	107	83	..	..	..
1851	110	86	..	103	..
1852	108	84	..	102	..
1853	123	99	..	114	..
1854	138	114	..	112	..
1855	133	109	..	96	..
1856	137	113	..	103	..
1857	142	118	..	104	..
1858	127	103	..	90	..
1859	128	104	..	101	..
1860	132	108	..	100	..
1861	131	107	..	101	..
1862	135	111	..	103	..
1863	137	113	..	101	..
1864	140	116	..	102	..
1865	135	111	..	97	..
1866	136	112	..	101	..
1867	133	109	..	98	..
1868	132	108	..	99	..
1869	131	107	..	99	..
1870	128	104	..	98	..
1871	133	109	..	104	..

TABLE X (*continued*)

Year.	I. Index of General Prices in the United Kingdom.	II. Index of Prices with Trend eliminated.	III. Moving 3-Year Averages of Column II.	IV. Index of Rates of Price Change.	V. Moving 3-Year Averages of Column IV.
1872	145	121	..	109	..
1873	147	124	..	101	..
1874	136	114	..	93	..
1875	128	107	..	94	..
1876	127	107	..	99	..
1877	125	106	..	98	..
1878	116	98	..	93	..
1879	111	94	97	96	..
1880	117	101	97	105	99
1881	113	98	99	97	100
1882	112	98	97	99	98
1883	109	96	94	97	96
1884	101	89	90	93	95
1885	96	85	85	95	95
1886	92	82	83	96	97
1887	91	82	83	99	99
1888	93	85	85	102	101
1889	96	89	88	103	102
1890	96	90	90	100	101
1891	96	91	89	100	98
1892	91	87	89	95	98
1893	91	88	86	100	96
1894	84	82	84	92	97
1895	83	82	82	99	96
1896	81	81	82	98	100
1897	83	82	82	102	101
1898	85	83	84	102	104
1899	91	88	89	107	106
1900	100	96	91	110	103
1901	93	88	90	93	101
1902	92	86	86	99	97
1903	92	85	85	100	100
1904	93	85	86	101	101
1905	96	87	88	103	104
1906	103	93	92	108	105
1907	107	96	91	104	101
1908	97	85	89	91	99
1909	99	86	87	102	99
1910	104	90	89	105	103
1911	107	92	93	103	105
1912	113	97	95	105	103
1913	113	96	96	100	102
1914	113	95	..	100	..

TABLE XI

INDEX OF PRICES OF MINERALS DIVIDED INTO INDEX OF PRICES
OF VEGETABLE FOODS IN THE UNITED KINGDOM
(Sauerbeck)

1850 96		1883 108
1851 97		1884 104
1852 100		1885 103
1853 95		1886 97
1854 104		1887 93
1855 110		1888 86
1856 99		1889 86
1857 97		1890 81
1858 91		1891 99
1859 87		1892 92
1860 102		1893 87
1861 112		1894 86
1862 108		1895 87
1863 93		1896 84
1864 82		1897 91
1865 92		1898 96
1866 104		1899 65
1867 132		1900 51
1868 133		1901 70
1869 102		1902 77
1870 99		1903 76
1871 101		1904 78
1872 80		1905 72
1873 75		1906 61
1874 90		1907 64
1875 92		1908 79
1876 119		1909 82
1877 107		1910 73
1878 128		1911 75
1879 119		1912 71
1880 113		1913 62
1881 109		1914 76
1882 106		

TABLE XII
Prices in the United States and Germany [1]

Year.	I. United States. Aldrich Report and Bureau of Labour. Recalculated to Base 1900 = 100.	II. Germany. (Herr Schmitz). Recalculated to Base 1900 = 100.
1860	111	112½
1861	111½	111
1862	127	114
1863	113½	116
1864	136	119
1865	111	111
1866	151	113½
1867	142	114½
1868	129	114
1869	125½	114
1870	130	111
1871	136½	117
1872	141	130
1873	135½	135
1874	132½	124
1875	126	116
1876	116	113
1877	116	113½
1878	111	104
1879	107	94½
1880	118½	105½
1881	117½	103
1882	120½	100
1883	118	98
1884	110	93½
1885	103	86½
1886	102	82
1887	103	84½
1888	104½	90
1889	104½	94½
1890	103	101
1891	102	98½
1892	96½	89
1893	96	86
1894	87	77½
1895	85	77
1896	82	77½
1897	81½	79½
1898	85	84½
1899	92½	92
1900	100	100
1901	99	94
1902	103	93
1903	103½	94
1904	103	94
1905	105	97
1906	111	106
1907	118	113
1908	111½	106½
1909	115	105

[1] From W. T. Layton, *Introduction to the Study of Prices*, p. 151.

TABLE XIII
BANK CREDITS IN THE UNITED KINGDOM
(In Millions)

Year.	I. Deposits of Bank of England and Joint-Stock Banks of the United Kingdom.	II. Deposits of Private Banks in the United Kingdom.	III. Sum of Columns I. and II.	IV. Gold Holdings of the Bank of England.	V. Excess of Column III. on Column IV.	VI. Increase in Each Year of Aggregate Deposits minus Increase in Gold Holdings.	VII. Moving 3-Year Average of Preceding Column.
1877	159	20	179	25·4	154	..	..
1878	332	41	373	23·9	349	195	..
1879	322	40	362	32·4	330	– 19	..
1880	335	42	377	27·6	349	19	10
1881	359	45	404	24·6	379	30	26
1882	382	48	430	22·0	408	29	26
1883	399	50	449	22·2	427	19	25
1884	423	53	476	22·9	453	26	20
1885	439	54	493	24·2	469	16	17
1886	444	56	500	21·0	479	10	15
1887	454	57	511	21·8	489	10	13
1888	470	59	529	20·8	508	19	22
1889	503	63	566	21·4	545	38	25
1890	519	65	584	21·8	563	18	33
1891	554	69	623	24·4	599	36	23
1892	568	70·9	638	25·5	613	14	15
1893	565	66·4	631	26·4	607	– 6	3
1894	579	63·9	643	34·3	609	2	13
1895	622	69·2	691	38·9	652	43	33
1896	704	47·3	751	44·3	707	55	37
1897	706	48·8	755	35·6	719	12	31
1898	739	39·9	779	33·6	745	26	24
1899	771	41·4	812	32·3	780	35	20
1900	771	42·1	813	33·3	780	0	16
1901	790	39·5	829	35·8	793	13	5
1902	797	34·5	831	35·6	795	2	6
1903	802	31·0	833	34·4	799	4	0
1904	798	28·3	826	34·4	792	– 7	8
1905	827	26·6	854	35·7	818	26	11
1906	839	27·4	866	33·9	832	14	25
1907	874	27·4	898	34·9	866	34	18
1908	879	26·8	906	32·7	873	7	19
1909	900	25·7	926	37·4	889	16	24
1910	942	26·8	969	31·3	938	49	32
1911	975	27·1	1002	32·4	970	32	41
1912	1015	26·7	1042	31·3	1011	41	37
1913	1058	27·1	1085	34·9	1050	39	50
1914	1157	32·8	1190	69·5	1120	70	..

These tables are based in the main on data collected in Appendix D of Mr. Layton's *Introduction to the Study of Prices*. I have been obliged to estimate the deposits of private banks for the years before 1891. The estimates are based on the assumption that, before that date, the deposits of these banks were increasing at the same rate as the deposits set out in Column I.

TABLE XIV

INDEX NUMBERS OF CREDITS OUTSTANDING IN THE UNITED KINGDOM

Column I. is derived from Column V. of Table XIII.
Column II. is obtained from Column I. by adding 3 to the figure for
1899, 6 to that for 1898, and so on ; and by subtracting 1 from the figure
for 1901, 2 from that for 1902, and so on.
Column IV. is obtained by dividing, for each year, the index number
for that year as given in Column I. by the index number for the preceding
year, multiplying by 100, and subtracting 3.

Year.	I. Index Number of Credits Outstanding. Base 1900 = 100	II. Index Number with Trend eliminated.	III. Moving 3-Year Average of Column II.	IV. Rate of Increase of Credits Outstanding (Trend removed).	V. Moving 3-Year Average of Column II.
1877	20	89	..	..	..
1878	45	111	102	..	..
1879	42	105	107	90	..
1880	45	105	105	104	100
1881	48	105	105	104	104
1882	52	106	105	105	103
1883	54	105	106	101	103
1884	58	106	105	104	102
1885	60	105	105	101	101
1886	61	103	103	99	100
1887	63	102	102	100	100
1888	65	101	102	100	102
1889	70	103	102	105	102
1890	72	102	103	100	103
1891	77	104	103	104	101
1892	78	102	102	98	100
1893	78	99	99	97	97
1894	78	96	98	97	99
1895	83	98	99	103	102
1896	91	103	101	106	102
1897	92	101	102	98	101
1898	95	101	102	100	100
1899	100	103	101	102	100
1900	100	100	101	97	99
1901	102	101	100	99	98
1902	102	100	100	97	98
1903	102	99	98	97	96
1904	100	96	98	95	98
1905	105	100	99	102	98
1906	106	100	101	98	101
1907	111	104	103	102	99
1908	112	104	104	98	100
1909	114	105	106	99	100
1910	120	110	109	102	100
1911	124	113	113	100	101
1912	129	117	117	101	101
1913	134	121	122	101	102
1914	143	129	..	104	..

TABLE XV

PROPORTION OF RESERVE TO LIABILITIES OF THE BANK OF ENGLAND

Year						Value	Year						Value
1850	.	.	.	.	.	59	1882	.	.	.	.	.	39
1851	.	.	.	.	.	52	1883	.	.	.	.	.	42
1852	.	.	.	.	.	63	1884	.	.	.	.	.	42
1853	.	.	.	.	.	46	1885	.	.	.	.	.	45
1854	.	.	.	.	.	46	1886	.	.	.	.	.	41
1855	.	.	.	.	.	47	1887	.	.	.	.	.	45
1856	.	.	.	.	.	34	1888	.	.	.	.	.	41
1857	.	.	.	.	.	30	1889	.	.	.	.	.	40
1858	.	.	.	.	.	58	1890	.	.	.	.	.	41
1859	.	.	.	.	.	49	1891	.	.	.	.	.	41
1860	.	.	.	.	.	40	1892	.	.	.	.	.	43
1861	.	.	.	.	.	41	1893	.	.	.	.	.	47
1862	.	.	.	.	.	45	1894	.	.	.	.	.	63
1863	.	.	.	.	.	39	1895	.	.	.	.	.	62
1864	.	.	.	.	.	36	1896	.	.	.	.	.	58
1865	.	.	.	.	.	38	1897	.	.	.	.	.	50
1866	.	.	.	.	.	30	1898	.	.	.	.	.	46
1867	.	.	.	.	.	49	1899	.	.	.	.	.	43
1868	.	.	.	.	.	46	1900	.	.	.	.	.	43
1869	.	.	.	.	.	43	1901	.	.	.	.	.	48
1870	.	.	.	.	.	47	1902	.	.	.	.	.	46
1871	.	.	.	.	.	48	1903	.	.	.	.	.	48
1872	.	.	.	.	.	41	1904	.	.	.	.	.	49
1873	.	.	.	.	.	41	1905	.	.	.	.	.	47
1874	.	.	.	.	.	43	1906	.	.	.	.	.	43
1875	.	.	.	.	.	43	1907	.	.	.	.	.	45
1876	.	.	.	.	.	52	1908	.	.	.	.	.	50
1877	.	.	.	.	.	43	1909	.	.	.	.	.	49
1878	.	.	.	.	.	37	1910	.	.	.	.	.	49
1879	.	.	.	.	.	49	1911	.	.	.	.	.	51
1880	.	.	.	.	.	48	1912	.	.	.	.	.	..
1881	.	.	.	.	.	43	1913	.	.	.	.	.	..

TABLE XVI

ANNUAL CLEARINGS OF THE LONDON BANKERS' CLEARING-HOUSE
(In Millions [1])

1870	.	.	.	.	.	3,914	1892	.	. .	.	.	.	6,482
1871	.	.	.	.	.	4,826	1893	.	.	.	.	.	6,478
1872	.	.	.	.	.	5,916	1894	.	.	.	.	.	6,337
1873	.	.	.	.	.	6,071	1895	.	.	.	.	.	7,593
1874	.	.	.	.	.	5,937	1896	.	.	.	.	.	7,575
1875	.	.	.	.	.	5,686	1897	.	.	.	.	.	7,491
1876	.	.	.	.	.	4,963	1898	.	.	.	.	.	8,097
1877	.	.	.	.	.	5,042	1899	.	.	.	.	.	9,150
1878	.	.	.	.	.	4,992	1900	.	.	.	.	.	8,960
1879	.	.	.	.	.	4,886	1901	.	.	.	.	.	9,561
1880	.	.	.	.	.	5,794	1902	.	.	.	.	.	10,029
1881	.	.	.	.	.	6,357	1903	.	.	.	.	.	10,120
1882	.	.	.	.	.	6,221	1904	.	.	.	.	.	10,564
1883	.	.	.	.	.	5,929	1905	.	.	.	.	.	12,288
1884	.	.	.	.	.	5,799	1906	.	.	.	.	.	12,711
1885	.	.	.	.	.	5,511	1907	.	.	.	.	.	12,730
1886	.	.	.	.	.	5,902	1908	.	.	.	.	.	12,120
1887	.	.	.	.	.	6,077	1909	.	.	.	.	.	13,525
1888	.	.	.	.	.	6,942	1910	.	.	.	.	.	14,659
1889	.	.	.	.	.	7,619	1911	.	.	.	.	.	14,614
1890	.	.	.	.	.	7,801	1912	.	.	.	.	.	15,962
1891	.	.	.	.	.	6,848	1913	.	.	.	.	.	16,436

[1] From the " Statistical Abstract of the U.K."

APPENDIX

TABLE XVII

AVERAGE ANNUAL RATES OF DISCOUNT OF GOOD 3-MONTHS
BANKERS' BILLS IN LONDON [1]

1845	3·00	1879	2·14
1846	3·75	1880	2·53
1847	5·87	1881	3·05
1848	3·25	1882	3·55
1849	2·25	1883	3·22
1850	2·25	1884	2·57
1851	3·00	1885	2·40
1852	1·87	1886	2·33
1853	3·50	1887	2·65
1854	4·87	1888	2·53
1855	4·55	1889	2·85
1856	5·50	1890	3·88
1857	6·65	1891	2·77
1858	2·75	1892	1·76
1859	2·50	1893	2·32
1860	4·00	1894	1·18
1861	5·00	1895	0·96
1862	2·25	1896	1·56
1863	4·25	1897	1·92
1864	7·00	1898	2·62
1865	5·32	1899	3·35
1866	6·41	1900	3·70
1867	2·66	1901	3·17
1868	2·46	1902	2·97
1869	3·37	1903	3·38
1870	3·28	1904	2·68
1871	2·89	1905	2·62
1872	4·08	1906	3·97
1873	4·70	1907	4·49
1874	3·56	1908	2·29
1875	3·14	1909	2·28
1876	2·26	1910	3·16
1877	2·62	1911	2·90
1878	3·59		

[1] From "The Rate of Discount and the Price of Consols", by T. T. Williams, *Journal of the Royal Statistical Society*, 1912, pp. 382-4.

TABLE XVIII

UNEMPLOYMENT AND REAL WAGES IN GREAT BRITAIN SINCE 1920

Years.	Quarters.	Dr. Bowley's Index-number of Rates of Money Wages. 1913 = 100.	Rates of Money Wages divided by Board of Trade Index-number of Wholesale Prices. 1913 = 100.	Rates of Money Wages divided by Board of Trade Cost of Living Index. 1913 = 100.	Trade Union Percentages of Unemployed.
1919	1	207	83	96	2·7
	2	209	86	101	2·2
	3	216	84	100	1·9
	4	221	77	91	2·9
1920	1	231	75	100	1·9
	2	250	77	101	1·1
	3	267	85	102	1·7
	4	273	96	101	5·0
1921	1	276	121	114	8·5
	2	268	133	121	20·9
	3	244	128	112	16·0
	4	228	131	115	16·0
1922	1	215	132	116	16·5
	2	202	126	111	16·4
	3	189	120	105	14·5
	4	178	114	100	14·1
1923	1	177	112	100	13·0
	2	177	110	105	11·2
	3	174	111	100	11·3
	4	173	106	98	10·4
1924	1	174	105	99	8·3
	2	177	108	104	7·2
	3	179	108	103	8·0
	4	179	105	99	8·8
1925	1	181	107	102	9·1
	2	181	113	105	10·6
	3	180	115	103	11·3
	4	180	117	102	11·1
1926	1	180	122	105	10·4
	2	180	124	107	12·6
	3	180	120	105	13·4
	4	180	120	101	13·0
1927	1	181	127	107	··

INDEX

INDEX

THE END